PATERNOSTER BIBLICAL MONOGRAPHS

The Appeal of Exodus

The Characters God, Moses and Israel
in the Rhetoric of the Book of Exodus

T0385281

PATERNOSTER BIBLICAL MONOGRAPHS

The Appeal of Exodus

The Characters God, Moses and Israel in the Rhetoric of the Book of Exodus

Stefan Kürle

First published 2013 by Paternoster

Paternoster is an imprint of Authentic Media
52 Presley Way, Crownhill, Milton Keynes, Bucks, MK8 0ES, UK

www.authenticmedia.co.uk
Authentic Media is a division of Koorong UK, a company limited by guarantee

09 08 07 06 05 04 03   8 7 6 5 4 3 2 1

British Library Cataloguing in Publication Data
A catalogue record for this book is available from the British Library

ISBN 978-1-84227-780-5

Typeset by Stefan Kürle
Printed and bound in Great Britain
for Paternoster

SERIES PREFACE

One of the major objectives of Paternoster is to serve biblical scholarship by providing a channel for the publication of theses and other monographs of high quality at affordable prices. Paternoster stands within the broad evangelical tradition of Christianity. Our authors would describe themselves as Christians who recognise the authority of the Bible, maintain the centrality of the gospel message and assent to the classical credal statements of Christian belief. There is diversity within this constituency; advances in scholarship are possible only if there is freedom for frank debate on controversial issues and for the publication of new and sometimes provocative proposals. What is offered in this series is the best of writing by committed Christians who are concerned to develop well-founded biblical scholarship in a spirit of loyalty to the historic faith.

SERIES EDITORS

to Birgit

My dwelling place shall be with them, and I will be their God, and they shall be my people. Then the nations will know that I am Yhwh who sanctifies Israel, when my sanctuary is in their midst forevermore.
(Ezek. 37:27–28)

CONTENTS

Series Preface   v

Series Editors   vi

Acknowledgements   xiii

Abbreviations   xv

CHAPTER 1 Introduction – Hermeneutical Reflections & Method   1

Reading and Identification   2

The Concept of Ethos   3

Direct and Indirect Characterisations   4

The First Encounter Between Character and Reader   5

The Relationship Between Literary Character and Historical Reality   5

Defining 'Reading'   6

A Shared Knowledge   7

A Functional Approach   8

The Organic Unity of Form and Content   11

The Cultural Conventions Shaping the Text   13

An Example: the Special Case of Law in Narrative   15

The Levels of Reading   17

Some Reflections on the Boundaries of Exodus   20

The Opening of Exodus   20

The End of Exodus   23

The Outline of the Study   27

CHAPTER 2 Yhwh – 'National Hero' and 'King'   29

The Rhetorical Function of Yhwh – the Interpretive Debate   29

Narrative Characterisation   35

   Direct Characterisation   35

      THE DIVINE NAME 'YHWH' AND ITS FUNCTION IN EXOD. 3–4   35

      THE EPITHETS IN EXOD. 34:6-7   43

      THE EPITHETS IN EXOD. 20:5-6   49

   Yhwh's Conflict with the Pharaoh   50

   The Introduction of Yhwh into the Plot of Exodus 60

   Yhwh's Conflicts with Israel (Exod. 15–17 and 32–34)   69

      IN THE WILDERNESS   70

      THE CREATION OF THE GOLDEN CALF   71

   Conclusion   74

Poetic Characterisation   77

Legal Characterisation   80

   The Laws as Direct Yhwh-Speech   85

   The Law Collections – a Divine Perspective on Israel   91

      YHWH'S PRESENCE   92

      LOYALTY TO YHWH   98

      RESTITUTION OR THE CONCERN FOR OTHERS   101

      BENEVOLENCE AS MOTIVATION   103

      SANCTION STATEMENTS   108

   The Implications of the Form of the Law Collection   116

      CIVIL AND RELIGIOUS LAWS – A MIXTURE   119

      HOLINESS AND SOCIAL ISSUES – EXOD. 22:20-23:12   121

   Conclusion   122

Yhwh, the King – a Conclusion   123

CHAPTER 3 Moses – the Mediator, Not the Hero   125

The Rhetorical Function of Moses – the Interpretive Debate   126

   H. Greßmann 1913   127

   G.W. Coats 1988   129

   S.D. McBride 1990   134

F. Crüsemann 1992 135

J.W. Watts 1998 138

T.B. Dozeman 2000 141

R. Rendtorff 2001 143

Conclusion 147

Opening the Mind – the Introduction of Moses as a Character in Exodus 148

  The Making of a Hero? 148

  The Call of a Mediator 157

    THE FIRST THEOPHANY AT HOREB 159

    THE DIALOGUE 160

    MOSES ON HIS WAY TO EGYPT 162

  Conclusion 164

Caught in the Middle – Moses the Mediator 167

  Moses and Yhwh 168

    MOSAIC OBEDIENCE 169

    MOSES IN THE DIVINE SPHERE 172

  Moses and Israel 179

  Conclusion 187

Moses: a Restored Character 189

The Reader and Moses – a Conclusion 193

CHAPTER 4 Israel – Between Ideal and Reality **196**

The Rhetorical Function of Israel – Some Perspectives 197

  P.D. Hanson 1986 197

  J. Assmann 1992 198

  J. Schreiner 1995 200

  R.G. Kratz 2000 202

  J.A. Davies 2004 204

  Conclusion 205

The Introduction of Israel Into the Plot of Exodus 207

The Development of Israel in Exodus 210

  Between Ideal and Reality 211

  A Change of Masters 215

'And they did just as Yhwh commanded them'   221

Conclusion   226

The Ideal Israel   227

   Israel – Between Ideal and Reality   227

      ISRAEL AS VASSAL   227

      THE ISRAELITE AS CITIZEN   282

      ISRAEL: A PRIESTLY NATION   229

   Israel in the Laws   234

      A PRIESTLY KINGDOM READING LAW   235

      THE INFLUENCE OF PAST EXPERIENCE   237

      ESTABLISHMENT OF A UNIFIED PEOPLE   239

      DIRECT ADDRESS OF THE IMPLIED READER   242

   Conclusion   244

'Israel' and Reader Identification – a Conclusion   245

CHAPTER 5 Summary and Conclusions   **248**

Reading Exodus – How Does the Book Work?   248

Reading Exodus – Broadening the Horizon   253

Bibliography   **257**

Biblical References   **281**

General Index   **286**

ACKNOWLEDGEMENTS

The work on this book would have been impossible without the support and encouragement of numerous people. Many of those must remain unmentioned which is not to depreciate their contribution in this work.

Firstly, I wish to express my gratitude to Prof. Gordon J. Wenham, who took on himself to guide my PhD project from which this book has grown. His generous help and support, together with his great competence and experience guided me through many difficult decisions and helped to retain the focus on the way. My thanks also to Prof. John J. Bimson, who acted as second supervisor. I wish to thank Prof. R.W.L Moberly who kindly commented on the early stages of my thesis. The University of Gloucestershire must receive my gratitude for providing an opportunity to pursue my interest in Exodus and also some of the funding. I owe gratitude also to Paternoster and Authentic Media and there especially to Dr. Robin Parry for accepting the manuscript and Rev. Dr. Derek Tidball and Dr. Mike Parsons for their patient guidance in preparing it for publication. Another institution must be mentioned, the Evangelische Hochschule Tabor in Marburg, Germany, which supported me with a wonderful and stimulating academic environment and helped to cut down my teaching requirements wherever possible so I could continue with my research. Great thanks also to Dr. Julie C. Möller who took the pains of reading my manuscript and used much red ink to make it readable. Other friends must find mention who all contributed in some way or the other: Rev. Dr. Richard Cleaves, Rev. Mark Evans, Simon Bramwell, Jean and Roger Gregory, Dr. Tillmann and Ute Krüger, Dr. Torsten Uhlig, Prof. Dr. Herbert Klement, Prof. Dr. Christoph Rösel, and Prof. Dr. Detlef Häußer. Thanks also to my extended family who played an important role in giving me the freedom and enabling the quietness necessary for theological research.

Above all, however, I would like to thank my wife, Birgit, to whom this book is dedicated. Without her love and support the entire adventure would not have been possible. Her patience has been overwhelming and her motivation has been vital. She and our children, Marit, Simeon and Jakob, have faithfully reminded me that there is more to this world than the book of Exodus.

Rolândia, June 2012, s.k.

ABBREVIATIONS

Biblical books are abbreviated according to "Instructions for contributors to the Journal of Biblical Literature" in: *Suppl. to Journal of Biblical Literature* 90.pt.3, 1971, 70.

Other abbreviations:

ANET	*Ancient Near Eastern Texts Relating to the Old Testament.* J. B. Pritchard, ed. (3d ed. Princeton, 1969)
ATD	Altes Testament Deutsch
Aufl.	Auflage
B	book of the covenant
BBR	*Bulletin for Biblical Research*
BC	Before Christ
Bd.	*Band*
BDB	F. Brown, S. R. Driver, and C. A. Briggs, *Hebrew and English Lexicon of the Old Testament* (Oxford: Oxford University Press, 1907; repr. with corrections, 1953)
bearb.	*bearbeitet(e)*
Bib	*Biblica*
BibInt	*Biblical Interpretation*
BJS	Brown Judaic Studies
BKAT	Biblischer Kommentar Altes Testament
BN	*Biblische Notizen*
BZ	*Biblische Zeitschrift*
BZAW	Beihefte zur Zeitschrift für die alttestamentliche Wissenschaft
ch.	chapter
c.	*circa*
cf.	*confer*
CBQ	*Catholic Biblical Quarterly*
CTJ	*Calvin Theological Journal*

DtH	Deuteronomistic History
E	Elohist
ed(s).	edited by, editor(s), edition(s)
e.g.	*exempli gratia*
EJTh	*European Journal of Theology*
erg.	*ergänzt*
erw.	*erweitert(e)*
esp.	especially
et al.	*et alii*
EThL	*Ephemerides Theologiae Louvaniensis*
etc.	*et cetera*
EvTh	*Evangelische Theologie*
ExpTim	*Expository Times*
ExR	*Exodus Rabbah* (or *Shemoth Rabbah*)
f(f).	the following page(s); the following verse(s)
FRLANT	Forschungen zur Religion und Literatur des Alten und Neuen Testaments
FS	*Festschrift für*
Ges-B	W. Gesenius and F. Buhl, *Hebräisches und Aramäisches Handwörterbuch über das Alte Testament* (unveränderter Neudruck der 1915 erschienenen 17. Auflage, Berlin: Springer, 1962)
HL	Hittite Laws
HALAT	L. Koehler, W. Baumgartner, and J. J. Stamm, eds., *Hebräisches und aramäisches Lexikon zum Alten Testament* (3rd ed., 5 vols., Leiden, 1967–1995)
HBS	Herder Biblische Studien
hif.	hif'il
Hrsg.	*Herausgeber*
HThKAT	Herders Theologischer Kommentar zum Alten Testament
HTR	*Harvard Theological Review*
HUCA	*Hebrew Union College Annual*
i.e.	*id est*
Interp.	*Interpretation*
J	Yahwist
JAOS	*Journal of the American Oriental Society*
JBL	*Journal for Biblical Literature*
JBTh	*Jahrbuch für Biblische Theologie*
Jdm	*Judaism*

JJS	*Journal of Jewish Studies*
JLR	*Journal of Law and Religion*
JSOT	*Journal for the Study of the Old Testament*
JSOTSup	Journal for the Study of the Old Testament Supplement Series
KBL	L. Koehler and W. Baumgartner, *Lexicon in Veteris Testamenti libros* (2nd ed., 2 vols., Leiden, 1958)
LE	Laws of Ešnunna
LH	Laws of Hammurabi
LNB	Neo-Babylonian Laws
LU	Laws of Ur-Namma
LXX	Septuagint
MAL A	Middle Assyrian Laws (tablet A)
MT	Masoretic Text
n.	footnote
Numen	*Numen: International Review for the History of Religions*
OBO	Orbis Biblicus et Orientalis
OTE	*Old Testament Essays*
p.	page
PRSt	*Perspectives in Religious Studies*
RB	*Revue Biblique*
repr.	reprint(ed)
SBLSP	*SBL Seminar Papers*
sc.	*scilicet*
SJOT	*Scandinavian Journal of the Old Testament*
THAT	E. Jenni and C. Westermann, eds., *Theologisches Handbuch zum Alten Testament*, (2 vols., München, 1971, 1976)
ThQ	*Theologische Quartalschrift*
ThZ	*Theologische Zeitschrift*
TO	Targum Onqelos
TOTC	Tyndale Old Testament Commentary
TNf	Targum Neofiti
TPsJ	Targum Pseudo Jonathan
TRE	Krause, Gerhard; Müller, Gerhard eds., *Theologische Real-enzyklopädie* (36 vols., Berlin, 1993-2006)
ThWAT	G. J. Botterweck, H. Ringgren, and H.-J. Fabry, eds., *Theologisches Wörterbuch zum Alten Testament* (8 vols., Stuttgart, 1970–1995)
TynBul	*Tyndale Bulletin*
vol(s).	volume(s)

VT	*Vetus Testamentum*
VWGTh	Veröffentlichungen der Wissenschaftlichen Gesellschaft für Theologie
WThJ	*Westminster Theological Journal*
ZAR	*Zeitschrift für altorientalische und biblische Rechtsgeschichte*
ZAW	*Zeitschrift für die alttestamentliche Wissenschaft*
ZThK	*Zeitschrift für Theologie und Kirche*

CHAPTER 1

INTRODUCTION – HERMENEUTICAL REFLECTIONS & METHOD

The book of Exodus is a crucial part of the Torah, the Jewish Tanach, and the Christian Bible. The texts in Exodus describe Israel as the people of the creator God, the God carrying the name Yhwh. Thus the book touches upon the foundational issues of identity and identification for all followers of this God. This, of course, has implications for the relation of those groups who consider the texts of Exodus to be sacred texts: Jews and Christians read this book and understand themselves as addressees. Within the dimension of identity, Exodus is part of the foundation of Jewish-Christian ethics. To live in the presence of Yhwh imposes certain attitudes and standards of behaviour; this is the argument in Exodus. This emphasis on ethics touches a central concern of our present day, as everyone is searching for values and their foundations. Quite often it is specifically the area of ethics which makes biblical theology relevant today. These considerations warrant a study of this ancient book and they will continue to do so as long as the Jewish people and the Christian church exist.

Of course, the book of Exodus has been the object of countless interpretive efforts, but the modern preoccupation with historical issues has obscured the view on the book itself. The disenchantment with the positivistic ideals of the 19th century also led to the disenchantment of the methodologies informed by them. The present study shares with numerous recent scholars the pessimism about the contribution of textual *genesis* to the understandings of the Hebrew Bible in general and of Exodus in particular.[1] But does the text of Exodus – as we have received it – actually make sense? Was it ever intended to be read or heard as a book? How can we as late modern readers do justice to an ancient book composed against the background of a different world view, different literary conventions, and general culture?

The present study attempts to grasp Exodus in its entirety. This will be done from the angle of the literary characters dominating the book. Furthermore, I

---

[1] Recently and from a non-suspicious vantage point Otto 2007, 9, 12–13 has formulated this for the entire Pentateuch: a reasonable historical-critical reading can only flow from a careful and reflected synchronic reading. The entire debate on the so called "Pentateuch crisis" continues to give rise to a great liberty in rejecting or at least doubting long held "consensuses". For a recent and lucid assessment see Fischer 2005. He even proposes the following: "Statt Texte mit Etiketten (wie 'P') zu versehen, ist es fruchtbarer, zu begreifen zu versuchen, *wie sie ihre Botschaft vermitteln und innerhalb ihres Zusammenhangs funktionieren.*" (101) which is close to my present concern termed "a functional approach".

propose a reading which takes Exodus on its own terms. This will be done from the vantage point of rhetorical-critical analysis. Hence the present study rests on a foundational concern with rhetorical issues which convinced me already in the early stages of the research of the centrality of the literary characters for the communication of the book. The aim is to investigate "the means by which a text establishes and manages its relationship to its audience in order to achieve a particular effect".[2] The 'text' will be Exodus in its extant form, i.e. with all its present unevenness and difficulties.

In this introduction I will argue for my concentration on the literary characters and my methodological decisions which are informed by a number of hermeneutical considerations. In a last step I will justify my focus on the forty chapters of Exodus. This seems to be called for by the multiple themes and subjects which, because of their nature, are not limited to the book of Exodus but run throughout the entire Pentateuch and often touch upon the issues of biblical theology.

Reading and Identification

As already mentioned, the present study focuses on the portrayal of the literary characters in the book of Exodus. In Exodus the three main characters – God, Moses, and Israel – dominate all of the text. Hence it follows that the concentration on these characters does not mean studying just part of the book. The entirety of the book constructs the narrative world in which these characters exist, develop and interact. Thus the aim to cover the whole book is met; or, to use a metaphor, the focus on characterisation becomes the spectacles through which the book is studied. But why give attention to the characters when there are other literary possibilities such as plot development, structure, spatio-temporal bounding, and the like?

Even a cursory reading shows that the concerns of Exodus are the earliest history of Israel and the establishment of Israel's relationship to God. Exodus is all about the definition of Israel's identity in relation to Yhwh and presents the implications thereof for their practical behaviour. Thus already at the stage of the *inventio* of the book[3] the subject of Exodus demands concentration on the characters. The study of these characters should then give insight into the ideational worlds of the author and of the readers for whom he wrote his book.[4] The following chapters will show how the message of Exodus unfolds along the

---

[2] This is the definition Patrick and Scult provide for the entire venture of rhetorical criticism (Patrick and Scult 1990, 12).

[3] On the *partes artes*, i.e. the five stages of rhetorical work and consideration (*inventio, dispositio, elocutio, memoria, actio*), see Plett 1991, 12–21 or any other introduction to ancient rhetorics.

[4] On the notion of the implied reader see p.9 below.

lines of character portrayal and development.[5] A few remarks are in order to settle a number issues that inevitably appear when talking about literary characters.

The Concept of Ethos

As this investigation is rhetorical-critical in nature – what this means precisely will be developed below – it is good advice to look at classical rhetorical theory and what it has to offer on the subject of character. As rhetorical theory is mainly concerned with oral communication, it does not explicitly mention literary characters. The self-characterisation of the speaker, however, the *ethos*,[6] was recognised as central for the effect of persuasion. Once the audience believes that the speaker's character is credible, it will be much more likely to accept the delivered content. Aristotle writes in his *rhetorica*:

> Persuasion is achieved by the speaker's personal character when the speech is so spoken as to make us think him credible. We believe good men more fully and more readily than others: this is true generally whatever the question is, and absolutely true where exact certainty is impossible and opinions are divided. This kind of persuasion, like the others, should be achieved by what the speaker says, not by what people think of his character before he begins to speak. It is not true, as some writers assume in their treatises on rhetoric, that the personal goodness revealed by the speaker contributes nothing to his power of persuasion; on the contrary, his character may almost be called the most effective means of persuasion he possesses. (I.2.1356)[7]

Abstracted from the oral realm, the force of a text depends on its author. Here we are in a sad situation, as we do not know much about our present author. Nevertheless, he uses the principle stated above by Aristotle. That is, he utilises personalities from Israel's past (including God) as characters in his book, endows them with direct speech, and lets their portraits influence the credibility of the speech's content. From this point of view it might have been quite desirable for the author to step back and leave the field to his characters. Of course, in the end it is the author who shapes the reader's perception of the characters and thus lends or withdraws credibility. But it becomes clear how important this literary characterisation is for the persuasiveness of the book's content.

Nevertheless, Aristotle's ideal that the listener should not be influenced by his preconceptions about the rhetor's *ethos* is not something with which the author of Exodus would agree. As the following investigation will show, it is ex-

---

[5] For a brief and lucid survey of issues revolving around character – from literary critical point of view – see Rimmon-Kenan 1983, 29ff.

[6] When I write of *ethos* (in italics) I am always using it in its technical sense. There are no implications whatsoever for any moral judgements or even qualities of the characters.

[7] Quote taken from McKeon 1941.

actly this preconception which most effectively influences the reader's willingness to accept certain contents. To illustrate this aspect I will briefly hint at a couple of the most striking examples; they will receive due attention later in the present chapter. The most obvious case is the character 'Yhwh' whose divinity assures, in an Israelite context, his credibility from the outset. Here, the author profits from the reader's prejudice about the reliability of God and strategically uses this to promote his view of the events narrated in his book. Interestingly, the author does not want to do the same with Moses. We can safely assume that the implied reader did have a positive preconception of Moses, but this is not supported for long in the course of reading Exodus. Rather, the reader should review and reshape his perception of Moses during the reading process.

Direct and Indirect Characterisations

Literary characters gain vividness for the reader by the actions in which they are portrayed and the judgements which the author passes. Sternberg offers a sizable list of rhetorical devices which contribute to this end which I call characterisation or character portrayal.[8] These modes of characterisation represent, by and large, stages between the poles of direct and indirect characterisations.[9] Direct characterisation is rather rare in biblical narrative compared with modern novelistic literature. This is, certainly, the case in Exodus; direct characterisation is largely limited to passages which serve a summarial function. There we find epithets of the divine and of human characters. Especially Yhwh receives this literary attention at marked points in the narrative: during his first encounter with Moses (Exod. 3), in the song at the *yam-suf* (Exod. 15), and after the sin of the people in Exod. 34. Moses is allowed to characterise himself in Exod. 3–4 with something like an epithet ('Who am I?', 'I am not eloquent' …). In the pharaoh's breast a stubborn heart beats. Israel is stiff-necked without any hope of improvement (Exod. 32–34). These comments on the characters are passed, in part, by the narrator and, in part, by the characters inside the story.[10] Especially in the latter case, it is left to the reader to decide whether or not he wants to accept the judgement. Moses proves to be the most ambiguous character in this respect, particularly in the first five chapters of the book.

The guidance of the reader's perception of the characters, however, is chiefly done through indirect characterisation. The reader must decide for himself what the qualities are which the characters' actions imply. When Moses shatters the tablets, the effect upon the portrait of Israel is obvious. Less obvious, but never-

---

[8] Cf. Sternberg 1987, 476–481.

[9] On this distinction see also Rimmon-Kenan 1983, 59–67. She uses the expressions 'direct definition' and 'indirect presentation'.

[10] It is also possible for a character inside the story to comment on another character. This direct characterisation often tells a lot about the first character and thus becomes indirect. The direct characterisation may, in this case, also carry less weight, as if it were uttered by the author/narrator himself (cf. Rimmon-Kenan 1983, 60).

theless perceptible, is the series of failures narrated before Moses' call. Divine patience is never expressed explicitly before Exod. 34, but the wilderness episodes of Exod. 15–17 make the same point. These are only a few examples of the manifold ways which guide the readers in their interpretations of the characters. The main part of the present thesis attempts to express the emerging picture of the main characters in Exodus and, also, to uncover the rhetorical strategies behind these pictures.

The First Encounter Between Character and Reader

As the plot of Exodus unfolds, the pictures of the characters inside the story become more complete, and the reader's perception of these characters is shaped. The introduction of the character into the story is a crucial step in the development of this character.[11] This is for several reasons. Firstly, as in everyday life, the initial meeting between two people is often the most decisive and influential in determining the quality of the later relationship. The first impression is generally the strongest, and it requires much effort to revise the conceptions formed then. Secondly, every introduction attempts to help the reader make a transition between the issues in his own world and those about which the author will be writing; it opens the door into the narrative world of the text. With regard to the process of reading it follows that the reader is least influenced at the beginning of a text. This may sound trivial, but here we will be able to observe the author struggling with the preconceptions of his implied reader. Hence, we might gain some insights into the rhetorical situation in which the book of Exodus was intended to serve as communication. Thirdly, and lastly, introductory paragraphs may already provide an indication of how this character will finally develop throughout the story. This is especially true for a character like God who will, by definition, not be too ambiguous.[12] With regard to the other main characters, Moses and Israel, there is certainly more tension between the impressions produced at first sight and their later development.

The Relationship Between Literary Character and Historical Reality

The objective here is not to follow the enlightenment obsession in Old Testament scholarship with the evaluation of the extent to which the portrayal of the characters can be called historical.[13] The results from these investigations tend

---

[11] Cf. Rimmon-Kenan 1983, 120. She refers to Perry 1979, 53 for a summary of psychological tests which demonstrate the influence of initial information on the process of perception. Perry concludes: "The continuation of the reading is actively adjusted to its initial stage. The details of the sequel are assimilated as best they can into a prepared framework where they undergo an assimilative change of meaning: Had this material stood on its own it would have had other implications than those now activated in it, in the context of meanings constructed at the beginning of the text-continuum."

[12] See my comments on M. Sternberg on this topic below (p.29).

[13] For a glimpse at the current debate on history and biblical interpretation see Bartholo-

to diverge widely, and the lack of any consensus with regard to a history of Israel suggests that the historical questions will remain unsettled for a while.[14] On
the basis of the hermeneutics developed in the following paragraphs, my main
objective will be to follow the description of the text and to evaluate the emerging portrait in terms of its literary function in the narrative and its communicative purpose. Or, in other words: I want to study the way in which the texts
shape the reader's response to the characters and the events linked with them.
That there is a link between the historical reality behind the text and the characters of the narrative, however, is indicated by the text itself. Exodus proposes to
give an account of the foundational period of Israel, which is essentially a historical subject. That Exodus is theologically interested and biased does no harm
to this fact. In referring to national history it is likely that the implied readers
shared some amount of knowledge about this common history. Apparently, the
text assumes that there indeed was a 'Moses', an 'Israel' in Egypt, a pharaoh, a
miracle at the *yam-suf*, an 'Israel' in the wilderness, etc. I will show that Exodus
does not claim to give the first account of these persons and events but to give a
certain interpretation of them. The history is presumed, the interpretation is disputed. Exodus is one part of this disputation.

Defining 'Reading'

Disagreements about the meaning of a text often stem more from the conflicting
aims of interpreters than from actual obscurities in the texts.[15] This, of course, is
true for any text, not just the Old Testament. In the following paragraphs I intend to give an overview of the hermeneutical convictions underlying the present study and thus my aims with this interpretation of Exodus. Furthermore, I
will provide an outline of the methodological tools that have been used in my
course of research. However, there is no space and need for a detailed description of the rhetorical-critical method itself. There is an abundance of books and
articles on the subject.[16] So it shall suffice to highlight only the aspects where
clarification might be necessary.

---

mew, et al. 2003.

[14] Especially, the character Moses has provoked some discussion in the past. For a few
remarks see the overview given p.126ff.

[15] Cf. Thiselton 1992, 49.

[16] To list only major contributions: Barton 1996, 198–219; The Bible and Culture Collective 1995; Howard 1994; Kennedy 1984; Muilenburg 1969; Patrick and Scult 1990;
Perelman and Olbrechts-Tyteca 1969; Plett 1991; Roth, W. 1999; Schnabel 1999; Trible
1994; Watson 1999; Watson and Hauser 1994; Wuellner 1987.

A Shared Knowledge

One important presupposition is that the implied reader did have a certain knowledge of his own history. That this is the case is evident from the text.[17] Exodus makes more sense when read according to this assumption. Further-more, to deny any shared knowledge between the author and the reader, i.e. a knowledge of their common history, would ultimately equate reading Exodus to reading a fictional literary work. A completely new world constructed by the au-thor requires no shared information, except perhaps for the well-known human condition in general. For Exodus, this seems impossible because of the author's play with the reader's premises, which can exist only if there is some sort of common denominator in history, something about which both reader and author know.[18]

Reading is always a process of interaction between the extra-textual knowl-edge that is brought to the reading and the message of the text.[19] With Gadamer, one might say that the merging of horizons creates meaning. This aspect of reading cannot be neglected, especially when the aim is to unearth the commu-nicative effects of Exodus. I will show that the process of interaction between author and implied reader works in Exodus at the levels of history and theology.

---

[17] Referring to Eco 1979, Rimmon-Kenan 1983, 117f writes: "Just as the reader parti-cipates in the production of the text's meaning, so the text shapes the reader. On the one hand, it 'selects' its appropriate reader, projects an image of such a reader, through its specific linguistic code, its style, the 'encyclopedia' it implicitly presupposes. On the other hand, just as the text pre-shapes a certain competence to be brought by the reader from the outside, so in the course of reading, it develops in the reader a specific compe-tence needed to come to grips with it, often inducing him to change his previous concep-tions and modify his outlook. The reader is thus both an image of a certain competence brought to the text and a structuring of such a competence within the text." This is preci-sely the case with Exodus and the historical competence it presupposes with its reader.

[18] Perry 1979, 36 calls these continuities 'frames' which are necessary for the reader to make sense of texts.

[19] In the case of the book of Exodus this assumption underlies at the study of the main texts of Exodus as 'polemical narrative' by Bosman 2005. He supposes a shared knowl-edge of author and intended reader in the various ancient Near Eastern myths which are deliberately alluded to and thus taken as conceptual foil on which the Exodus narrative gains much of its communicational significance. Though I feel the basis for Bosman's far-reaching general conclusions to be a bit narrow, he certainly points out a possibility for an overarching rhetorical strategy of the whole book which is not to be wiped away with a quick stroke. Nevertheless, I will only follow his line of approach in the area of ancient Near Eastern law collections, where the conceptual interrelationship can be re-garded as a scholarly consensus (see below p.80). This is mainly due to my focus on literary characterisation and not on the history of ancient Near Eastern literature in gen-eral.

We will observe the author trying to bring his influence to bear on his reader in the areas of national, social and political identities and practical personal behaviour. The implied bias of the reader is, of course, nothing that can be outlined with precision,[20] but a good number of hints are included in the text and await exposition.[21] In addition, Terence Fretheim urges readers to look at Exodus in the light of a previous reading of Genesis.[22] Here, again, the author of Exodus will be able to expect of his reader a certain amount of preconditioned perception of the shared history – this time specifically shaped by the reading of Genesis.

A Functional Approach

The definition of a method must begin with the nature of the object to be investigated. A method for looking at texts needs to do justice to the peculiarities of

---

[20] Beat Weber comments on this issue of uncertainty in his remarkable article on Exod. 1–2: "Das Element der Subjektivität wird auch bei diesem Ansatz, ähnlich wie beim historisch-kritischen, sich nicht gänzlich eliminieren lassen, zumal Dichtung ihre Wirkung oft auch der 'Fähigkeit zur Mehrdeutigkeit' verdankt und so in gewandelten Umständen neu gelesen werden will. Mehr analytische Präzision könnte auch weniger sein." (Weber 1990, 76)

[21] I am well aware of the likely opposition to my claim that the text was written with the assumption of previous knowledge on the implied reader's part. Sternberg, just to name one theorist, asserts that the effect of a shared knowledge between author and reader remains in authorial practice insignificant to the choice and presentation of the material. This belongs to what Sternberg calls 'poetic realities'. To explain, he states that even the Israelite "familiarity with the national past ... could hardly have been so complete as to rival the narrator's and prevent him from exploiting its lacunae for the arousal of narrative interest". (Sternberg 1987, 260f) Thus, the author would always have an unknown twist up his sleeve, so to speak, to create 'entertainment value'. This is the author's privilege as opposed to the audience which only receives the information that the narrator allows it to have. According to Sternberg, the awareness of these 'poetic realities' is the only effective means to avoid what he calls 'historical mysteries', i.e. the speculation about the content or amount of the historical (first) reader's previous knowledge. Of course, it is untenable to claim any sort of knowledge of the *real* reader's preconceptions unless we have the reader's written feedback. Nevertheless, there is the chance to derive from the extant text roughly what sort of knowledge the author supposed in his *implied* reader. Thus there is not much historical speculation necessary. And it is also Sternberg who argues for some sort of given that the biblical authors assumed with their original reader (e.g. cf. 132; 285f; 323). This assumed extratextual foreknowledge of the ending of a narrative, however, does not prevent the author from constructing suspense. How, when, and why will the (known) end be achieved in the narrative? That this creation of suspense actually worked – and still works today – Sternberg argues, convincingly, from a psychological perspective (261f). But that the author also plays with the reader's knowledge is something that works on a different level – the level of persuasion. It is the aim of this study not to speculate about the previous knowledge of the first readers but to focus on the communicative effect of the text for the implied reader.

[22] Cf. Fretheim 1991b.

those texts. Texts can be understood as a means of communication between a sender and his recipient, his reader or his audience.[23] Plett points out that within the rhetorical communication model the primacy lies with the recipient. Wolfgang Iser's legacy is that it has become common to be aware of the concept of the implied reader.[24] The implied reader is the text-immanent role which a concrete reader has to adopt in order to realise the potential of meaning offered in the text. The implied reader is thus part of the text. One may speak of him as the reader who was imagined by the author during the conception of the work. Throughout the present study I will use 'reader' and 'implied reader' almost as synonyms. It will be clear from the context when I deviate from this rule and speak of a concrete reader.

If a text is formulated from the perspective of the audience, everything else is subordinate to the intentionality of the effect. Hence, I want my rhetorical-critical approach to be understood as a functional method,[25] or as Booth puts it: "Rhetorical study is the study of use, of purpose pursued, targets hit or missed, practices illuminated for the sake not of pure knowledge, but of further (and improved) practice."[26] Texts, if one understands them as communication, always aim beyond mere information and toward exerting an influence on the reader. Vanhoozer agrees:

> All speech acts [...] are mission statements, words on a mission: to accomplish the purpose for which they have been sent. That purpose, according to relevance theory, is to alter the addressee's cognitive environment in some way. The 'where-

---

[23] Berger 1991, 131 is very cautious not to underestimate the differences between actual conversation and written texts: "Die Dialogsituation besteht nur der Form nach, nur fiktiv, der illokutive Charakter besteht nur in der Absicht des Autors. Es handelt sich immer nur um intendierte Kommunikation; Kommunikation vollzieht sich nicht zwischen Autor und Rezipienten, sondern unter den Rezipienten." Nevertheless, he values strongly the gain of a new perspective for the study of texts. The main difference between oral communication and a written text is the inevitable increase of indeterminacy with regard to the context, since with a written text a wider possible audience must be assumed and certain non-verbal aspects of communication are absent: "As soon as the message is written down, thus presupposing its preservation for non-immediate as well as immediate communication, we get a form of cultural semiotics where the code must take account of a wider range of receivers. The message must be expressed in a way which assumes an even lesser degree of contextual salience." (Jackson 1984, 32)

[24] Cf. Iser 1984, 63–67 (engl. Iser 1974; see also Iser 1979. For other theorists along these lines see Booth 1967 and Chatman 1978). What, in Germany, was called *Rezeptionsästhetik* has influenced American theorists and led to the development of reader-response criticism. Stanley Fish's radicalisation of Iser's approach has brought a helpful concept into discredit. I use certain aspects of *Rezeptionsästhetik* as commonsensical background of any reading process and do not embark on deep discussions or even conclusions with regard to literary theory. For a balanced and informed critique of both Iser's and Fish's contributions see Schmitz 2002, 103–110.

[25] Cf. Plett 1991, 4.

[26] Booth 1967, 441.

to' of communicative action is the reader; the 'wherefore' of communicative action is the reader's transformation (at a minimum, this means the reader will entertain a new thought).[27]

In highlighting the importance of the intentional nature and functional aspects of texts, this approach to rhetorical criticism goes beyond Muilenburg's concentration on the delimitation of the rhetorical unit and the discussion of its structure and style.[28] This is in line with W. Wuellner's hope that rhetorical criticism will be liberated from a 'rhetoric restrained', from being only concerned with finding rhetoric devices, from being reduced to stylistics.[29] He complains that some rhetorical criticism has become indistinguishable from literary criticism – a concern shared with a growing number of theorists.[30] Obviously such a liberation can lead in a number of directions, depending largely on the critic's agenda. In the present work, the emphasis will be placed on the intentionality of the text with its roots in the above mentioned communicational concerns. I will concentrate on the implied reader, and thus on the functional-persuasive aspects of certain textual features; chiefly the portrayal of the literary characters but other features will also be mentioned in passing.[31]

The method of rhetorical text-interpretation is the inversion of the process of rhetorical text-writing: a self-conscious author will assess his material, his audience and the exigency inviting his utterance. With all this in mind, he will use the rhetorical inventory at hand to achieve his desired effect with the audience

---

[27] Vanhoozer 2001, 22. With 'relevance theory' Vanhoozer is referring to the work of Sperber and Wilson 1995.

[28] Muilenburg's 1968 address (printed as Muilenburg 1969) catalysed the growing attention of biblical scholars towards the skilful artistry found in many texts of the Old Testament. Muilenburg, himself, discussed mainly the style and structure of a given textual unit, stressing that form and content must under no circumstances be separated. Classical rhetorical categories were not in his view. He rather referred to the textual phenomena as features of Hebrew, biblical or ancient Near Eastern convention.

[29] Wuellner 1987, 451.

[30] Cf. the programmatic articles Howard 1994 and The Bible and Culture Collective 1995.

[31] Only very recently I became aware of the more theoretical and philosophical works by Christof Hardmeier, who pursues to base Old Testament exegesis on a similar foundation. He speaks of the Old Testament texts as proposals by the actual authors to communicate. The reason for the existence (*raison d'être*) of a text is the author's intention to exert an (determined) influence on his audience. He arrives at very similar theoretical conclusions which are reflected in my actual practice. Given the multiplicity of research and creative thought on these issues this cannot be the place to enter into any detailed discussion here, but I am confident to assume that we encounter in this (and similar) proposals a way towards a theoretical basis which does justice to a hermeneutic of trust and humility towards the ancient documents. A helpful and concise starting point would be Hardmeier and Hunzinker-Rodewald 2006, who also present an up to date bibliography for further reading along these lines.

through the text he delivers. In classical rhetoric the desired effect is always the *persuadere*, which has two distinct aspects, neatly expressed in the German words *überzeugen* (convince) and *überreden* (persuade). The first highlights the intellectual aspect of persuasion (*docere*) and the latter the emotional (*delectare, movere*). The critic can assess the rhetorical strategies in a given text and thus deduce from it what the first audience might have understood while reading the text. "Er [the critic] spürt die formalen Wirkungen von Textappellen auf. Indem er die 'Appellstruktur der Texte' (Iser) formal-rhetorisch begründet, betreibt er gleichzeitig eine funktionale Textpsychologie."[32] In short, rhetorical criticism does not just assess what texts mean, but also how they mean.

The Organic Unity of Form and Content

Having stressed the importance of assessing how meaning is arrived at in a text, it is clear that form and content can never be separated in the interpretation of a text. This is in accordance with Trible's notion of the 'organic unity' of form and content, a notion leading her to formulate the motto for rhetorical criticism: "Proper articulation of the form-content yields proper articulation of the meaning."[33] Muilenburg states: "[A] responsible and proper articulation of the words in their linguistic patterns and in their precise formulations will reveal to us the texture and fabric of the writer's thought, not only what it is that he thinks, but as he thinks it."[34] Thus, even with a concentration on the literary characters, the structure of the book of Exodus, its relationship to known literary conventions of the Ancient Near East, the choice of the material incorporated in the argument, and the rhetorical devices used need to be kept in mind while reading Exodus.

In looking at the formal/structural features of a text one has to be careful not to lose sight of the persuasive nature of that text.[35] The recent preoccupation with finding very elaborate structures (especially chiasms) in large textual units does not consider the communicative functionality of the texts.[36] A recent example illustrating this interpretive fallacy is Meynet's book on rhetorical criticism. Discussing the mindset of the rhetorical critic he says that looking for the composition of the text can be very time consuming, "[b]ecause the most undeniable facts have the remarkable propriety of staying long hidden from one's gaze, even from the keen observer's, despite the fact that they are self-evi-

---

[32] Plett 1991, 6.

[33] Trible 1994, 91.

[34] Muilenburg 1969, 7.

[35] A similar point has been made by Möller 1999, 30 (= Möller 2003).

[36] A detailed discussion of the difficulties involved in proposing elaborate chiastic structures for the book of the covenant is found in Wright, D. P. 2004b. Wright suggests a set of avoidable fallacies regarding chiasms and, generally, is pessimistic about the interpretative worth of finding them, rightly so, when these structures are not methodologically controlled.

dent."[37] How can a structure be functional if it is so well hidden that even the trained critic has trouble finding it? What does this tell about the significance of the structure for the meaning of the text? A healthy counter-balance to this over-emphasis on elaborate structures is introduced by Watts, who argues convinc-ingly that many of the biblical texts have been written as texts intended for public, oral recitations and not, primarily, for scholarly reading.[38] Smaller struc-tures can be recognised by the listener and thus can unfold their rhetorical pur-pose. A similar point is made by Kennedy: "[A] speech or a text read aloud is presented linearly: the audience hears the words in progression without opportu-nity to review what has been said earlier, and an orally received text is charac-terized by a greater degree of repetition than a text intended to be read pri-vately."[39] The purpose of any structure must be to enhance our understanding of the material, not to distort that material; structure does not have an end in itself. This principle can serve as a faithful guide when evaluating the results of the re-cent fascination with structure in biblical studies.[40] The study of form always has to be balanced by considering the functionality of this form for the text. Nevertheless, the organic unity of form and content remains of utmost impor-tance.

This is why all the generically different material incorporated into Exodus is acknowledged in the present study. A major problem for traditional historical-critical research is the juxtaposition of such diverse material in Exodus. Nume-rous traditions, themes and genres seem to be connected only loosely with each other. In this light I put forward the following hypothesis: the book of Exodus is a carefully arranged literary work which serves to communicate a particular message. Very different kinds of material are used to reach this communicative aim. The nature and the ideational context of the interaction between author and audience gave rise to the present text of Exodus with all its literary and argu-mentative features. Thus the book of Exodus is not a mere collection of diverse and separable material but a purposefully created unit in which every part fulfils

---

[37] Meynet 1998, 171.

[38] See especially Watts 1999.

[39] Kennedy 1984, 37.

[40] Important studies for Exodus are Blum 1990, Schart 1990, Janowski 1993, 223ff, Smith 1997, and Park 2002. In his introduction (Zenger and Fabry 1998, 70) Zenger re-calls, primarily, the content but also gives much attention to the literary connectors and the plot. His attention to the connectors of the books of the Pentateuch is remarkable. Of course, the commentaries always assume some sort of overall structure for the book. Following Smith 1997, Propp 1999 sees Exodus as having a bipartite structure with the mid-point being the entire Song of the Sea (Exod. 15:1-21). The Song of the Sea begins with Egypt in the sea and summarises Exod. 1–14. It concludes with Israel camped around Yhwh's mountain sanctum, which anticipates the covenant and the construction of the tabernacle. Thus, the Song of the Sea both concludes the first half of Exodus and opens the second half. Dohmen 2004b places a particular emphasis on the issue of struc-ture. With good reason he sees the mid-point of Exodus after Exod. 18.

a role in constructing an overall argument. Due to the constraints of a manageable monograph I will focus only on the shaping of the literary characters throughout Exodus; especially in my reflections on God, a generic outline suggests itself.

This, of course, implies at the methodological level that I will concentrate on the received *Endtext* of Exodus. Seebass writes programmatically:

> Über alle Forschungsrichtungen hinweg, sie seien historisch-kritisch, konservativ, rhetorisch, strukturalistisch, semiotisch, literatur-ästhetisch oder kanonisch ..., verbreitet sich die Überzeugung, daß alle wissenschaftliche Arbeit beim Endstadium der Überlieferung (Childs: *canonical shape*!) einsetzen muß, daß ihm also eigene Untersuchungen zu widmen sind, nach denen erst Rückfragen in die Überlieferung hinein möglich werden. Rekonstruktionen bedürfen der Kontrolle ihres Erklärungswertes für das Endstadium.[41]

This present study shall be just that, a contribution to the understanding of the book of Exodus as it has been transmitted up to today.

The Cultural Conventions Shaping the Text

Biblical rhetorical criticism is often understood as a synchronic study of the text, that is, taking the text in its received form, without supposing earlier (usually perceived by historical critics as the more interesting) sources. And indeed, there is usually much consistency and unity of purpose in larger portions of the text which are well worth studying. Barton, however, complains that rhetorical criticism is sometimes used to force a sense of unity that is not there.[42] He suspects that the driving force behind rhetorical criticism might often be an apologetic one, to show that a text actually makes more sense than historical-critical scholars are prepared to admit. This point highlights the importance of the critic's hermeneutical decisions. The rhetorical critic will accept the speech-act theoretical point of view that says that pure historical reconstructions of textual origins do not help interpretation much. Thus Vanhoozer, helpfully, summarises his own hermeneutic:

> Typically, historical-critical commentaries describe either the history and process of a text's composition or 'what actually happened'. According to the traditional 'picture theory' of meaning, the literal sense would be what a word or sentence *referred* to. On my view, however, the literal sense refers to the illocutionary act performed by the author.[43]

---

[41] Seebass 1996, 188 (emphasis his). This is parallel to the concern of W. Moberly which is expressed in his exemplary monograph on Exod. 32–34 (Moberly 1983) and becoming more and more common place in newer (canonical) research as amply demonstrated by Steins 2006.

[42] Barton 1996, 204.

[43] Vanhoozer 2001, 21f. See also Dohmen's reflections on the genre 'biblical commentary' in the introduction to his commentary on Exodus (Dohmen 2004b, 29–33).

Vanhoozer introduces the terms 'thick' and 'thin' to qualify the different ways of interpreting illocutionary acts.[44] Thin interpretation omits the intentional and argumentative context that, in the first place, enables us to understand an utterance as communication. Form criticism, for instance, does not question the significance of the actual form used in a given text, whereas rhetorical criticism calls for understanding the text as an entity in its own right.[45] Hence, rhetorical criticism can be called an interpretive point of view which provides a 'thick' description of the text. This concentration on the given text, however, must be augmented by an awareness of the time and circumstances of its origin. Thus, it is important for rhetorical criticism not to end the analysis by describing the structure and consistency of a discourse but to take these results as a basis for establishing the communicative aim and power of the text. The function of a text and its exertion of influence upon the reader/hearer in a given culture and time are crucial for valuing the intention of a text and producing an interpretation with some claim to correctness.

Having stressed the reader and his cultural background, rhetorical criticism cannot, in my understanding, be a purely a-historic venture. This is not to say that the origin of a given discourse, the psychological and biographical situation of its author and its possible literary sources are being brought back into the picture. The concern is more with the cultural conventions and literary devices at the time of the text's creation. Eco cautions us not to read old texts according to the reading conventions of modern society:

> Der einfühlsame Leser, der das Kunstwerk der Vergangenheit in all seiner Frische aufnehmen will, darf es nicht nur im Lichte seiner eigenen Codes lesen (die vordem von der Erscheinung des Werkes und von dessen Assimilation seitens der Gesellschaft gespeist und redimensionalisiert worden sind): Er muß die rhetorische und ideologische Welt und die Kommunikationsumstände wiederfinden, von denen das Werk ausgegangen war. Die Philologie erfüllt diese Informationsaufgabe, durch die wir das Werk nicht in seiner akademischen Lektüre austrocknen, sondern die Bedingungen seiner Neuheit, unter denen es entstanden war, wiederfinden, in uns die jungfräuliche Situation rekonstruieren, in der sich derjenige befand, der sich dem Werk als erster näherte.[46]

Of great significance is the actual situation for which the text was written. In addition to this are the culture's value structure and world view which have direct implications for the uncontested premises of an argument. These things are so basic to the author and his implied audience that no elaboration or justifica-

---

[44] Of course Vanhoozer is not the first one using these terms. Already Geertz 1973 introduced the terms 'thick description' and 'thin description' in his field, anthropology.

[45] This is precisely the main thrust of Muilenburg's all important presidential address (Muilenburg 1969).

[46] Eco 1972, 191.

tion is necessary.[47] Watson and Hauser express this thought in their functional definition of rhetorical criticism:

> Rhetorical criticism is a form of literary criticism which uses our knowledge of the conventions of literary composition practiced in ancient Israel and its environment to discover and analyze the particular literary artistry found in a specific unit of Old Testament text. This analysis then provides a basis for discussing the message of the text and the impact it had on its audience.[48]

According to this definition, literary standards alien to ancient Hebrew conventions are not considered in the analysis of the text. The absence, however, of ancient texts describing these specific conventions means that they must be deduced from the very texts under scrutiny, in our case Exodus. This, clearly, calls for caution, as circular reasoning is very likely. Nevertheless, for a starting point, it seems safe to assume certain standards of communication which are true for all cultures and times. These standards will almost certainly be reflected in the canon of classical rhetorics. A further source of information about literary conventions can be found in the chronologically and culturally parallel texts from the ancient Near East. Sternberg, in his *Poetics,* offers such a work on which the present analysis will be partly based. From these two perspectives one can approach the question about culturally-conditioned conventions in Exodus.

An Example: the Special Case of Law in Narrative

One feature of Exodus is particularly striking for a reader who is shaped by the literary conventions of our present culture (late western modernism): the inclusion of legal material in a story. One possible way to address this issue is to discuss the interrelationship between the legal collections of the Old Testament and its ancient Near Eastern counterparts. This paragraph is not the place for an attempt to settle the issues,[49] and thus I will selectively build upon the work of

---

[47] Cf. Plett 1991, 3.

[48] Watson and Hauser 1994, 4.

[49] For a recent and very helpful discussion of comparative law studies in the ancient Near East refer to Levinson 1994. Wright, D. P. 2004a also provides an applied overview to the current discussions and gives himself a detailed and balanced contribution, arguing for a direct literary dependency between LH, LE and the casuistic collection of the book of the covenant. This of course has not gone unchallenged as the subsequent scholarly discussion has shown (Wright, D. P. 2003; Wells 2006; Wright, D. P. 2006). To decide whether a direct literary dependency or the respective drawing from a common Near Eastern legal tradition is more likely is way beyond my competence. That I follow the approach exemplified by Westbrook has mainly to do with the additional appeal of wider spread knowledge of the legal traditions in the ancient Near East for my assumption that the intended readers of the law collections where roughly aware of what was going on in the area of legal list science.

others. The discussion can, however, provide an example for the just mentioned cultural conventions which underlie the *inventio* of Exodus.

Westbrook's approach, which, among others, argues strongly for a common legal tradition in the ancient Near East, will serve as a starting point.[50] Given the scope of his study, Westbrook is not very interested in the literary framework of the law collections in Exodus. Instead, he constructs a new framework in which the covenant code and all other legal texts of the Pentateuch are part of a large ancient Near Eastern law tradition. Thus, he assumes a context working on an ideational level rather than on a literary level. This may serve as a fruitful vantage point for the present discussion.[51] Westbrook suggests that there was a great deal of very specific common knowledge spread among the people in and around Israel. This well-known legal tradition cut across many languages, cultures and historical borders and constituted the background of all law-writers and law-readers as well. It is this common knowledge which makes the comparative approach viable from a rhetorical-critical perspective: a preconditioned reader will automatically perceive differences and similarities – between his knowledge and the text – as constituting meaning, or, at least, as nuancing the surface content of the text. The backdrop of the rejected might-have-beens invests the choice of themes covered in the law collection with significance.

Beyond the level of the single regulation the author of Exodus can and will fall back on the conventions of legal writings, including their various communicational functions. One such function of an ancient Near Eastern law-collection is as propaganda. Watts argues that "the parallel contents reflect the similar goals of biblical and Mesopotamian law, namely, the characterization of the law-giver as just according to internationally recognized standards of law."[52] This suggestion is very much in line with my conclusions below (p.80ff) and shows the value of escaping modern reading conventions when approaching ancient texts.

---

[50] Cf. Westbrook 1988; Westbrook 1994; Westbrook 2003. Westbrook concentrates, mainly, on the similarities between biblical and Mesopotamian law, whereas others such as Greenberg and Paul stress the differences.

[51] One probably does not need to follow Westbrook's arguments entirely, especially in reconstructing texts by merging the many similar laws into one 'ideal' law/regulation. Another debatable issue is the 'scientific' *Sitz im Leben* which Westbrook assumes for the law collections in all ancient Near Eastern cultures. See also the criticism by Jackson 2006, 10–16 who accuses Westbrook of positivism and anachronism. This discussion, however, seems to be due to the differing interests the respective scholars pursue. Jackson's own theses receive a similar criticism on a different set of claims in the areas of orality, sociology and legal *praxis* (cf. Tomes 2008). All of these discussions betray the (natural) dependency of our results on our presuppositions and questions. However, to ponder the ideational level of law collections, as Westbrook does, helps in the present context to keep the focus on the meta-communicative level, which I attempt to explore.

[52] Watts 1996, 6.

The awareness, or even exploration, of this ideational room in which biblical literature was created is still a *desideratum* in many exegetical studies. Rhetorical criticism, however, contributes a methodological framework which is explicitly open to such considerations.

The Levels of Reading

The role of the implied reader in the *dispositio* of the text has already been mentioned. This implied reader is not necessarily an individual, hypothetical person. The author might also choose to imagine a mixed audience for which he composes his text. Amit provides an insightful reflection on different possible reading levels which are connected with different addressees. It is worth quoting in full:

> An examination of the rhetorical and formative functions of the biblical text brings us to a further issue: namely, that of the target audience. It seems reasonable to assume that the biblical story was simultaneously addressed to all levels of the people, from the simplest person, who was presumably an auditor-listener, to the educated reader. One may go even further, and argue that it was not a story intended only for a small community of intellectuals, lovers and consumers of literature. Its writing within a historiographical setting was done in order to transmit the ancestral tradition, and was intended to serve and to educate all levels of people. One may therefore conjecture that different levels of target audiences were taken into account in the editing and fashioning of this literature. The primary messages of a story, which were also addressed to the widest levels of the people, needed to be clear and understandable, so that there would be no mistaking the message, even without sophisticated exegesis, when it came to different kinds of audiences. ... The compositional sophistication involved in these methods of shaping is thus a means used by the biblical narrator in relation to the enlightened and refined audience. On the lower levels of reading, the story is understood as an imitation of reality, and the reader or listener tests what he is told in accordance with his ability to examine reality. He asks questions matching his own life wisdom and experience, such as: what happened and why, when and where? On this level, the biblical story is likely to be perceived as a simple dramatic narrative. But on the higher levels of reading it is interpreted far beyond the imitation of reality. On these levels, the episodes are likely to be perceived as motifs, the figures involved as archetypes, and the language as a highly stylized tool, filled with allusions, sound-patterns and word-plays. On these levels of reading, the reader activates his sensitivity to analogies, to niceties of changes within structures of repetition, to syntactical variations, to the use of nomenclature, and the like – that is, to all those techniques of composition whose discovery enriches the experience of reading, arouses the excitement of the reader at the manner of fashioning and, above all, deepens the message of the narrated materials.[53]

These reading levels can, indeed, be found throughout Exodus. The richness of some passages in Exodus invite a reading beyond the mere dramatic level of

---

[53] Amit 2003, 13.

the unfolding events. Numerous allusions betray complex intertextual and intra-textual networks which are able to express nuances as well as a fullness of meaning. Exodus is not, however, primarily a subversive text in that its main plot deceives the simple reader into understanding one thing while at the same time deconstructing this reading in a way only perceptible to a sophisticated reader. Exodus is largely homogeneous and consistent in its communication. Even in the initial portrayal of Moses, which is remarkably complex in its rhetorical strategy, the unity of purpose is given.

These various reading levels will be discussed in the present study. Important distinctions are to be made between the story level (i.e. the narrated world) and the literary level (i.e. a meta-level addressing the relations between text and reader). Further meta-levels are, for instance, theological, communicational or persuasive in nature, relationship based, or dealing with preconceptions. The awareness of these multiple levels prevents a narrow or thin reading of Exodus or its passages.[54]

I am speaking of an awareness which is essentially, in my opinion, the nature of rhetorical criticism. There is no rigid, step-by-step guide. One may speak of rhetorical criticism as an art-form,[55] which suggests the need for openness and intuition. Different theorists offer different approaches. Trible understands rhetorical criticism as an interpretive perspective. From her exploration of what she calls "Muilenburg rubric" (i.e. that "proper articulation of the form-content yields proper articulation of the meaning") she develops a helpful set of suggestions for where to start, what to do, and what to expect as the outcome.[56] Regarding form, rhetorical criticism puts more stress on the particular and less on the typical and conventional, although the latter aspects of a text are taken into account, as well. In accordance with Trible's reader-response hermeneutic the environment of a text (extrinsic issues) is less significant than its intrinsic properties: "Basically an intrinsic approach, it [rhetorical criticism] focuses on a text rather than on such factors as historical background, archaeological data, authorial intention, sociological setting or theological milieu. [...] Yet," Trible goes on to say, "no text is an island unto itself."[57] Nevertheless the intrinsic reading best identifies rhetorical-critical reading – a notion not uncommon with most rhetorical critics. As outlined above, the present study retains an emphasis on intentional discourse and the notion of Exodus as communication designed for a certain historical situation. This underlying hermeneutic differs from Trible's relativist point of view.

---

[54] An example for a multi-layered reading – reflecting the various possible audiences, and observing the observing the "how" of text-reader interaction would be for the burning bush episode Davies, O. 2006.

[55] Plett 1991, 6f.

[56] Trible 1994, 91–101.

[57] Trible 1994, 94.

The "articulation of meaning" (the second part of Muilenburg's motto) prompts Trible to define meaning from three points of view: that of the author, that of the text and that of the audience. Rhetorical criticism works somewhere between these alternatives: there is more than a single meaning but less than un-limited meanings. Texts reveal things about their author (resources, knowledge, issues, perspectives and skills). At the same time, what a text means can be other than what its author intended it to mean. The second centre for meaning is the text itself, in its content, interlocking structures and artistic configurations. For rhetorical critics texts are more than artistic objects: language has the power to specify and to signify meaningfully. The reader gives the text voice; he artic-ulates form-content in order to articulate meaning. Readers bring various skills, knowledge and sensitivities to the interpretation process, hence the multiplicity of readings for one text. But who is the reader (ancient, first audience; ideal or implied audience; contemporary reader; …)? Here I suggest that rhetorical crit-ics should be aiming for a maximum self-awareness of their presuppositions. This should prevent, as far as possible, the danger of reading the texts with a standard which is foreign to the text itself.

Regarding the words "proper articulation" Trible stresses that "not all articu-lation is valid, and not all valid articulation is equally valid."[58] But who defines "proper"? An alternative word-choice is the equally ambiguous "appropriate", which, again, is open to various definitions according to the presuppositions of each exegete. Trible suggests that this phrase simply intends to call the inter-preter to articulate carefully and with caution. She also insists that every appro-priate reading needs to account for all form-content. Finding meaning goes be-yond pure form-content analysis, but the results from the form-content analysis need to be incorporated into the 'articulation of meaning'.[59] This is expressed in Muilenburg's leading proposition, in particular the verb "to yield". So far, we have considered Trible's suggestion for a guideline for the exegete who uses rhetorical criticism. She recommends transparency and honesty about one's pre-suppositions, while remaining adamant about the importance of the unity of form and content of texts – the heart of rhetorical criticism. Thus her approach may be characterised as an interpretive perspective: it does not offer a specific methodology.[60] The present study will be guided by this rhetorical critical per-spective in its perception of Exodus.

---

[58] Trible 1994, 99.

[59] Cf. Dohmen 2004a who also argues that exegesis needs to yield a spectrum of possi-ble readings and to limit textual meanings.

[60] By contrast, Kennedy's understanding of rhetorical criticism offers an articulated pro-cedure which comes much closer to a specific methodology (Kennedy 1984). For my present purpose, rhetorical criticism as an interpretive framework, such as Trible under-stands it, is more effective. Kennedy's methodology has been specifically designed for the criticism of texts of whose historical and literary backgrounds are better known than these of the Torah.

Some Reflections on the Boundaries of Exodus

That Exodus is a literary unit of its own is something which has to be argued, although a recent resurgance of canonical criticism came to think of the "book" as the elementary unit in the process of reading the canon.[61] This, of course, presents a welcome theoretical support for my work but I hope to justify the delimitation of my object of research on exegetical grounds.

I take my lead from Weimar and Zenger who observe that Exodus can be understood as a unit: the book is included in the large Pentateuchal draft of history from creation to the conquest of Canaan ... "[und] doch kann das Buch aus dem größeren Erzählzusammenhang, in den es eingebunden ist herausgenommen und für sich selbst gestellt werden, da die Buchgrenzen zugleich deutliche Einschnitte im Erzählablauf anzeigen."[62] In the following, I will show that it makes sense to start reading Exodus with its first chapter and to end after its last.[63] This sets the horizon against which the following reflections on the literary characters are to be understood. Nevertheless, I will always keep in mind that there is a literary context larger than Exodus and, especially, that the knowledge of Genesis seems to be presupposed by the implied reader. Exodus was probably never transmitted apart from its Pentateuchal context; but the Torah was also never divided at different points in the narrative.

The Opening of Exodus

The book of Exodus derives its name ואלה שמות from the quote of Gen. 46:8a in Exod. 1:1a – a fitting start for a book in which the further fulfilment of the promises to the patriarchs is recorded. The genealogical list in Exod. 1:1-5 provides the reader with several significant allusions to the history of the sons of Jacob. The link with Gen. 46 is especially strong with the mention of the number of the family coming to Egypt (Gen. 46:27). Gen. 46 functions in the Joseph

---

[61] See Steins 2006, 58ff for detailed arguments. For the problems linked with the delimitation of rhetorical units and the subjectivity connected with this venture, see The Bible and Culture Collective 1995, 178f.

[62] Weimar and Zenger 1975, 11.

[63] Römer 2002, 221 supports the often noted narrative movement from slavery to service and concludes that Exodus is "eine klar erkennbare Einheit." The only difficult candidate for a literary unit would be Numbers. The demarcation of Numbers from its Pentateuchal context, however, has been shown by Olson 1985. The turning away from the various Pentateuchal sources running through the books of the Torah seems to mark a new trend in Old Testament criticism, so the death of the Yahwist has already been pronounced. (Cf. Gertz, Schmid and Witte 2002. One contributor to this collection, Auld 2002, 233f, considers Numbers to be an attachment to Leviticus and Leviticus, an attachment to Exodus.)

cycle as a conclusion to the previous narrative by bringing the plot to a halt for the reader. Benno Jacob states that one function of the Joseph cycle is to express why the בני יעקב deserve to carry the name בני ישראל.[64] This aim seems to be fulfilled in Gen. 46 (cf. v.8a!) – the brothers regained unity. The genealogical recollection marks the end of the time of Israel's split family in Canaan, expressing the transition of the entire family to Egypt. From Gen. 46:2-4 the reader knows that the meeting between Jacob and his son Joseph will work out positively. But more than that, this brief Yhwh speech prefigures what will happen in Egypt and that they will not remain there forever, which is exactly to what the beginning of Exodus alludes. The sons of Israel will become a great nation (גוי גדול).

It would have been sufficient to remind the reader of this divine forecast at the start of Exodus, but the author chose to list, explicitly, all the sons of Jacob as a clearer link to the patriarchal promises. It was this family that received the promise to flourish. Considering Jacob's remarks on the attribution בני ישראל in Gen. 46 and Exod. 1, it seems likely that the author of Exodus wants to take up the thread of the patriarchal promises of which the twelve sons – representing the twelve tribes, as Exod. 1:7 suggests – are heirs.[65]

But it is not only the list of names which establishes the literary connection between the patriarchal promises and the beginning of Exodus. The fruitfulness of the Israelites (Exod. 1:7) is expressed in terms which force the reader to recall the multiplication as part of the covenant and thus as the fulfilment of its promises: Exod. 1:7 פרו reflects Gen. 9:7; 17:6; 28:3; 35:11; 48:4 and וירבו alludes to Gen. 16:10; 17:2; 22:17; 26:4.20; 28:3; 35:11; 48:4.[66]

Leder, in his discussion of the themes dominating the beginning and end of the book of Exodus, goes a bit far when he takes the narrative Exod. 1:1-7 as "a word of blessing, [reminding] the reader that what God began with Abraham is being fulfilled in Egypt."[67] It is quite obvious from the narrative that Israel's stay in Egypt is not the best-case scenario. The distance from the land of the promise, together with the political heteronomy, are counterproductive to the full enjoyment of Yhwh's blessings.

In order to establish an *inclusio* keeping together Exod. 1 and 39–40, Leder argues for a theological link between the creation narrative, the opening of Exo-

---

[64] Cf. Jacob 1997, 3.

[65] The mention of the בית־יעקב in Gen. 46:27 provides another link between Genesis and Exodus. This Hebrew expression is only used again in Exod. 19:3. (Cf. Dohmen 2004b, 33, who considers the allusions to Gen. 46 to highlight the role of Exod. 1 and 19 in the macro structure of Exodus.)

[66] Cf. Leder 1999, 18, who regards the multiplication language in Exod. 1:7 as countering "death in Joseph's generation." In my opinion, this link is less prevalent because the patriarchs all died at some stage, which was never perceived in the Genesis narrative as a threat to the divine promises.

[67] Leder 1999, 18.

dus and the final consecration of the tabernacle at the end.[68] It is true that Exod. 1:7 (שרץ) establishes more of a connection with the creation narrative (Gen. 1:20-21) and the Noah-promise (Gen. 8:17; 9:7) than it does with the patriarchal promises. Also, the linkage between the narrative Eden and of the tabernacle itself has long been noticed.[69] But to carry into the beginning of Exodus the notion of Yhwh's presence as the divine 'blessing' seems unreasonable. The divine presence is a theme both in Gen. 1–2 and in Exod. 25–40, but not in Exod. 1:1-7, where the divine blessing is concretely narrowed down to the theme of multiplication. Leder's conclusion is that: "It is the particularist application of blessing, by reference to Israel's growth and priestly work in the Lord's mediate presence, that forms a frame for the Exodus narrative."[70] It seems doubtful whether this can be functional at the reading level, which he so strongly emphasises as being important. The link simply appears too weak to be rhetorically effective.[71] Houtman uses the terms 'prologue'/'introduction' for the passage Exod. 1:1-7. In addition to establishing the connection between Genesis and Exodus, their function would be to give the information needed to understand the developments from Exod. 1:8 onwards.[72]

If we are looking at *inclusio* as a means for establishing the textual unity of Exodus, we must look in a different direction which is less theologically centred and more literarily significant for the reading process. It is, again, Leder who provides a starting point in suggesting that Israel's building activities throughout Exodus form a possible framework motif.[73] Exod. 1:11 describes the building object as ערי מסכות (storage cities).[74] Exod. 25–40 refers, frequently, to the משכן (tabernacle/dwelling place). Thus we find the rhetorical device of assonance which is strengthened in its linking effect by the repetition of various forms of the root עבד (serve/work). Israel is picturedin both cases as working

---

[68] Leder 1999, 18f.

[69] Cf. Wenham 1986.

[70] Leder 1999, 19.

[71] Leder makes a second proposal for an *inclusio* in Exodus (Leder 1999, 19f). He sees a link between the filling of the land of Egypt (Exod. 1:7) and the filling of the tabernacle with God's glory (מלא). Here, again, he draws from Genesis (Gen. 1:28) in order to widen the scope of Exod. 1:7 so that it refers to the entire earth at the intertextual level. But the linkage, again, is mainly one of theological concepts at different levels, a device which can hardly account for an easily accessible communicative strategy.

[72] Cf. Houtman 1993, 220. A similar proposal has been forwarded by Vialle 2004, who considers 1:1–2:10 as prologue to the entire book, introducing the major themes of Exodus.

[73] Cf. Leder 1999, 20f. He suggests two more aspects of Exodus' framework: "from land of slavery to the land of service" and "from the mountain to the tabernacle." These lines of development are not so convincing, but in their cumulative weight they might be aspects which guide a reader.

[74] Cf. Hoffmeier 1997, 116–122 for a recent and balanced discussion of the implied historical aspects.

for a sovereign. Indeed many aspects of Exodus suggest a change in masters for Israel – from the very demanding and unsupportive pharaoh to the very caring, but no less demanding, God of the fathers.[75] The root עבד plays a major role in expressing this progressive element of the plot of Exodus. The completion of the construction of the pharaoh's storage cities is never recorded, whereas the completion of Yhwh's dwelling is elaborately narrated. The consecration of the tabernacle by Yhwh (Exod. 40:34-35) concludes the entire ('building-') plot and marks it as overwhelmingly successful. All this emphasises the contrast between the two projects and also Israel's role in the projects. As this framework is central to the plot of Exodus and functions mainly on the narrative level, without needing elevation at the theological level, we have found an *inclusio*-strategy which is likely to be effective rhetorically.

The End of Exodus

The transition from Genesis to Exodus is relatively clear, and that Exod. 1:1 presents a new beginning has already been argued. That Exodus reaches its conclusion in 40:38, however, is something which is less obvious. For a reader who knows the Pentateuch in its entirety, Exodus has several loose ends and many plots that do not end with the book.[76] At the level of the entire Pentateuch, one could speak of Exod. 19:1–Num. 10:10 as a major literary unit, which might be called 'Sinai composition'. This unit would, mainly, be based on the plot features of the travelling narrative. It opens with a major itinerary note in 19:1-2, including detailed chronological specifications. There is no report of other spatial movement until the narrative reaches Num. 10:11-13, which, again, includes detailed chronological remarks. Thus, there is a long literary delay in the description of the actual, physical move toward the land of promise. This portrayal of the people, thus, gives room for a description of the development of the relationship between them and their God. Despite arguments for treating this material as one, large block,[77] the present study will concentrate only on the part

---

[75] Cf. p.215 below.

[76] Cf. the discussion in Weimar and Zenger 1975, 11f, which expresses similar results: Though the story continuous "ist der Abschnitt Ex 40,36–38 offenkundig als Abschluß des Exodusbuches gedacht. Die Reflexion über die Funktion der Wolke für das Aufbrechen oder Nichtaufbrechen der Israeliten von ihrem jeweiligen Lagerplatz steht im jetzigen Zusammenhang literarisch wie syntaktisch merkwürdig isoliert da, greift bezeichnenderweise aber gerade auf Num 9,15–23 und damit auf das Ende der Sinaigeschichte vor, was gewiß deshalb geschehen ist, um trotz des Weiterlaufens der Sinaigeschichte vorgreifend deren Abschluss und zugleich den Abschluß des Buches Exodus zu gestalten." Similar results are found in studies focussing on the tabernacle construction pericopes (Exod. 25–40). The following shall be named as representatives: Hurowitz 1985; Hurowitz 1992; Timmer 2009.

[77] Cf. e.g. Wenham 1981, 14–18; Sailhamer 1992, 33; Zenger and Fabry 1998, 74–79.

which is included in the book of Exodus. Besides the practical consideration, there are strong arguments for treating Exodus as a unit of its own, which has its definite and rhetorically appropriate conclusion in Exod. 40.

The break between Exodus and Leviticus is obviously an ancient one as there are no text-critical witnesses for a different division.[78] Furthermore, 40:34-38 forms a proper literary closure of the book in its recapitulation of past experiences and its anticipation of leaving Sinai under the leadership of the now present God of the exodus. Leviticus begins by mentioning the אהל מועד in Lev. 1:1, picking up the theme from the last chapters of Exodus. However, Leviticus goes beyond the actual building of the sanctuary in the presence of Yhwh to a discussion of what this divine presence implies in liturgical and practical life. The break after Exod. 40:38 is also justified rhetorically. 40:34–38 is very iterative in its wording; an *epipher*[79] is the structuring principle:

[34] Then the cloud covered the tent of meeting   Yhwh's presence fills

and the glory of Yhwh filled the tabernacle.   the habitation

[35] And Moses could not enter the tent of meeting, because the cloud settled on it

and the glory of Yhwh filled the tabernacle.

[36] But when the cloud was lifted from the tabernacle, the   "on all their jour-
Israelites would set out   neys"

on all their journeys.

[37] But if the cloud was not lifted up, then they would not journey further until the day it was lifted up

[38] for the could of Yhwh was on the tabernacle by day, but fire would be on it at night in the sight of all the house of Israel

on all their journeys.

This feature belongs to an elevated style – without being elaborate – and, thus, signifies an emphasis of the worthy end of the book of Exodus. Repeti-

---

[78] To my knowledge, there are no manuscripts of the Pentateuch which either do not separate these two books, at all, or do separate them, but at a different point. If the reason for the division was motivated by material constraints, one would expect a variety of different divisions which would have left their traces in the textual witnesses. This, of course, is an *argumentum e silentio*. Nevertheless, the amount of documentary findings of pentateuchal material seems enough to justify a supporting role of this argument. Cf. Zenger's comments in Zenger and Fabry 1998, 68, 70.

[79] An *epipher* is also known as *antistrophe, epistrophe* and as *conversio* and is defined as a *repetitio*, with the repeated elements positioned at the end of two or more (sentence) units (Plett 1991, 35).

tion slows down the flow of information and, thus, helps the reader to rest and reflect, all the while creating clarity and directing the mind.[80] The first two verses (40:34-35) succinctly conclude the main theme of the preceding chapters by stating that Yhwh is, finally, living among the people in his finished habitation. 40:36-38, then resumes the journey. This is supported by a reintroduction of the fire and cloud theme at the start of the wilderness wanderings (13:21-22).

The cloud (הענן) forms a verbal link between these two concluding texts, thus, pointing to the presence of Yhwh both when the people rest and when they travel. The use of the cloud-metaphor at crucial points throughout the narrative warrants a closer look at this motif. Yhwh's presence, as expressed by the cloud-motif, comes with a number of different connotations and implications. The noun ענן "is most frequent in figures of speech or metaphors for transitoriness, immensity, and impenetrability."[81] Generally, metaphors lose their communicative power when they are limited to just one interpretation. In the case of Exodus, it seems that the author used all three connotations of the word to express the nature of Yhwh's theophanies. Nevertheless, depending on the respective context, one of the notions dominates the metaphor. All theophanies bear the characteristics (1) of the two extremes 'visibility' and 'impenetrability', (2) of the overwhelming immensity for the experience of the onlookers, and (3) of the temporal transitoriness of the appearance. This range of meanings works at the paradigmatic level. At the syntagmatic level a certain set of ideas is always linked with the cloud-motif. The 'cloud' guides, comes down, speaks, shines and confirms the position of the leaders. These ideas connected with ענן function at the text-semantic level as a device linking different passages in Exodus. Starting off the chain, Exod. 13:21-22 brings together the theophany with the theme of guidance. The text functions as a summary notice and anticipates the later continuous divine presence.[82] This summary function of Exod. 13:21–22 is highlighted by the poetic characteristics,[83] the separation from the preceding narrative by content, and the break in the chain of waw-consecutive forms. The attention of the reader is heightened as he expects the introduction of something new and, at the same time, the author ties the reader's expectation to the 'pillar' theme: the reader expects Yhwh's enduring presence with his people.

---

[80] Plett 1991, 33.

[81] Futato 2002, 465.

[82] Cf. Houtman 1996, 253. He translates: "By day the pillar of cloud never left its post and by night the pillar always went in front of the people" (similar to Luther Bibel 1984: "Niemals…"). This is also implied by the merism 'day – night' which expresses continuity.

[83] Observe that the two clauses in v.22 complement each other by contributing respectively to the verb לא־ימיש and to the prepositional object לפני העם. Further note the parallelism constructed with the threefold mention of the sequence 'by day' – 'by night' (cf. Houtman 1996, 253f).

The theme of guidance implies protection. This is narratively expressed by the context of the next occurrence of the cloud-motif. In Exod. 14:19.20.24 (19: עמוד הענן) the cloud is situated between the enemies and Israel and thus protecting them. Here, the immensity of the experience shocks the enemies, causing them to recognise the presence of Israel's god, and thus prompting them to flee the situation. The 'cloud' theme, linked with the presence of Yhwh as travel guide and protector, is, again, taken up only when the narrator anticipates the further wanderings in connection with Yhwh's consecrating[84] the newly-built sanctuary (Exod. 40:34.35.36.37.38). The link to the similar summary notice in Exod. 13:21-22 is made by taking up motifs: the fire, the pillar shape, and day-night. The cloud and the glory now settle among the people. Prior to this event the cloud stayed emphatically on Mount Sinai where it symbolised the impressive presence of Yhwh as source of the revelations to Moses. By mentioning the mode of communication with Moses the author recalls Yhwh's revelatory presence on Sinai and thus brings together the two main themes connected with the cloud: guiding-protecting and revelation-authorisation of the leaders.

The second main theme of revelation and authorisation deserves further exploration. In the relevant passages the cloud appears to be static: Exod. 16:10; 19:9.16; 24:15-16.18; 34:5. Exod. 16,10 mentions a new characteristic of the cloud; it is the place of revelation. The כבוד יהוה enters the cloud in order to confirm Moses' and Aaron's role as leaders. In this crisis-situation Yhwh interferes directly and visibly to strengthen the position of the appointed leaders. From Exod. 19:16 onward the cloud remains settled on Mount Sinai and is the explicit place of revelation to which only Moses has physical access. This revelatory aspect of the theophany continues to dominate the cloud-motif. Yhwh's presence with his covenant people is not only a guiding and supporting presence but, also, a demanding one, as becomes apparent when Yhwh makes his standards known. To be sure, revelation from Yhwh is not limited narratively to the simultaneous presence of the cloud, as e.g. Exod. 3:2-5 and 15:25 prove. But, the cloud motif describes Yhwh's presence as a metaphor for divine transitoriness, immensity and impenetrability.

As it appears, the book Exodus finds its appropriate end in Exod. 40:38. Here a number of themes and motifs, introduced and developed throughout the book, are repeated and brought together as the climax.[85] Yhwh has remembered his people and established a relationship with them, a relationship which is now settled enough to face new challenges. Of course, there is still enough unresolved material so that the remainder of the Sinai composition in the Pen-

---

[84] Cf. Houtman 2000, 599f, who argues against the interpretation that Yhwh entered the sanctuary in order to stay there forever.

[85] Park 2002, 141f, makes a strong case for a link between Exod. 24:15b-18a and 40:34-35. Further elements connected to the ending of Exodus may be found, but the case has been argued sufficiently for our purposes.

tateuch is thoroughly linked with Exodus. Nevertheless, Exodus should be regarded as a single, major unit inside the Pentateuch. The book stands in its own right, bringing to a conclusion an internal argument which is formulated with various literary genres such as plain narrative, dialogues, Yhwh-speeches, and poetry. Leder makes a theologically relevant observation regarding these structural considerations: "Remarkably, then, Exodus ends where Genesis begins. Or, to put it another way: The end of Exodus picks up where Adam's and Eve's sin created a disjunction between the presence of God and human history."[86]

The Outline of the Study

The hermeneutical and methodological presuppositions of the present study have been presented; the corpus which forms its base has been delineated. In the following three chapters I will look intensely at the literary characters Yhwh, Moses, and Israel. Each of these chapters includes a brief discussion of earlier approaches to the study of these characters, because every reading of a text is influenced, implicitly or explicitly, by earlier readings of the same texts. Although almost all of these approaches come from quite different hermeneutical and methodological presuppositions, the insights and problems discussed sharpen my perception of the same texts. The remaining elements of each of these chapters is dictated solely by the demands of the respective subject. A conclusion completes each chapter and summarises the findings from a certain perspective.

The chapter on Yhwh is structured along genre lines. Firstly, I will consider the contribution of the narrative parts of Exodus to the portrait of God. An initial focus will be on the epithets placed at important junctures of the book. The first encounter between reader and character deserves close attention, and the levels of interaction with the pharaoh and Israel will be examined. The poem of Exodus (Exod. 15:1-18) serves as a hinge between the narrative characterisation and the legal characterisation of Yhwh, and thus it will be discussed just before the legal parts of Exodus. This last part of the chapter concentrates on a neglected, but very important, element of the divine picture in Exodus. Although the legal collections say much about their recipients, they also reveal deep insights into the law-giver's nature and his concerns.

Moses is, usually, the first person in Exodus to attract a critic's attention. Here, I will specifically focus on the difference between his first appearance in Exod. 2–5 and his later development. There is remarkable tension in the Mosaic portrayal, which opens interesting insights into the implied reader's preconceptions. Here, we can closely trace the argumentative strategy of the author in his attempts to convince this reader. Furthermore, the paradigmatic qualities of the character Moses will be discussed.

---

[86] Leder 1999, 30.

Reader-identification is at the heart of the chapter on Israel. Israel, as a collective character, invites the implied reader's identification. The bridging of the historical gulf between the Israel of the narrative and the Israel of the implied reader is a key focus throughout this chapter. It will be shown that the complexity of this character is a central aspect of Exodus' rhetoric, which urges its readers to comply with the ideal the author sought to communicate with his book.

The size of Exodus as the textual base for this study dictates that not all pericopes can be treated with equal attention. In some cases I can rely on the work of others, whereas in other cases issues have to remain undiscussed. The last chapter, besides summarising the results, will point to these issues and other questions which deserve further enquiry.

A word must now be said about the difficulty of distributing the material between the characters in the presentation of the results. The main characters of Exodus are always linked with each other, often so inextricably that it is difficult to refrain from commenting on the characters which are not the subject of the respective chapter. This is especially true in the case of 'Yhwh'. Here, I often anticipate material which would also have its rightful place in a later chapter, but this is done in order to present a fuller argument. These instances become rarer as the argument unfolds. At some places there is the need to include a more detailed discussion of a problem or rhetorical feature of the text which has only supportive weight for the discussion of literary character. The nature of these comments, however, do not justify excursuses or their collection in a separate chapter. Thus, I ask for the patience of my readers to continue reading and to await the return to the proper argument.

CHAPTER 2

YHWH – 'NATIONAL HERO' AND 'KING'

Yhwh is the only character who features in all the different genres in Exodus. The direct and indirect characterisations of Yhwh[1] are divided along genre lines. Only in the poem (Exod. 15) and in two epithets (Exod. 20:5-6; 34:6-7) do we find direct comments on what Yhwh is like. In the narrative and in most of the legal portions of the text we get to know this character indirectly. The following discussion will cover the portrayal of Yhwh along the lines of the main generic distinctions found in Exodus, i.e. narrative (p.35ff), poetry (p.77ff) and legal material (p.80ff). This structure is helpful, mainly, because of the history of research on the book of Exodus. Earlier discussions of character tended to concentrate on narrative texts, so that I can draw on a number of studies in the construction of my argument. The 'legal' characterisation of Yhwh, however, opens up a new avenue which adds to the picture of God as Exodus paints it. Each part will focus on how the portrayal of God in Exodus is designed and how it influences the reading-process. But, first, a few remarks on the scholarly context of my research on Yhwh in Exodus are necessary.

The Rhetorical Function of Yhwh – the Interpretive Debate

Quite naturally, the portrayal of God finds mention in many Old Testament theologies. When it comes to the contribution of the book of Exodus the discussion usually centres around topics such as: 'the divine name', 'God's role in the exodus events', 'God's role in the covenant of Sinai', and 'the grace of God as expressed in Exod. 20:5 and 34:6–7'. Recent commentaries on Exodus provide good summaries of the interpretive debates on these issues.[2] However, as these discussions come nowhere near to a rhetorical-critical analysis of the literary character Yhwh, there is no need to review them here. At relevant points I will, of course, give due consideration to the scholarly context. Nevertheless, I wish to highlight a few contributions that influenced my reading of the text with regard to the divine character in Exodus.

Firstly, Sternberg in his *Poetics* writes perceptively on the literary implications of the generic divide between divine and human characters. God is not just another character in the Old Testament; the portrayal of God has its own laws:

---

[1] For this distinction see the introduction (p.4).

[2] See esp. Houtman's three extensive volumes and most recently Dohmen 2004b.

One does not play tricks with God's image ... Permanent ambiguation of
character ... is out of the question in the divine sphere. Paradoxically, divine
otherness breeds familiarity ('knowledge') by ideological fiat. Taken together,
then, all these practices of characterization dovetail with the essentials of
character: God's ways may remain mysterious but man is himself a mystery.[3]

With the last comment Sternberg hints at the common practice in biblical literature, which is to let the reader marvel at God's deeds in history – how and when
he will interfere in human affairs – but not at his nature which "tends to con-
stancy."[4] Even when God's deeds and his nature contradict each other in the
narrative the latter aspect is often neglected. By contrast, the characterisation of
humans as variable and inconsistent grabs the attention of the onlooker. To say
that the character God is portrayed as being constant does not mean that the
emerging picture is ironclad or unambiguous. Black-and-white rendering or
one-dimensionality of characters cannot be found in the Bible.[5] Or in Sternberg's words: "the gaps about God concentrate in what exactly he is up to at this
or that moment in time; those about man, in what he is in the first place or has
become in the process."[6] Thus Yhwh's nature as a literary character is generally
marked by stability. Hence, we should not expect too much of a development in
his depiction in the course of Exodus.

Reading the exodus narrative (Exod. 1–15) from a deconstructionist perspective, which explicitly discusses the narrative portrayal of Yhwh, may here serve
to highlight some hermeneutical dimensions involved when looking at the character Yhwh from a literary perspective. Eslinger asks if the reader of Exodus is
urged to evaluate the exodus event and, especially, if Yhwh's role in it is positive. In answer to his own question, Eslinger reads the text contrary to the common interpretive tradition which positively evaluates the exodus events. He ad-
mits that there are many texts in the Old Testament that judge the exodus events
in a very positive way, but that Exod. 1–15 do not do so. He rightly distinguishes between the omniscient and omnipotent (implied) narrator of the story
(created by the real author) and the characters inside the story who are "stuck
fast and firm within the limitations of their respective positions in their story environment."[7] We, the readers, are better off in that we can perceive the narrator's outside perspective.

Eslinger takes his start with a deconstruction of the poem in Exod. 15. From
the explicit temporal and situational *Verortung* of the song in 15:1+19, he concludes that the narrator distances himself from this situation and wants his
reader to understand that the reaction of the people in the song is exactly what is

---

[3] Sternberg 1987, 325.

[4] Sternberg 1987, 324.

[5] Cf. Sternberg 1987, 157f.

[6] Sternberg 1987, 324.

[7] Eslinger 1991, 47.

to be expected, psychologically, in this situation (parallel to 14:31). How else can they respond to this unexpected escape from near death by the Egyptian army? Thus the narrator "displays his separation from that time, place and state of mind."[8] This distancing can be found throughout the entire exodus narrative.[9] To substantiate his critical reading of the exodus events in Exod. 1–15 Eslinger provides few details. Basically, he constructs the text's highly critical attitude toward Yhwh by noting the irony between the lines. Throughout, Yhwh appears to be obsessed with self-glorification, at the cost of both the Israelites, whose suffering is prolonged, and the Egyptians, who are struck beyond measure. With reference to the title of his article ("Freedom or Knowledge? Perspective and Purpose in the Exodus Narrative") Eslinger writes: "In reward for the part they play in this divine comedy, both Israel and Egypt are rewarded with the knowledge, 'I am Yahweh'."[10]

The main purpose of Eslinger's piece is, clearly, the disclosure of wrong or unreflective reading conditions when approaching the Old Testament. And, indeed, it is important to take a step back and review these issues. Whence, then, comes the traditionally positive evaluation of the events? Eslinger attributes it to the lack of explicit evaluation provided by the narrator.[11] Further reasons could possibly be the assumption that the narrator goes along with his characters' evaluation of the events or the failure to distinguish between narrator and character. Finally, Eslinger lists the reader's religious preconceptions regarding salvation history which prevent him from reading the texts in their own contexts and from reading a text which is critical of the divine character. These are valid issues that need to be kept in mind when approaching the texts. The first three reasons concern the implicitness of written communication, especially narrative, and the differentiation between narrator and characters, which cautions us not to produce a flat reading of the text.[12] The last reason, however, the issue of our preconceptions, is a difficult one. Eslinger says that the characters in the story "react to appearance, [but] we perceive the reality."[13] Do we really or is reality far too complex to describe and to perceive? Is this why the exodus narrative has so many loose ends? Does Eslinger not fall into the same trap he accuses the 'triumphalists' of falling into, namely, the preoccupation with a certain concept of what is right and wrong, of what is good measure and what is not when

---

[8] Eslinger 1991, 51.

[9] "A careful study of Exodus 1–14 reveals no trace of triumphalism or congratulatory comment in the narrator's exposition." (Eslinger 1991, 51).

[10] Eslinger 1991, 58.

[11] "All narratorial comment is implicit, and must be deduced from the narrator's ordering of material, allusions to other passages, and contextualizations of the characters' utterances in the story." (Eslinger 1991, 51f).

[12] Indeed, one has to allow for ambiguity and the reader's involvement, as I will argue in the case of Moses.

[13] Eslinger 1991, 59.

it comes to judgement? When Eslinger thinks that divine self-reminding of the patriarchal covenant is far from enough as a response to Israel's oppression, can we detect a modern mind-set in Eslinger's reading of what counts as an appropriate reaction to the people's suffering? Besides this, it seems questionable whether the author, indeed, intended to criticise Yhwh's involvement in the exodus and whether the rhetorical strategy outlined by Eslinger really did function well. At least, the multiple positive readings throughout the reception history provide enough examples that the strategy did not work out as it should have.[14] At the meta-level, Eslinger's contribution highlights the many pitfalls of literary approaches to the Bible, which, thus, demand the multifaceted approach of rhetorical criticism.

Related more closely to the issues of the present chapter are Fretheim's introductory remarks in his commentary on Exodus. He considers the redactors' view of the God whom they portray. He relates the more abstract statements about God's nature (e.g. 34:6–7) and the hymnic material in Exod. 15 to the narrative picture which develops in Exodus: "The book of Exodus is concerned in a major way with the knowledge of Yhwh."[15] From the vantage point of this literary paradigm Fretheim looks into various theological issues in Exodus.[16] Here he touches upon a portrayal of the divine character in Exodus. In doing this he is very much in line with what I am trying to do in the present study.

---

[14] A few snippets of the history of reception from the passage Exod. 14–15 may be found and are partially explained in Steins 2007, 232–233. He, indeed, observes a "critical" reading of the passage in antiquity but these readings aim to justify God and his kindness and the "sensibility of the world." To read the text positively does not mean to read it uncritically (even in antiquity), as Eslinger suggests. A very critical reading when it comes to the portrayal of Yhwh in Exod. 1–15 can be found in McCarthy 2004. Throughout this article, McCarthy's reading points towards the modern mind set which assumes a Kantian ethic of justice. There seems to be an interpretive shortcut from the ancient text to a late-modern reading of it. Maybe we learn more about McCarthy's own ethics than about the ethics of the implicit author. Clearly, McCarthy raises questions that need to be addressed, but he does not pay much attention to ancient rhetorics normally involved in this kind of polemical narrative (he restricts his observations mainly on the plague narrative). For the reader of the entirety of Exodus, the portrayal of Yhwh will be much fuller and complex than the one McCarthy extracts from this brief passage. A much more balanced and literary attentive study is Ford 2006.

[15] Fretheim 1991a, 14.

[16] Cf. Fretheim 1991a, 12–22. That the strong emphasis on a theology of creation largely informs the content, form and structure of Exodus is not convincing. Who is able to determine if the first chapters of Genesis are shaped by covenant theology or even by wisdom concepts (cf. Schmid, K. 2002)? The support for his creation-theology claim is too general in order to persuade. That humans are necessary for redemption is basic common sense and does not necessarily point to a specific creation theology. Fretheim probably feels the need to take sides against the more Barthian emphasis on the transcendence and otherness of God. See also Weimar's theological conclusions on the linkage between creation and Sinai (Weimar 1988).

Hence Fretheim's discussion will be addressed later in more detail. One might consider the brief mention of these issues, as Fretheim offers them, to be sufficient for the literary genre of commentary, but, even given this allowance, he fails to provide an outline of the effect of this portrayal on the reading process.

Nevertheless, Fretheim contributes an important insight, namely the fact that the portrayal of Yhwh develops and can rightly be grasped only in contrast with the other characters of the book.[17] This may seem obvious from a literary-critical vantage point, but common readers tend to approach religious texts differently because they consider them sacred and because these texts speak of the God in whom they believe. Thus, it is valid to stress the point that even Yhwh develops throughout the unfolding plot of Exodus, at least, as perceived by the reader. This is in conjunction with Sternberg's general remarks above on the divine character, but only to a certain extent. An important issue for Fretheim is the notion that God, in his sovereignty, is not an unmoved mover but a character who is liable to change and suffering and who is dependent on human cooperation in order to achieve his goals.[18] This emphasis may be valid from the perspective of a modern exegete who argues for a less transcendent God. As my discussion will show, this perception of Yhwh is only partly true, and I will contend that for the large part Yhwh is indeed portrayed as being well above human non-compliance or even opposition. This, of course, does not mean that Yhwh is not portrayed as caring or as being involved in the sufferings of his people.[19]

James Watts, in his article on the legal characterisation of God in the Pentateuch, agrees with these general remarks, and, by introducing a new hermeneutical level, he polarises the narrator's depiction of a character with the character's self-depiction.[20] This peculiarity must be understood as a difference between the rhetorical effect of direct and that of indirect speech. As argued in the introduction,[21] the reader perceives direct speech under the influence of the *ethos* of the character speaking. In Exodus Yhwh's voice is 'heard' most[22] – especially when it comes to the utterance of the legal collections. The influence of the strategy which lets the reader 'hear' Yhwh speak the law will concern us below (p.80ff).

Coming from quite a different angle, Assmann provides an insight that illuminates the larger issues at stake in the Torah's portrayal of Yhwh. In his book

---

[17] Cf. Fretheim 1991a, 15.

[18] Cf. Fretheim 1991a, 16f.

[19] This awareness is also present in Fretheim's valuable discussion on the paradigmatic quality of the liberation from Egypt.

[20] Cf. Watts 1996, 2. With regard to this distinction one has to bear in mind that it is ultimately the narrator who controls all speech in his text. The characters do not have their say directly!

[21] Cf. above, p.3.

[22] One could go into statistical detail regarding the distribution of direct speech in Exodus (cf. Baum 2003 for an example).

on political theology and the development thereof he concludes that (secondary) religion is shaped by the spirit of politics.[23] To a certain extent this seems to be exactly what happened in Israel, and Exodus plays an important part in this construction of religion or theology. The author of Exodus, clearly, promotes an understanding of the relation between Yhwh and Israel along political lines. The term emphasised by Assmann is ברית or contract:

> Der politische Vertrag als Modell einer neuen Bestimmung des Beziehungsgeflechts von Gott, Volk und Individuum steht am Ursprung einer neuen Form von Religion, einer Religion, die nicht mehr in den politischen Ordnungen und Institutionen repräsentiert wird, sondern als eigenständige Ordnung neben der politischen Ordnung, ja zuweilen ihr kritisch entgegensteht. Dieser Schritt, den Israel vollzieht und im Bilde des Exodus formt und kommemoriert, ist die entscheidende Theologisierung des Politischen, die alle anderen Theologisierungen fundiert.[24]

From my point of view this picture of the development of Israel's theology can be supported by numerous features of the book of Exodus, not just the term ברית.[25] In Exodus we observe Yhwh adopting a people, redeeming them successfully from foreign political domination, providing an able leadership in the mediator Moses, and endowing them with law and order to ensure their wellbeing. Assmann's conception comes from the cultural sciences and deals, largely, with the interface between ideology and social reality. But these elements of culture tend to find their way into texts. That Exodus is one such successful example may be seen once the political relevance of much of the Old Testament

---

[23] On this distinction between primary and secondary religion he says: "Wir müssen also unterscheiden zwischen Religion, die zu den Grundbedingungen des menschlichen Daseins gehört, und Religion, die als eine reflexiv gewordene und sich über andere Religionen kritisch erhebende Form der wahren Gottesverehrung in Israel und anderswo entsteht. Wir wollen sie primäre und sekundäre Religionen nennen. Der Begriff »Entstehung von Religion« meint also nicht die Entstehung von Religion überhaupt, sondern von *sekundärer,* gesteigerter Religion. Sekundäre Religion entsteht dort, wo die Unterscheidung zwischen wahr und falsch getroffen und in den Raum des Religiösen eingeführt wird. Erst auf der Basis dieser Unterscheidung wird es möglich, sich von allen vorhergehenden religiösen Traditionen polemisch abzusetzen und auf den Ruinen der als »falsch« ausgegrenzten primären Religion das neue Gebäude einer sekundären Religion zu errichten." (Assmann 2000, 30f).

[24] Assmann 2000, 50.

[25] This has to be understood as speech act and not merely as metaphor. The ברית, as Exodus reports and understands it, is not just a verbal picture from the political sphere, adopted to show certain aspects of the relationship between God and Israel, but it creates the reality of this relationship (cf. Assmann 2000, 50: "Das politische Bündnis ist keine Metapher der Gott-Mensch-Beziehung, sondern die Sache selbst, die jeder kennt."). Of course, all speech about God is necessarily metaphorical (cf. Kaiser, G. 2001, 17f), but metaphors do not exclude speech acts and hence can become part of reality.

is considered together with the fact that it is, largely, shaped and influenced by the covenant theology as promoted by the *Endtext* of the Pentateuch. If Exodus, indeed, can be viewed in this conceptual framework, then the character Yhwh and his portrayal play crucial roles.[26]

Narrative Characterisation

The picture of Yhwh in Exodus unfolds, one might say, more than it develops. The strategy in this depiction is to fill in information in the course of the reading process. Because of the relative stability of Yhwh, introducing him maps out large parts of what will follow. No big surprises are expected.

As we have seen, there are two kinds of literary characterisation, direct and indirect. In biblical literature, indirect portrayal takes pride of place, whereas direct comments on a given character are rare. Exodus, however, provides for its readers at least three instances that should be called direct characterisations of Yhwh. This alone betrays the importance of God for the author of the book. I will, firstly, look into these instances of direct characterisation.

Quite consciously, the treatment of Exod. 3:15; 20:5f and 34:6-7 is presented here under the heading 'Narrative Characterisation.' It will be shown that these passages must be read within their narrative contexts as the perception of these formulas or epithets depends strongly on their literary environments. The placement of this often very detailed discussion – separate from the treatment of the indirect characterisation – is for practical reasons only, i.e. I hope that the present work turns out to be more readable. In a second move I will draw together the picture that evolves along with the plot and the results of the preliminary work on the direct epithets. After the crucial introduction of Yhwh we find two areas of conflict in Exodus. The plot development is driven in the first third of the book by the confrontation between Yhwh and the Egyptian king. The remainder of the book is concerned with the portrayal of Israel in the wilderness and with how the people's unstable relationship with Yhwh develops. These two areas of antagonism will provide the material for discussing the character Yhwh in the predominantly narrative parts of Exodus.

Direct Characterisation

THE DIVINE NAME 'YHWH' AND ITS FUNCTION IN EXOD. 3–4

The main issues discussed in the history of research[27] are how the divine name can be etymologically substantiated and to which period of Israelite history the

---

[26] For a perceptive critical evaluation of Assmann's main theses see Kaiser, G. 2001.

[27] For relatively recent summaries of the history of research see e.g Mayer 1958 or Kinyongo 1970; cf. also the incomplete but extensive list in Saebø 1981, 43f.

first appearance of the name can be linked. The multiplicity, and quite often ir-reconcilability, of the many answers suggests that a good deal of subjectivity has been brought to the issue; there simply seem to be too many open ends to form more than a hypothesis. This raises the question of whether or not the right questions were asked with respect to this, admittedly, difficult passage. Childs, in his succinct summary of the main contributions, centres mainly on the influential hypotheses of Albright, Freedman and Cross[28] which try to reconstruct the meaning of the divine name by analogy with ancient Near Eastern parallels. In opposition, he concludes that there is a need to take "seriously Israel's own tradition when it interprets the divine name in a manner which is in striking discontinuity with the Ancient Near Eastern parallels."[29] This different approach could be justified by the fact that the biblical text, itself, emphasises the newness of the name to Moses and not the postulated long history of its development from a Canaanite creation deity to the biblical Yhwh, as proposed, for example, by Cross.

By paying close attention to the immediate literary context, Childs' own approach to the interpretation of Exod. 3:13–15 goes in the right direction, yet in the end it is no more satisfactory than the other approaches. True to his favoured form-critical analysis, he examines different possibilities to find an oral context which is fitting for Exod. 3:13-22. He finds that none of the formal patterns in the Old Testament can serve as the background for the present passage.[30] The closest parallels to the present text are the divine commission and the enquiry after the divine name, when the authority of a true prophet is being disputed. This question of the true or false prophet would then, later, have been introduced into the E tradition which upheld a marked discontinuity regarding the revelation of the divine name in the era of Moses: "The point of the inquiry [sc. by the people as anticipated by Moses] is to elicit from Moses an answer which will serve as the ultimate test of his validity as a prophet."[31] This confirmation of Moses' prophetic office is, according to Childs, the main thrust of the passage which was shaped specifically by the need of the Elohist to retain his own blueprint of salvation history. Considering 3:15 Childs attempts to address the difficulties linked with the second answer to Moses' question in Exod. 3:13. During a new literary stage of the text the question would apparently have been understood, not as asking for information about the name, but, rather, as inquiring about the character behind the name. The explanation for the significance of the name or, put differently, its divine purpose would be v.15. This literary level was, according to Childs, the conflation of J and E, when E's revelation-

---

[28] Cf. Albright 1924; Freedman 1960; Cross 1962.

[29] Childs 1976, 64.

[30] Childs 1976, 67.

[31] Childs 1976, 68.

historical aspect regarding a new development in referring to God was increasingly obscured.[32]

The problem with Childs' reading is that he gives two different interpretations for one text, which he, then, presents as two different stages of textual development. This method, however, does not easily explain the likely interpretation by a reader of the final text, given the assumption that this reader does not read with modern, post-enlightenment preconceptions. Childs realises exactly this point of contention when he comments on the passage in its context.[33] He, nevertheless, remains at the story level of the text: he discusses Moses' expectations and the people's assumptions, but the author-reader level he has only reflected in his form-critical remarks outlined above and in some rather superficial observations scattered sparingly throughout the comments.[34] In the end, Childs never explains the possible message of the chapter for the implied readers.

The above discussion of Child's interpretation may suffice to highlight the questions which must be answered before a significant contribution to a rhetorical understanding of the present text can be made. It seems sound to follow a number of scholars who doubt the importance of scholarly etymology for the interpretation of Old Testament texts. Houtman, as the most explicit proponent, writes: "By explaining the name, the author makes te name serviceable to the narrative. ... It is thus evident that literary etymology is of major significance to interpretation; scholarly etymology is not, as a rule."[35] If one is to presuppose that the etymology of a name makes this name serviceable for the context the following question immediately arises: What function does the giving of the name in a particular form serve at this present point in the narrative?

As a starting point for an attempt to answer this question I choose the observations by Joachim Becker who proposes an interesting and valuable distinction regarding the "I am"-formula in the Old Testament. Besides the expression of mere self-presentation (*Selbstvorstellung*) Becker detects an additional aspect

---

[32] Cf. Childs 1976, 69f.

[33] "The literary and form-critical analysis ... confirmed the scholarly opinion that vv.13ff. reflect the special tradition of one early witness which connected the communication of the divine name to Moses' commission. However, it is now our task to hear this testimony as it found its place within ch.3. What is the import of the question in its present context?" Childs 1976, 75.

[34] Cf. the following note on Exod. 3:16–4:9: "However, the present writer has skilfully adapted his material within his own narrative, enriching the portrayal of prophetic resistance, and pointing the reader toward the plagues in which material these signs were originally at home." Or "...but the tempo of the narrative has quickened." Childs 1976, 78 + 79.

[35] Houtman 1993, 72. Expressing the same hesitation, Childs is quite right to doubt that God's answer, as recorded in 3:14a, is truly loaded with as much importance as modern exegetes attribute to this text (Childs 1976, 75).

suggesting authority and excellency. The use of "I am ...", with a gradual domi-
nance of the latter aspect, he calls *Autoritätsformel* or *Imponierformel*.[36] With
this authority formula the biblical authors answer a question that goes well beyond the common quest for identity ("Who are you?"). The formula is much
more an answer to the question of significance and gravity of the person. The
person is expressing self-confidence in his own being or his ability and power.
Though liberally used in the neighbourhood of ancient Israel by sovereigns and
gods, the use of the authority formula in the Old Testament, apart from a few
exceptions, seems to be limited to the divine.[37] Among these occurrences are
the oft repeated אני יהוה of the holiness code, as well as the so-called *Erweiswort*
(Zimmerli) in Ezechiel, and the many different formulations in Isa. 40–49.[38]
Not surprisingly, Exod. 3:14-15 finds mention in this context by Becker. He
considers אהיה אשר אהיה as bringing together two different connotations:[39] firstly, the rejection of a direct answer[40] and, secondly, the massiveness of the authority behind the exclamation.[41] God is just what he is. Here we find a very
useful distinction between the levels of meaning in this brief text.

But before I consider the rhetorical implications of the previous discussion, I
want to refer to another aspect of Becker's article, which is very profitable for
our understanding of this pericope. It concerns the negativity of the authority
formula, the assertion of unworthiness: the 'nobody' considers his apparent or
real insignificance.[42] In biblical language the idea is expressed by the question
"Who am I to ...?" Of course, a character can use this formula in the second or
third person to challenge the authority of someone else. A striking, and for our
present purpose, very significant example is the pharaoh demoting Yhwh: מי
יהוה ('Who is Yhwh ...?' Exod. 5:2a).[43] Here a lackof knowledge does not
cause the pharaoh to utter these words but, rather, mockery which expresses a

---

[36] Becker 1999, 46.

[37] As exceptions, which are few but telling, Becker notes Gen. 41:44; I Kgs. 19:2
(LXX); Isa. 47:8.10; Zeph. 2:15 (and possibly II Sam. 13:28) for the use of the authority
formula in the human realm (Becker 1999, 48).

[38] Becker 1999, 50–54.

[39] Cf. Becker 1999, 54.

[40] Cf. also Exod. 4:13; I Sam. 23:13; II Sam. 15:20 and II Kgs. 8:1.

[41] Cf. eg. Exod. 16:23; 33:19; Ezek. 12:25 and 36:20, where the idiom signifies the immensity of the modified action.

[42] Cf. Becker 1999, 49. Similar observations are found in Coats 1970 and Houtman
1993, 361. A thorough investigation into the interplay between this negation of the authority formula and its positive appearance in the context of Exod. 3:14f is beyond the
scope of the mentioned authors, but their observations, nevertheless, provide a good
basis for the present discussion. Owens 2004, 622f, on the other hand, provides a well
argued, though brief, theological exploration of the God who is "radically free".

[43] Cf. Job 21:15 and Prov 30:9 for a similar doubt in God.

lack of submission, thus highlighting, for the reader, the purpose of the narrative (to promote a certain knowledge of Yhwh, cf. Exod. 10:2).

Further below I will suggest that Moses' objections are just the foil on which Yhwh's character portrayal gains its clarity.[44] If we understand Exod. 3:11 as, in Becker's sense of the expression, a negative authority formula, this theory is strongly supported. The reader knows from the previous verses (3:7-10) that the author views God as the source of the message (3:8aα: ואדר להצילו), while Moses is the messenger. As already mentioned, Moses' assertion of unworthiness in Exod. 3:11 refers the reader back to the narrative on Moses' failure (Exod. 2:11-22). At least from the author's point of view, Moses, it seems, is not the right person for the task, for he has gambled away his authority.[45] God's response is full of confidence that Moses will succeed: 3:12a puts the stress again on the fact that this is a divine commission, and 3:12b looks to the future beyond the event of the Exodus. With God's authority, Moses will achieve what he had previously failed to achieve.

What, now, dominates these verses is this issue of authority. The author uses the dialogue to picture both Moses and Yhwh as being concerned about their respective authorities. But God emerges as the one who claims the highest authority. It is he, then, who authorises Moses. This, gradually, prepares the reader for the overwhelming self-revelation of God in his name *Yhwh*. Usually, God reveals himself in events when he enters into the realm of history. This will, also, be narrated when God reveals himself in, probably, the most momentous event in Israelite history, the exodus from Egypt (remember the knowing-Yhwh motif!). But here the author, who is about to narrate these identity-creating events, discusses the self-revelation of God in the linguistic realm. This may be called direct characterisation and does not usually occur in the Old Testament. As noted above, even Gen. 1–11 lacks a proper introduction of God; it is always assumed that the readers will know who this God is. But, here, in Exodus, it seems to be of utmost importance to the author to introduce God properly and emphatically.

Exod. 3:13 serves as trailer for the following intense and redundant verses. Whatever motivated Moses to ask this question – his own or his people's desire for knowledge or his doubt in the people's acceptance of him, for example[46] – it

---

[44] See p.63f.

[45] Houtman considers a host of different commentators who address the nature of Moses' reasons for his first objection (Houtman 1993, 360f). In the end he seems to decide that Moses was afraid to face the task (e.g.: "... the Moses of 3:11 who is overawed by his call and recoils from it...", p.362), i.e. his reasons were psychological. This might well be the case on the story level of the dialogue, but the communicative level is not being touched upon by this answer.

[46] There is no need to list all the different answers to this question. The variety and, often, irreconcilability of these answers again suggest that only hypotheses are possible. Cf. Houtman 1993, 366f. for a brief summary.

is important that the reader is forced to decide for himself what God's name actually is.[47] In all likelihood we can assume that the reader knows the tetragrammaton as the divine name.[48] Now he expects something new or this very name. But what does he get from the author? The author offers a play on words. My question was: What function does the giving of the name serve at this point in the narrative and in this particular form? Here we find the answer. The mere mention of the tetragrammaton would not have had the same effect upon the reader. Instead, the author uses the similarity of the verb היה with יהוה to force the reader to reflect upon the significance of the name in the present situation.[49] אהיה אשר אהיה can be understood as an authority formula, asBecker suggests. It, nevertheless, is difficult to translate the phrase accurately.[50] Ogden's interpretation is in line with Becker's: "On analogy with the preceding examples of the *idem per idem*, the intention in the phrase may well be to make a comprehensive statement in which God claims to be 'everything that I will be'."[51] Houtman makes a similar point when he writes:

> Perhaps the substance is as follows: I am so great and so incomparable that what I am cannot be articulated in a single term; it cannot be expressed by a name; do not ask concerning his name; one cannot speak about me at the level of 'What is his name?' After God has made Moses aware of this he tells Moses how he must answer the Israelites. He cannot report any names but he may provide material concerning the character of his superior.[52]

---

[47] This is another example of a literary gap which motivates the reader to become actively involved in the progression of the text. A similar device was the mention of the covenant of the fathers in Exod. 2:24, where God's remembering induces the same action in the reader.

[48] Cf. Otto 2007, 40f.

[49] Phillips and Phillips, as do I, interpret v.14b as a pun which serves a communicative function. They suggest that the idea for the pun was derived from Hos. 1:9. The deuteronomistic interest in the covenant led the editors of Exod. 3 to reutilise Hosea's pun for their own purposes: they wanted to reassure their readers that, after the fall of the northern kingdom, the presence of God is still with Judah, as long as the covenant is kept as it is set out in Exod. 19–24, 32–34 (Phillips and Phillips 1998). In Hosea and in Exodus the divine name was already known to the reader and was then connected with a significant word play by both the authors/editors. If there was a literary dependency – and if so, in which direction – it remains, in my opinion, unsolvable.

[50] An interesting attempt has been made by Pannell 2006, who sees the verbs as being cohortatives, thereby arriving at a very similar interpretation as I am though not considering literary aspects. However, to translate these cohortatives in a sensible manner into English would not greatly help a more immediate understanding of the text. Thus I will stay with the more open and ambiguous English indicative present. This approach is also followed by Schniedewind 2004, who, as well, provides an overview of the interpretative history regarding this subject.

[51] Ogden 1992, 112.

[52] Houtman 1993, 95.

Clearly, the phrase suggests the self-awareness of maximum authority and ability. This interpretation is supported when we view the phrase as a positive counterpart to Moses' implicit self-criticism in 3:11. The reader perceives the shift from the "Who am I?" to the strongly emphasised "I am" as enhancing Yhwh's worthiness at Moses' expense. Thus, the author deconstructs the perception of Moses as a national hero in order to highlight Yhwh's significance. If the reader learns anything from Exod. 3–4, it is that Yhwh, and Yhwh alone, is the one delivering Israel from Egypt and that Moses is only his mediator.[53]

In the comment just quoted, Houtman touches upon the rhetorical function of the phrase אהיה אשר אהיה. He suggests that it is here used to terminate the debate, and, thus, it serves as sort of a non-answer or the refusal of an answer. Other commentators interpret it the same way. Zimmerli views this figure of speech along with the similar expression "I will be gracious to whom I will be gracious, and will show mercy on whom I will show mercy." (Exod. 33:19). Thus, according to Zimmerli, this phrase, which reveals his name, stresses Yhwh's sovereignty and freedom: Yhwh is at nobody's disposal.[54] Thus, v.14 should be taken as a refusal to answer Moses' question.[55] Zimmerli observes: "[a]n der einzigen Stelle, an welcher das AT selber eine Erklärung des Jahwenamens zu geben versucht, verweigert es die Erklärung des Namens, die diesen in den Käfig einer Definition einsperren würde."[56] Krochmalnik is a bit less radical and considers Yhwh's answer as being "eher ausweichend" (rather evasive).[57] Other scholars, like Childs, picture Yhwh as receiving Moses' question with "utmost seriousness" and as offering "an elaborate answer."[58] Magne Saebø devotes an entire article to this issue and arrives at results similar to Childs'. "Yhwh's answer is – just like the remainder of the chapter – revelation and not obscuration."[59]

From a communicative point of view it seems pointless to try to decide between these 'alternatives'. Just as Moses' motivation for asking his questions remains outside the author's interest, so does God's motivation in answering the questions in the way he did. The important thing is that the reader gets the point of the authority formula. The obvious parallelism between v.14b and 15a suggests the link between this phrase and the divine name:

---

[53] This is supported by the discussion of the introduction of Moses in the narrative found on p.148ff below.

[54] Cf. Zimmerli 1999, 14f.

[55] In a very similar Otto 2007, 40 way argues the same in his analysis of the Exodus narrative.

[56] Zimmerli 1999, 15. Cf. also Rad 1962, 196 and Lundbom 1978. All stress Yhwh's freedom which is expressed in this grammatical construction.

[57] Krochmalnik 2000, 42. A much more explicit termination of the discussion on the divine name follows in v.15b (see below p.66).

[58] Cf. Childs 1976, 75 and esp. 76.

[59] Saebø 1981, 54.

כה־תאמר אל־בני ישראל ‏ ‏‏15a ‏‏‏‏‏‏‏‏‏‏‏‏‏‏‏‏‏‏‏‏‏‏ ‏14b ויאמר כה תאמר לבני ישראל

כה־תאמר אל־בני ישראל 15a	14b ויאמר כה תאמר לבני ישראל
יהוה אלהי אבתיכם אלהי	
אברהם אלהי יצחק ואלהי יעקב ‖	אהיה
שלחני אליכם ‖	שלחני אליכם

Here the reader realises that God will reveal no name other than the one
they already know (the God of the fathers). The reader has known all along the
name 'Yhwh' – either by reading it in Genesis or in Exod. 3:2 or by knowing
it from his own background. He is now taught how one should understand that
name. With respect to the patriarchs, God was the maker of promises, but now
he will be known, also, as the fulfiller of these promises. That the author wants
the reader to get this point is apparent when we consider the content of the
word play – or the literary etymology of Yhwh, if one wants to understand it
this way. In this point I follow von Soden[60] who takes the given linkage between יהוה and היה seriously. According to his research into similar sentence
names from the semitic linguistic environment of Israel, the divine name
should be 'translated' as *he proves to be*. In this respect Yhwh is no more or
less than other ascriptions of the same god: *'ēl 'elyōn, 'ēl šaddai, 'ēl 'ōlām* or
even *God of the fathers*. Thus, Yhwh is not really a name but more a disclosure about God. As such a non-Israelite would not necessarily identify the sentence *Yhwh* as referring specifically to the Israelite god. But for an Israelite
even the *he* by itself would be unambiguous and thus sufficient to identify this
Yhwh with the God of the fathers or with *'ēl šaddai*.[61] Thus, Yhwh does not
simply equate with "I am" – as the pun in v.14a suggests – and, consequently,
it should not be understood as an ontological proposition of a metaphysical
programme. Together with the immediate context it signifies a theo-political
programme.[62] God Yhwh is prepared to bring Israel out of Egypt; he con-
vinces himself that he will manage because he has the authority, and at the
same time, guards his sovereignty. The resoluteness of the divine speech
serves to finalise this point not only for Moses, at the story level, but also for
the reader. The tetragrammaton is used emphatically again in Exod. 6[63] and in
Exod. 34:6, the passage to which I will turn next.

---

[60] In his contribution to the debate Soden 1985, esp. 84 discusses the different results of
various comparative approaches to sentence names in the semitic language family. In
correspondence with the linguistic findings von Soden also argues on a theological level
for the meaning of Yhwh as "he proves to be" (*"er erweist sich"*) where the concretion
remains untold. Von Soden emends "as helper" (*"als Helfer"*). Thus, the name is really
a sentence ascribing this god relevance for one's wellbeing and thus can be called a
"praise-name" (*Dankname*).

[61] Soden 1985, 85.

[62] Cf. Krochmalnik 2000, 40,45 who uses this terminology.

[63] See p.57 below.

THE EPITHETS IN EXOD. 34:6-7

Although the reader first meets Exod. 20, I will discuss the divine epithets in the decalogue later since the picture emerges more clearly in this longer passage, which is more directly connected to its literary context.[64]

Given the often noted theological importance of the *Gnadenrede* in Exod. 34:6-7, the exegetical literature on these verses is astonishingly sparse, apparently because of the secondary nature of these verses in the eyes of most critics.[65] Two recent studies, however, attempt to overcome this shortcoming. Ruth Scoralick[66] submitted in 2002 a canonical and intertextual reading of the text, whereas Matthias Franz's 2003 thesis[67] concentrates on diachronic and comparative aspects. I will build especially upon Scoralick's results and draw out the implications for my present interests concerning the portrayal of Yhwh.

Scoralick's analysis is inspired by the awareness of the unwieldy position of Exod. 34:6-7 in its present context, a fact which contributed largely to the numerous hypotheses concerning a secondary introduction of the speech. The unevenness in the flow of the narrative is of special rhetorical relevance. Anything that influences the reading process in a marked way is important for our purposes. That these verses were meant to protrude from their context is suggested, also, by the almost irreconcilable content – divine grace (34:6-7a) paralleling Yhwh's determination to impose sanction (34:7b) – and by the density of the language.[68] Scoralick even speaks of reader-irritation that is intentionally evoked by these verses, and she points to the difficulty of deciding in whose mouth – Moses' or Yhwh's – the narrative puts this exclamation.[69] The reader is strongly involved with the text and must participate in the creation of meaning. That this is a desired rhetorical effect is likely for two reasons. Firstly, the style of the text is very similar to that which is characteristic of prayer,[70] a fact which

---

[64] Cf. Dohmen 2004b, 108, who speaks of 'relecture' when referring to the decalogue. Thus he also presupposes knowledge of Exod. 34 when reading Exod. 20.

[65] See, especially, the history of research provided by Franz 2003, 6–13. Earlier collections of previous research are to be found in Dentan 1963 and in Zenger 1971, 227ff. On the discussion of the pretextual usage (cultic *Sitz im Leben*) and the incorporation of Exod. 34:6-7 (and with it 33:19) in its present narrative context cf. Moberly 1983, 128–131. He argues, convincingly, that 34:6-7 is an integral and original part of the narrative, which might quite likely have been used later in the cult. An independent existence of these verses is highly unlikely.

[66] Scoralick 2002; see also her article (Scoralick 2001) which briefly summarises the same argument.

[67] Franz 2003.

[68] The poetic character of these verses implies the accompanying semantic openness and probability of less than literal intentions with the lexemes (cf. also Scoralick 2002, 44).

[69] Cf. Scoralick 2001, 151f.

[70] Scoralick 2002, 67f points to the specific hymnic style in the use of participles and polarising structure. The doubling of the divine name also fits the generic framework of

has already given rise to a number Jewish exegetical discussions.[71] Even if a reader takes Exod. 34:6-7 as divine speech, he is still left wondering if he is reading a hymnic portion of Moses' intercessory prayer or if Yhwh is teaching Moses how to pray. Secondly, it is assumed that parts of the statement about divine mercy are stock phrases from hymnic prayers in Israel and other ancient Near Eastern cultures.[72] Scoralick summarises the rhetorical effect:

> Vor diesem Hintergrund [sc. the usage of terms parallel to 34:6-7 in hymnic phrases] gewinnt die Gestaltung des Textes in Ex 34,5-7 eine eigene Dynamik für die Leser. In Ex 34,6 (weniger sicher in 7) verwendet der Text ein Repertoire, das den Lesern außertextweltlich vertraut ist. Die Wiederbegegnung mit den Formulierungen im Text hat einen Verfremdungseffekt. Zugleich wird eine Aktualisierung bewirkt, ein Element der Textwelt stellt einen direkten Bezug zur außertextlichen Wirklichkeit der Leser her. ... Das Erstaunliche an der Situation muß für die Hörer vor allen Dingen im sprechenden Subjekt liegen: Gott selbst.[73]

Especially, Exod. 34:5 (ויקרא בשם יהוה) is grammatically uncertain (who is the subject?) and, thus, prompts the reader to reflect upon the content. Who utters such words? Do these words speak of God or to God? Only Exod. 33:19 makes it more likely that Yhwh is speaking here, revealing himself. Hence, the text cannot be understood properly or evaluated according to its rhetorical function for the portrayal of Yhwh without its literary context.

To accompany the following discussion I here present my translation,[74] which should, already, communicate a rough idea of how I understand this passage:

ויעבר יהוה על־פניו	6	And Yhwh passed by before his face
ויקרא		and he shouted:
יהוה יהוה		Yhwh (is) Yhwh,
אל רחום וחנון		God compassionate and gracious,
ארך אפים ורב־חסד ואמת:		slow to anger and full of kindness and reliability:
נצר חסד לאלפים	7	guarding kindness for thousands (of generations)
נשא עון ופשע וחטאה		lifting guilt, transgression, and sin
ונקה לא ינקה		but who will surely not leave (it) unpunished,
פקד עון אבות על־בנים		observing the father's guilt with the sons

---

prayer.

[71] For references cf. Jacob 1997, 931 and Scoralick 2002, 82f.

[72] See esp. the influential article by Scharbert 1957. See also Noth 1978, 215, and Scoralick 2002, 58–60, 63ff. For a collection of abundant material from the cultural background of ancient Israel see Franz 2003, 43–110.

[73] Scoralick 2002, 81.

[74] For a thorough lexical and semantic analysis of key terms in Exod. 34:6-7 cf. Franz 2003, 112–151.

ועל־בני בנים   and with the sons' sons

על־שלשים ועל־רבעים: and with the third and fourth (generation).

Before I come to the contextual function of the two verses, I will briefly sketch my understanding of them. That these two verses must be taken together is obvious, but what is their precise relationship? I follow Scoralick in taking v.7 as an explication of v.6: "Stellt V. 6 Wesenseigenschaften Gottes vor Augen, so erläutert V. 7 daraus resultierende Handlungsweisen."[75] However, to denote 34:6 as referring to Yhwh's nature must be balanced by emphasising that the descriptions are all of a relational quality[76] and thus have immediate implications for the understanding of the literary context. The tension in 34:7 between the willingness to forgive and not to נקה (release from punishment) cannot and should not be resolved on any level.[77] At the rhetorical level, it functions as a metaphoric (poetic) expression of hope: the contrast between thousands of generations and three to four generations stresses the almost infinite excessiveness of God's grace and dominates the *Gnadenrede*.[78] Exod. 34:7a takes up the keyword חסד from the last part of v.6: the kindness of God extends to an unimaginable timespan.[79] Following Dohmen and Schenker, one can understand v.7b as an explication of the phrase ארך אפים (v.6): the slowness to anger causes Yhwh to wait several generations for punishment,[80] while observing how guilt develops in a household.[81] Franz provides an inter-

---

[75] Scoralick 2001, 146. Cf. also Jacob 1997, 969; Moberly 2002, 199, and Dohmen 2004b, 355.

[76] Cf. Dohmen 2004b, 354.

[77] On the numerous attempts to resolve or understand the tension see Scoralick 2002, 68–72. I do not follow Brueggemann's notion of an unpredictable God, which finds its clearest expression in Exod. 34:6–7 (cf. Brueggemann 1994, 947 and Brueggemann 1998, 215–228). The communicative interest of the larger text is quite different, especially when considering the context!

[78] So also Scoralick 2001, 146.

[79] For the different options regarding the numbers in Exod. 34:6-7 see Scoralick 2002, 60–63. She understands the 3–4 generations as the usual age range of a normal ancient Israelite household.

[80] Cf. Dohmen 1993, 180ff and Schenker 1990, 86ff.

[81] "Drei bis vier Generation umfaßt ein בית אב, der Lebenszusammenhang einer Familie. Drei bis vier Generationen sind auch das Maß des lebendigen Überlieferungszusammenhangs, des kommunikativen Gedächtnisses (mit J.Assmann). ... Im Bereich der Familie sind Auswirkungen von Verfehlungen des Familienoberhaupts unmittelbar und bleibend erfahrbar: ein Verständnis des פקד als strafend heimsuchen wäre verständlich, ohne daß unter V. 7b ein Strafaufschub zu verstehen wäre oder von einer notwendig implizierten Schuld der Nachkommen ausgegangen werden müsste." (Scoralick 2001, 148). Scoralick explicitly argues against the idea of an archaic Israelite concept of collective or transgenerational guilt as a primitive legal institution (German terms would be e.g. *Sippenhaftung, kollektive Haftungsgemeinschaft*). There is still considerable dis-

esting thought when he relates the phrase אֶרֶךְ אַפַּיִם to the teacher of wisdom at the royal court. He maintains that אֶרֶךְ אַפַּיִם is, specifically, not an epithet of a king:

> Mit אֶרֶךְ־אַפַּיִם wird ein sehr wenig königlicher Begriff für Gott verwendet. Statt seinen u.U. überfälligen Zorn über die Sünde der Menschen auszuleben, hält Gott ihn an und schaut zu. So haben die Mesopotamier nicht von ihren Göttern geredet; ein vergleichbares akkadisches Epitheton fehlt. ... Der Mensch ist geduldig aus Macht- oder Alternativlosigkeit. Gott aus selbstgewählter Gnade.[82]

This note shows that the kingly portrayal of God in Exodus[83] is left open for the demands of the conceptual divide between the spheres of man and god. The metaphorical talk of the kingly god does not rule out the talk of a patient god, who is slow to anger because of his graciousness.

The literary context, especially Exod. 32–34, which could be described as the conflict between Yhwh and Israel, supports this interpretation of the divine epithets of Exod. 34:6. The tension between the divine attributes of 34:6-7 already appears in the overture to the golden calf episode. The two contrasting scenes 32:1-6 and 32:7-14, create this very same tension: the sin of the people arouses the divine אַף, and the question arises whether this leads to the annihilation of the people. God, however, with his comment – "Now therefore let me alone, that my wrath (אַפִּי) may burn hot against them ..." (32:10) – almost invites Moses' intervention.[84] The ensuing dispute between Moses and Yhwh

---

pute how this is to be viewed in the light of Old Testament theology (cf. Franz 2003, 143–150, for an up-to-date discussion). For my present purpose, there is no immediate need to decide between one or the other option.

[82] Franz 2003, 123.

[83] See esp. 80 below.

[84] Cf. the even stronger translation of the targumim, which makes explicit the link to divine חֶסֶד – TO: "Stop your supplication before Me." TPsJ: "Stop your prayer and do not plead for mercy for them before Me."; TNf: "Abstain from before Me pleading for mercy for them." (quoted from Houtman 2000, 646) Houtman, himself, refutes the old interpretation that Yhwh points Moses to the option of intercession on behalf of the people. He, rightly, observes the dogmatic apprehensions that might have led to favour this reading, but, whatever these reasons might have been, from a rhetorical-critical point of view, the explicit prohibition almost always provokes disobedience (cf. the long tradition of this interpretation as reviewed in Tiemeyer 2007, 203). The reader is led into thinking, "what will happen if..." This notion, however, is not necessarily the main thrust of the prohibition. Thus, I take (with Dohmen 2004b, 303f) the main thrust of Exod. 32:10 as pointing the reader to the divine evaluation of the sin of the people: the threat of death suggests that the worship of the golden calf clearly has to be understood as violation of the law to worship Yhwh alone (Exod. 22:19). This overall interpretation is supported once we recognise the literary strategy to bring together Yhwh's consequent treatment of sin and Israel's election via the intercession of Moses (see p.187).

moves to a first theological highpoint in 33:19.[85] The actual Mosaic prayer for forgiveness starts with 33:12 and revolves around the root חן: מצא חן בעינים חן (33:12.13 [2x].16.17; 34:9). The favour of Yhwh is Moses' primary concern and seems to imply the quest for divine forgiveness. The *idem per idem* formulation of 33:19 (את־אשר ארחם – ורחמתי את־אשר אחן וחנתי את־אשר),[86] together with the emphasised mention of the tetragrammaton, refers the reader back to Exod. 3:14: God's grace is at no one's disposal.[87] This verse prepares the reader for the tension of Exod. 34:7. The movement from the impending anger in Exod. 32 to the explanation of Yhwh's slowness to anger in Exod. 34:7 is nicely commented on by Scoralick: "Der zu Beginn des Erzählbogens drohende Zorn Gottes kommt in der feierlichen Proklamation seiner Eigenschaft in Gestalt des 'langsam zum Zorn' vor. 'Noch friedfertiger läßt sich vom Zorn kaum reden' ...."[88] But even as 33:18f prepares the reader for the divine self-revelation, it, also, raises expectations that are not fulfilled. The effect of this irritation in the reader – the involvement into the narrative – has already been discussed.

The actual proclamation of the divine name, then, refines the portrayal of God, which is clearly linked to the previous divine picture in Exodus. The divine name, which again takes centre stage in 34:6 (the doubling of יהוה may best be understood as a nominal clause and thus as an allusion to Exod. 3:14[89] – an understanding which has been prepared by 33:19aβ), is explicated here to include a very strong notion of the divine willingness to forgive, without allowing the reader to think that Yhwh is weak and does not take sin seriously.[90] This expression of Yhwh's core attributes comes at a rhetorically significant place in the story. As Moberly puts it: "... the unparalleled cumulation of terms of mercy and forgiveness is a response to Moses' intercession in a context of Israel's paradigmatic apostasy ..."[91] The divine 'inclination' to be merciful, together with the honest confession of sin, open up the possibility for the existence of an inherently sinful Israel (cf. Exod. 32:9) in the presence of Yhwh. Exodus places these verses after the violation of the covenant. The rhetorical effects of surprise and enforcement of the statement are central. Yhwh is not only

---

[85] This has recently, in great detail and with great theological awareness also been argued by Seebass 2004, against many exegetes who separate v.19 from its context and view it only as preliminary to 34:6-7.

[86] "I will grant the grace that I will grant and show the compassion that I will show." Transl. by Sarna 1991, 214.

[87] See the discussion of the divine name in Exod. 3–4 above (p.35ff).

[88] Scoralick 2001, 148.

[89] An observation made by numerous scholars, see e.g. Jacob 1997, 960 or Childs 1976, 595.

[90] Cf. Schenker 1990, 89: "[G]ar keine Strafe wäre Komplizenschaft mit den bösen, sofortige Strafe würde mehr zerstören als aufbauen. In der Mitte liegt das Angebot der Umkehr und Bewährung."

[91] Moberly 2002, 193.

full of reliable mercy and slow to anger when the people are doing well![92] But in addition to this, that Exod. 34:6-7 comes after the lengthy discourse between Moses and Yhwh shows that the author wanted to safeguard the understanding of the passage against possible misuse. The dialogue in Exod. 32–34 brings together the need for intercession and confession with the willingness of Yhwh to forgive. The mere statement that God is merciful is not sufficient, as Moses' reaction to the divine self-revelation makes clear: he confesses the sin and pronounces the people as stubborn (34:9).[93] Scoralick expresses this point succinctly:

> [D]ie Eröffnung des Spannungsbogens [hat] ihre Entsprechung nicht nur in den Gottesprädikationen …, sondern [es bilden] sowohl die gebetsermöglichende Aktion Gottes in Ex 34,5f als auch der konkrete Vollzug durch Mose in Ex 34,8f zusammen mit der Antwort Gottes V 10 die theologische Antwort auf die Ausgangsproblematik der Kapitel Ex 32–34 …. Das bedeutet, daß keine Lösung auf einer begrifflichen Ebene vorgeführt wird. Die Gottesprädikationen bleiben notwendig eingebunden in das dialogische Geschehen in Ex 34 und fungieren nur so als 'Lösung' der Eingangsproblematik.[94]

The *Gnadenrede* in Exod. 34:6-7, thus, summarises the picture that has emerged indirectly throughout the narrative. The result for the reader is a memorable encounter with the "fullest account of the name and nature of God in the whole Bible."[95] The narrative clearly shows that Moses is a very privileged recipient of this divine revelation. But not only Moses is privileged here. It is more than mere eavesdropping which is intended for the implied reader. His rhetorically enhanced involvement with the narrative honours him, but it, also, obligates him to respond, so as not to violate the covenant. His suggested response is the hymnic praise to God.[96]

---

[92] Cf. Moberly 2002, 198.

[93] Sarna 1991, 214 reminds us, again, of the divine sovereignty which was expressed throughout the narrative: "In the religion of Israel there is no magical practice that is automatically effective in influencing divine behaviour."

[94] Scoralick 2002, 105.

[95] Moberly 2002, 198. For Moberly, the brief passage in Exod. 34 opens an avenue for the theological key question "How may we speak of God?" In his definition of knowing God as a relational activity or competence he is very close to Scoralick's talk of a 'dialogical event'.

[96] The involvement of the reader, in terms of literary reader-identification, will be discussed in detail below (see 245). In the various discussions of the legal parts of Exodus below, I will argue that the *imitatio dei* represents the ethical standard which is commended by the writer. This expression of the divine character plays, of course an important role in this concept as Wenham 1997, 26, writes: "Yet it is precisely these qualities that God looks for among his people: they are to reflect, even positively imitate, his character."

THE EPITHETS IN EXOD. 20:5-6

Another set of divine epithets is found in a context of sanction: the decalogue in Exod. 20:5-6. Here, the description of the divine nature is harnessed to motivate law observance. It is in its construction and content parallel to Exod. 34:6-7, as the following diagram demonstrates.

	Exod. 20:5-6	Exod. 34:6-7	
introductory speech 'formula'	<Exod. 20,1>	ויעבר יהוה על־פניו [6] ויקרא	introductory speech 'formula'
divine exclusive-ness	לא־תשתחוה להם [5] ולא תעבדם	<Exod. 34,14>	divine exclusive-ness
Yhwh is ... ... jealous	כי אנכי יהוה אלהיך אל קנא	יהוה יהוה אל רחום וחנון ארך אפים ורב־חסד ואמת:	Yhwh is ... ... compassion-ate
1st negative	פקד עון אבת על־בנים על־שלשים ועל־רבעים לשנאי:	נצר חסד לאלפים [7] נשא עון ופשע וחטאה ונקה לא ינקה פקד עון אבות על־בנים	1st positive
2nd positive	ועשה חסד לאלפים [6] לאהבי ולשמרי מצותי:	ועל־בני בנים על־שלשים ועל־רבעים:	2nd negative

The first part of the decalogue (20:2–6) revolves around the prohibition of the worship of gods other than Yhwh (5a). The plural personal pronouns refer to אלהים אחרים in 20:3 and, also, to פסל וכל־תמונה in 20:4. The reasons for judgement (כי) in 20:5b-6 are provided for both the first and second laws of the decalogue. Furthermore this passage quotes אנכי יהוה אלהיך and goes on to describe the divine nature, thereby, alluding in content to Yhwh's self-presentation in 20:2. Thus, structurally, Exod. 20:2 and 20:5b-6 frame the first and second laws.[97] The self-presentation is augmented by a retrospective view on the exodus and the wilderness wanderings; 20:5b-6 includes a glimpse into the future, referring to curse and blessing for later generations. The God of the exodus and the jealous God are one. Two aspects belong directly to the special relation between Yhwh and Israel: the historical exodus which singles out Israel as a chosen nation as well as Yhwh's jealousy which demands exclusive worship.[98] Hating (שנא) and loving (אהב) God are expressed by idolatry and

---

[97] Cf. also Dohmen 2004b, 107.

[98] Cf. Kratz 1994, 210f.

proper Yhwh-worship, respectively. Consequently, Kratz can formulate pointedly: "Das Halten der Gebote ist danach weder Bedingung noch Folge oder
(sachliche) Entsprechung zur anfänglichen Heilstat, sondern – sehr viel theo-
zentrischer gedacht – Vollzug des Anspruchs Jhwhs auf Ausschließlichkeit,
der aus der Heilstat abgeleitet wird."[99]

The previous discussion of Exod. 34:6-7 has shown that a collection of hymnic stock-phrases were employed to express the highly complex theological tension and imbalance between divine compassion and divine willingness to pursue
a perpetrator. In the decalogue, the talk of God's jealousy (Exod. 20:6a) finds
an explication in 5b-6. Or, in other words, the imbalance between the divine
commitment to forgive and the visiting of guilt interprets the divine nature, essentially, when it comes to intolerance toward the worship of other gods. According to Exod. 20:5b-6, divine jealousy implies the existence of God-lovers
and God-haters. The commandments are connected with an emotionally charged
metaphor. Despite the reversal of the two parts concerning the generations in
Exod. 20:5b–6, the emphasis is still on the חסד, and, hence, the same imbalance
between God's willingness to forgive and to punish dominates the picture. The
context of present sin in Exod. 32–34 leads to the inclusion of the phrase עון נשא
ופשע וחטאה, specifying what it means that Yhwh guards חסד for thousands of
generations. The specification of the same idea in Exod. 20:6 (ולשמרי מצותי),
however, widens and includes the commandments that follow in the remainder
of the decalogue and the book of the covenant.[100] The effect is that the reader
perceives the entire legislation in Exod. 20–23 as an expression of a life which
befits a "God-lover". The talk of a jealous God provides the ideational context
for the legal parts of Exodus. Thus both instances of the 'generation formula'
greatly influence the reading of the surrounding passages. The effect in guiding
the reading process is even greater for Exod. 20, as it precedes the material
upon which it comments. For an explication of these issues, see my passage on
the loyalty to Yhwh, p.98ff, below.

Yhwh's Conflict with the Pharaoh

In a study on the main characters of the book of Exodus one might expect a separate chapter on the character 'pharaoh'. This need is probably felt because of

---

[99] Kratz 1994, 211.

[100] Dohmen 2004b, 108f understands the parallel formulation לאהבי ולשמרי מצותי as providing the hinge between the main law of the decalogue and the other ensuing laws.

the major role he plays as Yhwh's adversary and, also, because of the theological implications of the hardening of his heart. Nevertheless, I feel that the Egyptian monarchs (Exodus mentions at least two of them) do not need a separate treatment in the present study, firstly, because they feature only in the first part of the book, and, secondly, because they serve as a counterfoil which develops the picture of Yhwh.[101] As a supporting character the pharaoh of the exodus is important, and in the following I will explicate the way in which this figure fits into the rhetorical strategy of Exodus.

In ancient Near Eastern cultures the distinction between the secular and the divine, or between the natural and the supernatural, is not straightforward. All forces of nature are divinely controlled. Yhwh's announcement of the final plague "... I will pass through the land of Egypt that night, and I will strike all the firstborn in the land of Egypt, both man and beast; and on all the gods of Egypt I will execute judgements: I am Yhwh." (12:12) – suggests that the main conflict in which the Israelites and the Egyptians find themselves is a divine conflict, maybe a mythological battle between the gods of different ethnic entities.[102] The text is not specific about the judgements upon the gods, but whatever they were,[103] the reader, surely, concludes that these gods were not powerful enough to protect their people. But as the plague story of Exodus unfolds it becomes quite clear that the conflict is actually between Yhwh and the monarch, while specific Egyptian gods remain anonymous.[104] In the Egyptian world view, the "Pharaoh was held to be divine and to be the guarantor of Egypt's welfare and security. But these disasters [sc. as narrated in the plague cycle] prove he is not in control and that he cannot protect his people."[105] This failure

---

[101] Cf. again Berge 2008, 20, who also interprets the plague narrative along these lines.

[102] The Song at the *yam suf*, especially in its rhetorical question (15:11), defines the relationship between Yhwh and the other gods as incomparable, thereby implicitly including the Egyptian gods. This does not mean that I support the position that a mythological battle has been condensed here in the form of an historical narrative (cf. Childs 1976, 143). In support of my interpretation cf. Rendtorff 2001, 55. For the literary function of this poem in the narrative and hence its importance for the perception of the previous material, see p.78.

[103] See Houtman 1996, 184, for a summary of previous attempts to fill this gap.

[104] One might suspect that here arises an instructive parallel to the anonymity of the pharaoh throughout the book. Above, I mentioned the ironic twist of this silence: those defeated are not mentioned by name in Egyptian war records, so the pharaoh and his gods are assigned the label 'loser' in the war against Yhwh. (Note the militaristic language, e.g. in expressions like "strong hand" and "outstreched arm". Cf. Hoffmeier 1997, 151.)

[105] Wenham 2003, 61. See also Shaw and Nicholson 1998, 151: "Sakral verstandenes Königtum und Göttlichkeit des Pharaoh waren Dreh- und Angelpunkt der äg. Gesellschaft und Religion." Houtman opposes the apologetic notion against the Egyptian gods as unlikely, but he gives no specific arguments for his reading (Houtman 1996, 21). Hoffmeier 1997, 149–155 differentiates: Not every plague can be connected with a certain Egyptian god or goddess. But he supports the general notion of critique of the lack of ability of these gods claimed by Wenham. Another fine contribution to this theme

goes to the heart of the function of the king, who was to defend and maintain cosmic order and harmony, *Ma'at*, and to battle chaos.[106] Hoffmeier quotes a number of Egyptian texts illustrating this principle and concludes:

> The legitimate king who rules by *m3't* can expect the Nile to flood properly and bring the fertility to the land, and additionally the sun and moon operate according to the created order. [...] What the plagues of Exodus show is the inability of the obstinate king to maintain *m3't*. Rather it is Yahweh and his agents, Moses and Aaron, who overcome in the cosmic struggle, demonstrating who really controls the forces of nature.[107]

Given the abundance of literature on the plague story (7:1–12:32)[108] there is no need to go into detail here. Even on a first and cursory reading of the narrative the impotence of the pharaoh and, together with him, the Egyptian gods is proven beyond doubt; a more detailed investigation would, simply, refine the overall picture developed here. More interesting from a rhetorical-critical angle is the question: For what reason did the author include such a lengthy proof of Yhwh's omnipotence? I propose that our author, again, needed some sort of foil against which the character Yhwh can take shape. Or, as Sternberg puts it in his unmistakable style:

> The plagues of Egypt ... offer ample opportunity for spatiotemporal bounding [sc. the speech-act in which God commits himself to perform a wonder together with a specific place or time] ... Foretelling, two-dimensional bounding, repetition in fulfilment, recurrence within a tenfold series: these combine to maximise the effect ('knowledge') of divine omnipotence on all observers, from God's stricken antagonists through the excepted Israelites to the narrator's audience."[109]

The centrality of this strategy to the book of Exodus becomes apparent when we consider Exod. 10,1–2:

> Then Yhwh said to Moses, 'Go in to the pharaoh, for I have hardened his heart and the heart of his servants, that I may show these signs of mine among them, and that you may tell in the hearing of your son and of your grandson how I have dealt harshly with the Egyptians and what signs I have done among them, that you may know that I am Yhwh.'

To quote Sternberg again: "The plagues thus come as an object lesson to three different audiences, whom he [sc. Yhwh] himself enumerates to Moses: 'the pharaoh and his servants,' 'you,' 'thy son and thy son's son,' all need to 'know

---

paying attention to literary as well as historico-cultural aspects is Cox 2006.

[106] Cf. Shaw and Nicholson 1998, 151.

[107] Hoffmeier 1997, 153.

[108] For a first overview, including ancient and modern literature, cf. Houtman 1996, 10ff. A recent contribution form a decidedly literary perspective with a fresh reading of the hardening motif, which comes to very similar results as I am, is Ford 2006.

[109] Sternberg 1987, 115.

that I am the Lord' (Exod. 10:1–2)."[110] Here, we encounter the only passage in Exodus which directly mentions the implied readers or the later generations.[111] Even more exciting is the direct statement from God himself of the author's purpose for recording these events: that his readers might know Yhwh. Of course, this is no new observation, but it is, nevertheless, often neglected. The concentration, rather, is on the various forms and literary sources that are thought to make up the plague story. In this context, Childs affirmingly refers to Moshe Greenberg:

> He [sc. Greenberg] sees the major theme of the plague story to revolve around the revelation by God of his nature to Pharaoh, to the Egyptians, and to all men. Even more important is recognizing how this theme fits into the movement of the book as a whole. The initial revelation of God's name met with human resistance and disbelief which created the tension of the narrative. The plagues function as demonstration of God's nature which shattered the resistance.[112]

The function of the plagues, at the story level, is to make Yhwh known (7:17; 8:18; 11:7); the removal of the plagues serves the same purpose, to make Yhwh known (8:6; 9:29).[113] As observed above, Exod. 10:1-2 suggests that this is not only the case for the story itself, but also at the rhetorical level for the communication between the author and his implied reader. Below, I will investigate whether there are any further clues which support this thought and what the knowledge of Yhwh might mean for the reader.

A set of passages, marked by the recurring statement that the hardness of the pharaoh's heart is "just as Yhwh had said" (כאשר דבר יהוה Exod. 7:13.22; 8:11. 15; 9:12.35),[114] provides the starting point for the present enquiry. Of course, this phrase is of worth only at the reading level of the text, as it guides the reading process. The use of a prediction-fulfilment pattern stresses the reliability of God for the reader. The occurrences of the phrase in the middle of the narrative complex remind the reader that the course of events unfolds exactly as they were meant to unfold. This being the case, the narrative arouses a bizarre feeling: each time a sign fails to achieve its stated goal, the reader is tempted to hope that the next sign would be effective.[115] This is a common sense expecta-

---

[110] Sternberg 1987, 103. For a detailed discussion of the various audiences of the plague narrative see Ford 2006, 113–123.

[111] But consider also Exod. 29:46, where there is no explicit mention of future generations. But the link via the tabernacle cult might provide the necessary continuity for more immediate identification of the readers.

[112] Childs 1976, 150, referring to Greenberg 1967.

[113] Cf. Childs 1976, 172.

[114] The construction is indeed very similar to the obedience formula discussed below (cf. p.170).

[115] An interesting theological treatment of this ambivalence can be found in Fretheim 1991a, 96–103. Fretheim, also commenting on the final redaction of the narrative, tries to resolve theologically the tension between Yhwh's foreknowledge and the king's lia-

tion of the reader, but the rule for reading this specific narrative is Yhwh's prediction, which is repeatedly called to mind by the refrain. Thus, the implied
reader is constantly encouraged to correct himself, and this communicates constantly the notion of divine control in the historical situation described.[116]

Whatever the theological implications behind the hardening motif,[117] it is
clear that the pharaoh's attitude is the counter-example in the narrative. It is left
to the reader to conclude what it positively means to know Yhwh. It will suffice
to mention only a few aspects of the literary construction of the king's counter-
attitude, especially in relation to the ongoing shaping of the character Yhwh.[118]

After the introduction of Yhwh as a determined and faithful character, the author describes the fulfilment (in the narrative's present) of the prediction given
by Yhwh in the dialogue with Moses (e.g. 3:18-20; 4:21). The actual conflict
between Yhwh and the pharaoh, which will dominate the narrative until Exod.
15, is introduced in 5:2 with the pharaoh's outright rejection of Yhwh's claim to
authority. The theme of knowing Yhwh is expressed clearly. The divine "I am"
from 3:14 is ridiculed by the Egyptian king: מי יהוה. Houtman comments: "It is
an insult aimed at YHWH. To Israelite ears Pharaoh's question must have soun-
ded like blasphemy."[119] The Pharaoh does not want to have anything to do with
this Yhwh: לא ידעתי את־יהוה. Furthermore, he does not intend to give up authority over Israel (את־ישראל לא אשלח). The problem is thatboth characters, Yhwh
and the pharaoh, claim the people of Israel. This is the driving force in the plot
from this point forward. The conflict, foreseen by Yhwh, begins immediately,
which, again, establishes Yhwh as being trustworthy in the eyes of the reader.
The reader will remember the specifics of the prediction: Yhwh's mighty hand
will be needed to free Israel. This had prepared the reader for the intensity of
the conflict, so the complications, narrated in Exod. 5, are not too surprising.
Nevertheless, the reader must surely suffer with the people and their "utter

---

bility and freedom of decision. This harmonisation is not necessary and deprives the text
of a possible rhetorical device that engages the reader.

[116] Also interesting is the mention of the divine promise to bring the people into the land
of promise, which also uses the marked phrase כאשר דבר יהוה (Exod. 12:25). The notion
of divine control is, thereby, extended beyond the actual exodus.

[117] I follow Jackson 2000, 245, in viewing the hardening of the pharaoh's heart as a self-
inflicted complication of Yhwh's struggle with the pharaoh. Childs 1976, 174, rightly,
includes an exegetical warning in his discussion: "Hardening was the vocabulary used
by the biblical writers to describe the resistance which prevented the signs from achieving their assigned task. The motif has been consistently over-interpreted by supposing
that it arose from a profoundly theological reflection and seeing it as a problem of free
will and predestination."

[118] With this, I hope to provide a few suggestions in answer to Dale Patrick's remark:
"Practically every commentary on Exodus discusses the theme of hardening carefully,
... but I have not found any mention of the dramatic import of the theme." (Patrick
1995, 115, n.18).

[119] Houtman 1993, 462.

sense of helplessness before the highly organized machinery of the system."[120] It seems that the narrator wants Israel to fall even deeper into despair so that the deliverance would appear all the more magnificent. Houtman comments fittingly:

> Now that the liberation of Israel truly depends solely on Him – cooperation from the side of the people can no longer be expected after 5:19-21 (the people play no further role in the confrontation with Pharaoh), and Moses is a despondent individual – the moment has come to really seize the initiative. The reader must be fully alerted to the fact that Israel's liberation is not the work of mortal man but purely and solely YHWH's doing.[121]

The ancient Jewish interpretation of the pharaoh's response in Targum Onkelos[122] and Targum Pseudo Jonathan[123] understood the entire situation in these terms: they embellished the conversation in a way that was, later, understood to promote Yhwh at the cost of deconstructing the pharaoh who is made to look stupid because he looks for Yhwh among the dead.[124] The whole purpose was to enlarge Yhwh's praise. Praise follows praiseworthy deeds, and, as Yhwh's deeds are signs here of his potency, they look all the more praiseworthy when there is appropriate and considerable challenge (cf. Exod. 9:15f). The author anticipates this scene even before the beginning of the plague narrative. At the end of Exod. 5 Moses' attempts to convince the pharaoh to let them go fail. God is significantly absent from the scene in Exod. 5, and the reader finds himself evaluating the situation from the perspective of the Israelites and that of Moses (5:21-23). Both perspectives accuse Yhwh of not being able to resolve the situation; things are worse than they were at the start. This literary situation can be compared with a different story in which the negative portrayal of Moses is used as a rhetorical device to effect the positive perception of Yhwh. Sternberg well observes the rhetorical force of Moses' doubts about Yhwh's ability to provide food to a large number of people (Num. 11:21-23):

> Dissonant voices are thus manipulated rather than eliminated in the interests of persuasive harmony. ... [T]he less credible a marvel before the fact the more

---

[120] Childs 1976, 106.

[121] Houtman 1993, 486.

[122] "And Pharaoh said, The name of the Lord is not known to me, that I should hearken to His word to send Israel away. The name of the Lord is not revealed to me, and Israel I shall not release." (Exod. 5:2 – translation taken from Etheridge 1968, 353)

[123] "But Pharaoh said: 'The name of the Lord has not been revealed to me that I should listen to his word and let Israel go. I have not found the name of the Lord written in the Book of the Angels. I do not fear him, and moreover I will not let Israel go." (Exod. 5:2 – translation taken from McNamara, Hayward and Maher 1994, 173)

[124] Cf. *ExR* V,14: "Thus did Moses and Aaron say to Pharaoh: 'Idiot! Is it the way of the dead to be sought for among the living, or are the living among the dead? Our God is living, whereas those thou dost mention are dead; yes, our God is a living God and an eternal king'." (Translation taken from Lehrman 1951.)

impressive its performance. So Moses' very stature actually enhances his value for the narrator. If even he turns sceptic, we reason, then the divine undertaking must be a tall order indeed. We are positively tempted into doubt … to maximize the effect of the denouement. The earth covered with quails, Moses never questions God's power again; nor, by implication from our spokesman, should we.[125]

The recording of inimical remarks can, thus, be a means of articulating a possible attitude on the part of the reader. As the story progresses in Num. 11 not only is the character put to shame but also the reader, because he also would have questioned God's power. Drawing the parallel to Exod. 5:21-23 – the Israelites' accusation and Moses' reaction to it – we might also conclude that here the implied reader's thoughts find expression in the text itself.

The author creates a certain atmosphere in Exod. 5:1-19 – probably a feeling of impotence and bitterness at the king's tyranny – which anticipates his reader's reaction and, then, he articulates that attitude in two complaints, one from the Israelites' foremen and the from Moses. We are positively tempted to doubt whether Yhwh has not taken on too great a task. In this doubt the reader is not alone; he is in the good company of Moses and the Israelites. It is only during the course of reading the plague narrative (Exod. 7:8–12:32) that the reader realises that Yhwh is actually able and willing to overpower the pharaoh. Of course, the author is aware that his reader already knows that God will be successful, but the narrative in 5:1-19 is specifically designed to draw the reader into the emotions of the story. The fast-moving pace of direct speech is quite different in its rhetorical force from, for example, the long monologues of Yhwh in Exod. 3+4 or the reporting style in the first two chapters. Once the reader is immersed into the plot, he is open to the guidance of the narrator. The result is that in the end the reader feels unsure. Whose fault was it that Moses and Aaron's visit to the pharaoh ended in a fiasco? Was it Moses' fault, as the Hebrews suggest? Was it God's fault, as Moses suggests? The answers cannot be found in the narrative. Even though the author prompts the questions, I am convinced that he considers them the wrong question to ask. This, at least, is suggested by Yhwh's response to Moses' complaint (Exod. 6:1). The rhetorical strategy that we observe is equivalent to a military pre-emptive strike in that a likely reading of the text is anticipated and, then, shown to be invalid. This engages the reader and focuses the reading process on the determination and potency of Yhwh, which seems to be the thrust behind the motif 'knowing Yhwh'.

Earlier, I asked what the knowledge of Yhwh might positively mean for the reader. In the previous discussion I concluded that divine determination and potency is part of the answer. This will now be delineated more fully. Exod. 6:1-8 is not really an answer to Moses' accusations. Yhwh does not seem prepared to be drawn into a discussion. The emphatic use of "now" (עתה) and the repetition

---

[125] Sternberg 1987, 113.

of his intention to exert pressure upon the pharaoh[126] – so that he drives the Israelites out of his country – both point to God's determination to bring about the change he intended from the start. Significant to our present interest, this Yhwh speech is framed by an *inclusio* in verses 2 and 8: אני יהוה (repeated in 6 and 7). This self-introduction comes as a surprise to the reader, for if he remembers something from the previous narrative, he will, surely, remember Exod. 3:13-15 and the link between this name and the mention of the patriarchal covenant. Even if we could safely assume two different sources, each with roughly the same idea, this repetition was not superfluous to the final redactor. Repetition serves mainly to induce comparison and emphasis. The most significant change between the two *Selbstvorstellungsformeln* in Exod. 3 and 6 is the phrase "but by my name I did not make myself known to them." (6:3b)

Whatever the historical implications are for the reconstruction of the Yhwh-belief in the Patriarchal and Mosaic periods, the rhetorical force is obvious and is, probably, best communicated in a paraphrase: "Just as you *now* have access to my name 'Yhwh', you will *now* experience the fulfilment of my land-promise to the fathers!" God appeared to the fathers (v.3a) and now reveals a new name to the oppressed people (v.3b). God established a covenant (v.4) and now remembers this covenant (v.5). The structural parallel highlights the progress God is about to initiate: "God reveals himself in a new posture, not only making a promise [as to the patriarchs; SK], but also fulfilling it,"[127] as Houtman interprets along the same lines. The message Moses has to deliver to the Israelites is framed by the mention of the divine name. Around the covenant formula (v.7) God's acts of deliverance and of giving the Israelites their promised land[128] are grouped. This speech anticipates the main events in early Israelite history, two of which are narrated in Exodus, the exodus from Egypt and the inclusion of Israel into the Patriarchal covenant. Hence, for the reader the knowledge-of-Yhwh motif is linked to the main themes of the book and connected to the display of a determined and potent God. The conclusion to which the reader is in-

---

[126] The phrase ביד חזקה is somewhat ambiguous as it can be translated "with a strong hand" (*beth instrumentalis*), "by power/violence" (taking ביד as compound preposition: with/by – the sense again being instrumental), or "because of a strong hand"/"because being forced" (a causal use of beth). The first two translations imply that the king will use force (ESV, Hyatt et al.), whereas the third suggests that the king himself is forced to let them go (Childs, Houtman et al.). Some commentators make a difference between the two phrases in v.1; e.g. Cassuto takes the first one as modifying Yhwh and the second, the pharaoh. I prefer Houtman or Childs and take it as an expression of Yhwh's putting the king under pressure (cf. the unambiguous Exod. 3:19; 13:9!).

[127] Houtman 1993, 487.

[128] See the three parallel verbs of deliverance in v.6 (יצא hif, נצל hif, גאל qal) and the two verbs expressing the act of giving the land to the people in v.8 (בוא hif, נתן qal).

vited by the rhetorics of the text is that Yhwh is stubborn and unfaltering[129] in bringing about his promises to the Patriarchs and to Israel as a people.

This link to the father's covenant is theologically important in terms of the continuity in the dealings between Yhwh and Israel. The dialogue between Moses and Yhwh in Exod. 6 reconfirms the patriarchal promise. Jackson argues, convincingly, from Genesis that the covenant with Abraham is developed into a "hereditary obligation/blessing."[130] Jackson writes, regarding the plot-strategy of Exodus:

> If we take the stories from Abram as a macro-narrative of the relations between God and the people, what we have observed thus far is the institution of a 'Contract' (in the Greimassian sense) in which God becomes the Subject of an hereditary obligation. At this point [sc. Exod. 2,23–25], an Opponent is presented, who threatens to impede Performance. The attitude of the new pharoah [sic] is presented not simply as an incident in the changing fortunes of the Israelites, but as directly relevant to the Contract God has undertaken.[131]

"The Contract God has undertaken" becomes the main theme of Exod. 5:22–7:7. In view of the new and severe threats described in Exod. 5:6-21, the doubts raised by Moses, the Israelites, and the reader – according to the observations above – concentrate on the concrete promises received by Moses during the encounter at the burning bush. The character 'Yhwh', on the other hand, reintroduces the larger context (6:2-8). God will, actually, bring about the promises of the old covenant and re-confirm to a new generation the land-promise to the fathers: "I will bring you into the land that I swore to give to Abraham, to Isaac, and to Jacob. I will give it to you for a possession. I am Yhwh." (Exod. 6:8)[132] From Yhwh's point of view, the deliverance from slavery is the prelude to the fulfilment of the land-promise. For the reader, historical facts are linked to a theological interpretation. At an ideational level, we find the author suggesting an element of continuity in Israel's history, which is dominating all historical particularities. What ensures the continuity? Exodus answers: continuity is ensured by Yhwh's self-binding promise to the hereditary covenant together with his willingness and potency to bring it into fruition for his people.

The motif of 'knowing Yhwh' and the 'I am'-formula are closely linked, not only in Exodus but, also, in the rest of the Old Testament, if not in the entire Bible. Rolf Rendtorff argues that the point behind the two motifs lies, not so

---

[129] It is possible to conclude from a comparison between the characters pharaoh and Yhwh that they are not much different when it comes to the determination with which they pursue their respective goals. Neither is prepared to give in to the other's 'arguments'. If it were not for the negative connotations of the term, one imagines speaking of the hardness of Yhwh's heart.

[130] Cf. Jackson 2000, 243f.

[131] Jackson 2000, 244.

[132] Cf. Jackson 2000, 245.

much in the attributes or personality of this God, but in the reference to the divinity of Yhwh: "... es soll ... nicht erkannt werden, wer oder wie Jhwh ist, sondern, daß *er* es ist, der in dem, was angekündigt wird, handelt und der sich darin als er selbst erweist."[133] Thus, according to Exodus, Yhwh wants to be known as the God who acts on behalf of his people and who does so successfully, even though the superpower, Egypt, and its mighty king need to be overcome.[134] Taking this idea further, the notion might be suggested that Yhwh is not only a mighty god – or even the mightiest – but also the only god who truly deserves to be called 'god'. As the story unfolds, the example of the acceptance of Jithro balances that of the ignorance of the pharaoh (Exod. 18:9-12). Appearing only twice, Jithro is a marginal character in Exodus, but his presence is nevertheless crucial. The contrast between the stubborn, ignorant and less than helpful Egyptian monarch[135] and this Midianite priest exemplifies the way non-Israelite people should respond to Yhwh's representatives, be they Moses or Israel as a nation. In reaction to his hearing the story of the exodus from Egypt he states: "Now I know that Yhwh is greater than all gods." (18:11) As his offering and eating with Aaron and the elders of Israel show, he is, effectively, taken into the people of God.[136] The Egyptians could have responded in the way that the Midianite responded. The knowledge of Yhwh among the other nations was developed as a theme, including a more clearly-expressed monolatric theology.[137] According to Exodus this knowledge is based on the knowledge of Yhwh's deeds in history, the exodus events, specifically. Jithro was compelled by a mere narration of the events; the reader of Exodus finds himself in the very same situation. Thus, we can conclude that Jithro functions as a point of undivided identification in the rhetorical setup of the book. In him, a non-Israelite, the whole purpose of the narration of the exodus events comes to fruition.

---

[133] Rendtorff 2001, 178.

[134] Later in the Old Testament we find Ezekiel using the knowledge formula extensively and applying the same notion to the negative experience of the exile, this, of course, being a considerably different theological emphasis than the more triumphant one in the Pentateuch.

[135] Fretheim 1991a, 195, views the contrast between Aram and Midian, but, on the functional side, I find the contrast between the pharaoh and Jithro much more fruitful and convincing, especially given the allusion to the knowledge motif. On this see also Ber 2008.

[136] Exod. 18:12 seems strangely misplaced in the plot, given that the sanctuary has not been built yet and instructions for the offerings have not been received. The reader will nevertheless know the preconditions from his own worship. Eating with the elders in God's presence is developed in 24:9-11 and, here, the covenant context provides the link between right worship and belonging to the chosen people.

[137] Some texts are more concerned with this than others, at least on an abstract level. That, for all biblical writers, Yhwh is the one and only god is apparent, but it would be anachronistic to use the term monotheism in this theology.

The first area of conflict touched upon in the book of Exodus, from a rheto-rical-critical point of view, is very similar function to the dialogue between Moses and Yhwh: the portrayal of Yhwh takes shape against the backdrop of another character, this time the Egyptian sovereign. The reader concludes that Yhwh is not only determined and faithful but, also, potent. The hardening of the pharaoh's heart is a strategy to provide an abundance of literary opportunities for this depiction of Yhwh – he controls everything and, in the end, succeeds. The rhetorical device, which is central for this communicative effect, is the knowing-Yhwh motif which has been shown to apply to both the story level of the text and the reader's level.

The Introduction of Yhwh into the Plot of Exodus

It is striking how quietly the author starts off the work in which Yhwh will later play the major role. But this reticence of the author to introduce God explicitly as character is a common biblical feature, as Sternberg, with a view toward the author-reader relationship, describes:

> [I]t would be awkward if not offensive to open by introducing to the audience the God of their fathers, however dim or even misguided their actual conception of him. Only a Pharaoh, as it were, requires information on 'Who is the Lord, that I should listen to his voice?' (Exod. 5:2). The rhetoric of solidarity indicates a more oblique line of unfolding, whereby the narrator first pretends to assume his rea-der's knowledge-ability and then slips in the necessary premises, under dramatic guise and often with corrective or polemical intent, as the need for them arises. For another thing, it would be equally bad policy to reduce God to a series of epithets, as if he were one's neighbour rather than a unique and enigmatic power, knowable only through his incursions into history.[138]

Though Sternberg, here, reflects on the beginning of Genesis in particular, his observations are very fitting for the situation in Exodus. The reader only learns in a piecemeal fashion about the character 'God', his relationship with Israel, and his intentions for Israel. The truth of the last sentence, quoted above, is of particular importance to the theological significance of the following discus-sion: I do not wish to diminish the divine obscurity and otherness as it is dis-played in Exodus. Nevertheless, it remains the task of this chapter to systemati-se and categorise to a certain extent this complex testimony. But this will not be accomplished in a biblical-theological manner, by collecting the facts about God that are touched upon in Exodus. Rather, the aim is to explicate the inter-play of silence and explicitness in the book's description of God and its sup-posed influence upon the reader.[139]

---

[138] Sternberg 1987, 323.

[139] This concentration on the reader is the more interesting aspect when it comes to the character 'God'. As observed above, God does not really change very much in biblical literature. But the author still needs to apply this 'known' character to the different sit-

The growth of the people thematised in the first chapter, apparently, should be understood as being Yhwh's work, but this is communicated only implicitly through the example of the midwives who are being blessed by God for their courageous support of the Israelite progeny (Exod. 1:17.20-21).[140] Yhwh stays in the background, a literary device used to contrast him with the pharaoh. Exod. 1 displays the king of Egypt, on the one hand, as frantic, fearful and malicious,[141] and as busy ushering in political decisions; he is, thus, actively opposed to God. On the other hand, God is passively opposed to the pharaoh, and much more successfully. This contrast is established by the portrayals of the Egyptian king and of the Israelite midwives and it forces the reader to judge the situation morally. The pharaoh is adorned with direct speech in Exod. 1 (the midwives are only reacting, cf. 1:19) which contributes to his fervent busyness. Yet this activity is not blessed with success, as the entire chapter strongly emphasises. Quite the opposite, the midwives are not only successful in delivering strong and healthy babies, but they are, also, blessed directly by God, his only action explicitly mentioned in this chapter. Underscoring this reading of the text, the author withholds the name of the actual pharaoh, whereas he explicitly names two midwives who are representing Yhwh's will to sustain his people.[142] One of the important themes of Exodus thus surfaces: fear of God (1:17.21) leads to blessing (1:21), but work against God will never bring success.

This all happens in a very subtle way. Although being pictured as present in the multiplication issue which dominates the first chapter, God is not the central character yet. Yhwh, as character, is not mentioned explicitly until Exod. 2:23-

---

uations he is describing in his text. Doing this, he will, of course, presuppose a certain knowledge on the part of the reader. Cf. Owens 2004, 619–621, who observes the same creative tension regarding the portrayal of God at the beginning of Exodus.

[140] That Yhwh remains largely in the background may also be attributed to the wisdom setting which the first two chapters of Exodus betray (cf. Childs 1963 and, from a different perspective, Weber 1990, 73–75).

[141] Jacob 1997, 40 even designates this pharaoh as being insane ("jener Wahnsinnige"), ushering idiotic decrees ("idiotischer Dekret"). This characterisation is probably a little radical, though the text certainly gives a very negative and ironic picture of the king.

[142] "To remain nameless is to remain faceless, with hardly a life of one's own. Accordingly, a character's emergence from anonymity may correlate with a rise in importance." So writes Sternberg 1987, 330. This generalised rule is certainly true in this incident: the pharaohs of the book of Exodus are interchangeable, for none of them carries a name. They are nothing but typical characters, important only in their hardheaded opposition to Yhwh. In an insightful discussion of the Egyptian habit of not mentioning the names of the conquered monarchs in their records (*damnatio memoriae*), Hoffmeier concludes similarly that Exodus anonymises the pharaohs as "a nice piece of irony", suggesting that they are to be delivered to annihilation in human memory, whereas Yhwh's name becomes great (Hoffmeier 1997, 109–112).

25.[143] His introduction comes about significantly with a cluster of four occurrences of the term אלהים in 2:24-25. The death of God's opponent, the Egyptian king, is recorded briefly, but the situation for the Israelites does not change. This is recorded in a comparatively wordy manner: four times the Hebrew's difficulties are mentioned (2:22-23: אנח/זעק/שועה/נאקה).[144] But the most important change is expressed in words of care and concern: God listens, remembers, perceives and knows. The narrative pace slows down, which hints at the importance of the text.

After a brief, concluding notice about Gershom, Moses' first son (Exod. 2:22), the author takes a big step forward in the narrated time and upward into the heavenly realm. God now enters the story line in an impressive way. Exod. 2:23-25 not only forms the important base for the following discussion between Moses and Yhwh, but it, also, functions as an interpretive key for understanding the preceding narration. The construction ויזכר אלהים את־בריתו את־אברהם את־יצחק ואת־יעקב (2:24b), which can be understood as a simpleanthropomorphism, is much more than that at the communicative level between author and reader. By using the mere word 'remember' (זכר) the author induces the same mental action inside the reader's mind. The reader is urged to recall God's covenant, the knowledge of which is clearly presupposed, either from common knowledge or from previously reading Genesis. The reader then fills in the actual content of this covenant. On this foil the previous narrative receives its theological evaluation. The abundant increase in Israelite population (Exod. 1:7.9.12) can now be understood as an obvious result of Yhwh fulfilling his promise to Abraham and his sons as recorded in Gen. 17:6; 28:3; 35:11. The narrative adds theological significance to the events retold in Exod. 1:1–2:22. The introduction of Yhwh (2:23-25) puts the smaller units, each with its own message, under the roof of an overarching theological rationale, the patriarchal covenant. However, this interpretation is only initiated by the author; the reader must recognise it for himself. The involvement of the reader in the process of constructing meaning is good rhetorical practice, as he might be inclined to adopt this theological paradigm for other parts of his national history, as well. As I will show at different points in this study, this is exactly what the author offered his implied reader in giving

---

[143] This brief passage received quite varied attention in the major commentaries. Childs 1976, 32f, interprets Exod. 2:23-25 as relating back to the previously stated misery of the Israelites, after the two scenes from Moses' life. Very briefly, he suggests that the reader might ask himself what God's plan will be for his people. Houtman 1993, 322f, refers to its narrative function as the turning point in the narrative: God cares and is ready to enter the action. Rendtorff 1997, 14, suggests that "…these verses are to be understood as an integral part of an overarching concept of the Pentateuch". He links them to the remembering of God in Gen. 9:14-16.

[144] Cf. Jacob 1997, 41f, on the significance of the fourfold mention of nouns and action verbs in these few verses. Especially, the fourfold reference to אלהים captivates Jacob's attention.

him an example from the earliest times of Israel to evaluate historical developments.

Given these considerations, the retrospective aspect of Exod. 2:24b is not the
one and only aim of the author: He also offers an interpretive paradigm for the
future. The immediate context makes clear that Israel's being a slave-nation
should be at the centre of attention. The author now contextualises this oppression explicitly using the covenant between Yhwh and the fathers and as the
reader remembers the contents of this covenant his expectations develop. The
reader's perspective is thus dependent upon the covenant. He will, therefore,
evaluate Israel's slavery as being totally unacceptable to God. God promised
Abraham the land of Canaan and a sovereign nation (cf. Gen. 15:18-20; 17:4-
8), yet neither promise had been fulfilled at the time of the author's narration.
This discrepancy between *status quo* and promise is what drives the reader's interest in the following chapters of Exodus.

After the short, but intense, overture to the actual introduction of the character 'Yhwh', the author utilises the compositional device of dialogue to fill in the
gaps of the reader's understanding. In this dialogue, however, the two participants are not of equal importance, so far as the author is concerned. One character (Moses) serves as background for the other (Yhwh).[145] This passage is
mainly about Yhwh, whose picture is clarified against the background of Moses' resistance. That is, the author utilises the narrative, and in this case especially the dialogue, to point out the central aspects of Yhwh's being and the divine purpose for the people. Furthermore, the dialogue enables the author to
forecast or anticipate the crucial events. When future events finally take place
the reader will remind himself of the prediction and intuitively compare it with
the report of the actual occurrence. Since the forecast is given by Yhwh – with
Moses only anticipating the people's reaction (3:13; 4:1[146]) – the author claims

---

[145] Beach-Verhey 2005 hints in a similar direction. Rendtorff, however, is convinced of
the opposite: "So haben die Kapitel Ex 3 und 6 in mehrfacher Hinsicht eine grundle-
gende Funktion. Sie führen Mose ein, der von jetzt an die beherrschende Gestalt bis zum
Ende des Pentateuch sein wird. Sie verbinden mit der Person des Mose die ausdrückli-
che Kundgabe des Yhwh-Namens an Israel. Und sie kündigen die bevorstehende Befreiung Israels aus der Knechtschaft an, ebenfalls in unmittelbarer Verbindung mit Mose."
(Rendtorff 1999, 39) In my opinion these chapters serve to introduce Yhwh more than
Moses. A view between Rendtorff's and my own position is being held by Fischer 2007,
who understands the described physical movement in Exod. 3:1-6 as being paralleled by
the continuing literary togetherness of messenger and God throughout the following narrative (227). In detail as well, Fischer arrives at a more positive Mosaic picture than I
do. In the end, however, in Fischer's article the main thrust of the literary effort of Exod.
3–4 is towards the characterisation of Yhwh, and here he arrives at the same conclusions
as I do.

[146] In Exod. 4 the contrast is most obvious. Moses anticipates the people will react with
utter disbelief (cf. 4:1). Yhwh rather expects that they will believe (cf. 4:5 and v.8+9
which also imply that they will believe Moses). And as 4:31 states, simply and clear:

the highest authority for his prediction and, thus, establishes the measure against which the actual fulfilment will be evaluated.

In the following I will investigate in more detail the rhetorically relevant features of the dialogue between Yhwh and Moses including its immediate narrative context, in order to substantiate my claims that the text's rhetorical function refines the initial portrayal of Yhwh.

The first encounter between Yhwh and Moses (Exod. 3:1–4:31) is connected to the previous narrative by the introduction of Yhwh in 2:23-25, which has already been discussed. This section ends quite abruptly and cryptically with the elliptic phrase וידע אלהים ("and God knew"). This ending was clearly not satisfying to many ancient and modern readers, resulting in various emendations to the text.[147] These proposed solutions suggest that the author achieved his aim with this rhetorical trick. Such a conspicuous ellipsis challenges the reader to fill in the blank. And he does. Beside the standard function of ellipses – the raising of attention and expectation – the reader is encouraged to reflect, in much the same way he did when remembering the contents of the divine promises of the fathers. Here, the reader must wonder what exactly God knew, thus entering the mind of the character God. The effect may be called the adoption of the divine perspective. The reader will try to think about the difficulties in Egypt just as he supposes Yhwh might have thought about it. Clearly, the author has little control over this thinking process, for his portrayal of Yhwh is quite undeveloped as yet, but the involvement of the reader in the reading process is certainly reinforced, no matter how subconscious it might be. Whatever the reader might conclude, he will either be confirmed or corrected. The rhetorical strategy of this brief passage with the ominous ending is apparent now: By inviting the reader to engage with the text's likely progression, the author can be sure that his reader is concentrating mainly on Yhwh and on the unfolding of Yhwh's plan.

Exod. 2:24-25 provides, in a nutshell, the terminology, as well as the subject, of the ensuing dialogue. The verbs (ידע, ראה, שמע) in this passage are taken up in the first proper divine address to Moses (3:7+9). The self-introduction of Yhwh in 3:6 refers the reader back to the definition of the covenant that he was earlier encouraged to remember (2:24b).[148] This connection prompts the reader to anticipate the theme of the following conversation: how is the covenant linked to the situation of oppression? The setting of the dialogue (3:1-6) includes two

---

"And the people believed." Here, the author closes the issue once and for all; Yhwh was right and Moses was wrong.

[147] The Septuagint, for instance resolves the problem of the missing object: καὶ ἐγνώσθη αὐτοῖς ("and was known by them"). Other translations amend the text in other ways; cf. the brief discussion in Houtman 1993, 332.

[148] The structure of repetition here is enactment/report, to use Sternberg's categories. The functional quality of this repetition is obvious; there is no natural or internal reason for this, almost verbatim, redundancy (cf. Sternberg 1987, 409ff).

concepts known to any Israelite reader: the 'mountain of God' and divine holiness. Both themes are so crucial to the Jewish concept of God that there is no mistaking the theophany as referring to any other divinity, an idea which might have arisen by the settling of Moses in Midian and, in particular, in the household of a Midianite priest (cf. 3:1). Thus four elements – each of which are probably known to the intended reader – are being drawn together in the following dialogue: the caring God of the Israelites, their oppression in Egypt, the covenant of their ancestors, and a political refugee, called Moses. The communicative aim of the author will be to reshape his reader's understanding concerning the relationship of these four 'elements'.

A rough outline of this relationship is presented in the first part of Moses' commissioning (3:7-10). This text is highly redundant and forms a parallel structure:[149]

a	God's perception of the situation (v.7)	I have surely seen the affliction of my people who are in Egypt and have heard their cry because of their taskmasters. I know their sufferings,
b	God's resolution to free the Israelites (v.8)	and I have come down to deliver them out of the hand of the Egyptians and to bring them up out of that land to a good and broad land, [...]
a'	God's perception of the situation (v.9)	And now, behold, the cry of the people of Israel has come to me, and I have also seen the oppression with which the Egyptians oppress them.
b'	God's commission of Moses to realise the resolution (v.10)	Come, I will send you to the pharaoh that you may bring my people, the children of Israel, out of Egypt.

This parallelism allows the author to express two aspects of the deliverance: God initiates and Moses executes. The text forces the reader to interpret the exodus as, predominantly, Yhwh's concern: there is a strong emphasis on God being attentive to their problems, together with a dominant use of the first person in verbs and pronouns. Only at the very end is Moses referred to by the use of two imperatives, but again it is God who sends him. As stated above, in this dialogue, Moses' objections function as a foil against which the portrayal of

---

[149] Cf. Houtman 1993, 324, who also observes this parallelism but is more concerned to (refute) sensibly the idea that these verses present us with a literary doublet rather than an explanation of the parallelism's significance.

Yhwh emerges brighter and clearer.[150] The author uses the remainder of the conversation to stress that Moses will not go on his own authority but on Yhwh's: God sends Moses, and it is God who defines the purpose of the exodus, which ultimately is to serve Yhwh (v.12).

The second of Moses' objections (3:13-22) provides the opportunity for developing the portrayal of Yhwh in a way which became classic for both Jewish and Christian theology. The divine name takes centre stage in reflections on how Yhwh must be understood. Even in Exodus, the name of God, in certain ways and places, becomes a shortcut referring the reader back to the picture painted in Exod. 3. Often this phenomenon is linked with the motif of knowing Yhwh, a crucial concept in the unfolding drama of Exodus, especially in the plague narrative.[151] Above, I already reflected upon the tetragrammaton 'Yhwh' and its contribution to the refinement of Yhwh's character portrayal. It is clear that the reflection upon the divine name, as presented by the author in Exod. 3, communicates the crucial role that Yhwh will play in the events of the exodus. Exod. 3:15 presents Yhwh as the determined authority who will sovereignly bring about the exodus of Israel from Egypt. The author achieves his purposes by downplaying the character Moses – who now acts only because Yhwh authorises him – and, thus, highlighting Yhwh's profile.[152] The reason for this strategy lies in the assumption the author makes regarding his reader's bias. Below (p.148ff), I will argue that the author presumes – as does his implied reader – a picture of Moses which is too positive. The emphasis on Yhwh in Exod. 1–5 balances this preconception and establishes a new picture of Moses which replaces the old one. The author presents the god, called Yhwh, as being beyond human disposal but, also, as a god who, nevertheless, cares for his people and is willing to deliver them from Egypt. The continuity between Yhwh, the God of the exodus, and the God of the patriarchs is established beyond any doubt. This theme runs through all of Exod. 2:23–4:31. What is new to the portrayal of God after 3:14-15 is that he used to be known as the maker of promises, but he will now be known, also, as the fulfiller of these promises. This is the new understanding of the tetragrammaton which the author sought to com-

---

[150] This emphasis is supported by the first of Moses' objections (3:11). The short phrase מי אנכי reminds the reader of the tension between the obvious destiny of Moses as born deliverer – a picture suggested by the form and style of the birth story (2:1-10) – and his first failed attempt to act as deliverer in 2:11-15. The reader must, indeed, agree with Moses that he, from all Israelites, could not and should not be the chosen deliverer. Moses is void of all authority, married into a non-Israelite family, and shepherds as a political refugee with a pending death-penalty in a country far from his oppressed brothers. For more detail about Moses' portrayal in the beginning of Exodus refer to p.148ff.

[151] See p.54ff below.

[152] This rhetorical feature has been described also by Berge 2008, 17–21.

municate. But as soon as this becomes clear, the name-issue is dropped[153] and the author, immediately, returns to the planning of the exodus.

Exod. 3:16 is linked to the heart of the message to Moses with almost verbatim repetition of 3:6+8. For the third time, as if it were a refrain, it is said that Yhwh heard the Israelites, saw their oppression, and cares. The message of Moses is recalled,[154] but, here, a new perspective comes into view: the reaction of the different recipients to God's intentions. The elders of Israel will listen, that is they will obey (3:18aα), but the pharaoh will not listen or obey (3:19a). Thus, in Exod. 3:16-22 the author prepares the reader for the plague and exodus narratives.[155] Rhetorically, this passage pre-programmes the reader for receiving Exod. 6–15. Here, things are made explicit which are present only implicitly in the unfolding larger narrative. The interpretation suggested by the author is clearly a theological one, focussing on the determination of Yhwh not just to remember the covenant of the patriarchs but, also, to fulfil it. The dialogue between Yhwh and Moses has precisely this function: it prepares the reader for the actual narration of the exodus events, so that the theo-political programme is recognised in the reading process.

The portrayal of Yhwh that emerges from this dialogue warrants the present discussion. Prediction automatically invites comparison with the report of the actual events. The concerns in the dialogue are clear: Moses is occupied with the reception of his message by the Israelites (Exod. 4:1-17), whereas Yhwh clearly expects a hardened heart in the Egyptian monarch (3:18a). Exod. 4:21 ("Now that you are ready to return to Egypt, remember to do before the pharaoh all the miracles I have empowered you to do.") supports the observation that Yhwh is concerned with the pharaoh's reception of the message. It, therefore, comes as a surprise that the signs introduced in 4:2-9 are intended for convincing not only the Israelites but also the pharaoh. Additionally, the prediction in 3:19 prepares the reader for who will actually listen to Moses and who will not. Exod. 4:21 seems to be a turning point: Moses is, finally, ready to be Yhwh's emissary. The pharaoh again becomes the centre of attention, and the author offers another forecast of the events that are about to come. The conflict, which has already been introduced, implicitly in the first chapter of Exodus and explicitly in 3:19-20, is now clearly expressed with a chiasm (4:22-23).

---

[153] This is clear from the last part of v.15. The reference to all future generations ends any further discussion of the divine name.

[154] The command "say to them" (ואמרת אל...) is taken up from the previous section (3:13-15), where it dominates the conversation, occurring four times. It is also repeated in v.16 and 18.

[155] Interestingly, the forecast highlights a later event which is referred to only briefly, the 'plundering of the Egyptians' (cf. Exod. 11:2; 12:35-36). This odd event, which has troubled many interpreters, seems to be merely a memorable division marker in the larger narrative. Its reappearance occurs at significant structural breaks in the narrative.

²² וְאָמַרְתָּ אֶל־פַּרְעֹה כֹּה אָמַר
יהוה
בְּנִי בְכֹרִי יִשְׂרָאֵל
וָאֹמַר אֵלֶיךָ שַׁלַּח אֶת־בְּנִי
וְיַעַבְדֵנִי
וַתְּמָאֵן לְשַׁלְּחוֹ
הִנֵּה אָנֹכִי הֹרֵג אֶת־בִּנְךָ בְּכֹרֶךָ

Then you shall say to the pharaoh: So says Yhwh:

My son, my firstborn is Israel.
> Therefore I say to you: **let my son go**,
>>   that he may serve me.
>   But because you have **refused to let him go**,
>   see – I will kill **your son, your firstborn!**

The dense language of this forecast conditions the reader's perception of the real conflict which dominates the first 15 chapters of Exodus. The importance of the ensuing events is expressed: Yhwh considers Israel as his firstborn, as his most important son. And, indeed, only after the cruel slaughter of every first-born in Egypt is the pharaoh prepared to let the Israelites serve their God (Exod. 12:12).

Although the dialogue in Exod. 4 focuses much more on Moses and his problems (more so than in Exod. 3), in the end the author makes sure that the reader gets the message: Yhwh's forecasts are fail-safe. The Israelites believed Moses; they listened to him and obeyed the mediated commands (4:31).[156] This is precisely what Moses did not expect.[157] Here, again, we find that the author establishes a picture of a reliable Yhwh at Moses' expense. The *ethos*[158] of Yhwh has been established and refined; his role in the subsequent larger narrative has been outlined. Every divine action will now be interpreted within the theological framework established in Exod. 1–4.

The debate between Moses and Yhwh regarding who will be the more difficult recipient of the divine message, Israel or the pharaoh, provides a sensible

---

[156] That the author calls the people בני ישראל is significant, for only here at the pericope's end (v.29.31) is this way of referring to the Israelites resumed. Since Exod. 3, where the expression was used regularly, one finds the more general term העם. Thus, these last verses serve as a conclusion to the entire unit, Exod. 2:23–4:31. Exod. 2:23-25 begins with the mention of the affliction of the sons of Israel and God's caring for them. It ends with the hope of deliverance, which is so strong that the sons of Israel worship, even though nothing material has happened as the following narrative will make clear.

[157] The accumulation of the verb אמן (hif) in the first section of Exod. 4 is striking (4:1.5.8 [twice] and 9). The subject is always the Israelite people. Moses very much doubts the trust of the people, whereas Yhwh seems not to worry. As mentioned previously, important for the rhetorical effect of the chapter is the last occurrence of אמן (hif) in 4:31. This is an almost laconic note, but it has an enormous effect for the retrospective evaluation of the dialogue. Its briefness contributes to this effect: ויאמן העם. Two words suffice to qualify Moses' objections as ludicrous. The puzzling pericope in Exod. 4:24-26 will be discussed below (p.163), as this threat upon the messenger's life tells more about the messenger himself than about Yhwh. For the rhetorical force of such inimical remarks see p.55 below.

[158] For this term refer to my introduction, p.3.

outline for the subsequent discussion of the narrative portrayal of Yhwh. But, before I go into the details of the conflict between Yhwh and the pharaoh, I will, briefly summarise the outcome of the previous section. As we have seen, it is the literary unit Exod. 2:23–4:31 which, primarily, serves to introduce Yhwh to the reader of Exodus. At many places it is obvious that the author presupposes a good deal of knowledge about Yhwh by his implied reader. Especially, the dense passage dealing with the divine name demonstrates that the author felt the need to guide his reader to a *new* understanding of the tetragrammaton. This name is now linked with the notion of the authority and the ability of God to fulfil the old promises to the patriarchs. This picture is, then, refined by the contrast with Moses and the validity of predictions regarding the welcome of the divine messenger. The author establishes a picture of Yhwh which will guide the reader to a certain perception of the actual plague and exodus narratives. This introductory portrayal of Yhwh is further refined as the plot of Exodus unfolds.

Yhwh's Conflicts with Israel (Exod. 15–17 and 32–34)

Exodus relates two major conflicts between Israel and Yhwh. The first one takes place during the wilderness wanderings between the *yam suf* and Mount Sinai. The second is prompted by the people's creation of the golden calf about 40 days after the great theophany at Sinai. In the first incident, I propose that Israel is yet another foil against which the portrayal of Yhwh takes shape. The second conflict focuses more on the relationship between Yhwh and Israel.[159] The seminal passage Exod. 34:6-7, which is of major importance in this second conflict, has already been discussed above (p.43ff). Thus, below, I will bring together the results of my discussion of the epithets with the narrative picture drawn in Exod. 32–34.

Both narrative blocks are chiefly concerned with the present of the implied reader, not the narrative setting in the past. They are not meant to satisfy chronistic interests. As Houtman puts it for the wilderness wanderings:

> A closer look shows that the stories were not written for providing a report of Israel's stay in the desert, but are intended for instruction of the Israel of the

---

[159] I, however, do not follow Dozeman 1996, whose basic thesis consists of the development from a presentation of the exodus to a more nuanced and fully-developed story. This initial presentation he calls the "pre-exilic liturgy of the exodus," where "all powers other than God are impersonal abstractions" and not genuinely independent characters (especially the pharaoh and Israel). And, in the fully developed story, secondary characters function over against or in conjunction with God in a way that is more characteristic of relational power, where divine action and thus the outcome of the story are influenced more by other persons in the story than simply by the deity. Even if this movement could be detected in the narratives, I doubt very much that this is a major communicative strategy in the present form of the text.

future. The writer relates that history to deliver a message to that later Israel. That
intent colours the way the history is presented.[160]

And, indeed, it appears that the two passages, whose suspense is mainly carried
by the antagonism of Israel, strongly influenced the implied reader's outlook on
his own situation. Both texts stress the divine goodness toward Israel, despite
several shortcomings in the people's responsiveness to Yhwh's presence. For
the wilderness episodes, the message for the implied reader is less obvious,
whereas the author includes more hints for reader-identification in the golden
calf scene (Exod. 32–34).[161]

IN THE WILDERNESS

As I will argue below (p.209f), the picture of Israel in Exod. 1–12 is marked by
significant passivity. As soon as the exodus starts, however, the people become
quite involved. The pre-Sinai portion of the wilderness wanderings includes
three of the so-called murmuring or rebellion stories,[162] which centre around
three locations: Mara, the Wilderness of Sin, and Rephidim. Although the criticism of Moses as leader and mediator is at the heart of all these stories, the people ultimately attack Yhwh, as stressed, explicitly, by Moses (cf. 16:7-8; 17:2).
The behaviour of the people confronts the reader with a counter-programme, to
use Jobling's terminology.[163] The Israelites glorify the blessings of Egypt so
much that they want to return, thereby diametrically opposing Yhwh's main-
programme, which is to lead them into the land of the promise. One could even
suspect that the author portrays Israel as, in effect, assuming the pharaoh's role
as God's chief adversary.[164] The literary role of Israel is, indeed, quite similar to
the pharaoh's role in providing an adversary that highlights the portrayal of the
divine. Hence, for the implied reader, I suspect that there is not much suspense
produced by the tension between the divine main-programme and the Israelite
counter-programme; the reader is prepared for the people to falter and become
anxious (cf. Exod. 13:17). A further indication that the people's rebellion – a
rebellion which prevents the fulfilment of the patriarchal promises – is not at the
centre of attention is Yhwh's astonishing lack of any substantial reaction to their

---

[160] Houtman 1996, 299. The communicative end for Houtman is a rather vague and generalised notion of Yhwh's caring for the faithful in their 'wilderness experiences' – a
call for perseverance. Yhwh did this for a rebellious Israel, he will do so for the faithful
implied reader.

[161] For more on reader-identification see p.215 below.

[162] For a detailed discussion of this type scene see p.179f below.

[163] Jobling's definition of a 'narrative programme': "... the sequence of events, carried
out or merely conceptualised, whereby an actor in the narrative seeks to bring about
some result." (Jobling 1986, 38) He, himself, finds three programmes for the wilderness
narratives in the Pentateuch, dominating both Exodus and Numbers (cf. Jobling
1986, 31–65).

[164] Cf. Houtman 1996, 300.

actions and complaints. Yhwh simply resolves the problem.[165] Hence the literary strategy behind these conflicting programmes cannot be the creation of suspense at the plot level. But, even if suspense were one of the communicative effects intended for the telling of the first leg of the wilderness wanderings, the people's rebellions are, chiefly, opportunities to refine the portrayal of Yhwh. This new aspect of the picture vividly describes Yhwh's ability to bring about, against all odds, the fulfilment of the patriarchal promises. In the plague narrative, the author proves that Yhwh is able to deal with the political superpower of the time. These occasions provide sufficient evidence for the reader to conclude that Yhwh deserves to be Israel's new master; he can provide military success (14:19-31 and 17:8-16),[166] and can also supply them with an abundance of life's necessities, exemplified by water (15:25.27; 17:6), meat and bread (16:13.21).

This notion of God, the supplier, well suits the overall concern of Exod. 1–18, with its focus on the knowledge-of-Yhwh theme. The knowing-Yhwh motif reappears in the context of the Manna pericope (Exod. 16), which is the central part of the three murmuring stories.[167] Exod. 16:6-7 combines the exodus – the subject linked with this motif until now – and the provision of food, and it ascribes both acts to Yhwh.[168] Yhwh's potency in the wilderness pericopes is intended to impress the reader deeply. This power is shown in the conflict with the Egyptian ruler, but there it is destructive power. In the wilderness, it is being used for a positive end, which is to present the life-sustaining Yhwh. The greater the problem, the greater the positive effect of the solution. There is no need to go into any detail here, as the narratives are straightforward, and the point is clear. The implications of these pericopes upon the portrayals of Moses and Israel will be discussed below (p.179 and 219). I will, therefore, leave the derness texts and move on to Exod. 32–34.

---

[165] The brief comment about the breaking of the Sabbath (Exod. 16:28f) is not a reaction to the initial complaint. In the post-Sinai murmuring stories in Numbers there is always a threat or judgement communicated to the people by Aaron or Moses. One might attribute this to the fact that the law has been given between the two scenes, but the references to מצות, חק/חקים, תורה and משפת (15:26; 16:28) suggest differently (cf. Houtman 1996, 301 who also finds that Israel was aware of Yhwh's will prior to Sinai).

[166] These two parts nicely frame our stories of rebellion nicely (see p.180 below).

[167] Cf. also Moberly 2007, who provides a lucid reading of this often separated passage by the earlier methods of literary criticism.

[168] Jacob 1997, 461 notes an intriguing link between the quail in Exod. 16 and the plague of the locusts (both are flying things appearing in crowds) in Exod. 10. Exod. 10:2 makes explicit reference to the knowledge of Yhwh using the phrase וידעתם כי־אני יהוה, which appears only here and in 16:2 and also in 6:7. This refers the reader back to the Yhwh-name issue and, hence, links the whole pericope with the divine character. The provision of food is, thus, an event modifying the previous knowledge of this character.

THE CREATION OF THE GOLDEN CALF

The crisis of the calf has been used by the author to clarify his vision of the identities of all characters involved and the relationships between them.[169] Israel is and will continue to be a stiff-necked people (Exod. 32:9; 33:3.5 and 34:9; see p.211ff below). Moses emerges as the paradigmatic intercessor and the approved mediator of the divine word, including his words of forgiveness. And Yhwh is the merciful God, slow to anger but willing to punish (see p.43ff above). In the end we find a people observing the Sabbath as a covenant sign and keenly building a sanctuary to make real the divine presence among them. This positive outcome clearly shows that Israel is still part of the patriarchal covenant, which was the ultimate reason for the divinely initiated exodus from Egypt. This picture in Exodus is of Israel's foundational history. But it is also the paradigmatic picture of Israel's endangered and fragile relationship with Yhwh. It presents an extreme violation of the foundations of the relationship and balances it with the possibilities of a renewed relationship based on the merciful attitude of God.[170]

The centrality of 32–34 for the rhetoric of the entire book is obvious.[171] In the following, I will discuss the role that the portrayal of Yhwh plays in this communication.

The conflict is set up for the reader by the beginning of the decalogue (Exod. 20:2-6), by the prohibition of god-images (at the very beginning of the book of the covenant, 20:23), and by the expression of the divine willingness to dwell continuously among the people (29:45f). The reader is encouraged to imagine the tabernacle and the consecration of the priests and is, thus, immersed in the preparations for the divine presence with Israel.[172] Therefore, for the reader the narrative is stringent: everything that happens on the mountain brings Israel closer to perpetuate what they had already experienced in a paradigmatic way in the great theophany (Exod. 24). The reader observes Yhwh doing everything necessary to fulfil his promises. So, for him, the reaction of the people to Moses' stay on the mountain must come as a big surprise. The contrast is striking. The details of how this contrast is rhetorically created are laid down by Scoralick, and I can safely build upon her results.[173] The people's desire for the visi-

---

[169] Cf. Scoralick 2002, 90.

[170] Cf. Rendtorff 1999, 59. He links the later generations to the stiff-necked Israel.

[171] For a recent summary of research on these chapters cf. Schmid, K. 2001.

[172] Dohmen 2004b, 242–245 argues strongly that this rhetorical effect underlies the instructions for the tabernacle. He speaks of an *Inszenierung des Raumes*, which prompts the reader to picture the place in his mind's eye and thus to position himself in the imagined space.

[173] Cf. Scoralick 2002, 92ff. One example may suffice: "Darin wird eine Darstellungstechnik der Kapitel 32–34 greifbar. Oberflächliche Ähnlichkeiten (auf lexematischer wie konzeptioneller Ebene) können tiefgreifende Gegensätze überspannen. Analoges kann Gegensätze verdecken. Ablesbar ist das an dem Verlangen des Volkes nach Gottes-

ble presence of God is at the core of the presentation of the divine character, thus far. They want to have the God of the exodus at their disposal, visible and 'real' in their midst (32:1.4). The people know nothing of the conversation between Moses and Yhwh, but the reader does. For him the reaction of the people appears as the "Identitätsverlust des Volkes, das seine Geschichte im Interesse vermeintlicher Zukunftssicherung mißdeutet und so JHWH aus Vergangenheit, Gegenwart und Zukunft ausgeschaltet hat, indem er zunächst verdrängt und dann ersetzt wurde."[174] This interpretation of Israel's behaviour touches upon the paradigmatic quality of the text. Exodus, subsequently, offers a model for how Yhwh can be regenerated as *the* integral part of Israel's identity. The offering of a new identity for the people – or as the author portrays it, the old and true identity – is inextricably linked to Yhwh, his actions and his nature. This outlook became relevant throughout Israel's history.

Exod. 32–34 offers a concept of God that integrates the ideals demanded by the divine proximity and the reality of a people inclined to sin. The highpoint of this portrayal is the abstract formulation of the balance between mercy and taking sin or desecration seriously. As shown above, the balance is not an equal one: the emphasis of 34:6-7 is, clearly, on mercy and forgiveness. Nevertheless, the recapitulation of significant parts of the book of the covenant in Exod. 34:11-26[175] just after actually granting forgiveness stresses Yhwh's concern with the fitness of the people to be in his dangerous presence (see 33:1-6). The brief account concerning the sons of Levi (32:25-29) and the enigmatic verse 32:35 (together with 32:33-34) point in a similar direction. But again, the brevity of these two passages shows that the punishment aspect is consciously downplayed. At the end of the larger narrative, the mercifulness of Yhwh clearly dominates. The opportunity for a new beginning becomes part of Israel's identity as described in Exod. 34.

The reasons for the success of Moses' intercession are something the reader is indirectly invited to ponder with the phrasing of 32:30bβ: אולי אכפרה בעד חטאתכם. The word 'perhaps' indicates probability, and, hence, the overwhelming statement of divine patience and willingness to forgive is far from predictable for the reader.[176] This results in a tension between the divine commitment

---

gegenwart, das in der Herstellung des Kalbes fehlgeleitet ist, später jedoch eine legitime Erfüllung findet (in der Gegenwart des Mose und dem Heiligtum als 'mitwanderndem Sinai')."

[174] Scoralick 2002, 93. Cf. also Slivniak 2008, for a deconstructionist reading of the passage, commenting on the various oppositions in the text.

[175] Thereby, understanding this passage as a *pars pro toto* construction. For this interpretation see Dohmen 2004b, 365: "Kurzfassung des Bundesbuches". There are a host of different conclusions for the understanding of this passage, but they are not crucial for our point and, thus, remain unmentioned (For details see the groundbreaking work by Jörn Halbe, Halbe 1975).

[176] Cf. Dohmen 2004b, 363: "In Ex 34,9 schließt sich der Bogen hin zum Anfang in Ex 32,30, insofern die in diesem Rahmen aufleuchtende Frage der Vergebung Gottes

to Israel, which has dominated the narrative until now, and the seriousness of the covenant breach. In the narrative, Moses is given the role of communicating the earlier divine concern for the בני ישראל, i.e. that they are included in the covenant of the fathers (32:11.13). The parts of the dialogue regarding the association of the people (Moses' people in 32:7.9[העם הזה] *versus* Yhwh's people in 32:11.12[14]) allude to the crucial verses of Exod. 19:5-6 where the belonging of Israel is a major part of Yhwh's agenda. Moses also 'reminds' Yhwh of the issue at stake (32:12): God will risk the ideational outcome of the plagues and exodus events if he kills his people in the desert. The severity of the people's sin, however, demands divine action, otherwise Yhwh would contradict his own principles and be considered weak and inconsistent.

Both extremes of the divine nature are in tension but are, nevertheless, present which opens up the possibility for the existence of the people in Yhwh's presence. To express this tension without creating a schizophrenic picture of God the author utilises Moses' intercessory prayer. The divine command, in Exod. 32:10 ועתה הניחה לי (Leave me alone...), actually carries the rhetorical intent to invite Moses' intercession. The reader, as well, expects Moses to interfere.[177] Moses' prayer on behalf of Israel clearly does not just come out of Moses' commitment to his mediating role or an emotional concern for the people's future existence, it has been invited by God so he, actually, can return and be patient and gracious with his people.

Both aspects of Yhwh's nature, expressed in *abstracta* in Exod. 34:6-7, are divided narratively and brought into dialogue with each other. At the end, the offer to uphold the covenant (Exod. 34:10-28) unites the two aspects. The covenant in Exod. 34 does not replace the one in Exod. 24; by concentrating on the land and the festival calendar it shows, rather, the divine willingness to prepare the basis on which Israel can fulfil its part of the covenant.[178]

The rhetorical effect of the narrative and the ideational suspense in the portrayal of Yhwh emphasise that Yhwh is gracious and good. For the implied reader, who might doubt that Yhwh is still cohabiting with the Israelites of his

---

das ganze dazwischenliegende Stück zusammenhält."

[177] The rhetorical effect of what has been called foreknowledge in biblical narrative can be clearly seen in the interpreters' reactions on these texts. Tiemeyer 2007 works her way through Jewish and Christian interpretations of the narratives of Noah and the flood generation, Abraham and his concern for the Sodomites and then Moses intercession on Sinai. Commentators throughout the centuries and cultures ponder the question what the foreknowledge of imminent judgement ought to do with the initiated. Even in the case of Noah, of whom the narrative does not report any action on behalf of the doomed, this question arises. Hence, we can conclude that our author did construct the dialogue between Yhwh and Moses consciously in a way that invites the active interpretative involvement of the reader in terms of evaluation, at least, by suggesting the question, "What would I have done in Moses' place?"

[178] Cf. Halbe 1975, 226f and Dohmen 2004b, 364f.

day, the hope arises that this God really is present. The mercifulness of Yhwh is, however, balanced by the implications of Yhwh's continuous presence for the implied reader.[179]

Conclusion

The previous discussion was concerned with the picture of the character Yhwh that emerges when reading the narrative parts of Exodus. The investigation began by looking at the direct characterisation of Yhwh in the epithets which are placed at key points in the unfolding plot. These epithets are significantly linked with the tetragrammaton. The divine name, thus, functions as a reminder for the reader to recall the different divine attributes expressed in these epithets. They are also linked at the contextual level. Without the literary surroundings the epithets remain abstract and difficult to interpret.

The character Yhwh is introduced quietly, so as not to offend the implied reader, whose previous knowledge serves as the background on which the author develops his picture of God. There are four elements to the story: the caring Israelite God, the oppression of Israel in Egypt, the covenant of their ancestors, and a political refugee, called Moses. Each one of these particulars is, probably, well known to the intended reader. The communicative aim of the author is, hence, to reshape his reader's understanding of the relationship between these four 'elements'. Hieke observes the same interplay between the unfolding story and the theological conception of Yhwh in Exodus. The result, quite in line with my own findings, of this mental interaction is a multi-layered and complex, but balanced, divine picture which has strong influence on the reading process in which the reader is kept constantly open to new aspects of the divine character.[180]

Throughout the book, the author's strategy in his character-portrayal is the interplay between silence and explicitness. In Exod. 1–2 Yhwh works between the scenes, so the reader has to discover and explicate the divine involvement in history, even in the narrated history. This hidden activity of Yhwh can offer a theological paradigm for other parts of the reader's national history, past or present. In the dialogue between Moses and Yhwh (Exod. 3–4) the author points out the most crucial aspects of Yhwh's being, thereby defining the divine purpose for the people. Furthermore, the dialogue enables the author to forecast

---

[179] In this passage one can, perhaps better than anywhere else in the Old Testament, see how a narrative can hold together theologies that would be mutually exclusive in many types of systematic theology. Ellington 2005 offers an interesting insight into the issues involved, mainly concerning the actual open theism vs. traditional theism debate. Another very insightful treatment (in defence of traditional theism) is the metaphysically finetuned reading in Owens 2004.

[180] Hieke 2007.

or anticipate the crucial events in the subsequent scenes. This, also, refines the initial portrayal of Yhwh given in the overture (2:23-25).

The remainder of the lengthy narrative focuses on certain conflicts which further refine the divine picture. One could trace the imagery of "God's hand", which dominates exactly the parts of Exodus where Yhwh is portrayed as proactive in bringing about his will.[181] In relation to the pharaoh, Yhwh's ability to execute what he promised is strongly emphasised. Two longer literary blocks are concerned with the relationship developing between Israel and Yhwh. In the wilderness, the willingness and ability of Yhwh to bring about his promises are expressed in the provision of life's basic needs. If these aspects of the picture of Yhwh in Exodus are brought together and viewed against the backdrop of the ancient Near Eastern concept of the king, one can assume that the author wanted to give the impression that Yhwh is the able and efficient king of Israel. Though this kingly portrayal is never explicit in the narrative, it is present between the lines and strongly supported by the poetic and legal parts of Exodus (cf. p.80ff).[182]

With the offer of the patriarchal covenant and the acceptance of the people at Mount Sinai, the relationship gains a new conceptual quality. The divine epithets of jealousy and compassion or mercy now guide the reader through the narrative. Everyday life is ruled by the spatial proximity to God and the ensuing need for holiness. Life-preserving divine forgiveness forms the basis of Israel's identity as the chosen nation which is, nevertheless, in Yhwh's dangerous presence.

In conclusion, the narrative portrayal of Yhwh turns out to be a major aspect of the author's rhetorical strategy, in that it provides points of ideational reflection at certain stages in the unfolding drama. These instances – often theologically rich – specify the interpretation of history which is otherwise given only implicitly.

Leaving the narrative portrayal of Yhwh behind, we come to the poetic and legal characterisations of Yhwh, which receive pride of place in the second part of the book of Exodus. There, Yhwh is speaking with the language of law. This new genre will uniquely shape the portrayal of Yhwh. But, firstly, to Exod. 15, the poem within the exodus narrative. Here the centrality of the character Yhwh

---

[181] See the study Seely 2004. Seely finds a significant concentration of this hand-imagery in the following parts of Exodus: 3-4; 5-13; 14-15; 16; 24 and 33. This metaphor seems to be a special literary feature of Exodus as other occurrences outside the book are sparse in Genesis to 2 Kings.

[182] Interestingly, one study attempts to convince that Yhwh in Exodus is not portrayed as king but as father (in relation to Israel, the son). Kim 2004 discusses this after some remarks about the overall theological theme of Exodus (which he defines as worship of Yhwh), but fails to support his view with any passage from Exodus. He takes his proofs mainly from Deuteronomy and the (latter) prophets, which I find rather odd in an article on Exodus.

comes to the fore. The song of Moses, alone, justifies a detailed analysis of the divine character in Exodus, thus, making the teaching about Yhwh at least one of the main concerns of the book.

Poetic Characterisation

The song at the *yam-suf* presents the reader with a poetic version[183] of the drowning of the Egyptian forces. A first suggestion as to what the function of the poem is for the narrative and for the portrayal of Yhwh is found in the contrasts and similarities between the prose account and the poetic reflection of the victory at the *yam suf*. Watts provides a brief, but exhaustive, collection of plot relations and semantic and thematic connections.[184] I will only recall the aspects relevant for our present purposes. When comparing the distribution of roles in Exod. 14 and 15, it is striking to note that the only two active characters in the poem are Yhwh and the Egyptians (but only to record their utter failure to achieve their agenda, 15:9-10).[185] Moses does not appear at all (except in his role as poet in the narrative frame), and Israel is pictured only as the passive recipient of the promised land in Exod. 15:12-17. This concentration on Yhwh alone is significant in its communicative force. As Watts has shown, the reader is drawn into the narrative by the song and, therefore, becomes one of the people who came to believe Yhwh under the impression of the events at the sea (14:31!) and later also under the events surrounding the conquest of Canaan:

> The psalm moves from the temporal perspective of the narrative, in which the land's settlement lies in the future, to that of the readers, for whom it is in the past. The effect of the move is to allow the readers to join in the celebration at the sea from their own temporal perspective.[186]

Thus, the song recommends, in its concentration on Yhwh, a specific evaluation of history which goes beyond the narrative. Certain aspects of the divine portrait in the poem support this rhetorical function. The previous narrative of Exod. 1–14 introduces the horizon of the land promise at structurally crucial

---

[183] The poetic quality of this passage is obvious, but it is difficult to say more than this regarding a specific genre. It contains at least hymnic and (historically) descriptive parts. Houtman 1996, 244f is opposed to looking into a *Sitz im Leben* of the song. Benno Jakob (Jacob 1997, 429f) provides a comprehensive description of the poetic values of the text. The strophic arrangement is far from obvious and has led to a considerable array of proposals (cf. Houtman 1996, 246f for a collection, Howell 1989 and Fokkelman 1998, 24–53 provide their own very detailed approaches). I follow Jacob's appealing description of the song's structure (see his commentary Jacob 1997, 431–433) which, itself, almost swings aloft to poetic qualities.

[184] Cf. Watts 1992, 41–55.

[185] Cf. Shreckhise 2007, whose close reading of some formal rhetorical features of the poem, highlights the same point.

[186] Watts 1992, 51.

points (Exod. 3:17; 6:6-8; 13:5). "The Song of the Sea celebrates the fulfilment of this two-part promise in Yahweh's victory at the sea (15.1-11) and the conquest of the land and the Temple mount (15.12-18) ..."[187] The recollection of the land promise to the fathers is closely linked with the passages concerned with the divine name (see especially Exod. 15:1-3) and is, thus, identified with it. This connection becomes even clearer in the second part of Exodus (23:20-33; 34:10-16). Thus, Exod. 15 is not only a bridge between the narrated events and the reader's present reality in Canaan but also a bridge between the two large parts of Exodus. The attention on Israel in the song's latter part prepares the reader for the new focus on the relationship of Yhwh and Israel.[188] As with other hymns set in narrative texts,[189] Exod. 15:1-18.21 concludes a narrative strand – the exodus narrative – and introduces the ensuing literary developments. Thus, the poem serves more or less the same function as the *yam-suf* narrative. In general, poetic bits set inside narrative slow down the pace of the story,[190] which, in our case, is especially necessary given the brevity of the account of the events at the *yam-suf*. The reader's attention is directed to the divine level (God's fury, Exod. 15:7[8-10?[191]] *versus* God's steadfast love, 15:13), which happens in any song of praise. Here the poem is formulated as an outburst of joy and worship after the experiences of salvation and a confession of faith.[192]

These functional considerations suggest that the results of my study up to this point should appear, in one form or another, in this poem. I argued that a certain picture of Yhwh is constructed for the implied reader from the beginning of the book. Thus, if the psalm is, indeed, functionally some sort of literary hinge or summary, as well as a preview[193] at a structurally important point in the narrative, it may, also, function as a test case for the present enquiry.

The portrait of Yhwh which emerges from the song is a hymnic one in language, selectiveness and ambiguity. The poem begins with a focus on Yhwh

---

[187] Watts 1992, 48.

[188] This is a literary movement which can, also, be detected in the portrayal of Israel (see 210 below).

[189] Cf. Sailhamer 1992, 35–37, who neither mentions Exod. 15, nor develops his point.

[190] Other songs outside the psalms are often found at structurally exposed places (cf. Zenger and Fabry 1998, 310). See also Patterson 2004, who offers a brief overview of the various inset hymns in narrative, also from other ancient near eastern literature. His own detailed treatment of the interrelationship of poem and narrative in the case of Exod. 14–15, however, fails to draw the draw the communicational implications for the reading process.

[191] Cf. Noth 1978, 99.

[192] Cf. Houtman 1996, 230f.

[193] Cf. also Fokkelman 1998, 28: "…v.11 rise[s] above the masses of water and clouds of dust being kicked up before and after, and exclusively refer[s] to the greatness of the true God, who has just redeemed Israel and in doing so gave it its identity."

and his divine name. Four different ways to refer to the divine are employed
(יהוה, יה, אל, אלהי) before Yhwh is described in 15:3, a first highpoint of the
poem, as a man of war (יהוה איש מלחמה), which takes up the name issue from
Exod. 3 and 6 (יהוה שמו – a nominal clause). Thus the theme of the entire song is
introduced in the first section. The divine name reappears at the end of each of
the five strophes (15:3.6.11.16.18),[194] which reminds the reader of the centrality
of Yhwh in all events touched upon in the psalm. I have argued above that the
divine self-presentation with the *idem per idem* formula in Exod. 3:14 and its
immediate context express an entire theo-political programme. This programme
is linked to the tetragrammaton, and each time the name is repeated the reader
will recall this notion. One of these instances is in the first strophe of the psalm.
The preceding context provides the evidence that Yhwh, actually, brought about
the theo-political programme that the author connects with the divine name. The
divine victory at the *yam-suf* has been stylised to express the success of the
programme. I proposed that the conflict between Yhwh and the Egyptian monarch can be viewed as a metaphysical battle. The author uses the plague narrative to prove the inability of the pharaoh to uphold the all-decisive *Maʿat*. The
Song of the Sea, with its most explicit link to the narrative of Exod. 14 in 15:4-
5, recalls the failure of the Egyptians in the conflict. The picture of the drowning Egyptian army is refined in the third strophe of the song which recalls the
megalomania of the pharaoh in the only appearance of an active character other
than God (15:9). The plans of the pharaoh are framed by two parallel occurrences of the divine רוח (15:8.10) which prepare and bring about the watery
grave of the mighty pharaoh. This strophe ends in a very dense eulogy of
Yhwh's singularity (15:11), again, setting Yhwh in the context of other gods,
who are less powerful. The other divine attributes provide numerous links at
multiple levels to various parts of the book. The awesomeness of God (נורא) is
semantically linked to the fear described as an appropriate response of a Yhwh-
worshipper. This is spread throughout the entire narrative, but is rhetorically
prominent in the opening of the book with the epithets of the midwives (cf.
Exod. 1:17.21; 3:6; 9:30; 14:31; 15:11; 20:20; 34:10 [possibly 34:30]). The attribution of holiness (קדש) points the reader to a dominant theme in the latter
part of the book, especially the requirements of sacredness in the sanctuary. The
wonders, mentioned at the very end of the verse, relate back to the plagues (cf.
Exod. 3:20) and to the events linked with the conquest which especially comes
into view in the context of the renewal of the covenant (cf. 34:10). Thus this
conceptually central verse of the poem highlights Yhwh as the central figure in
the plague and wilderness narratives, which I termed, above, as the willingness
and ability of Yhwh to bring about his promises. This can be supported from the

---

[194] The verses 6, 11 and 16 are marked poetically as well. Fokkelman 1998, 26f observes
in each of these verses a staircase parallelism in which the first line of the stanza is elaborated using the following pattern: a b / cd > a b / e f. He also stresses the centrality of
v.11 on prosodic grounds. Fokkelman calls these three verses the "thematic power supply of the work of art." (27)

fact that the only two anthropomorphisms which dominate the song (breath and hand/arm) are conceptually linked with creation (the giving of life) and omnipotence (the maintenance of life and the fighting of life-threatening powers).[195]

The last two strophes (15:12-16 and 17-18) open the horizon toward the future of Israel. The conquest points to the land of the promise and the sanctuary (מקדש), to the continuous worship of Yhwh in the cult, which is familiar to the implied reader. These allusions are in the reader's present and, thus, create a rhetorical immediacy and relevance for him. As mentioned above, the reader-identification is a specific function of inset hymns. The final verse of the Song at the Sea is a climax, in that it summarises the praise with the expression מלך יהוה. That Yhwh is king forever is exactly how the author of Exodus wants his implied reader to think about Yhwh. Throughout, Exodus offers a distinguished, kingly portrayal of God. The reader learned about the contrast between two kings, the pharaoh and Yhwh. They appear in the song as the drowning king and the everlasting king. The language applied to Yhwh often evokes notions of sovereignty, both inside the psalm and in its narrative context. In relation to Israel, Yhwh proves himself to be an able protector and supporter and, later, a wise law-giver. This last aspect of the divine portrayal will be the concern of the next section on the legal characterisation of Yhwh.

With regard to the plot development the poem in Exod. 15 is unnecessary.[196] But, for the rhetorical strategy of the book, it is central. It causes the reader to slow down and reflect upon his earlier reading, all the while preparing the reader for the subsequent material, which draws him into the story even more (see p.234ff below).

Legal Characterisation[197]

The legal genre takes a prominent place in Exodus. In the following pages I will develop the contribution of the legal material to the portrait of Yhwh. This contribution is essential for the communicational strategy of the book. The characterisation of a literary character always emerges from the complexity of the literary piece. Nevertheless, the present discussion is manageable only when this complexity is broken up and different aspects of Yhwh's characterisation are

---

[195] Cf. Jacob 1997, 433: "Das Geschehen ist sein Odem, und in dem Gericht zeigt sich seine große Hand."

[196] Cf. Watts 1992, 42.

[197] There is not much of a history of research to be covered here. Most scholars touch on the issue in passing, often without much attention to detail. Thus I have decided to incorporate the most appropriate of these remarks at the relevant points of the discussion. James Watts' article (Watts 1996) serves as starting point for the following discussion and will be referred to throughout the present section, as cues for a more detailed investigation. Watts highlights certain aspects, but the scope of his article does not go beyond a general treatment of the entire Pentateuch.

discussed separately. This is an unfortunate simplification for the sake of a structured presentation. Thus, one must keep in mind that the reader of the Exodus law collections draws his conclusions about the divine character unconsciously and in a less structured manner. The textual corpus which I intend to discuss here is the decalogue (Exod. 20:1-17) and the book of the covenant (Exod. 20:22–23:33). The laws given in the context of the reinitiation of the covenant in Exod. 34:11-26 are, primarily, a summary of the book of the covenant, and thus there is no new contribution to the divine portrayal.

For the modern reader, who is somewhat familiar with the Pentateuch, it seems perfectly acceptable that Yhwh gave Israel the law as the last authority in matters of right or wrong. But, that a god would take the societal role of lawgiver is astonishingly different from other ancient Near Eastern cultures, where the king issues the law and, ultimately, presides over its implementation.[198] This, of course, is done on behalf of and in the name of the deity, as Roth summarises: "Whether or not the king was always himself an active participant in the administration of the legal system, he was always its guardian, for the application of justice was the highest trust given by the gods to a legitimate king."[199] Being adorned by the gods with this function of moral leader and sustainer of the divinely approved and fixed ideals of justice, the king is, also, answerable to the gods for achieving justice and order.[200] But law does not emanate from the gods, nor is it subject to divine capriciousness. Rather, it is perceived as also being binding in the divine realm.[201]

The law and justice functions of an ancient Near Eastern king are not something theoretical but have had an immense impact on society. As mentioned above, the king's god-given task is to care for the rights of the orphans and widows. These are the members of society who do not have access to familial support and, thus, do not have the means of gaining justice through this channel. The king's responsibility is to be approachable and to uphold justice for these groups.[202] That the law can have a host of different communicative functions besides the societal function is obvious, but this phenomenon cannot be dis-

---

[198] Cf. also Crüsemann 1992, 24: "Es handelt sich nicht um göttliche, sondern eben um königliche Setzung. Das gilt bis in die Einzelformulierungen und wird immer wieder mit durchaus großem Selbstbewußtsein festgestellt."

[199] Roth 1997, 5.

[200] Cf. Roth 1997, 5 who, in support of this idea, quotes two prophecies commissioned by the god Addu to be delivered to Zimri-Lim of Mari. Being present for a potential appeal and rendering justice are what Addu asks of the king.

[201] Cf. Crüsemann 1992, 24.

[202] Cf. Kaiser, O. 2003, 42ff, who quotes Egyptian and Old Testament sources in support of his theory. The right of direct appeal to the king, by anyone, is more than an ideal or unkept promise. At least in the second millennium BC the societies of the levant were still of a manageable size so that the king could attend to the legal questions of his people. Later, in the larger cities, we must assume a more distant sort of government.

cussed in depth in the present study.[203] Here, it suffices to note that besides its social regulative functions, the law served the direct personal and political interests of the legislative, to term it anachronistically. Considering similar aspects in Hammurabi's law collection, the assyriologist Jean Bottéro writes: "What Hammurabi wanted to collect in his 'Code', as he tells us in so many words when he talks of verdicts, was a selection of the principal decisions of law, the most just decisions, the wisest, the most sagacious, the most worthy of an experienced ruler."[204] By introducing a set of laws, he desired to make his mark against his predecessors and, thus, to commend himself as a high profile ruler who is worthy of his subjects' admiration and support. The Mesopotamian kings placed great emphasis on the idea that *they* were the source of the law, which they ordered to be written on stelas. This indicates that they hoped for some positive effect coming from this information.

Two possibilities come to mind. They expected to achieve either a greater willingness to abide by the law on the part of their subjects or a greater admiration because of the wonderful laws they issued. Both options touch directly upon the issue of *ethos*, as the classic rhetors referred to it: the first option implies a very positive *ethos* previous to the *inventio* of the text, whereas the latter implies the hope that this positive characterisation will be the result of the text. Obviously, these options are not mutually exclusive, as both can go hand in hand. Compared with its Mesopotamian context, the situation, as portrayed in Exodus, is quite different in early Israel. Here, we do not find a human king, but a god taking up a certain societal role of the king. We find Yhwh depicted as Is-

---

[203] In the specific quest for the function of the law collections of Exodus Hanson's list of six different possible uses of rules (Hanson 1977, 138ff) could serve as a starting point: (1) Laws can provide an archive of past values for the sake of the future. (2) They can, in an argumentative setting, provide reasons for making judgements on moral issues. (3) Laws can positively initiate desired action. (4) They can awake or moderate emotions. (5) They may provide a fresh perspective on relationships. (6) Lastly, they may express ideals. To add another possibility which is mentioned by Sternberg: rules, insofar as they belong to the realm of ideology, may serve to establish a certain worldview. In this respect they perform a similar function to wisdom literature (Sternberg 1987, 41). This final possibility suggests a general function which includes many aspects of Hanson's six functions.

[204] Bottéro 1992, 165. Cf. also Assmann 2000, 179f who puts it nicely: "[D]ie monumentale Aufzeichnung soll den König als Gesetzgeber kommemorieren, nicht die Rechtspraxis auf eine ein für allemal bindende einheitliche Legitimitätsgrundlage stellen. Es handelt sich um ein Denkmal, nicht um einen Kodex. Die Schrift verewigt die Gerechtigkeit von König Hammurapi. Die zahlreichen Fluchformeln des Epilogs schützen das Denkmal, nicht das Recht. Wer das Recht bricht, wird bestraft; wer es aber Hammurapi abspricht, indem er das Denkmal beschädigt oder seinen eigenen Namen daraufschreibt, wird verflucht."

rael's king, yet without the sociological implications.[205] This picture of Yhwh has large implications at the rhetorical level, especially as the law collections are part of a larger literary work. In this context, the divine portrait emerging from the law will be described.

Again, the likely preconceptions of the implied reader become relevant. For a 'good Israelite' reader of Exodus the nature of the law-giver implies his positive *ethos*: God is wise, good and able from the start. Thus the main purpose of the strategy of putting all the law in Yhwh's mouth is to heighten the authority behind the law. But the picture does not emerge so clearly if one considers the inevitable rhetorical implications of this literary strategy regarding the *ethos* of

---

[205] That Yhwh is in certain aspects pictured as king does not necessarily imply that the societal system of Israel can be termed a theocracy. The term θεοκρατία was coined by Josephus (*Contra Apionem*, 2, 165) to refer to the special mode of the societal constitution of ancient Israel. It was only from the 17th century onwards that this term was used more frequently (cf. Lang 2001, 178f). In the secularisation mood of the Enlightenment it soon gained strongly negative connotations (cf. only Voltaire ou Rousseau). Quite in line with Josephus' ideals, theocracy was later used to refer to a state in which the ruler belongs to the group of priests and religion was the main responsibility of the state (e.g. M. Weber). The current discussion of the term 'theocracy' in the study of religion – as well as in the media (cf. esp. the coverage of Iran and similar attempts to rule; Auffarth 2000, 485) – illustrates the ambiguity of the word. According to Lang a theocracy "...besteht darin, daß unter den Aufgaben des Staates die Ausübung und Förderung einer bestimmten Religion einen sehr hohen, wenn nicht den höchsten Rang einnimmt. ... Der theokratische Staat besteht um der Religion willen." (Lang 2001, 179f) This definition may be relevant for modern societies, but for our purposes it neglects the common worldview of the ancient Near Eastern cultures which is totally opposed to all secularisation. There is no world apart from the religious world. Life is immersed in religion. This may, of course, lead to a hierocracy (which is basically what Josephus meant), including the notions of an unchangeable word of god, a priesthood communicating the divine will, and the potential of misuse of power. Wellhausen has offered a definition of (an Islamic) theocracy which points in this direction: "Man kann die Theokratie definieren als das Gemeinwesen an dessen Spitze nicht der König und die angemaßte und ererbte Gewalt steht, sondern der Prophet und das Recht Gottes." (*Das arabische Reich und sein Sturz*, 1902, 5-6, quoted in Lang 2001, 181). The prophet is, of course, Muhammad and the law is the untranslatable Quran. But it can also lead to a more democratic ideal in which everyone is responsible to the same god and hierarchies are levelled out because one divine law applies to all, including the king. This seems to be the vision of Deuteronomy, esp. with its criticism of the establishment and its rhetorically urgent call to re-interpret the law (cf. McConville 2002). This we may call a theocracy, but it is not what is usually implied by this term (cf. also Assmann 2000, 48f). Exodus, in my view, prepares one for Deuteronomy, in that it even deconstructs a potentially kingly picture of Moses (see my chapter on Moses, below) and urges the Israelites that there is one law applicable to all social classes. True, this is an ideal picture of Israel's statehood and the misinterpretation of the concept 'theocracy' dominated life and reality in Israel, as the prophets suggest, but what we have in the Pentateuch seems to communicate ideals and thus reshape society.

the speaker: "Speeches always characterize their speaker by providing the basis for inferring the kind of person who talks this way. So the law codes, voiced directly by God, provide a powerful impression of the divine character."[206] Inevitably, the reader learns something about the character of the speaker of the law.[207] The author seems to be doing exactly what he does not need to do: he is commending Yhwh as a high-profile ruler who is worthy of his subjects' admiration and support. Here, we observe an interplay of different rhetorical levels. This makes it difficult to assign a single function to the legal collections of Exodus, if not those of the entire Pentateuch.[208] Regarding the speaker's *ethos*, the author of Exodus, apparently, wants his reader to conclude that Yhwh assumes his royal place rightfully. Rhetorically speaking, considerable parts of his book are shaped along the lines of the most telling literary expressions of kingship known by the ancient Near Eastern societies: the 'law code' or, to use a less misleading term, the 'law collection'.[209]

For the following detailed discussion I take my start with Watts' exploration of the legal characterisation of God. Approaching the subject from different angles, he concludes that the Pentateuch's writers depicted "God as author, revisor, and interpreter of law ... by exemplifying the wisdom of the just ruler".[210] He reaches his conclusion by comparing the ancient Near Eastern concepts of kingship, as found in their law collections, and the divine self-portrayal in the law collections of the Pentateuch. Watts argues, convincingly, that the kingly portrait of God emerges from multiple layers in the legal collections. He mentions four of them: the authority inherent in the action of promulgating law, the

---

[206] Watts 1996, 1. The importance of the fact that Old Testament law is divine law (*Gottesgesetz*) has come to the fore in the old discussion (from 1955 onwards) whether one should speak of retaliation in respect to Old Testament law, or rather in terms of the "*Tun-Ergehen-Zusammenhang*", which Koch defined in the context of law as the inherent consequences of a crime (cf. Koch 1955). Recently, Graupner has, again, stressed the consequences of our perception of the law for our concept/image of Yhwh (Graupner 2005, 461).

[207] The term 'book of the covenant' has been established for Exod. 20:22–23:33 on the grounds of 24:7. As Dohmen 2004b, 148 rightly stresses, one must not forget that this represents "verschriftlichte Gottesrede", thus the oral character of the communication needs to be considered in discussing the features of the text.

[208] This is a notion to which Watts would probably not subscribe. He summarises the functional aspect of law: "[The] characterization of the law-speaker is, as it is in Mesopotamian codes, a primary goal of biblical law." (Watts 1996, 11, cf. also 6)

[209] To the modern reader 'law code' implies a well-structured set of laws which attempts to achieve the highest level of comprehensiveness possible. Measured against this standard, all ancient law writings fail in every aspect. Cf. Soden 1985, 125f and also Bottéro who even argues against the designation 'law', in the modern sense of the term (Bottéro 1992, 160ff). The expression 'law collection', instead of 'law code', nevertheless seems to capture the essence of these texts, for they, actually, dealt with legal issues.

[210] Watts 1996, 14.

relationship between law-giver and law-recipient in the covenant, the types of sanctions motivating obedience, and, lastly, the presence of contradiction between different law collections. All this constructs a picture of Yhwh which is effectively communicated through the medium of the legal genre. Watts' illuminating work may serve as a point of departure into the detailed investigation of the relevance of the Exodus law collections for the characterisation of God.[211] But, additionally, I propose the importance of two other aspects, not explicitly touched upon by Watts: the choice of themes included in the law collections and the order in which they appear.

The Laws as Direct Yhwh-Speech

In the present section I wish to highlight the implications of the author's strategy of putting the laws into God's mouth.[212] This topic is a significant part of the author's communication, as made clear by the reflection in Exod. 20:18-21. The motifs of fear and standing far off frame v.19, the centre of this passage which focuses on who should speak to the people directly. This text contributes more to the characterisations of Israel and Moses than to that of Yhwh, but the author goes on to have his reader 'listen' directly to Yhwh. Deuteronomy, with its mediated voicing of the law, demonstrates that he could have decided differently.[213] Exod. 20:22 continues with another speech-formula which introduces Yhwh as speaker (ויאמר יהוה) and then quotes his direct speech.[214] Thus, the reader is in a different position from the people; he perceives Yhwh's law directly, without mediation through Moses. The reader never escapes the direct address of Yhwh. Note that in Exodus and Deuteronomy there is no difference regarding the ultimate source of the laws, but there is a significant difference in the rhetorical strategy of Deuteronomy where Yhwh steps back behind Moses.

---

[211] The following thoughts will be developed mainly in interaction with Watts' work.

[212] Kaiser, O. 2003, 46f, also asks why the Pentateuch's laws are attributed to Yhwh. He argues, largely, from a historical perspective, that there was no king during and after exile who could issue a law collection for Israel. That this chronological localisation is debatable is clear, but the rhetorical implications of this strategy remain, largely, the same no matter the period of Israel's history in which the text is being read. Baker 2005 provides a helpful review of differing positions in the history of recent interpretations of the Decalogue. He also opts to take the divine attribution of the Decalogue seriously, but fails to draw any conclusions on the communicational aspect of this literary strategy.

[213] Watts is aware of this (Watts 1998 - on the legal characterisation of Moses). Here Watts concentrates on Deuteronomy, whereas his article on Yhwh argues almost entirely from Exodus, Leviticus and Numbers.

[214] As Sternberg puts it generally: "[T]he range of available options invests each choice with significance against the background of rejected might-have-beens." (Sternberg 1987, 387) This, of course, is a fundamental principle of the structuralist movement in the following of F. de Saussure.

This, of course, has a considerable effect upon the readers' perception of emphasis. And, indeed, by allowing God to speak the law in Exodus our author invests Yhwh with the authority that is inherent in the relationship between lawgiver and law-recipient. Whether an actual reader of Exodus counts himself as a law-recipient, depends, largely, on his perception of his relationship with Yhwh.[215] It can be assumed that the implied reader thought of himself a law-recipient.

A further effect achieved by this literary strategy is discovered by comparing Yhwh's law collections with those of Israel's ancient Near Eastern law collections neighbours. These collections were always formulated as the king's direct speech. For this parallel to work rhetorically, we need to assume that all participants – speakers and hearers alike – had a certain amount of common knowledge in this area. Deut. 4:6-8 demonstrates that the Israelites – or, at least, the implied readers of the Pentateuch – were aware of the other legal traditions around them.

> Keep them and do them, for that will be your wisdom and your understanding in
> the sight of the peoples, who, when they hear all these statutes, will say, 'Surely
> this great nation is a wise and understanding people.' For what great nation is
> there that has a god so near to it as Yhwh our God is to us, whenever we call upon
> him? And what great nation is there, that has statutes and rules so righteous as all
> this law that I set before you today?

This awareness means that at least an indirect comparison happened somewhere in the reading process. It is my understanding that this comparison was intended by the author and should shape the reader's perception of the text. It follows that the author moves Yhwh's characterisation[216] close to the function of the ancient Near Eastern king. This prompts the question, how far this similarity is drawn out in Exodus' presentation of Yhwh. In the following I will discuss the most important areas of similarity and dissimilarity and their implications for the portrayal of Yhwh. First, I will reflect further on the difference between the biblical and the ancient Near Eastern societies' understandings of the duties of the king. Second, the implications of localising the biblical law in a covenant setting will be highlighted.

Comparing the legislative role of kings in the ancient Mesopotamian cultures and in Israel, one finds a difference significant for the rhetorical presentation of

---

[215] The whole discussion of Jews and Christians reading Exodus becomes important here.

[216] As already observed above, it is not appropriate to consider the characterisation of Yhwh in his direct speech as stemming from a different source than the characterisation in the narrative parts. All characterisation, whether narrative or legal, is done by the same author. Having this in mind it seems less fitting to adopt Watts' terminology of Yhwh's "self-characterization", even when conceding the possibility that there could be disagreement between the author's (personal) view of a character and the presentation of the character itself (Watts 1996, 2).

Yhwh in Exodus. Oriental research has defined a pattern of legislative practices common to ancient Near Eastern cultures. At the beginning of his reign, the Babylonian king would issue a so called *mišarum*-act (*mīšaram šakānum*), later followed, toward the end of his reign, by a larger law collection, published in his name. The single rules of these *mišarum*-acts (*ṣimdatum*), mainly, dealt with matters directly relevant to the social and economic reality of the people: price fixing, alleviation of the worst excesses of debt-slavery, and the like. These statutory orders commonly adjusted former rules and were, especially, characterised by their making life easier for the people.[217] The retrospective orientation of the *mišarum*-act, in that it tries to provide relief from earlier social shortcomings, is different from the law collection's strong claim to continuity in both temporal directions. The latter takes up content from earlier collections and, also, explicitly states its claim to be valid, even into the far future. Jackson states that besides the content of these two legal modes also their outer forms (the material on which they were written and the literary composition enfolded between prologue and epilogue) support the difference in temporal terms.[218] Thus, the Babylonian kings did not only have the right to promulgate *ad-hoc* decisions like the *mišarum*-acts, but they, also, produced enduring documents like the large collections which were engraved in stone and copied time and time again.

In contrast, the Israelite kings did not have the legislative right to issuing lasting laws during their periods of government – from the biblical literature's point of view, at least – but they could nevertheless partake in a *mišarum*-like activity, as can be deduced from the *mišpaṭ hammelek,* given in 1 Sam. 8:9-18 and Deut. 17:14-20.[219] This restriction on the legislative responsibility of the human royals of Israel is, also, illustrated by the temporal limitation connected with all non-divine law. As Jackson convincingly argues, the acts of legislation initiated by humans, as they are scattered throughout the Bible (cf. also Jithro's suggestions in Exod. 18), are all temporally limited. In conclusion, Jackson summarises:

> ...[T]here is no claim, however, that the measures themselves have been mandated by God. Such measures are ad hoc; like the Babylonian *mišarum*-act, they do not create enduring law. Nevertheless, by the very fact that they use a religious legitimation – specifically, a *berit* with God as guarantor (Jer. 34:15-16) in the case of Zedekiah, a curse in the case of Nehemiah – an element of continuity is introduced, the continuity that attaches to the (divine) person of the guarantor.[220]

---

[217] Cf. e.g Soden 1985, 126f and Kraus 1984. These *mišarum*-acts could not be found during or after Assyrian times.

[218] Cf. Jackson 2000, 147.

[219] See de Vaux 1965, 150 and Jackson 2000, 148f, for further discussions and bibliography. Eckart Otto points in a similar direction when he states that "Israel in der Gerichtsorganisation sehr eigenständige Wege gegangen ist, die den königlich-staatlichen Einfluß auf die Ortsgerichte gering hielten." (Otto 1991, 150f; he also offers a list of more recent literature.)

[220] Jackson 2000, 162.

The role of passing enduring law seems to have been limited, in the Israelite society, to Yhwh. The human kings of Israel, apparently, did not publish any considerable law collections, which emphasises the idea that Yhwh had the sole right to legislate in Israel. Another hint in the same direction is the Israelite kings' responsibility for the continuous implementation of the eternal divine law, as e.g. Kings and Chronicles make abundantly clear.[221] The formulaic phrase for establishing this connection – "to do what is right in the eyes of Yhwh" (עשה + הישר בעיני יהוה or עשה + הישר בעיני [where the suffix denotes Yhwh]) – is introduced in Deuteronomy,[222] where the link between whatever is pleasing to Yhwh and his law, as quoted by Moses, is established.

Thus, on the surface we find in the claim of eternality a strong similarity between the divine Israelite law collections and those of their ancient Near Eastern counterparts. But, looking deeper into the textual evidence reveals that the ancient Near Eastern collections were far from being eternal: Bottéro argues that the importance of Hammurabi's collection does not equal the Magna Carta or the Code Napoleon, for example. The different copies of Hammurabi's collection (LH) throughout history seem to be nothing more than practice texts for scribes. Compared to the other law collections, previous and subsequent,[223] Hammurabi's, merely, seems to be one among many, valid for a certain time and soon to be replaced.

> Considering the situation in Mesopotamia ..., i.e. the absence of a lasting legislation promulgated at once for everyone until it would have been revoked, it is certain that the prescriptions of the 'Code' of Hammurabi had become outdated at the latest from the moment that the political and administrative situation of the country changed, if they ever did have some legislative value.[224]

This change happened, at the latest, by the end of Hammurabi's dynasty (the start of the Kassite period, ca. 1600), if not already by his death.

On the one hand, we have the ancient Near Eastern idea of a king who secures his reputation by publishing a wonderful law collection. He claims its eternal relevance but in the end this is not achieved. On the other hand, we have the Israelite idea of a divine legislator who publishes a law collection which is binding for every king throughout Israelite history. The only rationale securing the longevity of the Israelite law collections is the divinity of Yhwh. Thus, it is

---

[221] See 1 Ki. 11:33.38; 14:8; 15:5.11; 22:43; 2 Ki. 10:30; 12:3; 14:3; 15:3.34; 16:2; 18:3; 22:2; 2 Chr. 20:32; 24:2; 25:2; 26:4; 27:2; 28:1; 29:2 and 34:2. See also the stipulation in Deut. 17:18, which requires each king to have his own copy of the divine law that has been validated by the priests.

[222] Cf. Deut. 13:19 for a general correlation, Deut. 12:25 for a case of ritual law, and Deut. 21:9 for legal procedures.

[223] Our knowledge of legal collections from the ancient Near East stretches from the Laws of Ur-Namma, ca. 2100, until the middle of the first century.

[224] Bottéro 1992, 160.

again the *ethos* of the divine that shapes the Israelite perception of law. Exodus, clearly, conditions the Israelite reader to regard everything that comes out of God's mouth as trustworthy and of enduring quality. The contrast with the ancient Near Eastern mode of handling law intensifies this rhetorical effect by playing on the idea of Israel being superior to the other nations, a notion displayed explicitly in other parts of the Pentateuch. The portrayal of Yhwh as king of Israel, especially given the biblical differentiation between the restricted legislative role of the human Israelite kings, makes the divine kingship a socially practicable notion. For a reader who knows about the biblical ideal of kingship in Israel, king Yhwh supersedes, at least in legal issues, any human on the throne in Jerusalem.

It remains to be seen whether the differences highlighted above can function rhetorically. If they do, the implication is that the reader of Exodus must be aware of these realities in Israel and its cultural environment. The reader then learns that Yhwh supersedes, in significance and power, the royals of the cultural environment, which, again, heightens the probability of agreement and compliance on his part. But, contrast only works when there is a perceivable amount of similarity which establishes the cognitive link in the first place. Hence, I will focus, briefly, on the similarities between the Israelite legislature and that of its ancient Near Eastern counterparts.

Apart from the differences between the relatively abstract categories of divine *versus* human, one should recognise the implications which result from comparison between the narrative and covenantal settings of the law. It is in this area that we encounter more similarities with ancient Near Eastern practices of the king.

The authority to legislate is not necessarily substantiated on grounds of a creation theology, i.e. that God, as creator, has an inherent right to issue law. But "[f]or the most part, the Pentateuch's laws derive their authority from more immediate relationships."[225] In Exodus, more than in other books of the Pentateuch, this connection is made most explicit. The relationship with the people expected to live under the law is defined in Exodus by Yhwh's actions in the past and future on behalf of Israel. In addition, this relationship is, also, defined as the covenant relationship between Yhwh and Israel: obedience on Israel's part is stipulated and agreed upon by the people (Exod. 19:5.8). The implication is that there is an explicit agreement on Yhwh's role as law-giver. Exodus even places the acceptance of the legislator prior to the recipients' exact knowledge of the content of the law.[226] The notion that Israel owes Yhwh obedience is not much different from what we find in the ancient Near Eastern law collections' literary framework, i.e. their prologues and epilogues. Here, the king claims military and other achievements on behalf of his subjects. The recollection of

---

[225] Watts 1996, 3.

[226] Cf. Watts 1996, 3f.

the great deeds of the ruler should justify the people's obedience. Exodus utilises a similar logic by recording the events of the exodus from Egypt. In law collections of Exodus this strategy is made explicit in the occasional motive-clauses which encourage law obedience (e.g. Exod. 19:4; 20:2.12.22; [22:21 + 23:9; 23:15]; 23:20-33; 34:10). The obvious rhetorical effect is to transfer Yhwh's *ethos*, as displayed in his actions for his people, to his role as law-giver. The reader will, presumably, have at least some sort of recollection of Yhwh's great deeds (especially after reading the first part of Exod). To link these stories with the motivation to observe the law will lead the reader into a holistic perception of reality in which law and history are inextricably connected. On these grounds, it is logical to accept Yhwh's legislative authority.

The covenantal setting of the law has a similar structural logic: the division of roles in a covenant implies that the lord has power to initiate stipulations, whereas the vassals, defined as the receiving party, are expected to show obedience. The keeping of these stipulations defines the existence of the covenant. Given the many political treaties known from the ancient Near Eastern world, one can again assume a good amount of common knowledge among the population of the Levant, including the implied reader of Exodus. Watts can, thus, propose that casting the relationship between Israel and their God into the terms of a covenant will inevitably characterise the initiator of the covenant "as the kind of person who accepts and abides by such conventions."[227] The Exodus law collections are connected in a literary way with the covenant between Yhwh and Israel links the two pictures of Yhwh: law-giver, on the one hand, and guarantor of the covenant, on the other. To be sure, both functions evoke the concept of 'king', but the relationships expressed by these royal functions are quite different. To merge the two is quite an unusual strategy in the ancient Near Eastern world. Usually, there are subjects living under the law of their king or there are national entities being connected through a covenant. But there is no people covenanted to their king or a law collection ruling the relationship between two political powers. That we can observe these two relationships between Yhwh and Israel at the same time seems to be one of the reasons for the often contradictory results in the many studies on the similarities between the biblical texts and the ancient Near Eastern law collections and covenants. The parallels between these show the difficulties involved if one addresses just one of these options while interpreting the biblical texts. Nowhere does the picture fit perfectly. This seems due to the mix created by the biblical authors.[228] That this mixture was intended shows its rhetorical implication: the reader knows that he stands in that formal covenant relationship with God, who enforces the law

---

[227] Watts 1996, 4.

[228] An additional complication arises when one considers the implications of Exod. 19:1-6 which describes the people as a kingly priesthood. The relationship between Yhwh and Israel cannot, apparently, be expressed by a single metaphor. Cf. p.227 below for more detail.

promulgated inside this covenant setting. As argued above, the reader was already made aware by the author of Exodus that it was the covenant between Yhwh and the Patriarchs which motivated Yhwh to act on behalf of their descendants in the first place. Thus, he will perceive the law recorded in Exodus as belonging to this covenant. The author equates the characteristics of the covenant God with the God portrayed as law-giver. The rhetorical force of this strategy is that a reader who wants to belong to the covenant people will, very likely, also, be prepared to accept the legislative authority of Yhwh.

The specific picture given in Exodus regarding the source of Israelite law bears consequences for the perception of Yhwh. Yhwh, known as the God of the Patriarchal covenant, corresponds to the ancient Near Eastern ideal of the just king in that he gives eternal and good law and he enforces it. This connection of two realms suggests a literary strategy on the part of the author which utilises allusions to known concepts in order to give his text maximum effect. It is not new or astonishing in the ancient Near Eastern world that Yhwh, a god, appears as final authority in the determination of humanly impossible legal decisions.[229] But that a god would actually take up and, thus, supersede the legislative authority of a king does not coincide with the legal concept of the time. This contrast encourages the reader to think of Yhwh in a new way, a way which goes beyond the conventional talk about the divine. In merging the concepts of the covenant God and the legislating king the author suggests that Yhwh is a worthy king, able to order the social and religious life of his followers who, also, happen to be his covenant partners. Thus, one purpose of the present literary strategy is the shaping of Yhwh's *ethos*, which, in turn, effects the content and force of the law given by him.

To substantiate this result I will now turn to the other aspects of Yhwh's characterisation in the legal parts of Exodus.

The Law Collections – a Divine Perspective on Israel

Further implications follow from the fact that the law is always placed in Yhwh's mouth. Regarding the content of the regulations, it is, again, the backdrop of the rejected might-have-beens[230] that invest the choice of themes covered in the law collection with significance. Here, we find two important aspects: the already-discussed literary strategy of having Yhwh utter the law and the mixture of 'civil' and 'religious' regulations. The latter aspect relates to the form of the collections in Exodus and will be discussed in the corresponding chapter, below.

---

[229] Cf. e.g. the 'divine River Ordeal' to which so many law collections of Mesopotamian origin refer to (LU ¶13+14; LH ¶2+132; MAL A ¶17,22, 24–25).

[230] Cf. p.85, n.214.

The 'rejected might-have-been', in the first case, is the common tradition of the human king publishing his (temporally limited) law collection with no recourse to the divine sphere other than the general approval of the gods as mentioned previously. The legislator of the Exodus law collections, on the other hand, is Yhwh. The thesis put forward here is that the legislator's character is invariably and directly linked with the content of the collection; it qualifies the themes and concerns covered as *divine*.[231] It is, thus, a divine perspective the author presents to his implied reader. Again, we see an interplay between the divine source, characterising the law, and the law, itself, enabling the reader to learn about the character of God. Everything communicated by the law in Exodus is qualified by the divine perspective, whether values, ideals, desired actions, concerns, culture, perspectives on relationships or other judgements. The following discussion will attempt to explicate this divine perspective according to major themes. The present selection of themes – Yhwh's presence, loyalty to Yhwh, restitution or concern for others, benevolence as motivation, sanction – tries to cover the aspects of the Exodus law collections which relate, specifically, to the characterisation of Yhwh, even though a number of other themes, legal or theological, remain unmentioned.

YHWH'S PRESENCE

Yhwh states emphatically:

> I will dwell among the people of Israel and will be their God. And they shall know that I am Yhwh their God, who brought them out of the land of Egypt that I might dwell among them. I am Yhwh their God. (Exod. 29:45-46)

This seminal sentence in Exodus directly links the presence of Yhwh to the knowledge that Yhwh is the Israelite's god, the god who established a covenant with them (cf. Gen. 17:8; Exod. 6:7-8). A large part of Exodus is concerned with the provisions for enabling Yhwh's presence among the people, making divine presence one of the major themes of the book. Hence, it should not surprise us to find this theme in the legal parts of the book as well. As it will be argued later, the sequence of the laws in the book of the covenant has its implications for the characterisation of Yhwh. I will anticipate a later discussion to highlight the importance of the theme of the divine presence for the perception of the book of the covenant.[232] In any written communication the beginning and the end of a given unit are of special rhetorical relevance. Thus, it is significant that the collection starts off with the altar law (Exod. 20:24-26), clarifying the intentions of Yhwh to be present among the people, and ends in a reflection on the consequences of his guiding presence (Exod. 23:20-33).

---

[231] To show the dependence of Israelite legislation upon their conception of Yhwh is one of Paul Hanson's main interests (cf. Hanson 1986).

[232] Cf. Crüsemann, who stresses the importance of the three occurrences of מקום in B (Crüsemann 1992, 201).

Two religious concepts, common to all ancient Near Eastern cultures, are touched upon in the so-called altar law. First is the notion that a deity can be present both in its heavenly realm and on earth, commonly in a sanctuary.[233] Second is the conviction that the deity's presence needs to be ensured in order to receive the divine blessing.[234]

The altar law links these concepts with the most fundamental commandment in the Old Testament, the command to worship Yhwh alone. Given the characterisation of Yhwh, it is no surprise that the particularisation of this basic principle is the subject of the beginning of the book of the covenant. The deity is introduced: worship is the core of every religion, and *ergo* the divine character will be expressed, among other things, by the way the sanctuary is furnished. According to Exod. 20:22–26 the monolatric principle has to find its expression in the place of worship[235] which helps to ensure the divine presence among the people. In the following, I will demonstrate how the brief paragraph in 20:22-26 constitutes a well-rounded unit[236] and stresses the need for a proper place of worship as precondition for Yhwh's presence. 20:22a refers the reader back to 19:3b.4,[237] and the בני ישראל are the ultimate addressees which are taken up again in 21:1 (לפניהם). All of this suggests that 20:22a functions as a general in-

---

[233] Cf. Hutter 1996, 80–86 and also Pitkänen 2000, 22ff for a summary of the ancient Near Eastern evidence for this notion. That gods are present in heaven is evident from various mythologies as well as from their associations with physical phenomena as sun, moon, stars etc. The earthly presence of the gods is bound to god-images (cf. Niehr 1998, 43). The ancient Near Eastern Temple, where the god-image is situated, is understood as an interface between heaven and earth. Hutter speaks of an integration of spheres which was initiated by a set of rituals (Hutter 1996, 83).

[234] This aspect can be deduced from the extinct lamentations of the ancient Near East which bewail the fall of cities: their gods left and withdrew their protective presence (cf. Block 1988, 125–161 and Niehaus 1995, 136–140). Another hint is found in ancient Near Eastern reflections on offerings, which provide the basis for the principle of *do ut des* (cf. Hutter 1996, 94–96).

[235] Jacob 1997, 614–616 provides a very specific limitation of the applicability of the law: he limits Exod. 20:24 to the festival of 24:1 on the basis of the relative clause אשר אזכיר את־שמי. The regulation to build a stationary altar of stone would then refer to the specific time after crossing the Jordan (ואם – should notbe translated as "whenever"), the more permanent stone signifying the *stabilitas loci* of a settled community. Again, Jacob qualifies the altar as the one on Mt. Ebal (cf. Deut. 27:5-6; Josh. 8:30-31 [617f]). In my present interpretation I suggest that the context implies a more general understanding of the law. Cf. also Childs 1976, 466, who argues this for the current context. On the diachronic level, of course, he maintains its original independence and argues for the antiquity of the law compared to its present context.

[236] Aware of the likely opposition of many scholars, Cf. Childs 1976, 465 summarises: "...the overwhelming number of critical commentaries (Bäntsch, Noth, Te Stroete, etc.) judge vv. 22–23 to be later redactional framework, and therefore without exegetical significance." On Jacob and his very context-oriented interpretation, see below.

[237] Cf. Houtman 2000, 103.

troduction to the book of the covenant. 20:22b, – however, "You yourselves have seen how from heaven I spoke with you" – is tied to the subsequent verses, as it provides an example of Yhwh's immediate presence from the literary context. The Israelites have seen – and, implicitly, heard – Yhwh's presence (Exod. 19). This theophany is perceived by the reader as an instance of what 20:24b alludes to: Yhwh came to them and blessed them with his presence, even though he usually dwells in heaven and not on earth. Crüsemann widens the scope of this connection between Yhwh's self-attestation (20:24b) and his presence to include the literary context:

> [Gottes] Gegenwart ist … nicht ohne sein Wort zu haben, das Wort, durch welches sein Name verkündigt wird. … Seine Selbstverkündigung entscheidet über seine Präsenz. Erst sie läßt den traditionell heiligen Ort zu dem werden, was er immer schon zu sein beansprucht hat, den Ort seiner Gegenwart. Und was der Inhalt dieser Selbstverkündigung ist, zeigt der Text, an dessen Spitze sie steht: Sie gewinnt ihre entscheidende Gestalt im Bundesbuch selbst, das als Ich-Rede Gottes konzipiert ist.[238]

In other words, Yhwh is present among his worshippers wherever he chooses to appear (בוא "come"[239]) and to accept the offerings.[240] The force and centrality of this phrase becomes clear once we recognise the contrast between the non-Israelite and the Israelite forms of worship. In the surrounding cultures, worship and the corresponding sacrifices served to guarantee the benevolence of the gods. The gods' presence would be ensured with the help of figurines or other images. We see the rhetoric of the passage at work: Yhwh chooses freely where and when he wants to appear (20:24b), as the previous narration of the theophany and audition of the decalogue have shown (20:22b). His intention to bless is assumed, and thus Israelites who trust in this God have no need to produce images of his presence or to follow religious practices to win his benevolence. Yhwh lives in the heavens – and, despite this, is active on earth, i.e. his presence is a matter of his will and power and is not dependent upon god-images.

Given the viability of the argumentation above, Houtman's translation of Exod. 20:23 – "*Therefore* you may make nothing …"[241] – correctly highlights

---

[238] Crüsemann 1992, 204f

[239] On the further implications of Yhwh's appearance at local altars, see Pitkänen 2000, 54ff, who argues that the altar-law is not in competition either with the later so called 'centralisation' of worship at the Jerusalem temple or with the previous mobile sanctuary.

[240] It is common Old Testament practice to link these two kinds of sacrifices. The עלה, a burnt offering reserved for Yhwh alone, expresses wholehearted worship, and the שלם exemplifies the harmonic relationship between deity and the one bringing the offering (cf. Houtman 1997, 53f). It appears that the offerings are only mentioned here to highlight the setting of worship; there is no deeper theological significance.

[241] Houtman 2000, 98+104 (my italics).

the semantic relationship between 20:22b and 20:23-26. The unity of the following verses is hinted at by the intriguing use of עשה (four times, twice in the prohibitions and twice in the positive statements): "You shall not *make* gods of silver ... gods of gold you must not *make* ... an altar of earth you shall *make* ... whenever you *make* an altar of stone ..." An altar is sufficient for worship, and, therefore, images of his presence are superfluous.[242] This thought might well be the rationale behind the unhewn nature of the material for the altar. The temptation to equip the stones with images or figures[243] would, then, bring the finished and elaborate altar in proximity to other ancient Near Eastern styles of altar construction (esp. Canaanite).[244]

As we saw, the rhetoric of the altar law depends largely on Yhwh's freely choosing the place of his appearance, i.e. the place of his presence (20:24b: בכל־המקום ... אבוא אליך וברכתיך: "In every place ... I will come to you and bless you."). Yhwh, himself, must decide where he desires to be present with his blessing benevolence. Hence, the reader meets a god who is willing to be present among the בני ישראל, the covenant people, and he isassured that the divine presence means blessing. The author utilises three ways to communicate this willingness of Yhwh to be present among the people. Firstly, the reader encounters another instance of the already stressed theme of the exclusivity of the Yhwh-worship.[245] Secondly, a contrast is built which brings together the different cultural ideas of securing the divine presence at places of worship. In other words, Yhwh's presence is not at man's disposal. Nevertheless, Yhwh binds his presence with the right way of worship which is expressed by the outer appearance of the sanctuary, the sign of his otherness and his freedom. Thirdly, with Pitkänen,[246] I suggest that the omission of any statutory penalty in the altar law is rhetorically relevant. The reader deduces that it is possible to set up an altar anywhere he desires but that he is also prohibited from setting up *mazzeboth* or

---

[242] On this theological connection between 20:23 and 20:24-26, see Keil 1983, 519f. Keil's comments on the earthen nature of the altar appear slightly embellished in their theological relevance. For a discussion of the functional similarities and dissimilarities between Israel's and other ancient Near Eastern cultures' places of worship cf. Pitkänen 2000, 35ff.

[243] So says Jacob 1997, 617 following Rashbam and Maimonides. Pitkänen 2000, 49, hints in the same direction: "In other words, an altar as described in Ex 20:22–26 acts as a locus at which Yahweh's presence is manifested. Then, since in the ancient Near East images acted as a locus of a god's presence, an earthen altar in Israel serves a purpose analogous to that of ancient Near Eastern god images. Furthermore, this implies that god images are not necessary, but an earthen altar is enough to secure Yahweh's presence and blessing."

[244] Cf. Childs 1976, 467 and Durham 1987, 320, who both refer to Conrad 1968. The reference to avoiding nakedness in worship (v.26) would support this cultural contrast and would be a preventive measure against heathen worship.

[245] Cf. the notes on the theme "Loyalty to Yhwh" in the following section.

[246] Pitkänen 2000, 55.

god-images to force Yhwh – and, implicitly, his blessing – to be present. But the prohibition will not be enforced by a direct legal threat. The implication of the verses is that only buildings in the right place are accompanied with Yhwh's presence and blessing. Yhwh will not let himself be forced to realise his benevolent presence. Once Yhwh is willing to be present, it suffices to offer thanks on a simple earthen altar. Thus, it is not a negative fear of a certain consequence which motivates law keeping, here, but the hope for a positive outcome.

At the beginning of the book of the covenant the author points to the presence of Yhwh in the cult places. That the divine presence is not limited to a worship setting becomes obvious in the epilogue to the book of the covenant.[247] Yhwh will – through the mediation of his 'messenger' (מלאך) – be present among the travelling and settling people in a more general, protective way.

Exod. 23:(13).14-33 constitutes the final section of the book of the covenant. Throughout the section the author shifts his perspective from the wilderness at Sinai to the future wanderings and the final settlement in the land of promise.[248] Three festivals are prescribed and additional requirements for sacrifices are mentioned (23:14–19).[249] The actual epilogue (23:20-33) begins with הנה which marks a significant break in style, all the while continuing with general exhortations on obedience – without specific new regulations – and a motivating glimpse into a blessed future. The only regulations found are well known to the reader and provide him with a thematic link to the altar law (23:24-25a). The new feature is the expansion of the concrete blessings (23:25b-26: the Israelites' water, bread, health are blessed[250] and progeny and a long life-span are prom-

---

[247] This opposes Crüsemann 1992, 210f, who understands the מקום in 23:20 as signifying the place of worship, in this case, specifically, the temple in Jerusalem (so already Nachmanides cf. Houtman 2000, 273). Hence, the way to the sanctuary (23:20), as well as the way back (into the multi-cultural every day life setting of the people), will be guided by God's messenger (23:23). The text would then speak of the guarding presence of Yhwh outside the holy places of worship. This interpretation can only be supported by Crüsemann's redaction critical treatment of 23:20-33. It hinges on his excluding small, but significant, parts from 23:21.23.32-33 and all of Exod. 24–31 as later 'historising' attachments which transfer the authority of an old text (the book of the covenant plus its setting at Sinai) to the later text, probably from the time of the Assyrian domination (cf. Crüsemann 1992, 209–213).

[248] Houtman perceives this point also (Houtman 2000, 270 – the entire book of the covenant points to the settlement in Canaan), but in his interpretation he remains at the narrative's level. From within the narrative the land of promise is future and from the reader's point of view it, almost certainly, is present. This distinction is important for the interpretation of the text.

[249] For a discussion of the structure see Houtman 2000, 259.

[250] The blessings of v.25b may be allusions to the events of the wilderness wanderings preceding and following the stay at Mt. Sinai. All of the blessings described in 23:25-26 allude to the theme of populating the land of Canaan: the supply of nourishment, health and a long life-span have a beneficial effect on the birthrate which is the theme of v.26a

ised) which have been included in the altar law merely in a generic way (cf. וברכתיך – "and I will bless you", 20:24b).[251] By elaborating on the blessings, the author stresses Yhwh's positive intentions with his covenant people. The presence of Yhwh is not a threat which leads to requirements for the people, because Yhwh is a god who blesses the ones belonging to him.

Considering the rhetorical force of the text, we encounter a more ambivalent picture. On the one hand, the text is framed by the theme of Yhwh's endangered presence (23:20-24 and 32f). The presence of the Canaanites threatens the presence of Yhwh because of the likely temptation of Israel to commit idolatry. The presence of Yhwh can be secured only by proper religious loyalty and exclusivity in worship. On the other hand, we find the emphasis on Yhwh's initiative to remove the Canaanites from the land[252] – it is Yhwh's terror-arousing presence which drives them out (v.27-30) – and his benevolent blessing which enables the Israelites to replace them in the end. Given these two aspects, the reader is led to evaluate the divine presence as both a threat and a blessing:[253] a threat to ignite his own loyalty to Yhwh and a blessing (the land without the likely snare of the Canaanite religion) to provide a situation conducive for this desired loyalty.[254] This two-way strategy of provoking law obedience is already present within the decalogue and altar law[255] at the beginning of the book of the covenant, but it seems rhetorically more effective here, because it addresses multiple layers in the human constitution. Here, the element of hope is added to the per-

---

and 29-30.

[251] Several verbal and thematic links establish the parallel between the altar-law and the closure of the book of the covenant: the place chosen by Yhwh (20:24bα המקום אשר || 23:20b המקום אשר הכנתי); the blessing promised (20:24bβ וברכתיך || 23:25aβ וברך) the indirect and direct mention of other gods (20:23 || 23:24.32); the theme of worship (throughout); and the nature of the forbidden altar which is parallel to Canaanite altars (cf. n.244 above).

[252] An exception is the brief mention of Israel's involvement in v.31. The picture is quite different in Deut. 7:17-24 where the Israelites shall do this task with Yhwh's help (cf. Houtman 2000, 272).

[253] Köckert observes a similar ambivalence, which he traces back to the different installations of the Abrahamic covenant. Especially instructive is his interpretation of Gen. 17, the content of which he links with the P material in the latter Pentateuch (41f). Parallel to the circumcision as an inward sign of the established covenant, the Sabbath marks the holiness of the people to the outside world. This holiness comes from Yhwh who consecrates his people for himself: "Nicht Israel heiligt sich, sofern es das Sabbatgebot hält, sondern indem Israel Sabbat feiert, wird für jedermann erkennbar, daß Jahwe es geheiligt hat." (Köckert 1989, 54f)

[254] Jackson 2000, 248f, uses the term *berit* for this reciprocal relationship. Israel is already committed to Yhwh and, thus, must abstain from any covenant with the inhabitants of Canaan.

[255] As argued above, it is his more theoretical willingness to be present which enforces the altar law in a positive way.

suasive force of the passage. This element is, of course, only rhetorically effective because of the support of Yhwh's character which has implicitly been described throughout the book of the covenant as benevolent and reliable, as will be described below. Yhwh's accompanying presence becomes Israel's blessing.

The previous discussion has shown the centrality of the theme of divine presence for the book of the covenant. We meet the theme at the rhetorically relevant positions at the beginning and the end, hence constituting an *inclusio* around the collection which highlights the basis/rationale for the collection: it is Yhwh's proximity that requires a certain behaviour and attitude. Obedience to the law establishes the ground on which Yhwh's presence is of a benevolent character rather than being a threat to the well-being of the people. This threat, which can only be read between the lines, will become substantial and explicit when we consider the theme of loyalty to Yhwh.

LOYALTY TO YHWH

A number of direct attributes of Yhwh are linked to the central theme of Yhwh's demand for loyalty, which is the predominant theme from the beginning of the desert wanderings onwards. In the context of the Mara-incident (Exod. 15:22-26) we find Yhwh demanding undivided attention to his will:

> If you will diligently listen to the voice of Yhwh your God, and do that which is right in his eyes, and give ear to his commandments and keep all his statutes, I will put none of the diseases on you that I put on the Egyptians, for I am Yhwh, your healer. (Exod. 15:25b-26)

This densely phrased Yhwh-speech introduces the loyalty-theme into the ideational world of Exodus.[256] The attribution of Yhwh as healer (אני יהוה רפאך) refers to the past deeds on behalf of his people. Firstly, of course, the context makes clear that Yhwh made the urgently needed water drinkable, thus, preventing likely diseases. Secondly, but not less explicitly, reference is made to the plagues brought upon the Egyptians,[257] thereby provoking the reader to recall again the Exodus events, i.e., everything that Yhwh had done on behalf of his people thus far. Yhwh is the one who brought the Israelites out of the land of disease. Even though the text does not mention any legal content of the 'statute and rule' (Exod. 15:25a) presented to the Israelites, the rhetorical link between

---

[256] Note the legal language of the brief passage: מצוה (commandment) and חק (statute). In its structure it, also, bears some poetic aspects. The reflective nature (commenting of the previously narrated events) of this brief text has also been observed by Berge 2008, 5–7.

[257] Possibly the link is made to Exod. 9:10-11. It is significant that in Deut. the diseases brought upon the Egyptians become almost proverbial: בשחין מצרים (boils of Egypt; Deut. 28:27) and את כל־מדוה מצרים (sickness of Egypt; Deut. 28:60). Itis, clearly, not a singular concept, but gained in referential significance. Hence, the brief description of Yhwh as healer would be meaningful to the readers.

deliverance and legislation is made. Loyalty could be motivated by the benevolence of Yhwh.[258]

The very same emphasis dominates the first part of the decalogue.[259]

I am Yhwh your God, who brought you out of the land of Egypt, out of the house of slavery. You shall have no other gods before me. You shall not make for yourself a carved image, or any likeness of anything that is in heaven above, or that is in the earth beneath, or that is in the water under the earth. You shall not bow down to them or serve them, for I, Yhwh, your God am a jealous God, visiting the iniquity of the fathers on the children to the third and the fourth generation of those who hate me, but showing steadfast love to thousands of those who love me and keep my commandments. (Exod. 20:2-6)

By casting these verses in the form of direct (apodictic) prohibitions and a direct characterisation of Yhwh, the author colours the entire picture of the following Yhwh-speeches with loyalty. Everything that follows will be read against this backdrop. The direct characterisation of these few verses provides the basis for the prohibitions in that it is designed to justify the monolatric attitude of the book of the covenant. Yhwh is the one who brought Israel out of the land of oppression and servitude (Exod. 20:2). This qualifies Yhwh as the God of the Exodus and, thus, explicitly links the two main aspects of divine activity encountered so far in the plot of Exodus, deliverance and legislation.[260] Keeping in mind that the covenant is an expression of the relationship between Yhwh and Israel, both aspects – deliverance and legislation – provide the basis for this relationship. Exod. 20:2 serves as an introduction to the following law but, also, as rhetorically effective recapitulation of all preceding events. This recapitulation focuses entirely on Yhwh's actions on Israel's behalf.[261] To present Yhwh as the God to whom Israel owes its freedom utilises the emotional forces of thankfulness[262] and awe. A thankful reader is more likely to be attentive to the stipulations and motivated to lead a life that is pleasing to God, his deliverer. The awe initiated by the brief statement is closely connected to the thankfulness it prompts. The awe is produced, first, by the quality of the divine action and,

---

[258] Cf. p.103 below.

[259] On the structure and implications of Exod. 20:5-6 in the portrayal of Yhwh see p.49 above.

[260] The introductory formula in Exod. 20:2 links the decalogue with the previous narrative in that the reader knows already much about Yhwh and will link these preconceptions (at least in part, informed by the first 19 chapters of Exod) with the following texts. Cf. Jacob 1997, 553 who uses this fact to argue (according to his Jewish tradition but, in my view, less convincingly) that Exod. 20:2 be read as the first commandment. Exod. 20:2 represents, in my understanding, the rhetorical device of referencing a phrase with its mnemonic function of recalling previously communicated knowledge to link otherwise separated strands of the narrative.

[261] Cf. Childs 1976, 401.

[262] Cf. Houtman 2000, 16f.

second, by the recognition that he did all this on behalf of this small and, seemingly, insignificant people. The reference to Egypt supports this last aspect in that it implies the contrast not only between the pharaoh and Yhwh but, also, between the slave lords and the slaves who are now free. The motivation for loyalty is thus heightened; the reader is conditioned to perceive the remainder of the book as the rightful demands of the new lord, Yhwh.

The theme of loyalty is, also, emphatically taken up at the end of the book of the covenant. The so-called epilogue to the law collection (23:20-33) reflects the language and concern of the beginning of the decalogue. This thematic *inclusio* suggests the subject's significance for the author of Exodus. The general command to refrain from idolatrous worship given in the decalogue is now specified to include the gods of the inhabitants of the country promised to them.[263] Viewed at the level of the narrative, this, obviously, constitutes a glimpse into the future. At the level of the communication between author and intended reader, it, most likely, presents a present issue. The obvious presence of these two logically separated levels is a constituent for the rhetorical force of the passage. The author, hereby, presents the ideal relationship between Israel and Yhwh.

Another direct characterisation of Yhwh is the mention of his jealous nature. Whereas loyalty was positively motivated by an emotional link to thankfulness, we find that loyalty can, also, be negatively motivated by stressing Yhwh's jealous nature, which imposes an implicit threat on the non-compliant, disloyal reader. Thus the theme of Yhwh's jealousy is related to loyalty in much the same way that thankfulness is related to loyalty. It is again in the decalogue where we find the statement of Yhwh's jealousy (קנא) which functions as a motive-clause for the second commandment:

> You shall not bow down to them or serve them, for I, Yhwh, your God am a jealous God (כי אנכי יהוה אלהיך אל קנא), visiting the iniquity of the fathers on the children to the third and the fourth generation of those who hate me, but showing steadfast love to thousands of those who love me and keep my commandments. (Exod. 20:5-6)

The formulation is quite similar to Yhwh's self-introduction in 20:2 (... אנכי יהוה אלהיך). Whatever the exact theological implications,[264] it is obvious that the loyalty to Yhwh is the heart of the second commandment. The loyalty is specified here as undivided loyalty, and the corresponding emotion, if Israel behaves disloyally, is jealousy,[265] an image that is conceptually connected to the holiness

---

[263] Cf. above p.92ff.

[264] Cf. the brief summary of scholarly opinions on Exod. 20:4-6 by Childs 1976, 404ff.

[265] Jacob defines קנא, in the present context, as a very positive zeal of God who is concerned about this own reputation as well as that of Israel. It is parallel to the term's use in the realm of marriage: "'Eifersüchtig' wäre eine schlechte Wiedergabe, denn diese האנק ist nicht der tadelnswerte Affekt einer egoistischen Leidenschaft, die das Weib für

of Yhwh.[266] Given this emphasis in the first words that Yhwh addresses to the people at Sinai, it comes as no surprise that, after recalling the first and most explicit act of disloyalty, Exod. 34:14 uses the very same language to express Yhwh's claim to undivided loyalty: "… for you shall worship no other god, for Yhwh, whose name is 'Jealous' (קנא), is a jealous (קנא) God." Here, the plot of Exodus turns back on itself by closing the verbal link between the beginning of the decalogue and the theological significance of the golden calf episode.[267]

At the rhetorical level, the direct characterisation of Yhwh as a benevolent, as well as jealous, God enforces the desire to behave loyally. Both characterisations are connected with strong emotional forces, thankfulness and fear. By linking Yhwh's actions in the past with the installation of the covenant the author manages to positively shape the attitude of the reader toward accepting everything that comes out of the mouth of Yhwh. This leads the reader, at the ideational level, to perceive law keeping as an expression of the required loyalty.

RESTITUTION OR THE CONCERN FOR OTHERS

Beyond the direct characterisation of Yhwh in the legal parts of Exodus, we, also, need to consider the content of the law collection which does not refer directly to the person of Yhwh. With respect to the decalogue Childs observes: "The commandments were not arbitrary stipulations which had unwittingly assumed an importance. Rather, they reflected the essential character of God himself."[268] This statement can be extended to the other legal parts of Exodus.[269] The effect of characterisation through the content of a commandment has already been observed above, when considering the link between the desired loyalty of Israel and the cultic commandments of the prohibition of foreign worship

---

sich allein haben will,… Der götzendienerische Abfall von IHM gleicht der Untreue des Weibes, die sich zur Dirne macht. Gottes 'unduldsamer' Eifer ist also das Gegenteil von unsittlicher Lauheit und Schwäche und der Schmerz darüber, wie die geliebte Person der Treue Hohn spricht und den Eifer herausfordert …" (Jacob 1997, 561).

[266] Cf. Josh. 24:19: But Joshua said to the people, "You are not able to serve Yhwh, for he is a holy God. He is a jealous God; he will not forgive your transgressions or your sins."

[267] The reader encounters a similar *inclusio,* featuring the theme of loyalty to Yhwh, in Exod. 20:7 and 23:13. The misuse of the divine name or the use of names of other gods would be a major breach of the expected loyalty. I include a more detailed discussion below, under the heading, The Implications of the Form of the Law Collection, p.116.

[268] Childs 1976, 397.

[269] Childs would not agree to this because of his distinction between the decalogue, which is "direct, unmediated communication of Yahweh himself", and all other regulations of the Torah (Childs 1976, 397). This distinction cannot be sustained from my point of view, because of the obvious strategy of the author to put all law directly into Yhwh's mouth. Thus, for the reader of the extant text all law is direct divine communication and is covered by the same divine authority.

in all forms (Exod. 20:2-6). There the link to characterisation was explicit, whereas the following comments arise from the assumption that a similar rhetorical force is linked to the content of a regulation even, if it is there only implicitly.

Meinrad Limbeck argues, convincingly, that the biblical texts concerned with the legal actions of Yhwh endorse a concept of law which displays Yhwh's positive, life-enabling and life-sustaining attitude.[270] The regulations of Exodus should be understood as Yhwh's means to express his desire for life and to enable behaviour that protects life and sustains the divinely-given order of the universe. In support, Limbeck investigates the following two features of the *mišpatim* of Exod. 21:18–22:16: the principle of restitution and the possibility of understanding the book of the covenant as an articulation of Yhwh's binding benevolence, i.e. the divine interest in the well-being of the people which in turn requires obedience (*"Artikulation eines verpflichtenden Wohlwollens"*[271]).

The principle of restitution touches on the great importance assigned by the ancient Near Eastern world to material possessions which guaranteed personal security in times of need caused by age, illness or a lean harvest.[272] Hence, importance was attached to the subject by all ancient Near Eastern law collections, including the *mišpatim*. A ruler's concern with and consequent treatment of this issue would be received with great interest by the people.

---

[270] Cf. Limbeck 1997, 16 and *passim*. Even when God punishes he only does so with the pedagogical intent to bring those affected back and to encourage appropriate actions. This observation is theologically very significant and helpful. Limbeck tries to formulate this insight in a reflection on the verb פקד. His theological distinction between God caring and God punishing may be valid on the conceptual level, though the way he tries to communicate this on the verbal level seems artificial, if not outright impossible from a linguistic point of view. A verb which is listed with the following array of English equivalents – "attend to, take note of, care for, punish, muster, assemble, record, enroll, commit, appoint, call to account, avenge" (Williams 1997, 657) – can hardly carry all of its possible aspects in every given context. Limbeck tries to limit the number of translations to the more or less positive German equivalents of the caring aspect (*sich kümmern*), while rejecting a translation from the semantic field of 'punish' (*strafen/heimsuchen*) as unbiblical. To me, the caring attitude of Yhwh is aptly mirrored in the terms of punishment, commonly used biblically and extrabiblically in languages other than Hebrew, while Limbeck's differentiation (or better polarisation) appears rather artificial, for he can write: "...er [God] war ganz offensichtlich nicht willens, es *hinzunehmen*, wenn ein Mensch zum Widersacher seines alle umfassenden Wohl-wollens wurde." (Limbeck 1997, 17, his italics) He suggests that Yhwh can 'care' without any explicit pedagogical intent, which sounds more like a simple 'punishment'. Of course, given the unfortunate misconception of Yhwh's attitude toward mankind, against which he argues in his book, the aspiration to correct it is valid, though the means are difficult to sustain.

[271] Limbeck 1997, 31.

[272] For a general treatment on the dealings with social problems cf. Yaron 1993.

Interesting, with regard to the rhetorical implications, is the deviance of the *mišpatim* (specifically their so called y^e šallem-laws [from שלם pi. 'make compensation'], Exod. 21:37–22:16[273]) from the common idea that restitution is linked to the social status of the harmed.[274] The driving-force of the statutory sentence (*Rechtsfolgebestimmung*) is not Yhwh's desire to punish or merely to deter, but, rather, the desire to recompense the wronged and, thus, to restore his well-being. These reparation-payments were not intended to multiply the possessions of the wronged party, which seems to be at least one aspect of the Mesopotamian regulations with their clauses distinguishing between temple or royal possessions and private property.[275] The king would, in this case, uphold the interests of the institutionalised aspects of society and prioritise them at the expense of the private household. That Yhwh's laws did not make such a distinction reveals much about Yhwh's attitude toward Israel. Of course, this tells the reader more about the author's perception of Israel,[276] but it nevertheless, also, gives an important hint in the characterisation of Yhwh, especially as recommended by the author. It almost works similar to the classical *captatio benevolentiae* in its effect to compliment or even to flatter the audience by not making them feel inferior to the ruler in this respect. The issue of material possessions ensured the utmost attention of the reader, and the deviation from the (most likely well-known) norm showed Yhwh in the best possible light. Yhwh was concerned only with the well-being of his people, and he ensured this well-being by providing means to restore it if an individual was damaged by a fellow member of society.

BENEVOLENCE AS MOTIVATION

The second aspect mentioned above, which is rather cryptically termed by Limbeck "*verpflichtendes Wohlwollen*"[277] ('binding benevolence'), concentrates on Yhwh's intentions for the reception of the book of the covenant. Here, we meet another more or less explicit linkage between Yhwh's character and the content of the Exodus laws. Limbeck discusses various laws and how they could have been perceived by their original readers. In conclusion, he states that the

---

[273] Crüsemann suggests that these regulations are not limited to their specifics but are rather examples of a 'Grundsatzregelung' (Crüsemann 1992, 193). Given that this suggestion is probably not very disputed, the rhetorical consequences concluded in the following are even more appropriate, especially considering their general implications.

[274] Limbeck draws his more general conclusions from a comparison of Exod. 21:33–22:5 with LH ¶8 and MAL ¶¶3.4 (Limbeck 1997, 20f).

[275] Here, I do not touch upon the differences made between the free man and the slave (cf. 21:20f.26f.32), which are rooted in the nature of ancient Near Eastern debt-slavery. The dominating culture would not have perceived these differences as unjust and to introduce modern concepts of slavery would be hopelessly anachronistic (cf. Chirichigno 1993 and Dandamaev 1984).

[276] Cf. the corresponding chapter below (p.234).

[277] Limbeck 1997, 26ff.

spirit of the law can only be upheld when these regulations are read as expressions of the divine will to do good for the people.[278] The laws of the book of the covenant are open to misuse by the powerful at the expense of the underprivileged. To use them this way would, certainly, be outside the author's intentions and, implicitly, Yhwh's intentions, which, according to E. Otto, is the 'ethic of solidarity'.[279] The positive intentions of the law-giver are apparent at the text level in the regulations containing motive-clauses (or similarly functioning phrases), in the concentration on groups representing the margins of society, and in legal ideas that are difficult to enforce. The interesting observation for the present context is that the author of the book of the covenant wants his readers to orientate their actions by Yhwh's own behaviour.[280]

> And the foreigner you shall not maltreat, neither shall you oppress him, for foreigners you have been in the land of Egypt. The widow and the orphan you shall not afflict. If you indeed afflict him, if then he indeed cries out to me, I will indeed listen to his crying. And it will be kindled my anger, and I will kill you with the sword, and your wives shall become widows and your children, orphans. (Exod. 22:20-23)

> If you lend money to (any of) my people, to the poor among you, you shall not be like a creditor to him, and you shall not exact interest from him. If ever you take your neighbour's cloak in pledge, you shall return it at sunset, for it is his only covering, and it is his cloak for his skin; in what else shall he sleep? And if it is that he cries to me, I will listen, for I am compassionate. (Exod. 22:24-26)

> If you meet your enemy's ox or his donkey going astray, you shall bring it back to him. If you see the donkey of one who hates you lying down under its burden, you shall refrain from leaving him with it; you shall rescue it with him. (Exod. 23:4-5)

> You shall not bend the justice of your poor in his lawsuit. Keep far from a word of deceit, and do not kill the innocent and righteous, for I will not justify the wrong. And you shall take no bribe, for a bribe makes blind the seeing and it will pervert the cause of those who are in the right. (Exod. 23:6-8)

Yhwh will hear the oppressed's cries and this hearing implies that he will uphold their rights which have been infringed upon by the oppressor addressed by the law. This applies to the foreigner, widow or orphan, as well as to the poor

---

[278] Cf. Limbeck 1997, 26–31.

[279] Cf. Otto 1991, 167.

[280] Considering the different motive-clauses in the other legal parts of the Pentateuch, we encounter an interesting fact in Exodus. The clause אני יהוה אלהיכם ("I am Yhwh, your god"), which is so frequent in Lev. 18–20; 23–26, does not appear in the Exodus law texts, but only in references to the Exodus events (6:7; 16:12), where it provides the information that it was Yhwh, and no other god, who brought them out of slavery. In Leviticus the mere name is used to motivate law-obedience; there seems no need to argue that Yhwh is the Israelite god.

person needing to borrow money (Exod. 22:22+26).[281] Even more explicit is the
characterisation of Yhwh as the one who will never pervert justice. Thus, Yhwh
becomes the model of justice for the Israelite community. These regulations
contrast God himself (the righteous and caring God) with the offender to encourage obedience by posing a threat for an eventual perpetrator. These 'sentences' are not so much a statutory penalty (it is not possible to give them into
the hand of an executive) as they are more a rhetorical threat intended to effect
an emotional force.[282] This characterises God's interest in these issues of righ-
teousness and loving care and helps to make less abstract the idea of a God who
desires the well-being of all humans. The phrase כִּי־חַנּוּן אָנִי (22:26 "for I am
compassionate") achieves the same effect in a more straightforward way. The
emotion that is desired on the part of Israel is here mentioned directly. God is
compassionate and this informs his ideals of law and justice. The result of
God's listening to the oppressed is not mentioned in this case but will easily be
supplied by the reader according to the previous regulation.[283] The rhetorical
device of encouraging law obedience by appealing to the emotions of the readers works especially well when these emotions are, also, endorsed by God. This
support, from the highest authority available, reflects the divine character.
Again one can observe how important the characterisation of Yhwh is for the
legal corpus of Exodus. The reverse and equally valid conclusion is that the perception of Yhwh's character is shaped by the way the legal corpus is written.

Yhwh's concern that all members of society care for each other's welfare is a
dominant feature of the book of the covenant.[284] Exod. 23:4-5 makes this point

---

[281] Widows, orphans, the resident alien, and the poor are some of the typically underprivileged persons in the Old Testament, as the motif-like phraseology of the following
passages shows: Deut. 10:18; 24:17; 27:19; Ps. 146:9; Isa. 1:17.23; Jer. 7:6; 22:3; Ezek.
22:7; Zech. 7:10; Mal. 3:5. Cf. also Houtman 2000, 217f. Given that this stylistic device
of *merismus* is active in Exod. 22:21, it is nevertheless also used in a literal sense here:
the repetition of the widows and orphans in v.23 only works on rhetorical grounds if
widows and orphans are really meant by these words. The link to reality, here, is supported by the common ancient Near Eastern notion of the king showing compassion toward the poor and weak. For a telling quotation from a Hittite hymn cf. Otto 1991, 166.
Especially with respect to the justice for the poor, Otto views the role of Yhwh as parallel to the role of the ancient Near Eastern king.

[282] For a more detailed analysis of the rhetorical strategy used here see the chapter on
sanction statements below (p.108ff).

[283] These 'gaps' (cf. Sternberg) allow for the readers' participation and serve to encourage engagement at a deeper level than would be possible with an explicit text. The presence of such gaps in 'law texts' shows the model of legal writing behind the book of the
covenant is different than the model which informs today's legal texts in the western
hemisphere. This demands a different reading strategy, as has been suggested above.

[284] This may already be seen in the fourth commandment of the Decalogue to honour
ones parents, as has been pointed out by Beulke 2004, who considers this law as applying primarily to the elderly parents.

in a very powerful way.[285] Even though no explicit mention is made of Yhwh's character, the mere content of the law makes clear that Yhwh's benevolence is the motivation behind these two exhortations. Both mention emotional worst-case scenarios. To help a friend or a family member in these exemplary situations would be regarded as a matter of course. No regulation would be necessary in this case. But "your enemy" and "the one who hates you"[286] are not the natural recipients of one's benevolence. Maybe this is why v.4f break up the thematic sequence of 23:1-3 and 6-8.[287] Not only shall *Justitia* be blindfolded, but the book of the covenant requires that one look after the well-being of others, without respect of person.[288] The rhetorical strategy, here, is one of directness where implicitness in expression is expected: איב as well as שנא are quite explicit words. The use of the two *imperfect absolutus* forms pointedly stress the required action, and, most interesting, we find mention of what one would normally do in cases like that: וחדלת מעזב לו ("and desist from leaving it to him"). Here, the reader must feel caught. Furthermore, v.5 seems to be deliberately artistic in its choice of words. The rhetorical devices of *paronomasia*[289] and *polyptoton*[290] used in v.5b provide a play on words and leave the reader in

---

[285] Otto arrives at the same conclusion via a different avenue. He compares the *Wirkungsgeschichte* of the book of the covenant's ethical appeals (of course, they belong, for him, to the deuteronomistic redaction of the book of the covenant) with the long-term effects of the *mišarum* acts of the old Babylonian epoch. The actual social impact of these regulations, which attempted to bring together (the practice of) law and (the ideal of) justice, can no longer be traced (Otto 1991, 167f).

[286] Speculating why the difficult relationships arose in the first place is futile and adds nothing to the understanding of the text (e.g. TPsJ: "whom you despise because of a fault that only you know of"; Cf. Houtman 1997, 263 for a brief recollection of the discussion).

[287] Jackson offers a different rationale: "The message of the literary structure, taken as a whole, is that enmity must neither subvert the administration of justice, nor interfere with the observance of ethical behaviour." (Jackson 2000, 224) Jackson reads the text 'from the inside out', i.e. takes the explicit theme of enmity in v.4-5 into the framework of 1-3 and 6-8, where this theme is not present in the same way. From my point of view, this construction is less probable than the unifying theme of impartiality.

[288] Houtman 1997, 265 is quite right to reject the understanding that we observe here, the expression of some theoretical ideal of love for one's enemy. It is, rather, the practical concern for another's basis of livelihood, whether enemy or friend.

[289] The play on semantically different usages of the same root. Commonly understood, a *paronomasia* plays with a slight change in part of a word to create a (usually extreme) semantic tension (cf. Plett 1991, 38).

[290] The use of the same root in different grammatical forms.

uncertainty because of the created ambiguity.[291] All of this, of course, helps to make the point appealing in the emotional world of the reader. This is not what one would expect from a legal text which – at least by modern standards – should be devoted to clarity and unambiguousness. The effect of heightened attention is amplified by the immediate context dealing with court-room issues.

The fourth law quoted above, also, touches upon the theme of benevolence. The proper administration of justice restores well-being where it has been violated and is, thus, an act of benevolence toward the wronged party. Exod. 23:6-8 uses the rhetorical device of contrast: possible injustice in a court situation is set against the justice upheld by the ultimate authority. The sentence דיקכי לא־אץ ארשׁע (23:7b "I will not justify the wrong-doer") is another first-person speech of Yhwh with which the author of the book of the covenant looks above the horizon of the inner-worldly matters covered in the law. The person presiding over the judicial court must be aware of his responsibility to the ultimate judge: God will not justify a perpetrator. This statement is, apparently, intended to function as a motive-clause to put pressure on the legal *personae* of Israel to reproduce God's attitude toward justice. As in the previous case, we encounter a gap[292] in that the reader needs to supply the detail of why this statement – "I will not justify the wrong-doer" – should prevent them from doing the opposite. The most likely options for filling this 'rhetorical' gap are the desire to imitate God or the fear of consequences in the case of unjust judgements. We need not decide on either one, for in both cases it is the character 'Yhwh' who stands in the background and implies law-keeping. The judge or other judicial representative is under the same accountability to Yhwh, even as is the 'normal' citizen to whom all other regulations of the book of the covenant apply.

In Exod. 23:1-8, the reader can detect a meta-communicational level in that the practice of law and order in Israel is raised as an issue. Crüsemann hints at this additional level, commenting on Exod. 23:1-8:

> Das Gotteswort in v.7b formuliert, worum es zuallererst gehen muß: daß Schuldige und Unschuldige zu je ihrem Recht kommen. So wie Gott im Gegenüber zu Unterdrückten und Armen gnädig ist (22,26), so ist er derjenige, der nicht recht-

---

[291] The verb עזב is used twice with two, almost opposite meanings: first, the addressee shall not *leave* the troubled party alone, then the action of helping is described as *freeing/restoring* (the donkey from the heavy load to enable it to get to its feet again). There is an open discussion whether there are two different roots of עזב here (or even in general; cf. Ges-B; BDB; *KBL*; *THAT*, II, 249; *ThWAT*, V, 1200f). Whatever the case, the text offers this accumulation of עזב, a fact that certainly works on the rhetorical level. Houtman dismisses the idea of a pun here, but without any reasoning (Houtman 1997, 268). In the end it remains difficult to reproduce the rhetorical nuances in translation, which has been the case in general from the Targumim and the LXX onwards.

[292] Cf. n.283 above!

fertigt und nicht gerecht spricht, wo es um den Schuldigen geht. Das zu verhin-
dern ist Absicht des vorliegenden Textes wie des gesamten Bundesbuchs.[293]

Yhwh becomes the example for the people regarding judicial issues, which is
displayed concretely in the present passage referring to court decisions but,
also, throughout the book of the covenant in the very content of the laws included in the book of the covenant. The theme of justice in Israel, which dominates the legal parts of Exodus at the formal level, is invariably linked with the
divine character at the content level. The introduction of Yhwh into the legal
collection enhances the rhetorical force by constructing it entirely as divine
speech. At essential points, the author refers to divine characteristics, such as
his benevolence, and encourages the reader to adopt this attribute, even on the
threat of consequences, which is why Limbeck's term 'binding benevolence' is
so apt.

SANCTION STATEMENTS

Sanction depends, by its very nature, on the prior characterisation of the person
uttering it for its effectiveness, i.e., its persuasive power.[294] This rhetorical relationship between sanction and character warrants the discussion of the issue in
the present context. I will discuss two different groups of sanction clauses found
in Exodus, guilt- and shame-oriented sanctions. It will emerge that the rhetorical
strategies on which they draw depend heavily on the cultural and societal background of the legal collection.

Guilt-Oriented Sanction

In the legal parts of Exodus we find several clauses which are apparently designed to motivate law obedience. There are four types of sanction statements
found in the book of the covenant: death penalty, compensation, the calculable
loss of property and the implicit withdrawal of blessing. Several very severe
offences carry the consequence of death for the perpetrator. The most common
formulation in this case is the intense מוֹת יוּמָת (cf. Exod. 21:12.15.16.17; 22:18;
31:14.15). Murder (cf. also 21:14.29), disrespectful behaviour against parents,
slave-trading, certain sexual abuses, and religious offences (especially profanation of holy things or days; cf. 28:35.43; 30:20-21; 35:2) can be penalised with
death. It may be deduced that the reader should be introduced to the value-

---

[293] Crüsemann 1992, 222.

[294] Jackson also refers to this link but considers it as being a lower developmental level
in legal reasoning (Jackson 2000, 112). Proper justification would not have been important, since as the *auctoritas* of the legislator would provide enough gravity to imply obedience. Only in later, more developed law collections would one find motive-clauses.
Jackson links this proposed development to Piaget's research on the development of
children. I do not agree that societies which are the ultimate source of law, necessarily
develop along the same lines or take similar developmental steps as humans do while
growing up. Jackson's equation seems oversimplified and is unconvincing.

system of the law-giver by exemplary mention of the most serious offences. The sanction of compensation,[295] often connected with the recurrent phrase שלם ישלם, is found in the rather homogeneous unit 20:18–22:16. Compensation for the loss of the injured party in the cases of bodily harm seems to be ruled by the *ius talionis* which secures the appropriateness of the sanction (21:22-27[296]). In the case of theft we find 'over'-compensation (21:37; 22:3.6.8). With the slave-laws the calculable loss of property functions as sanction (21:11 and also 21:21-22).[297] These statements of sanction are quite explicitly attached to a concrete statement of offence.[298] This is what a modern reader – and probably, also, an ancient Israelite reader – would expect from the formulation of most law collections. But we find two larger blocks of material which, arguably, also belong to the group of sanction statements in Exodus because of their similar rhetorical function. In Exod. 23:20-33 and in 34:10-26 indirect sanction is expressed by the implicit withdrawal of blessing. The rhetorical strategy is not to impose a

---

[295] Cf. the section on benevolence on p.103. Otto's chronological stratification of the Israelite law system, moving from an '*innergentalem Restitutionsrecht*' to a '*intergentalem Sanktionsrecht*' (Otto 1988, 61ff), would consequently exclude the *jᵉšallēm*-laws from the discussion of 'sanction'. Because I am working from an entirely different understanding of the nature of the biblical text and, hence, an entirely different hermeneutic and because my aim is not to write a history of law of the ancient Near East, I find no need to discuss pre-textual forms. For a critical discussion of Otto's theses cf. Osumi 1991, 11ff and Crüsemann 1992, 178f. Viewed from a different set of premises, there is no need to create an opposition between compensation and sanction, for compensation is, in my opinion, logical at the level of sanction. Its rhetorical aim is to motivate law obedience.

[296] Exod. 21:22-27 is a complex example: A specific law gives the subject (21:22), then the principle of *talion* is provided (23-25), and two further examples for its application are provided (26-27). That monetary compensation is meant has been rightly argued by a number of ancient and recent scholars. For a thorough discussion see Jacob 1997, 661–673. For recent literature cf. Otto 1994, 73–81. Dohmen 2004b, 165f, however, considers the *talio* as compensation for the cases where material compensation is not possible. Interesting for the present context is Jacob's evaluation that the ancient Near Eastern law-codes' *talio* principles ultimately intend to restore the honour of the injured party. The social status of the involved parties dictates the exact measures for the expiation of the dishonouring act. Here we find another example of a shame-oriented culture which treats offences according to an entirely different cultural or ideological framework than modern western cultures do. This fact often contributes to the puzzlement of modern readers of ancient texts.

[297] See also LE ¶49, which treats theft of slaves as parallel to other thefts. Roth is right to understand *iredde* here as meaning "to bring along for the stolen slave another slave of the same value" (Roth 1997, 70, n.26), i.e. double compensation.

[298] Crüsemann concludes his section on the Mišpatim with a stimulating discussion of the differences between the modern western concept of retaliation in criminal law and the Mišpatim's model of "*Täter-Opfer-Ausgleich*", with its attempt to restore the rights and property of the wronged party (cf. Crüsemann 1992, 198f). The same argument has been re-emphasised more recently by Graupner 2005, 466–470.

threat by mentioning a punishment for a specific offence, but, rather, to paint a picture of national well-being whose realisation is dependent on obedience.

The closure of the book of the covenant, Exod. 23:20-33, refers in a general way to law-obedience: ועשית כל אשר אדבר (... and do all that I said ...; 23:22aβ). That this includes the entire book of the covenant is suggested by the only explicit law mentioned in the context:

> Do not prostrate yourself before their gods nor serve them, nor act according their works, rather you shall pull them down entirely and destroy their *mazzeboth* entirely. You shall serve the Yhwh your God, and he will bless your bread and your water, and I will take sickness away from your midst. None will miscarry or be sterile in your land. The number of your days I will make full. (Exod. 23:24-26)

The parallels in theme to the altar law (Exod. 20:24) are obvious and have been discussed above.[299] Hence, we can view this allusion to the beginning of the book of the covenant as *inclusio*, inviting the reader to view the entire enfolded law collection as "all that Yhwh said".[300]

Exod. 34:10-20, again, recalls many connections with 23:20-33.[301] The exhortation to keep Yhwh's words or laws (23:22aβ || 34:11a) makes the explicit connection to legal sanction. That this happens in the ideational context of a covenant does not necessarily affect the rhetorical force of these longer, implicit sanction statements, which must be viewed as quite similar in their rhetorical force to the more explicit sanction statements dealt with previously. But beyond the 'normal' psychological effect of fear induced by a rhetoric of sanction, the longer sections offer a theological reasoning for the law. Watts makes this notion concrete by stating that this kind of sanction[302] "provide[s] the most extended depictions of God's willingness to bless or curse in response to Israel's behaviour. The speeches characterize their speaker as wishing to reward but willing to punish in order to maintain the covenant."[303]

---

[299] See p.96ff.

[300] This, of course, is nothing new, for as we saw before, the shaping of the entire law collection as direct divine utterance is dominant for the reader.

[301] The immediate literary context, alone, makes the parallel obvious: there is the mention of the major festivals (Exod. 23:13-17 || 34:10-16) and the puzzling commands of 23:17-18 || 34:25-26, though in reverse order.

[302] Watts' category of 'divine sanction' is a rather vague generic term. It may include even the entire book of Deuteronomy (cf. Watts 1999, 57ff) as well as the brief passages of the various law collections in the Torah.

[303] Watts 1996, 9. Watts observes, in the case of the Exodus law collections, that sanction can be scattered in motivational clauses, but its main expressions are found in the larger groups of blessings and curses that conclude the legal collections of the Pentateuch (Exod. 23:20-33; Lev. 26; Deut. 27–28). We need to keep in mind his proposal of a pentateuchal rhetoric of story, list and divine sanction (cf. Watts 1999). To sum up his main results: The narrative parts ('story') are to ground the legal lists in authoritative

The result – at the ideational level – is, in my opinion, what Eckart Otto terms 'theologising of law' (*Theologisierung des Rechts*).[304] Israel's law is in-extricably bound to the divine law giver. A further rhetorical analysis of the sanction elements in the book of the covenant will establish this result and pro-vide an even stronger link to the theme of divine character, which is still the driving force of the present discussion.

Shame-Oriented Sanction

When reading the book of the covenant rhetorically, it emerges that 'proper' sanction – the threat of certain punishment (or the withdrawal of blessing) – is just one possible way to motivate law obedience. Other motive-clauses use a different rhetorical technique. They touch upon the psychological effects of awe, thankfulness and logic. The structure of their motivational force is reflec-ted in the following paraphrases: "you know how I (i.e. God) am, so behave in the same way" (e.g. 22:26; 23:7); "you know how life can be from your own ex-perience, so ..." (e.g. 22:21-23 [+25-26]; 20:20 ‖ 23:9); and "you know me (i.e. God) from past experiences, therefore abide by my law" (e.g. 20:22). To under-stand the rhetorical device behind this kind of motive-clause I would like to draw attention to a study by Lyn Bechtel,[305] who, informed by anthropological and psychological studies, introduces two categories of sanction found in bibli-cal texts: shame as sanction and punishment as sanction. The rhetorical force behind the 'proper' sanctions, as named above, is clearly the fear aroused by impending punishment, and hence this rhetorical force is based on the concept of 'guilt'.[306] The other forms of motive-clauses mentioned may well fit into

---

common history. So the stories function as legitimation of the origin of the law and its application to Israel. The lists record the desired results in the addressees' present life-style, are focused on the ideal and are therefore aimed at belief and behaviour. By at-taching blessings and curses ('divine sanction') to story and law-list, religion is drawn in to increase the power of persuasion. Sanction aims to motivate.

[304] Cf. Otto 1991, 165.

[305] Cf. Bechtel 1991. She draws greatly on works published in the 1950s and earlier. It is only recently that psychologists have developed a new interest in the subject (personal communication with the missiologist Prof. Dr. Klaus W. Müller, Gießen). The important book by Mary Douglas (Douglas 1973) and several later anthropological and missio-logical studies affirm the importance of the concepts of guilt and shame in the fabric of a culture. Assmann 2000, 134ff, observes a similar phenomenon in Egypt and, also, in Is-rael. He adds a new dimension to the difference between a diachronic and a synchronic orientation of guilt or shame respectively. Clines 2007, 7–8, uses the same categories as Bechtel to shed additional light on the rationale of certain sanctions in the book of the covenant. For a recent general overview see Wiher 2003.

[306] Bechtel considers the emotional function of guilt as "accompanied by the fear of pun-ishment." Guilt is invoked by an injury of one's conscience: "the internalized, societal and parental prohibitions or boundaries that cannot be transgressed (as opposed to the internalized goals and ideals)." (Bechtel 1991, 53)

Bechtel's 'shame'-category: "The emotional response of shame relates to the anxiety aroused by 'inadequacy' or 'failure' to live up to internalized, societal and parental goals and ideals."[307] Guilt relates to prohibitions, whereas shame relates to the violation of ideals. As an example of shame as sanction from the Torah, Bechtel mentions Deut. 25:1-3 and 5-10.[308] Apart from these obvious examples outside of Exodus, I consider the rhetorical force of the specified passages, above, as being, partly, dependent on shame and, partly, linked to the character of Yhwh, the one in whose mouth the laws are placed and whose person is supposed to guarantee justice in Israel.

Significantly, we find an appeal to the reader's emotions in the introductory sentence to the book of the covenant: "You have seen how from heaven I spoke with you, therefore you must not make in my presence …" (Exod. 20:22b+23). Apart from recalling the past narrative at the beginning of a new unit, the author places his addressee rhetorically in the midst of the people standing there at Sinai, the people who have heard and seen the terrifying presence of Yhwh. In my opinion, Houtman's interpretation is valid: he suspects the reader adds the following thought in his imagination: "weil ich euch sehen ließ, wer ich bin (s. 20,22), und ihr wißt, wer ich bin, darum sollt ihr …"[309] The knowledge of the divine person provides the reason for law obedience. The reader feels responsible to Yhwh because of the (covenant) relationship on which Exodus bases law obedience.[310] A relationship is based on mutual knowledge, and the reader knows certain facts about Yhwh which are provided by the author in the earlier parts of his book. This god, as portrayed in these chapters, is a mighty king who has a motherly concern for his people. Disobedience of his law should lead to shame because of the discrepancy between the people's trespassing the law and Yhwh's acts for their well-being. Inadequacy – according to Bechtel, one of the emotions closely related to shame – will be felt: 'how can such a person belong to this god's covenant people?' Highlighting the appeal to shame in this single 'law' might appear a little ambitious, nevertheless, it is at least one aspect which motivates law obedience here.

The picture of law-motivation in the book of the covenant is further clarified when we look at the other instances where law is not sanctioned by the threat of concrete punishment: 22:26; 23:7 and 22:21-23 (+25-26); 22:20 ‖ 23:9. The reasoning of the first two passages is very similar to the that found in 20:22. Yhwh

---

[307] This is the definition she accepts (Bechtel 1991, 49).

[308] Cf. Bechtel 1991, 57ff and 61f. These references from the Torah are certainly appropriate and make a valid point in her discussion; nevertheless they do not go far enough. The concept of shame as sanction is not limited to the actual presence of the Hebrew words for 'shame'.

[309] Houtman 1997, 51. Obviously, the contrast between heaven and the material god-images is the dominant rhetorical device used in this passage. This, nevertheless, does not exclude the interpretation given below – it just serves on a different level.

[310] Cf. Limbeck 1997, 33. See also the paragraph on loyalty above (p.98)!

is compassionate and will not justify the wrong. Hence, any behaviour lacking compassion and any partial judgement will not be set against a legal standard but against a theological one. Because it addresses the sphere of human existence it goes much deeper than the threats of compensation or loss of property.[311] The remaining passages have already been discussed above from a different angle.[312] There, it was clear that Yhwh's character – and, hence, his behaviour – is the rod against which the Israelite's actions will be measured. Furthermore the reader is threatened with being shamed. This conclusion is reinforced by a number of observations on the regulation found in Exod. 22:21-23:

> You shall not mistreat any widow or fatherless child. If you do mistreat them, and they cry out to me, I will surely hear their cry, and my wrath will burn, and I will kill you with the sword, and your wives shall become widows and your children fatherless.

Firstly, one may point to its highly repetitive structure: 22:20 draws the parallel between the foreigner in Israel and Israel's former status as foreigners (cf. the repetition in 23:9) – a motivation from retrospect.[313] 22:21-23 use a similar structure in paralleling prospectively: if you maltreat widows or orphans, your family will be widowed and orphaned. This formulation is logically redundant if the oppressor is killed. It implies immediately that the spouse and children receive the status described. This redundant way of putting things is highly effective, rhetorically, in that it evokes all the emotions that are linked with the theme 'widows and orphans'. The anger that befalls a person who thinks that someone else could maltreat their spouse or children is the very same anger that Yhwh feels. In the prospective case of infringement the reader will feel intense shame, "for that is certainly not a thing to be done in Israel" (cf. Gen. 34:7). The strategy of drawing from easily imaginable real-life situations (becoming a widow or orphan; having no cover for the night) and – collective, if not personal – past experiences (being slaves in Egypt) of the reader has nothing to do with sanction proper. There is no statutory sentence here but an appeal to the

---

[311] For Sneed 1999, 502, this is a definite shortcoming of the law in Exodus (and in other parts of the Old Testament). On Exod. 22 he comments, "Note also that this is in apodictic form, and thus there is no fixed penalty for the violation of this value, except perhaps shame. No doubt the collectors knew it would not to be enforced. And that may be the point." (504) Or: "It was in the self-interest of the royal or priestly rule to protect the resident aliens since they needed their cheap labor." (504). The lack of proper judgements would provide reason enough to suspect the authors of the Pentateuch as guarding their power by half-heartedly mentioning the potential of divine judgement.

[312] Cf. p.104 above.

[313] This motivation bears upon the characterisation of Israel which will be dealt with in the corresponding paragraphs below (cf. p.234).

emotions of disgrace and fear of what 'the others' will think of oneself if such a thing were done.[314]

Surprisingly, given the relation between shame and personal honour, we find that the appeal to shame as sanction in Exodus is not distinct from the 'theologising of law', to which I already referred. All instances of shame as sanction refer to Yhwh as the leading principle for ethical behaviour. That this could have been done otherwise is suggested by Deuteronomy's mention of shaming sanction without specific reference to the divine sphere (Deut. 25:1-3. 5-10). How is the association with the divine character for this kind of sanction to be explained? The reason may be found in the specific communicative interest of Exodus. Shame works especially well as sanction when it is used in a group-oriented society in which honour, personal standing, pride and respect are the highest values. Bechtel argues that this was the case for ancient Israel. Inevitably, there is potential for the misuse of shaming in such a culture.[315] Exodus seems to set up barriers against such a misuse. We can learn from many cultures that an honour-shame paradigm consolidates the already-existing social layering[316] – a fact which can, for instance, be seen in the different sanctions for the same offence, depending on the social status of the wronged person (e.g. LE ¶¶23-24, 52-57(58?); CH ¶¶8, 196-214).[317] That there was a similar situation in the Israel, which the author of Exodus has in mind, is suggested by a notion of discontent expressed in the regulations betraying an ideal of unity and equality[318] among the people. The author's social ideal is based on the idea that every-

---

[314] "The functions of the sanction of shame are primarily: 1. as a means of social control which attempts to repress aggressive or undesirable behavior; 2. as a pressure that preserves social cohesion in the community through rejection and the creation of social distance between the deviant members and the social group; 3. as an important means of dominating others and manipulating social status." (Bechtel 1991, 53).

[315] Cf. the reason given for the restriction to forty strokes in Deut. 25:3.

[316] This interpretation may be underscored by the fact that modern societies which have not been strongly influenced by western reformation and enlightenment thought – like many Asian cultures – are, usually, rigidly layered societies. The notions of honour and pride forbid mixing with lower levels of society, and the interests within peer-groups tend to be much more important than abstract ideas of justice and morality.

[317] Cf. also Jakob's remarks on the *ius talionis*, already referred to above (p.109 n.296). Especially relevant in the present context is his discussion of the different honour assigned to the different classes appearing in LH ¶¶202–205 (*awīlum, muškēnum.* and *wardum*). Not a monetary compensation for the restoration of damaged property is made but some sort of re-establishment of the honour of the struck person.

[318] Cf. regulations like Exod. 21:12 (in its generality); 22:20-26+23:9 (in their care for the underprivileged); and 23:3+6 (both extremes mentioned). Besides these regulations inside of the book of the covenant, the principle is already stated in Exod. 12:49 (see also the parallels in Lev. 16:29; 17:15; Num. 9:14; 15:15-16). For Deuteronomy cf. Otto 1991, 167, who draws on Lohfink 1990: "Wurde das Recht nicht staatlich aufgesogen, so konnte es Fehlentwicklungen im Staate entgegentreten, zu einer kritischen Instanz werden und wie im Deuteronomium die Einheit des Volkes im Gotteswillen begründen,

one is equally part of the divinely-chosen nation.[319] This is the point where the theologising of law comes into play. The author of Exodus justifies law by linking law with the divine, which is different from the ancient Near Eastern justification of law,[320] or as Otto puts it:

> In der Königszeit entwickelte Israel Motive der theologischen Rechtsbegründung, die denen der atlbabylonischen Keilschrifttexte verwandt, aber doch charakteristisch von ihnen geschieden waren. Mit sozialer Differenzierung israelitischer Gesellschaft wurde die Integration der Armen und Schwachen zu einer Aufgabe des Rechts, die es in seiner Frühzeit nicht gehabt hatte und die nun zum Einfallstor einer umfassenden Theologisierung des Rechts und der Ausbildung eines sozialen Ethos der Solidarität Gottes mit den Schwachen wurde.[321]

Hence, we detect in Exodus a new persuasive level: the authority of an ideational principle based on the personality of Yhwh, i.e. his solidarity with the weak. The specific portrayal of Yhwh in Exodus enables the author to move this way. The effectiveness of this principle does not rely on the threat of exclusion from society and is, thus, more guilt- than shame-oriented.[322] If violated, the ethos does not pose imminent social danger to the perpetrator, but it catches him in the sphere of guilt and sin which is present in the human-divine relationship. This retreat to a means of sanction, other than shame, can effectively work against the potential misuse of shaming. Otto describes the social effects of this innovative justification of law:

> Die Überwindung des Grabens zwischen Recht und Gerechtigkeit wird im Gegensatz zum altbabylonischen Recht der *mīšarum*-Akte nicht in einem zeitweiligen Außerkraftsetzen des Rechts zugunsten der Schwachen gesucht, sondern in der Aufforderung zu ethischem Handeln zugunsten der Armen im Rahmen des bestehenden Rechts. Wurde im Gegensatz zum altbabylonischen Recht, das dem König die Šamaš-Funktion der Rechtsdurchsetzung zuwies, im israelitischen Recht JHWH zum Subjekt der Rechtsdurchsetzung, so war das Recht in Israel auch davor geschützt, in staatlicher Organisation aufzugehen und ihr dienstbar zu werden.[323]

---

wo es in den sozialen und politischen Konflikten zerbrach."

[319] See p.239 below!

[320] That this represents quite a discontinuity with the ancient Near Eastern mode of the justification of law (*Rechtsbegründung*), which is strongly based on kingly ideology, was discussed above (cf. p.85).

[321] Otto 1991, 165. Of course, we can detect Otto's evaluation of the different redactional layers in the legal collections of the Pentateuch, but his comment on the last redaction is certainly valid. The theologising of law has infiltrated the book of Exodus, and it cannot be neglected.

[322] The call for impartiality in court (Exod. 23:2f.6-8) is probably the most marked sign of this guilt-oriented approach to justify norms. The honour of the accused or accuser is not to be considered in the decision.

[323] Otto 1991, 167.

At the foundation lies a change of ideational perspectives which needs to be communicated. To this end, the author uses the portrayal of Yhwh as the ultimate source of law, including the divine concern for the underprivileged and the description of the relationship between the people and Yhwh as covenant.

This does not mean that the author can do without using the rhetorical force of shaming, but he introduces Yhwh as one in front of whom the reader does not want to be humiliated. Of course, this works only as long as Yhwh is known to the reader and only as soon as he internalises the underlying ideals. These ideals are expressed in all their complexity in the character Yhwh. The picture of him emerging from the legal collections of Exodus provides the reader with the divine perspective on several issues, including the everyday ones.

Before I conclude the chapter on the legal characterisation of Yhwh, I want to do justice to the principle claim of rhetorical criticism that content, form and function belong together in any given text. Thus, the following section will concentrate on the internal framework of the legal parts of Exodus and its implications for the portrayal of the divine character.

The Implications of the Form of the Law Collection

The fact that the book of the covenant appears as law collection in a well-known format enforces the ideational link between the ancient Near Eastern king and Yhwh, which has been argued above (p.85f). Before I come to the distinctions between biblical and other legal collections I will briefly discuss some generic issues.

The form of the major law collection in Exodus, the book of the covenant, resembles quite closely the forms of other ancient Near Eastern legal collections. Of course, there are remarkable differences concerning the prologues and epilogues, but, on the functional level, the prologue is mirrored in the preceding exodus narrative (or, narrowed down, Exod. 19) and the epilogue, in the blessing-curse-scheme toward the end of the collection. The actual corpus of the different laws is – at least concerning formal aspects – parallel to the book of the covenant. The most prominent feature I am alluding to is the rather unsystematic sequence of laws in the book of the covenant, as well as in the ancient Near Eastern lists.

A brief reflection on the structural analysis of the law collections will provide the hermeneutical rationale behind the following discussion. Quite the opposite of many biblical critics with regard to the book of the covenant, most of the orientalists do not attempt to find a meaningful structure in the cuneiform lists, be they legal or not. After many failures to find structures in these collections, the consensus emerged that in these lists there is no all inclusive, systematic structure perceivable. The legal collections seem to be rather arbitrary collections, jumping from theme to theme. Martha Roth, however, finds groups with a certain thematic congruity. Describing how these minor structures might be formed, she summarises that

> [in] any one collection, there is a complex interplay of literary and compositional principles, of legal requirements, and of unusual cases and common circumstances. Associative principles draw law provisions together into larger blocks, and certain cases in the provisions serve as bridges linking together such blocks. [...] Within these larger groups of laws, two compositional principles – presentation of polar cases with maximal variation and juxtaposition of individual legal cases – dictate sequencing of the provisions.[324]

Hence, one can expect smaller units which might even be linked by some sort of logic, but the parallels between the ancient Near Eastern collections and book of the covenant suggest that aiming for more than that is mere speculation. This notion can be supported from a rhetorical-critical perspective: structures that are so elaborate that even a most dedicated reader hardly finds them will probably not be observed by a hearer or casual reader of the text. It is important to keep in mind that texts need to viewed from an internal perspective, not an external one.[325] Discussions about the inner structure of the book of the covenant and the laws in Exod. 34 circulate mostly among German scholars such as Crüsemann, Halbe, Osumi, and Schwienhorst-Schönberger,[326] each of whom have published on the redaction history of the legal collections in Exodus. All of them find chiastic constructions and parallel panels, though there is considerable dispute about the details and the chronological sequencing of the distinct parts of the law collections. In addition, the process-like nature of reading texts becomes a stumbling block to these studies, as the rhetorical effect of the arrangement of the material in the book of the covenant depends largely on its perception. Clearly, the proposed structures mentioned have rights in themselves, but for our present concerns – a structure's influence on the perception of Yhwh – they

---

[324] Roth, M. T. 1997, 3f. She is referring mainly to authors who turn to the structures in the laws of Ešnunna for evidence, but the context of her argument is a general one, implying that similar features are to be found in other collections.

[325] Menakhem Perry observed rightly that "[the] conception of a literary text by most researchers has been essentially static. The text is observed from above, as though it were given instantaneously in its entirety, without due consideration of its dependence on a process of reading." (Perry 1979, n.p.) This accusation is a general comment on the practice of literary studies, but it quite often applies to biblical studies as well.

[326] Their main publications include: Halbe 1975; Schwienhorst-Schönberger 1990; Osumi 1991; and Crüsemann 1992. Halbe presents the most restrained structure, which might be due to the early date of his research. One must not forget Sprinkle 1994, who also discusses larger structures in the book of the covenant (esp. 199–203) but without using diachronic arguments. His huge chiasm (A-H + H'-A') for the book of the covenant and a parallel-panel structure is another example of the unhealthy practice of finding very elaborate structures in large textual corpora. That he finds two totally different structures for the same text highlights the ambiguity and subjectivity in this kind of structural analysis.

are far too complicated and, thus, from a rhetorical perspective, more or less irrelevant.

The previous discussion attempted to set a framework in which structural observations make sense for a rhetorically concerned study. To proceed with a positive contribution I want to mention again an effect of structure which invokes cognitive connections with genre conventions or other known texts.[327] The proximity between the legal collections in Exodus and the ancient Near Eastern law compilations is a fact which can safely be taken for granted.[328] Of course, a lot of details are still being disputed. The structural parallels between the different literatures, in their lack of order and their selective choice of subjects, nevertheless, provide enough ground for some conclusions which are not too dependent on questionable connections. Westbrook[329] and Fitzpatrick-McKinley[330] would describe the book of the covenant according to the general format of ancient Near Eastern list science. A number of assyriologists, among them Bottéro,[331] Kraus,[332] and Klengel,[333] have argued for a similarity of form between the law collection of Hammurabi and the widespread list literature of the ancient Near East, such as omen texts and medical texts. The latter are understood as collections of casuistically formulated examples, and they show as little thematic ordering as the collection of Hammurabi (LH).[334] Thus, the very lack of logical over-all structures and all encyclopaedic claims by the book of the covenant moves its legal collections into the proximity of these other 'lists'. For this proximity to be effective rhetorically, there is no need to assume that the implied reader was familiar with the ancient Near Eastern list literature. Given the widespread use of this genre, the reader will understand that the book of the covenant is exactly this: an example of a list. The recognition of genre reshapes the process of reading, and, in our case, the reader will expect an unstructured, selective collection of law.

---

[327] Cf. my discussion on the presupposed knowledge of the implied readers, p.86 above.

[328] There have been numerous attempts to explain certain literary dependencies between extant law lists from the ANE and biblical material. Wright, D. P. 2004a, provides a thorough analysis in the case of the laws concerning the goring ox. This article reflects well the current discussions in this field and his conclusions are based on a detailed and balanced analysis of the relevant texts.

[329] Westbrook 1994 and Westbrook 1988.

[330] Fitzpatrick-McKinley 1999.

[331] Bottéro 1992, 156–182.

[332] Kraus 1960.

[333] Klengel 1992, 184–194.

[334] From these formal features a *Sitz im Leben* is being deduced: the House of the Tablets, which is the place for learning and science in ancient Mesopotamia. I will not go into any detail regarding the literary or social function of the law collections in Exodus. That this is an important issue was made clear at the start, but the benefit for the characterisation of Yhwh is less obvious.

So far, the discussion of the structure – or better, the lack thereof – was a discussion on a generic level. But the book of the covenant certainly has its structure, even if it is not readily apparent to our modern eyes. My hesitation concerning large chiasms or complex parallel panels has been expressed,[335] but certain other aspects of the form of the book of the covenant are, nevertheless, striking and have implications for the portrayal of the character in whose mouth the text has been placed. Two of them will be mentioned here, firstly, the inclusion of 'civil' with 'religious' regulations, and, secondly, the structure of a small but rhetorically crucial part of the book of the covenant, Exod. 22:20–23:12.

CIVIL AND RELIGIOUS LAWS – A MIXTURE

As has been seen in the previous section, the divine perspective finds its expression in the choice of themes covered in the law collections of Exodus. I have discussed in detail, above, both the socially related 'civil' laws, which are very much in line with the ancient Near Eastern parallel texts, and the religiously concerned stipulations.[336] That these two are connected in the book of the covenant is, however, a special feature in the Old Testament. Besides the law collections, there is a good amount of extant literature from the ancient Near East which records religious provisions: e.g. commemorative inscriptions relating to the founding of cults contain instructions for (re-)building the sanctuary or for the provision of cult supplies.[337] But these cultic provisions are never included in the major law collections such as LE, LH, LNB and HL.

Against this backdrop, it seems significant that in the book of the covenant we find both civil and religious regulations[338] – an innovative strategy for the compilation of a law collection. This suggests that the divine nature of the law-

---

[335] Again, I would like to refer to the article by Wright (Wright, D. P. 2004b), who comments on the various and differing attempts to find a reasonable structure of the book of the covenant. His criticism is viable and does justice to the text as we have it in the Hebrew Bible. Wright's own solution to the extant form of this text is a source-critical one in that he proposes a direct dependance in content and order of the casuistic laws on the law collection of Hammurabi (LH). This may well be the case, but this only shifts the problem a little and leaves us with two questions: Why did the author of LH create this sequence and not another? And: Why did the adaptor responsible for the book of the covenant copy this sequence as found? A source-critical approach will not be able to suggest answers.

[336] On the implications of the structure of the cultic framework of the book of the covenant cf. p.92–98, and on a number of the socially concerned laws see p.101ff and p.103ff.

[337] Cf. Watts 1996, 6f. He, again, notes as the literary purpose of these inscriptions a ruler's self-commendation as a devout worshipper, thereby guaranteeing perpetual service to the gods.

[338] That these regulations can be distinguished by any person of any culture is clear, but in the presentation of the Pentateuch it is not possible to provide a reconstruction of separate codes, one secular and one religious (cf. Weisman 1995, 411f!).

giver has something to do with these regulations. On an ideational level, the juxtaposition of 'profane' and religious legislation as expressed in Exodus[339] highlights a core-element of the biblical world view. Watts summarises this notion: God, himself, "guarantees the sacred equilibrium between heaven and earth."[340] In most ancient Near Eastern cultures this would have been the duty of the king in his quasi-priestly position between the divine and the human realm.[341] The benefits of an ordered universe affect the well-being of all. It is this possible positive outcome which helps to establish the *ethos* of the person responsible for making "wise provisions guaranteeing perpetual services to the gods",[342] which, in our case, would be the law-giver himself, Yhwh. In Exodus, the overall rhetorical effect is, again, that Yhwh appears in a positive light: he gives provisions to maintain order and repel chaos, which in turn legitimates his authority as law giver.[343]

This rhetoric is nuanced by the references to the cult in the framework of the book of the covenant (Exod. 20:22-26 and 23:13-33). In all ancient Near Eastern world views the cult secures order and fights chaos. The altar law and the festive calendar both contain core elements of the cult, and in their present shape in the book of the covenant, both delegate the responsibility for establishing what the Egyptians called *Ma'at* to the people.[344] Yhwh provides the means by which the maintenance of the cosmic order can be achieved. Each and every Israelite can, then, contribute to this order by adhering to these principles.[345]

---

[339] The detailed building instructions for the tabernacle must be mentioned here as well, but only in their functional dimension. Regarding their formal aspects it seems difficult to define them as 'law'.

[340] Watts 1996, 7.

[341] For a further reflection on this cf. Assmann 1992, 248ff, who suggests three possible concepts of *Tun-Ergehen* in ancient world views.

[342] Watts 1996, 7.

[343] Cf. Watts 1996, 7, who refers to the law collections of the entire Pentateuch, which, of course, provides more material to support his argument. In the book of the covenant one cannot only speak of a mixture of cultic and profane issues in 22:17 and the framework of the book of the covenant. Exod. 22:17+19 refers to magic practices and sacrifices to gods other than Yhwh. Dohmen 2004b, 172, argues, convincingly, that these laws, along with the *môt jûmāt*-laws of 21:12-17, are, basically, concerned with keeping together the society by guaranteeing the basic values that uphold the people. That religious issues are mentioned is significant and supports the point I am making. The order of the world and of society can only be secured when those violating foundational values are cut off from the people. Exod. 22:27-30 and 23:10-12 will be discussed in the next section.

[344] Cf. Fretheim 1991a, 203f for a very brief mention of this balance.

[345] This 'democratic' sort of sharing responsibilities is part of the discussion in the chapter below on Israel.

HOLINESS AND SOCIAL ISSUES – EXOD. 22:20-23:12

In the following brief discussion I would like to show that, at the communicative level, the text Exod. 22:20–23:12 is of utmost importance for the understanding of the book of the covenant and, in turn, for the portrayal of Yhwh.

To start with the obvious, there is a framework constructed in Exod. 22:20
and 23:9 by the repetition of the key word גר, alluding to the past experience of
Israel as גר in Egypt. Halbe understands this frameworkas providing the theme
of the entire unit and introduces the term *Sammlung 'ger'* (collection '*ger*') for
this unit.[346] 'Collection' well reflects the more cumulative nature of the text.
Despite the clear resemblances between 22:20 and 23:9, the unit does not end
with 23:9. I suggest that 23:10-12 belong to this collection as well.[347] These
verses express the concern of an institutionalised support of the weak and poor.
The relevance for our present discussion surfaces once we see the numerous
linkages between the divine character and the laws: 22:21-23 end with the reference to Yhwh's anger; 22:24-26 conclude with a note on Yhwh's compassion;
and 23:1-8 contrast an unbiased Yhwh with a potentially partial human judge.
These passages have been discussed above, so there is no need to go into any
detail here. In the context of form, it is significant that these laws, covering a
variety of issues, are accumulated here in one spot near the end of the book of
the covenant. In addition to these more socially related laws, the author includes
two blocks of a cultic concern, Exod. 22:27-30 and 23:10-12, which intermingle
with the others.

The more or less ceremonial section (Exod. 22:27-30) hardly appears to be
linked thematically with the surrounding material. The key to the interpretation
of this brief passage lies in v.30a – ואנשי־קדש תהיון לי – the "concluding formula", as Houtman calls it.[348] This phrase concludes the previous couple of
verses in that it provides the rationale for the stipulations given and, also, the
brief 'holiness-law' in v.30b. As such v.30a serves as a key phrase to prompt
the reader to establish the link between the commandments and the divine status
of the people of Israel. The surrounding material thus receives a theological
perspective in that the behaviour commanded is part of that which becomes a

---

[346] Cf. Halbe 1975, 422f.

[347] The link to the preceding section is provided again by the recurrent use of words
from the semantic field of the underprivileged (אביון, בן־אמה, גר). The mention of גר at the
end of 23:12 is quite surprising, given the beginning of the list in this verse. The other
subjects mentioned are all logically linked with the domain of work, whereas this is not
necessarily the case with the גר. (Jacob 1997, 725 finds it necessary to include the גר in
the chiasm in 23:11-12: "the needy of your people ... animals of the field" – "your bull,
your donkey ... son of your female slave, the גר". This may be the reason for including a
second element at the end of verse 12, but it does not provide a specific reason to include גר.) The effect of surprise appears to be deliberate, especially as it is placed at the
end of the entire section: Exod. 22:20–23:12 start and end with the same word.

[348] Cf. Houtman 2000, 234.

priestly kingdom and a holy nation (Exod. 19:6).[349] Compared to the extensive laws on holiness requirements in other parts of the Pentateuch (e.g. esp. Lev. 17–26), Exod. 22:27-30 only touches upon a limited few.[350] It appears, however, that these selected stipulations in the middle of a 'profane' context were enough for the author to link the holiness of Israel to their everyday life.

The same connection is supported by Exod. 23:10-12. That 23:12 explicitly refers to the seventh day is significant in the light of the other parts of the collection. The reader, having read all the preceding material, will remember the introduction to the Sabbath in the decalogue (Exod. 20:8-11 and also Exod. 16) and, thus, connect the idea of the holiness of this day with its social implications. Both cultic inclusions suggest an ideational connection between the social concerns of the book of the covenant and the divine character which is stereotypically linked with holiness. Thus, Yhwh's holiness and Yhwh's concern for the underprivileged come together in the reader's mind by way of the author's communicative strategy. The strategy used here works on a formal level: varied material has been brought together which suggests a meaning which goes beyond that of its parts. That this happens toward the end of the book of the covenant is part of the strategy and can have two effects on the reading process. Firstly, the transition from the main part of the book of the covenant into the framework is made smoother,[351] thereby subconsciously sneaking in the truth – through the back door, as it were – that God is, also, socially concerned. And, secondly, as it almost comes as an afterthought, the strategy may urge the reader to review, mentally, the earlier material and to establish the linkage consciously.

Conclusion

With regard to the portrayal of the character Yhwh, the previous discussion covered the third generic division in the book of Exodus, the legal collections. The relevance for the present enquiry has been developed, mainly, from the fact that Exodus presents its legal collections as direct divine speech. Consequently, the *ethos* of the law-speaker comes into focus. It has been argued that this rhetorical strategy leads the reader toward a new understanding of the relevance of the promoted Yhwh-religion for his everyday life. The author suggests, by merging the metaphors of the covenant god and the legislating king, that Yhwh is a worthy king, able to order the social and religious life of his followers who, also, happen to be his covenant partners. This ordering action is for the direct benefit of the people living in the realm of the king, that is, in Yhwh's presence.

---

[349] Cf. Houtman 2000, 230 and also Dohmen 2004b, 179.

[350] Houtman 1997, 246 uses the phrase "Sorge um Jhwh" (or: "treating Yhwh respectfully" Houtman 2000, 230) so that Exod. 22:27-30 is made "to express total consecration to YHWH."

[351] Compare the harsh and marked break between the introduction to the book of the covenant and Exod. 21:1.

Through the laws the reader is being introduced to God's perspective on Israel. To a modern reader, it appears as though the author wanted to bring together two conceptual levels, the social and profane sphere with the religious sphere. To an ancient reader who has not been influenced by the Kantian idea of a dichotomous world, the merging of these levels is presumably nothing especially noteworthy. Against the ancient Near Eastern background, however, the idea that a god gives a law which is applicable for all, regardless of their social standing, establishes a new perception of the role of the divine in society and in everyday life. For the author, it is the perception of Yhwh – his role, his ideas, his preferences – which redefines the relationship between the two levels and thus invests each social or profane decision with a religious significance.

This aspect was, also, established in our last step, the reflections upon the form of the collection. It has become clear that Yhwh's divine nature is an essential part of his kingly portrait. Holiness and social issues are at the heart of Yhwh's concerns. Thus, a mixture of religious and more profane stipulations is needed to reflect this reality. For the reader, it must be clear that his cultic life as well as his social life is governed by the same God, and, thus, these areas cannot be separated. It is the author's merit to create a narrative that asserts such an influence upon the reader. Further reflections on the processes of reader-identification will follow below in the chapter on the character Israel.

Yhwh, the King – a Conclusion

Jan Assmann has proposed that in Israel, as in other cultures, one can find a process which can be called the theologising of political concepts.[352] Of course, Assmann's claim goes well beyond the rhetorics of religious talk or writings, but it nicely captures what the author of Exodus presents to his implied reader. With Exodus, he offers a record of the history of Israel's foundational period. This narration is dominated by three characters: Yhwh, Moses and Israel. In the following chapters the interplay between these characters will be increasingly at the heart of the discussion. The portrayal of Moses and Israel in Exodus will strongly support the claims of the present chapter, namely that Yhwh is pictured as *the* hero and king of Israel. The author of Exodus claims that Israel's political existence depends solely on the divine initiative – a focus of the first part of Exodus (Exod. 1–18). Yhwh is the (military) hero who brought the people out of Egyptian domination. Yhwh is the king who supports and sustains them in times of great need. In the latter part of Exodus, the focus shifts to a different aspect of the kingly portrayal of Yhwh, the specifics of his relation to his people. Again, the author promotes Yhwh, this time as a king who successfully establishes law and order among his people and who, also, offers possible contact with the divine realm in the cult of the tabernacle. The political concept of king and the different roles connected with this social position are used to develop a

---

[352] Cf. Assmann 2000.

picture of a god who is involved heavily with the history and culture of Israel. Hence, Exodus offers guidance at a variety of conceptual levels. At the theological level, the God of the exodus and of the covenant is linked to the God of Genesis, i.e. the God of creation and of the fathers. At the historiographic level, the founding elements in Israel's history are, inextricably, linked with the activity of this same God. At the social level, Yhwh is introduced as the ultimate source of law, and, thus, a rhetoric of *imitatio dei* and divine sanction can be introduced as governing the life of any Israelite, and this in a far more holistic way than mere kingly legislation.

The portrait of Yhwh, painted in kingly colours, is expressed using all generic features present in Exodus. The respective genres contribute decisively to the perception of the message. Most explicitly, however, the poem in Exod. 15 speaks of Yhwh's kingship. Here, the implied reader is invited to join the narrative, and, at a religious level, Yhwh becomes the focus of the reader's worship.

The question emerges whether the author of Exodus developed his kingly portrait of Yhwh from scratch or whether he merely refined an existing metaphor for the talk about God. From a rhetorical-critical perspective, I believe there is no way to decide on this issue. The preconceptions the author suspected to be with his implied reader – regarding the role of Yhwh in the events – are not as clear as they are for the character Moses, for example. In the case of Moses, there is clearly a tension between the implied reader's conception of his role and the picture of him that emerges from the book. In the case of Yhwh, I find no such apparent tension. An area of dispute between the author and his implied reader might have been the issue of exclusivity with regard to worship. An emphasis throughout Exodus is clearly on the singularity of Yhwh's role in history and the cult. Especially, the concentration on the decalogue and the book of the covenant together with the golden calf narrative point to this background. The kingly portrait of Yhwh, however, is not touched by this likely rhetorical situation in which the text was created. Nevertheless, it is relevant to note the centrality of Yhwh's kingly portrait for the book's overall rhetorical strategy. The influence of the divine picture will provide a base on which the other main characters' contribution to the rhetorics of Exodus will be evaluated.

CHAPTER 3

MOSES – THE MEDIATOR, NOT THE HERO

Moses is the leading character in Exodus. One could view the entire Pentateuch as Moses' biography and in doing so would do justice to much of the material covered in the Torah. The focus of the author of Exodus on this one character may indicate that he is the one to copy, the example or model for the reader. To what extent this is the case and how the author attempted to achieve his aims will be the concern of the present chapter.

As I suggested in the previous chapter, following Sternberg's discussion, the character 'Yhwh' does not show significant alteration within the plot of Exodus. Moses, on the contrary, is – as a human character – always in transition. Beyond this liability to change, Moses, also, appears to be the most ambiguous character in Exodus. Again, according to Sternberg, this is a common literary feature of biblical character portrayal: "With biblical man … there is usually a distance – and often a clash – between the impression produced on his first appearance and the one left after his last."[1] This effect is due to what he calls "the biblical poetics of ambiguity."[2] Not all data is given in order to comprehend a character fully. In other words, the author and the reader do not necessarily move along at the same pace. Quite often the reader of Exodus has to readjust his mental image of Moses in the process of reading. The main aim of this chapter is to explicate the implications of this portrayal for the reader, his values and preconceptions.

Given this objective, together with my hypothesis that Exodus is all about the encouragement to a law-abiding lifestyle, certain questions are unavoidable and await answers:

- How paradigmatic is Moses in the rhetoric of Exodus? His ambiguity suggests that he serves as an example both in a positive and a negative way. But does he not, also, have a special, singular role in which the paradigmatic function of his portrayal is limited?

- What is the point in reading the Pentateuch as a biography of Moses? Usually a biography provides a good example for others to follow; i.e. it is more or less idealistic (presenting a prototype, archetype). But it may, also, be intended to rehabilitate a person (explaining circumstances, char-

---

[1] Sternberg 1987, 326.

[2] Cf. Sternberg 1987, 325 and his Ch. 5.

acter traits, etc.) or to present the reader with a negative example, which has a repulsive effect. What, exactly, is happening in Moses' case? And for whom is this communication intended?

- The implied (and real) reader, living in post-mosaic times, will experience a certain social fabric consisting of numerous institutions which quite likely try to find their legitimation in Israel's history, and, most likely, do so in the beginnings of it all centring around Moses. What are the implications for the rhetorical force of Exodus in such a setting?

To start off the discussion I shall give a review of recent approaches to the rhetorical function of the literary character 'Moses' in Exodus. Before an enquiry into several aspects central to his vocation, I shall devote a few paragraphs to the introduction of him into the plot of Exodus. This is fundamental to understanding the author's rhetorical strategy with Moses.

The Rhetorical Function of Moses – the Interpretive Debate

There are not many studies dealing with Moses as literary character in his own right. George Coats devotes an entire monograph to the Moses traditions and begins the specific literary investigations into Moses with Hugo Greßmann.[3] True to the historical-critical paradigm, the research usually goes into questions of discovering the historical reality behind the texts in order to reconstruct some sort of a satisfying picture of this person which is preconditioned by modern conventions of historiography.[4] The other option attempts to use the differences

---

[3] Cf. Coats 1988, 28.

[4] There are a number of exhaustive and thorough overviews of past scholarly research on (the historical) Moses available. Cf. Osswald 1962; Smend 1959; Schmid, H. 1986, 1–54 or Coats 1988, 10–42. Symptomatic of his principle outlook, Schmid writes in the context of reviewing the 'canonical approach' and 'stylistic criticism': "Beide mit guten theologischen Gründen die Endgestalt des Textes berücksichtigenden Betrachtungsweisen mögen zur Erfassung eines freilich nicht genau definierbaren 'Canonical Moses' beitragen, zur überlieferungsgeschichtlichen und geschichtlichen Erkenntnis der Mosegestalt führen sie nicht (höchstens bei Moberly)." (38) Crüsemann verbalises the chief difficulty facing the historicist with the minimalistic remains of what we can know about this historical person Moses: "Wie eigentlich konnte aus jenem Anfang, über den wir so wenig wissen, das werden, was die Bibel mit dem Namen Mose verbindet? Ist man auf das Problem erst einmal ernsthaft aufmerksam geworden, verwundert, wie selten so gefragt wurde. Der Bann des Historismus muß erstaunlich stark sein, wenn man mit dem Anfang auch schon die Folgen, mit Auslöser bereits die Wirkung zu haben glaubte." (Crüsemann 1992, 76f) Crüsemann, himself, is very pessimistic about what we really can unearth about Moses, but he asks the right question – why has Moses become the leading figure of the Pentateuch or even the entire religion and culture of Judaism? Or, in other words, what substantiates the authority of Moses and his speeches? Dijkstra 2006 approaches the same question: How became Moses (with such a difficult to reconstruct history) such a dominant figure of memory? Again, Dijkstra's study is set firmly in the historical-critical mould and, thus, does not contribute much to my present set of questions.

in the Moses traditions for a reconstruction of the textual history. Rolf Rendtorff dismisses this paradigm as irrelevant for answering the question of who Moses is – the Moses who dominates the fundamental beginnings of Israel as retold in Exodus to Deuteronomy. Hence, he pursues searching for the 'big picture' of Moses in the Torah, attempting to discover what these texts try to convey to their readers in their presentation of Moses.[5] While Rendtorff explicitly addresses the question I am interested in, James Watts attempts to trace the influence of the rhetoric of the Pentateuch, mainly in the legal parts of Deuteronomy, on the characterisation of Moses. This study certainly provides many points of contact beneficial to me, especially with its concentration on the legal collections. The other authors discussed are not specifically interested in rhetorical analysis but contribute, in their way, to the general picture.

H. Greßmann 1913

Hugo Greßmann's analysis has been called the 'pace-setter' of literary investigations into the Moses traditions.[6] The *Wirkungsgeschichte* of this study justifies a brief description of his thesis in the present context, although, he is far from considering the present shape of the tradition.[7] In the pursuit of a glimpse into the historical Moses Greßmann uses literary analysis and inquires into the oral stages of the traditions. His finding is that the genre of all the Moses narratives is *Sage* (what Greßmann means is probably best translated as 'tale'[8]):

---

[5] "Was bringen diese Texte mit dem Bild zum Ausdruck, das sie von Mose zeichnen? Entsprechend der Komplexität der Texte und der Unterschiedlichkeit der in ihnen aufgenommenen und verarbeiteten Traditionen ist dieses Bild keineswegs einheitlich und widerspruchsfrei. Gleichwohl fügen sich die verschiedenen Element [sic] zu einem Gesamtbild zusammen." (Rendtorff 2001, 121) It seems significant that an Old Testament theology coming from a canonical approach includes an entire chapter on the role of Moses. Moses is the one person dominating the Torah and, thus, certainly, deserves explicit treatment in a description of Old Testament faith. This is not a given among scholars, as a quick look into the tables of contents of various Old Testament theologies betrays.

[6] Cf. Coats 1988, 28.

[7] This can be exemplified by his comments on the narrative of Moses' call in Exod. 2–4 and 6–7: "Die Erzählung von Moses Berufung ist so, wie sie gegenwärtig lautet, unlesbar und unverständlich, weil verschiedene Rezensionen, Varianten und Zusätze in ein buntes Durcheinander gewirrt sind; lesbar und verständlich wird sie erst, wenn man sie in die zusammengehörigen Abschnitte zerlegt und diese dann stereoskopisch hintereinander schaut. Bisweilen wird freilich gefordert, man dürfe die Schichten nicht nur abtragen, sondern man müsse sie auch wieder an ihren Ort zurückbringen, oder ohne Bild gesprochen, man solle die Quellenschichten nicht nur in der Vereinzelung betrachten, sondern auch den jetzigen Zusammenhang würdigen, in dem sie uns überliefert sind. Diese Forderung ist prinzipiell abzulehnen, weil sie Unmögliches verlangt." (Greßmann 1913, 22).

[8] This is how Coats 1988, 219, n.65 translates the German 'Sage'.

"Alle Erzählungen ... über Mose und seine Zeit sind ihrer literarischen Art nach als Sagen zu betrachten ... Klingen diese Schicksale nicht wie ein Märchen aus längst entschwundenen Tagen?"[9] Greßmann highlights, in these tales, the miraculous elements in the derogatory style *en vogue* among the rationalist circles in the German academia of his time. Thus, he lets Moses appear as the divine hero of a fairy tale.[10] In the narratives which are less fairy tale in nature Greßmann misses the connection to political realities which must have existed in Mosaic times. This, again, gives rise to serious doubts about the historical reliability of the accounts.[11] With this, the early 20th century historian betrays his reductionist view of what constitutes historiography and judges the Mosaic narratives in the light of his rationalist preconceptions. Interestingly, Greßmann tries to envisage the first recipients of the *Sagen* he singled out. The pre-enlightenment understanding of causality is to blame for the present mixture of the miraculous and the factual and, hence, every *Sage* carries some kind of historical kernel. Greßmann attempts to identify the kernels and motifs, which carry the weight of the narrative. To get results, he establishes categories for assessing the historical reliability of these motifs: they are distinguished in typical and singular motifs, the former, reflecting fantasy and, the latter, being closer to reality.[12] This enables him to uncover what he calls '*Ursagen*' which are the only reliable sources for a historical reconstruction of Moses and his time.[13] His reconstruction of the textual genesis is not essential to our present discussion so I will leave it to one side.

Obviously, Greßmann is dependent on the traditional source-critical assumptions and, thus, his arguments stand and fall with this framework. Nevertheless, it is intriguing how he reconstructs the interests of the original authors. After reading about the reconstruction of the content of an *Ursage*, Greßmann's reader observes an interplay between modern anticipation (this is what a 'historian' would make of this kernel) and what the actual redactor made of it. The new point of reference (Greßmann's anticipations) provides the contrast in which the narrator's motivations and interests clearly appear. The following example illustrates what happens here:

> Als Mose zum Priester Jethro kommt und bei ihm in die Lehre geht, da erwartet man, daß er den Beruf des Priesters lernt und sich für sein späteres Priesteramt vorbereitet. Aber die Sage, die im Kreise der Hirten vorgetragen wird, macht ihn

---

[9] Greßmann 1913, 360.

[10] Cf. Greßmann 1913, 360f.

[11] Cf. Greßmann 1913, 361–363.

[12] Cf. Greßmann 1913, 364. That the typical motif in its fixed form is further from historical reality is an arbitrary assumption, which seems based on the modern concept of historiography. Beyond these two groups he accepts the value of the glimpses into the cultural reality reflected by the texts (*kulturelle Motive*).

[13] Cf. Greßmann 1913, 367.

zum Hirten, verheiratet ihn und läßt ihn Kinder zeugen. So ist auch hier das Familienidyll zum Thema des Erzählers geworden.[14]

This approach is, of course, feasible and does justice to the literary genre which Greßmann envisages for the Moses traditions. But, given the final shape of the biblical text, the picture of Moses does not emerge along these lines. Greßmann's opposition to the final shape of the Pentateuch has already been mentioned above and, with this assumption, he prevents himself from seeing many aspects of the texts into which I shall later enquire. It is obvious how strong the influence of the genre, as defined by the scholar, is to the picture of Moses which he develops from the sources. Greßmann defines the Moses traditions as *Sagen*, which leads him to view the extant texts as heaps of rubble[15] in which he digs. As an historian he unearths the historic kernel and thus makes the texts readable for us by constructing new literary contexts. This less appreciative view of the work of the final redactor is rooted in the paradigm of source criticism and is almost intrinsic to German Old Testament scholarship of the early 20th century.

G.W. Coats 1988

The work of Greßmann provides George Wesley Coats with a starting point in his designation of some Mosaic traditions as *Heldensagen*.[16] So Coats proposes as his basic thesis: "The Moses narratives can be understood, bracketed together, as heroic saga."[17] As the title of his study betrays, he finds a balance to the picture of a purely heroic Moses – which in Coats' opinion is, essentially, a literary attribute[18] – by tracing the literary description of his dependence upon Yhwh. The Moses narratives merge with other confessional traditions about Yhwh's mighty acts. These two opposing traditions, taken together, give the Pentateuch its present structure.

Coats' literary avenue makes his work profitable for the present discussion as he touches on aspects relevant from a rhetorical-critical point of view. His

---

[14] Greßmann 1913, 366.

[15] Cf. n.7 above. Or it may be the opposite dependency, but as there is always something of a hermeneutic circle, it does not really matter which assumption came first.

[16] Cf. Coats 1988, 29 referring to Greßmann 1913, 378, but see also 360f.

[17] Coats 1988, 36.

[18] That 'heroic' is mainly a literary concept becomes most obvious in his search for a *Sitz im Leben* of the tradition: "The point, however, is that insofar as setting is concerned, Moses as leader in heroic form emerges first in a literary construct. The literary, folkloristic depiction of this tradition about Israel's salvation cannot be imagined without Moses. And indeed, Moses may be implied at all points, even in the cultic forms. But in fact, Moses appears first and strongest in a literary setting. The literature describes him as heroic man and man of God. And it does so not because the image fits any particular office or any particular institution, but because that image was a folkloristic convention for narrating the deeds of past leaders." (Coats 1988, 139).

"goals are to determine how the traditions conceived Moses, how they put that image in literary form, and how that form communicated to Israel the importance of the man and his time."[19] Thus, he brings a set of questions to the text which are quite similar to the ones which I am asking in this current chapter. The following summary of his position centres around the rhetorical-critical implications of his approach and will help to specify my research questions.

The Moses traditions give a heroic picture of the man, because the people telling his story benefited from his actions; i.e. there is a national interest to uphold a positive picture of this man. According to Coats, a tale or a legend only has a heroic dimension when it attempts to identify the hero with the people by showing that the hero serves the best interests of the people. The comparison with other literary heroes is used to define to what extent Moses fits the common picture of such a hero, which "would be a figure of folk tradition that meets certain kinds of needs for the folk, such as a representative for courage, leadership, and honor."[20] There is no need to go into any detail with the similarities that are highlighted, but a significant point of difference, Coats stresses, is our hero's relationship to the divine sphere.[21] As already mentioned, the equilibrium Coats wants to keep is the following: "Moses is not simply an instrument in the hands of God. But he is also not the redeemer who initiates the salvation of the people. He fights for his people. But he does not make them into a people. They remain the people of God."[22] This would be true inside the heroic traditions which Coats isolates and even more so on the final redactional level of the Pentateuch. In addition to this content-oriented aspect, his use of the generic term 'saga', including his comment on the pragmatics of the genre, is interesting from a rhetorical point of view: "... a long prose, usually episodic narration built around a plot or a succession of plots ... [is intended] to *capture the audience* by the tensions in its story-line, thus, to *entertain its audience* with the skill of its storytelling."[23] This definition leaves out the notion of a-historicity which dominates the German term *Sage* as we saw in the discussion of Greßmann, above, but includes a functional statement: the narrative is told to effect entertainment which, in turn, is reflected in the episodic nature of narration. Both features would have originated in the *Sitz im Leben* of the ancient story teller.

As indicated above, Coats inquires into the question of which literary role is best reflected by the character Moses. The typical literary hero 'Moses' is portrayed along the lines of the heroic saga, which dictates numerous generic elements. In working out the details of his thesis, Coats remains, basically, within a

---

[19] Coats 1988, 34.

[20] Coats 1988, 40. Cf. also his general comments on the heroic legend (125).

[21] Cf. Coats 1988, 39–41.

[22] Coats 1988, 41.

[23] Coats 1988, 42 (italics mine).

form-critical and tradition-historical paradigm. This, often, leads him to consider the Moses traditions, apart from their present literary context, as single 'tales'. To highlight the typical heroic description of Moses, Coats compares the biblical account with other heroic literature, such as Sargon of Akkad's hymn or the *Nibelungenlied*. Scattered legendary features are collected and brought into contact with the heroic Moses. This leads him to oppose all efforts to belittle the importance given to Moses in biblical traditions. Thus, he criticises von Rad's conclusion that all Moses stories are not really about the man, but focus on Yhwh: "[I]t is not necessary to reduce the role played by the man Moses in these stories in order to emphasize the role of God for the weight of the narration. Indeed, it is precisely in the dialectic established by these two poles that the strongest dynamic in the Moses stories appears."[24] He refers, affirmingly, to a dissertation by Schnutenhaus, who claims that Moses, as a messenger, cannot be understood apart from his relationships to God, who sent him, and to the people to whom he was delivering the message. An example of how Coats establishes this 'dialectic' from the texts is his well-argued discussion of the stereotypical mention of the messenger's mouth in many biblical call narratives, i.e., an element not necessarily part of the heroic genre.[25] Here, he balances his description of the Mosaic character as heroic: "The stereotype demands objection in order to set up a reassurance related to the mouth of the subject."[26] So Moses' fourth objection in Exod. 3–4 is a generic prerequisite functioning as a mere catchword for the following reassurance of the divine authorisation of the messenger's message. As such, it would not point to a historical reality in terms of a speech defect on Moses' part. This reading is unusual, compared with Coats' tendency to fit the texts into the pattern of 'heroic literature' (which would have been possible here, cf. the typical 'heroic flaw'). It, nevertheless, provides him with a reason to write: "God's presence underwrites Moses' mission and authority. And it is out of that presence that his heroic relationship with his people is possible."[27] I very much doubt that an adopted authority suits a hero, in the traditional sense. A 'normal' hero proves his abilities and does not disqualify himself. Although this conflict in the tradition, as read by Coats, leads him to propose a deliberate dialectic in the portrayal of Moses; it becomes questionable whether the generic designation of Moses as 'hero' is a fortunate term to use for this character – at least in Exodus. As I attempt to show, there are certain features of the Moses-portrayal alluding to him as a heroic character, but, on the final redactional level, these allusions appear to be referring to a preconception on the part of the implied reader. This the author felt the need to correct, using the genre of *Heldensage* with a counter generic function.

---

[24] Coats 1988, 32, and in conclusion 155.

[25] Cf. Coats 1988, 68f.

[26] Coats 1988, 68. This reading is quite similar to the function I propose for the Moses speeches in the call narrative (see below).

[27] Coats 1988, 69.

Throughout his study, Coats collects material to support a separation of two traditions in the Pentateuch (or Hexateuch): one, portraying Moses, his mighty deeds and the people's reaction to these in a heroic fashion, the other, collecting confessional statements about Yhwh's acts on his people's behalf.[28] In the latter tradition, Coats finds Moses to be the mediator of the divine acts and covenant. In its communicational concern "[i]t functions as a necessary complement for the heroic saga, designed to ensure that the Moses narration should never move beyond its commitment to describe a human creature who works for the commitment of his people to God."[29] Thus, the more folkloric character of the heroic saga, with its interest in the beneficial actions of a heroic character, is complemented by the much more theological reflections stemming from a cultic setting. Throughout his study, Coats traces the distribution of the two traditions, generally, along the common lines of division between JE and P. The functional purpose of the folkloric, heroic JE portrait of Moses is "to facilitate the belief of the people in God."[30] This sounds a bit general or, even, vacuous. Coats becomes a little more specific in writing: "Moses' position is a position that enables the people to fear the Lord. Thus, to stand in proper awe and intimacy with God is to recognize the authority of Moses."[31] The character Moses thus serves the author on the literary-functional level as an example, inviting imitation and, also, as mediator in bringing the people in closer proximity to their God. This is very similar to the medieval concept of saints standing between the believer and the distant deity, which was brought about by centuries of concentration on the transcendental aspects of God. Expressing a more theological implication, Coats summarises:

> In order to see Moses fully, but also in order to understand the character of God's mighty act, the tension must not be broken. To break it would produce a transcendental divine history unencumbered even by the instrumentality of human involvement, or a human history devoid of divine involvement or even focused on elevating human involvement to the world of the divine (so, Exod. 32.1).[32]

This fine theological balance – Coats would argue – is already present in the JE description of Moses as heroic but from my point of view it appears clearly only

---

[28] This division of material into the two traditions can, for example, be found in Coats' discussion of the 'two' call narratives, the variations in the Midianite material, his distinction of two forms of the plague narrative or his separation of traditions along the traditional source critical results (esp. in the reed sea pericope and the wilderness pericopes), to name but a few.

[29] Coats 1988, 156. For the wilderness pericopes this is specified thus: "In P, it is fair to say that Moses and Aaron are really only supporting characters for stories about God's intervention on behalf of his people and his leadership for those people through the wilderness" (124).

[30] Coats 1988, 157.

[31] Coats 1988, 165.

[32] Coats 1988, 160.

when considering the textual arrangement after the P redaction. After this, the step towards the final form of the texts is not very far. What Coats detects after a form-critical analysis of the received traditions, the tension between the heroic and confessional, remains part of the final textual shape. Thus, our rhetorical analysis of the received text will need to observe the effect of this tension irrespective of how it might have originated – by a more or less arbitrary conflation of two opposing traditions, or by the process of critical evaluation and correction of earlier material, either as a rhetorical device used consciously by the 'final redactor' or not. How does this tension linked with the character affect the reading process? That it is simply designed to capture the attention of the audience and please its curiosity, as Coats' mention of the entertainment value of the texts may suggest, does not seem very obvious. Even Coats does not come back to this point. More likely is that the effect must be sought in the inception of reader-identification. This notion can be found between the lines of Coats' monograph,[33] but, again, it does not go very far beyond this implicit stage. Coats' most significant contribution is – from a rhetorical-critical viewpoint – the highlighting of the tension in the literary relationship between Moses and Yhwh. A simplified picture of Moses cannot be maintained alongside the complexity of human and divine action[34] into which the reader is drawn. Unfortunately, Coats does not go into any detail regarding the relationship between Yhwh and the people, although this, also, is quite certainly characterised by a similar complexity. The literary function of the heroic portrayal might have been an opportunity to ponder this question.

This brief sketch of Coats' theses focuses quite narrowly on just a part of his results, but in this, it tries to highlight the results touching the theme at the heart of the present discussion. The article by McBride, discussed next, explicitly

---

[33] An important aspect of Coats' hero is, for example, that he is connected to the Israelite people by way of "bringing boons to his people." (Coats 1988, 40) As hero Moses must act for the benefit of the people: "The giant can be no hero, not even an effective anti-hero for folk tradition unless he is hero for the people ... His heroic quality makes sense only insofar as it serves the edification of the community." (Coats 1988, 41) Taken together with the assumption that the heroic tradition derives from the folk and not from some sort of sociologically definable institution, what are the rhetorical implications? It seems that identification is the primary goal here. To portray Moses as always acting for the good of his people can be understood as a rhetorical attempt to initiate a similar behaviour via the emotional motivations of awe and, probably, thankfulness.

[34] Cf: "The heroic man acts so that his acts make public the acts of God. The tradition thus does not alter the form and genre of the heroic saga. Even with the image of Moses as man of God, and the themes that depict God's mighty acts, the form of the Moses narration remains as it was. Heroic saga is the narrative display of the hero as the man of God. And this display belongs to the exquisite art of Israel's storytelling." (Coats 1988, 167f)

criticises Coats' account of a heroic picture of Moses and stresses the importance of the function of a mediator in order to describe the character Moses.

S.D. McBride 1990

Opposed to Coats, Dean McBride is not prepared to support the idea of an early
Moses saga which interprets Moses as a popular hero, like Samson or David,
whose exploits accentuate his personal power and charisma. Moses represents
God, not himself. "In effect Moses is not even the protagonist of his own story."[35] McBride's article is, in essence, a brief overview covering the texts in
which Moses features as character. He does not give much detail in support of
his thesis but offers a general, sometimes associative, reading which must be
further substantiated from the text to be strong enough to carry the weight of the
argument. The exodus and wilderness episodes in Exodus to Numbers. are concerned with Mosaic authority, whereas the Sinai traditions, according to
McBride, are grouped around the theme of the divine presence with the people,
with Moses, as the one having intimate access to Yhwh, serving as the "model
for Israel's institutional formation as the people set apart, chosen, holy to Yahweh"[36] – a picture which is highlighted in Exod. 32–34. Moses is portrayed here
as becoming more and more associated with patriarchal traits and he is given
the task of bringing the people into the land of the promise. How Moses' role as
the pre-eminent mediator and model-leader for Israel is best represented in Israelite society would be the theme stressed by the last redactional layers of the
Pentateuch. McBride finds that the answers to this question meet in two *foci*,
expressed by the terms charisma and tradition. Unfortunately, he only hints in
the various directions and does so, merely, on a narrative level. Crüsemann's
detailed study covers the subject in a much more penetrating way.

As indicated above, McBride perceives Moses' authority as transcendent, i.e.
when Moses acts, he acts for God; when he speaks, he speaks for God. Contrary
to Coats, McBride does not allow, at all, for a picture in which Moses is a
leader in his own right. McBride is quite right to balance the literary genre of
the heroic with inner biblical material of other heroic figures, something which
would add depth to Coats' analysis, but the arguments in his brief article present
us with little more than suggestions in a particular direction. From my point of
view, Coats has made us more sensitive to the intricate balance of human action
and divine initiative. Even on the final level of redaction this balance is dominant and does require the reader's attention. This balance is, nevertheless, open
to the addition of McBride's notion of transcendental authority, with its stress

---

[35] McBride 1990, 230.
[36] McBride 1990, 234.

upon the mediator role of Moses, a role which is only marginally discussed by Coats.

F. Crüsemann 1992

Frank Crüsemann, true to the subtitle of his book on the Torah – *Theologie und Sozialgeschichte des alttestamentlichen Gesetzes* – seeks to unearth the way in which Israel authorised its social-legal institutions, for example, the law and the courts. In other words, the question is: who in Israel's history could claim to speak within Moses' authority and, thus, to represent 'Moses'? Hermeneuti-cally, Crüsemann positions himself firmly inside the historical-critical paradigm of dating the biblical texts in order to develop his picture of history, but this question is not the question of the present project and has to be addressed, in my opinion, only as an afterthought. Crüsemann also presents us with possible readings of the Mosaic traditions and hence provides a scenario of how these texts could have been used. His use of the Moses traditions represents a focus on one possible rhetorical function of these texts. It is the function of support-ing, from hindsight, a given institution (in this case, some sort of legal office) in order to stabilise or break down reality – essentially the texts are read etiologi-cally. Whatever the truth of Crüsemann's reconstruction of Israelite society may be, it is likely that certain readers tried to use the biblical traditions about Moses to substantiate their claims to legal authority. And, as the previous reviews and, also, the later discussion will show, in Exodus the character Moses is indeed linked with the themes of authority and divine legitimation. But I will contest that this rhetorical function (etiology) is what the texts betray to be their inten-ded communicative aim.

Coats, coming from a literary, form-critical perspective, finds the biblical Moses to be a heroic figure. Crüsemann's sociological vantage-point focuses, naturally, on the societal roles that are linked with Moses, i.e. on the extra-textual realities that are reflected in this presentation of Moses. Both focal points need to be considered in a rhetorical-critical reading of Exodus because both reflect parts of the reading process, the form of the text itself and the his-torical reality of the reader.

In the following, I shall briefly sketch Crüsemann's conclusions. For the pre-monarchic period, he is very skeptical about finding any sources for the legal institution of a *Rechtsgemeinde* in the city gate as envisioned in the Bible. In-stead the picture of a practice of self-aid (*Selbsthilfe*) and negotiation (*Verhand-lung*) without a mediating official would emerge.[37] The norms regulating these early informal proceedings seem to be self-evident without the need of some

---

[37] The textual basis for this conclusion being Gen. 31; 34; Judg. 17–18; 19–21; 2Sam. 14 (cf. Crüsemann 1992, 85–94). The difficulty is that the events narrated in these pas-sages are far removed from everyday issues and further that the main interest of the texts is not to tell how exactly the legal settlement was achieved. Both objections Crüsemann raises himself (93f).

sort of recourse to a divinely given law.[38] So for early times Crüsemann sees no influence of a Mosaic tradition in Israel, for there was no social institution in need of such a person to legitimise itself.

The legal administration in the gate is one of the innovations coming with the establishment of the monarchy.[39] One aspect of the social realities in preexilic times is, according to Crüsemann, reflected in the attempt of the Pentateuchal law collections to bring the law into the hands of all the people as opposed to leaving it to the state.[40] Yet, this does not account for the picture of Moses as the one on whom the law hangs and the one who communicates the divine will. So, parallel to the more democratic notion mentioned before, Crüsemann finds in Exod. 18 the establishment of a centralised organisation of justice in monarchic Israel. In Moses' person different functions, which are otherwise distributed to different offices/people, are intertwined. The king cannot bear the load of the Mosaic example and thus judges in civil service (*beamtete Richter*) are the other candidates. Considering 2 Chr. 19:5-7, Crüsemann concludes that only the Jerusalem main court (installed by Jehoshaphat) could claim Mosaic judicial authority and that this is legitimised by texts like Exod. 18 and Deut. 1:9-18:

> Nicht der König, sondern 'Mose' vermittelt das israelitische Recht, das letztlich von Gott kommt. Fragt man, wer diesen 'Mose' in der Königszeit repräsentiert und in seinem Namen sprechen konnte, kommt als einzige Instanz dieses Obergericht in Jerusalem in Frage, das sich offensichtlich mosaisch legitimiert sieht und im Namen des Mose spricht.[41]

So Moses reflects and legitimises this institution, an institution of far-ranging responsibilities: "Mose steht für eine Institution, die die Kompetenz in besonders schwierigen, also im bisherigen Recht nicht zu lösenden Fällen hat, welche also Präzendenzfälle [*sic*] an sich zieht. Zugleich aber befragt er Gott, wie es Propheten oder Priester tun."[42] Another precedent, literarily linked with Moses, from the pre-state situation of Israel is the tribal leaders. Moses' recollection of the events described in Exod. 18 in Deut. 1:9-18 is simply that he introduced and, hence, legitimised a new role for the already wise and perceptive tribal leaders who can from now on also administer justice: "Die traditionelle Führungsschicht Israels, und zwar die seiner traditionellen Verbände, übernimmt danach mosaische Aufgaben."[43] These tribal leaders take on many of the Mosaic duties and, hence, work with Mosaic authority, especially in their accounta-

---

[38] Cf. Crüsemann 1992, 94f "Das frühe Recht war kein Gottesrecht." In this context he also mentions Jackson's category of a "selfexecuting law" (cf. Jackson 1989, 197ff).

[39] Cf. Crüsemann 1992, 96ff.

[40] Cf. Crüsemann 1992, 104.

[41] Crüsemann 1992, 121.

[42] Crüsemann 1992, 108.

[43] Crüsemann 1992, 110.

bility before God. For the monarchic period the Mosaic traditions would mainly support institutions balancing the power of the king:

> Während das Ziel des vorexilischen Textes Ex 18 die Legitimierung der Einsetzung von beamteten Richtern ist, läßt er zugleich deutlich erkennen, daß eine mit 'Mose' bezeichnete Autorität hinter dem Vorgang steht, die die Rechtsfunktion des Königs mit der wichtiger Heiligtümer und ihrer Priester bzw. Propheten verbindet.[44]

For exilic and post-exilic times the account of Num. 11 becomes relevant.[45] According to Crüsemann, the emphasis here is, also, on the traditional leaders partaking in the Mosaic spirit and hence in Moses' ability and legitimation, but the view goes beyond that group: "Die traditionelle Führungsschicht des Volkes, ja potentiell das gesamte Volk (Num 11:29) muß zu 'Mose' werden, um die Krise zu überwinden und ein Weiterleben zu gewährleisten."[46] The crisis, of course, is the downfall of the kingdom. Here, Crüsemann touches upon the communicative intention of the texts in the exilic/post-exilic context that he imagines for them: Moses becomes a model to follow, a paradigmatic character who exemplifies a certain attitude which is apparently desirable, socially and religiously. In summary of his discussion of the postexilic texts, Crüsemann writes:

> Daß dem 'Mose' der späten Erzählungen über gewichtige göttliche Rechtsentscheidungen keine historische faßbare Größe entspricht, hängt nun wohl nicht zuletzt daran, daß dieser Mose an den Sinai gehört und damit in jene ferne Vergangenheit, lange vor den eigenen Staat und weit vor die herrschende Fremdmacht [sc. Greece]. Nur als Gestalt der Tradition und gerade nicht als eine der Gegenwart konnte er die Rolle spielen, die er gespielt hat ... Er steht für die Möglichkeit und Notwendigkeit, die divergierenden Gruppeninteressen und Traditionen besonders zwischen Priestern und Laien zusammenzuführen. Er ist damit keine in Israel aufweisbare Größe, aber steht auch nicht wie Abraham für das Ganze. Mose ist also letztlich keine Institution, geht keinesfalls in denen auf, die sich auf ihn berufen. Er ist vielmehr die Bedingung der Möglichkeit, daß seine Tora alle Institutionen überleben wird und sich gerade darin bewährt. ... [Mose] ist die Tradition von der Erneuerung der Tradition und als solcher der nicht "real existierende", aber gerade und nur so höchst wirksame Grund der Freiheit.[47]

What the Torah presents as 'Moses' is larger than life-size, an exemplary leader no institution of later Israel can exhaust. For Crüsemann, Moses is an ideal, and only as such is he able to hold together the diverging interests in Israel throughout all time. The result is exactly what Coats formulates at the end of his review of sociologically oriented studies on Moses. Using Eichrodt's words:

---

[44] Crüsemann 1992, 112.

[45] Num. 11 is considered to be part of a deuteronomistic redaction (Crüsemann 1992, 111).

[46] Crüsemann 1992, 113.

[47] Crüsemann 1992, 131.

It is characteristic of Moses that it should be impossible to classify him in any of the ordinary categories applicable to a leader of a nation; he is neither a king, nor a commander of an army, nor a tribal chieftain, nor a priest, nor an inspired seer and medicine man. To some extent he belongs to all these categories; but none of them adequately explains his position.[48]

Crüsemann makes the best of this situation and presents a fitting theological conclusion that, for as much – or as little, to be honest – as we know from Israelite history, there is no social reality fitting the picture given in the Torah of Moses.

What, for Coats, is a generic hero is, for Crüsemann, either an etiological construct to legitimate a present institution or a hypothetical ideal. Both attempts to penetrate the literary figure of Moses depend on the previous historical-critical reconstruction of texts and, hence, the creation of new literary contexts. I have already indicated my pessimism about the viability of these constructions and am convinced that a reading of the received text of Exodus will provide a picture of Moses which is neither heroic nor etiological. The texts may have been read throughout history to legitimise certain political or social interests, but I doubt very much that the rhetoric of the texts encourages such a reading. Crüsemann's theological reading of Moses as an idealised example to encourage unity among the exiles and returnees is a much more likely function supported by the texts. This, of course, may have to do with the inclination of Crüsemann to view the final redaction of the Torah in exilic/postexilic times, and, hence, drives him to consider the entire text in its canonical shape. I shall follow Crüsemann and pursue the different roles indicated by the presentation of Moses in Exodus. The openness of Moses' character to include so many roles appears to be the result of a conscious rhetorical strategy.

J.W. Watts 1998

In an article specifically coming from a rhetorical-critical vantage point, James W. Watts presents a picture of the figure of Moses based, mainly, on a discussion of Deuteronomy. He stresses, rightly, the importance of the characterisation of the lawgiver for the persuasive effect of the law. Knowing about the source of law helps one to appreciate its demands, especially if the authority of the law-giver is established: "Pentateuchal laws therefore join narratives in characterizing law-speakers as part of a rhetoric of persuasion."[49] Here, we find the reason why Watts mainly looks into Deuteronomy to unfold the legal characterisation of Moses: in Deuteronomy the law is put into the mouth of Moses, whereas in the other books of the Pentateuch the reader hears Yhwh uttering the law.

---

[48] Eichrodt 1961, I, 289, quoted in Coats 1988, 26.

[49] Watts 1998, 415.

To portray the 'legal' Moses, Watts analyses Deuteronomy's depiction of his different roles, beginning with a discussion of Moses as king. Watts argues in his earlier article on the legal characterisation of Yhwh[50] that the presentation of the divinely-given law presents Yhwh as the ideal ruler or king. The presentation of Moses as lawgiver in Deuteronomy, on the other hand, cuts down any kingly notions to give pride of place to Moses as prophet and teacher or scribe. One indicator of this is the concrete description of Moses: "Though Moses' self-characterization in Deuteronomy is neither humble nor apologetic, it stops short of royal self-aggrandizement."[51] The second role for Moses in Deuteronomy is, likely, that of a prophet (cf. Deut. 18:15.18; 34:10). According to Exodus-Numbers and Deuteronomy Moses possesses a "delegated authority to give the law to Israel":[52] both Yhwh and Israel chose him to mediate between them. "This double delegation of authority to Moses maximises his rhetorical power in Deuteronomy. When both God and Israel have appointed him to speak for them, who is left to challenge his words?"[53] This, of course, is true not only for Deuteronomy. Watts argues that, reading Deuteronomy in isolation from the preceding books of the Pentateuch, results in an image of Moses as lawgiver, suppressing his portrayal as prophet. But in the overall structure of the Pentateuch, Moses appears just as a prophet, a repeater of previously given law, and not more than that.[54] Here, the argument rests, mainly, on Watts' very general attribution of voice throughout the 'poems of sanction' in the Pentateuch as laid out in his *Reading Law*, 1999. Moses' role in this large context is the verbalisation of threats and promises in relation to law obedience: "The Pentateuch then does not present itself on the whole as 'the law of Moses,' but rather as 'the law of YHWH.' God speaks the law and God alone. Moses announces its consequences, as did Israel's lesser prophets."[55]

From the rhetorical function of sanction (i.e. motivation), Watts concludes that here must be a proximity to wisdom literature, whose key concern is also motivation. Moses becomes the "paradigmatic instructor."[56] Here, Watts can, of course, draw on the many points of contact between wisdom literature and the book of Deuteronomy (cf. his sources: Blenkinsopp, Carmichael, Weinfeld), but he does so only superficially. The remainder of his article is a discussion of the role of Moses as scribe and, mainly, focusses on the way Moses teaches, amends and interprets law. Watts stresses the fact that Yhwh remains throughout the ultimate lawgiver, a role never taken on by Moses in the description of the Pentateuch, especially of Deuteronomy. A scribe's authority depends, large-

---

[50] Cf. Watts 1996.

[51] Watts 1998, 417.

[52] Watts 1998, 418.

[53] Watts 1998, 419.

[54] Cf. McBride's notion of the transcendental authority of Moses.

[55] Watts 1998, 422.

[56] Cf. Watts 1998, 422.

ly, on the accuracy of the transmission of the tradition. But comparing the earlier law and the modifications Deuteronomy brings, we find some tension: Moses can be quite bold in introducing changes. Watts traces this rhetoric of change in law in Deuteronomy and comes to the conclusion that Deuteronomy actually tries to conceal legal innovations by prohibiting exactly this (cf. Deut. 13:1), so that "the overall force of Deuteronomy's rhetoric aims at identifying divine law and its interpretive tradition as one and the same thing. [Hence] Deuteronomy works to merge the voice of YHWH and Moses into a unifying rhetoric of authority."[57] However, this would only be true for Deuteronomy. For the entire Pentateuch Watts' postulate of the rhetorical strategy of the larger structure becomes his hermeneutical principle: the larger context distinguishes between the voices of Yhwh and Moses "and accords them separate functions, as speaker of law and speaker of sanctions respectively."[58] Obviously, this conclusion only works if one accepts Watts' generalising genre divisions across the Pentateuch (i.e. story, list, sanction). At the level of the Pentateuch, Moses' role as scribe – writing, interpreting and applying the law – would, then, bridge the gap between Yhwh's and Moses' relations to the law "by making him [sc. Moses] the only authorized tradent of divine law. ... There is no access to divine law except through him."[59]

The greatest weakness in Watts argumentation is his use of the phrase 'lawgiver'. There seems to be a conflation of ideas, the actual legislative speech-act and the mere communicating of law in the mediation context. Though Watts tries to separate these two ideas, it is not clear whether he actually sees Moses portrayed in Deuteronomy as lawgiver or not. I follow his thesis when he states that it is debatable if Moses is really pictured as legislator in Deuteronomy. Moses, surely, speaks law, such as that on the story level of Exodus, except for the decalogue, but the ultimate source of the law is Yhwh, not Moses, as Watts, himself, observes often: "The law comes from YHWH through Moses ..."[60] From my point of view, this calls into question the entire concept of drawing up a 'legal characterisation' of Moses. In the discussion of Moses in Deuteronomy the concept of 'reliable characters', as defined by Kissling, seems to be a more fruitful perspective. Kissling poses the question of how Moses presents the law in Deuteronomy.[61] Thus, the question is one of the characterisation of the mediator, interpreter and *Tradent* Moses, which Watts discusses under the heading "Moses as scribe". For the present discussion of the literary presentation of Moses in Exodus the attribution of a scribal role to Moses is not relevant. Nevertheless, Watts' reflections on the different aspects of Moses the mediator, especially the nature of his authorisation and, hence, his relationship to the other

---

[57] Watts 1998, 425.

[58] Watts 1998, 425.

[59] Watts 1998, 425.

[60] Watts 1998, 417.

[61] Cf. Kissling 1996.

main characters of the plot, are of value. Another point which deserves mention is Watts' overall result concerning the ambiguity of the presentation of Moses in Deuteronomy, something which applies to the Moses of Exodus, as well. Ambiguity seems to appear more obviously when reading on the synchronic level, as many historical-critical approaches tend to separate texts diachronically in order to avoid tensions. Characters become much more idealised and 'flat' when robbed of their complexity, or even, their enigmatic features. This reading sets Watts apart from mainstream research and provides helpful insights into the communicational aspects of the texts.

T.B. Dozeman 2000

With his aim "to interpret the literary significance of Moses' shining skin and veil within the larger setting of the life of Moses in the Pentateuch,"[62] Thomas B. Dozeman touches on only a very small textual part of Exodus, but he does provide in the course of his essentially semiotic discussion some valuable insights into the general presentation of Moses. The heart of the issue is, again, Mosaic authority. Dozeman sets out to prove that both the shining skin and the veil (Exod. 34:29-35) are 'masks' and that they contribute to the understanding of Mosaic authority. This masking would establish Moses as the "unique mediator of divine law" in the Pentateuch and, hence, influence the picture which develops while reading the Pentateuch.

Dozeman approves of Coats' view that regards Moses' masking as a transfiguration which establishes Mosaic authority as arising from involvement in God's power.[63] A wider definition of 'mask' includes the veil (מסוה) of Moses as a simple mask without a face.[64] The same applies to the shining skin of Moses which can be interpreted, on the ritual level, as functioning as a mask. This interpretation goes back to Greßmann,[65] who, also, understood the veil as being a ritual mask. Moses' shining face would be a 'mask of concretion', representing the deity which invades and transforms Moses,[66] all the while concealing Moses' private, everyday identity. The veil would, then, be a 'mask of concealment', displaying an inherent quality in Moses to the outside world, while again hiding his everyday identity: "The veil separates Moses from other Israelites, signifying his social authority … It designates Moses as the lawgiver, who administers divinely revealed legislation into the life of Israel."[67] The masks of Moses are interpreted as the means by which his special role of standing be-

---

[62] Dozeman 2000, 22.

[63] Cf. Coats 1988, 138.

[64] Cf. Dozeman 2000, 25. His definition of 'mask' is derived from mainly anthropological studies.

[65] Cf. Greßmann 1913, 246–251.

[66] Dozeman stresses that Moses is not deified, Dozeman 2000, 27, n. 33.

[67] Dozeman 2000, 28.

tween the people and Yhwh is expressed. Moses remains hidden and points the onlooker to God. This is related to McBride's concept of transcendent authority: Moses steps entirely into the background while God features dominantly.[68] This has consequences for the perception of Moses: "A central feature of Mosaic authority is that power does not arise from the profane character of Moses. Instead, Mosaic authority is transcendent. … [Moses' authority] arises not from his own personality or charisma but only in his role as a channel for divine teaching."[69]

Having argued for his reading of the masking of Moses, Dozeman goes on to trace two different inner-biblical interpretations of Moses' masking: first, the pre-Priestly (linked to Deuteronomy) and, second, the Priestly (P). A new text (the 'older tradition' of the Tent of Meeting) is created, consisting of Exod. 33, Num. 11–12 and Deut. 31. In this context, the masking of Moses is clearly linked to this 'oracular tent shrine', which points to Moses' unique authority in his role as the channel of revelation. There is no revelation in the Tent of Meeting independent of him.[70] P, on the other hand (Exod. 35–Num. 10), conflates the Tent of Meeting and the Tabernacle into a single cult at the one central tent in the camp. According to this priestly account the functions of the shining face and the veil of Moses are transferred to the sanctuary which, now, represents God's glory – God not residing in the person of Moses, but in the cult: "As consequence, the authority of Moses, for the Priestly writers, resides in his successful completion of the Tabernacle cult. He is the cult founder. Moses' action allows for the *Kābôd* Yahweh to enter the sanctuary and thus to dwell with Israel."[71] Moses' unique cultic role is played down further in that the Aaronic and Levitic priesthoods become authoritative figures within the tabernacle tradition. Finally, Dozeman attempts to relate his findings to a reader of the final text of the Pentateuch, who must find his way through the tensions between the two distinct interpretations of Mosaic authority. The two traditions create confusion on the reader's part, which in turn produces a dynamic of openness. Thus, the text develops a framework, finding its borders with the pre-Priestly and the Priestly interpretations. In a good irenic manner, Dozeman finishes his article thus: "The solutions [to this openness] are potentially infinite as long as neither claim on Moses is embraced to the exclusion of the other."[72]

Dozeman's detailed discussion of the various aspects of the pre-Priestly passages is, partly, based on shaky arguments which, in my view, are not able to bear the weight of his conclusions. He appears to find similarities between texts

---

[68] This is opposed to Zivotofsky's interpretation and to many of the early Jewish understandings of the character of Moses. They greatly emphasise Moses' outstanding personality and ability to be the leader of the people (cf. p.152 below).

[69] Dozeman 2000, 29.

[70] Cf. Dozeman 2000, 38.

[71] Dozeman 2000, 44.

[72] Dozeman 2000, 45.

that appear forced and to base his observation of literary developments on points of dissimilarity, essentially arguing from silence. Furthermore, Dozeman seems to be basing his discussion on source-critically constructed texts. Once the reader of the final text comes into focus, the entire discussion must go in a different direction, for he has already read the prescription of the building of the tabernacle before arriving at Exod. 32 (i.e. he has read the 'Priestly account' already). In addition, the mention of the shining skin and the veil are not verbally present outside Exod. 34, but Dozeman links these concepts with his interpretation of the double masking on the level of the *significat*, i.e., the different aspects of Moses' authority. The theme of Mosaic authority is almost always linked to the theme of the masks. This is reading on a very abstract level. Even given an original audience that is accustomed to cultic images and allusions, I doubt that the theme of masking should so strongly control our reading in this way. The theme of Mosaic authority, indeed, seems to be a dominating feature of the texts, and the masking of Moses as linked with his authority is only secondary. Keeping this in mind, Dozeman's conclusion appears to be quite fruitful for our further discussion: Moses is not a character in his own right, but always points to Yhwh.[73] As he formulates it:

> The two masks symbolize his unique status. They become permanent features in his characterisation, witnessed by all Israelites. Yet the interaction of the masks ensures that Moses is not a popular hero. Although the veil directs attention to Moses as its wearer, removal reveals divine light, not the person.[74]

R. Rendtorff 2001

In analysing the text's communicative aims, Rolf Rendtorff traces the text's depiction of Moses' different roles of national saviour, mediator of the covenant, paradigmatic prophet, suffering intercessor and God's servant. This review of Rendtorff's position concentrates, mainly, on his remarks on Exodus material and tries to explicate the rhetorical aspects of his analysis.[75]

Moses has been singled out among the Israelites and prepared for his special role in a spectacular way, as is noted in his birth story ('the saved saviour') and his later meeting with Yhwh in the wilderness. On the literary level the call narrative, which consists, basically, of a lengthy dialogue (3:7–4:17), links Israel's

---

[73] Again McBride's ideas balance Coats' heroic picture of Moses are affirmed.

[74] Dozeman 2000, 39.

[75] In an important essay, Rendtorff, dealing mainly with aspects of Exod. 2 and 3, already states programatically: "I will try to imagine how the readers or listeners received and understood the biblical texts in their final form." (Rendtorff 1997, 11) There he suggests that the Moses narrative can be read on two levels. The inner-plot level is not the only one which exerts influence on the readers. But "[t]he reader knows certain things that are not explicitly told." (12) Although this specific knowledge is difficult to define, its presence cannot be disputed and the exegete has to take into account this additional level.

prehistory with their national beginnings.[76] Here, Rendtorff hints at the intimate relationship between Moses and God, a theme he comes back to time and time again. The immediacy of this relationship is unparalleled in biblical literature, except perhaps for Abraham's relationship to God. But Abraham stood alone before God, whereas Moses stands as mediator between Israel and Yhwh.[77] This 'in-between office' of Moses bears significant implications; it has a political aspect (bringing freedom from Egyptian domination), a religious aspect (revealing Yhwh's name, nature, and Torah), and a prophetic aspect (revealing God's will to the pharaoh [4:22] and being sent by God [שלח 3:10.12][78]). Rendtorff stresses that the character is not idealised. Moses opposes this call, doubting the people's acceptance of him ("What if they don't believe me ..." 4:1), pleading that he is unable to speak convincingly (4:10), and categorically refusing to take on the task (4:13). This theme of Moses not really wanting the job is present throughout the story, especially when the people grumble in the wilderness about his leadership qualities.

Even as Israel's early history unfolds under Moses' leadership, Israel's religion unfolds under his mediatorship. Through Moses comes the basic document of Israelite faith, the Torah, which remains linked to Moses' name throughout all of Israel's literary history, even though Moses is never portrayed as the founder of the Israelite religion. This aspect deserves closer attention than Rendtorff can devote to it in his brief overview and will be dealt with below in further detail. The same is true of the ingenious rhetorical device to portray the fact that the Torah[79] was mediated by Moses and didn't come to Israel directly from God, for it was not only God's will but, also, the people's explicit desire (Exod. 20:18–19).[80]

Rendtorff maintains that the Torah is inseparably linked with the covenant. Moses, again, acts as mediator between the two parties. Besides receiving the

---

[76] Rendtorff notes the self-presentation of Yhwh as the God of the fathers (3:6.14; 6:2-3) and the theme of land, which had been promised to the fathers (6:8).

[77] Concluding his remarks on Deuteronomy: "Mit dem Deuteronomium steht auch die Gestalt des Mose beherrschend und prägend am Ende des Pentateuch. Im Rückblick zeigt sich, daß er überhaupt die beherrschende Gestalt des Pentateuch ist. Vier von den fünf Büchern des Pentateuch handeln von ihm. Vor ihm ragen zwei andere Gestalten heraus: Noah und Abraham. Was aber Mose von diesen beiden unterscheidet, ist vor allem, daß er es nicht nur als einzelner mit Gott zu tun hat, sondern daß er zwischen Gott und Israel steht." (Rendtorff 1999, 85).

[78] Note the formula, "Thus speaks the Lord...", throughout the plague narrative.

[79] In the present context Rendtorff uses 'Torah' as something different from the Pentateuch, referring to the specific content of the divine revelation ("Weisung Gottes") to Moses as it is recorded in the Pentateuch (cf. Rendtorff 2001, 61f).

[80] This was already observed by Dozeman 1989, 54 and, quoting him, Watts 1998, 418, n. 16. Both of them were aware of some sort of rhetorical significance, but never elaborated on what exactly this is.

terms and conditions and besides his involvement in the initiation ceremony
(Exod. 24), Moses' role as mediator of the covenant is most explicit after the
golden calf incident where the covenant is broken and renewed (Exod. 32; 34).
This connection between the covenant/Torah and Moses was so effective, that
in the later literary history both are known with the attribute 'Mosaic'.

Another role Moses takes on in the portrayal of the Pentateuch (especially in
Numbers and Deuteronomy) is the paradigmatic prophet. Exodus refers to this
theme in a more hidden way, using the motif of sending (שלח Exod. 3:10.12)
and the prophetic formula, 'Thus says the Lord' (כה־אמר יהוה 4:22; 5:1; 7:17.26;
8:16; 9:1.13; 10:3; 11:4; 32:27). In the perception of the Pentateuch, Moses is
the benchmark for other prophets, but he remains, by virtue of his meeting face
to face, in a class of his own (cf. especially Num. 12:6-8). This proposition of
Moses preceding and superseding almost every institution in later Israel runs
through the remainder of Rendtorff's discussion and hints at the rhetorical effect
of the literary presentation of Moses in the Pentateuch.

Two things are most noteworthy when Moses' relationship with God is examined: his suffering and his intercession. Already, in the call narrative, Moses
is characterised as suffering under the weight of his role (Exod. 3:12; 4:1.10
and 13). Moses' discontent arises, especially, in situations when things go
wrong: the workload for the people gets worse (5:22) or the murmuring at
Mara, which is directed against him (15:22-23; and similar 17:2-3 for example.
Further examples are found in Numbers). In these situations Moses complains
to God and always receives an answer which supports his leadership role and
establishes him as mediator. That things get better for the people when Moses
brings the crucial issues before Yhwh is another feature of Moses' character,
which is strongly emphasised in the golden calf episode (Exod. 32–34). Here,
his intercession manages to turn away God's imminent wrath by reminding him
of his promises to the fathers. Here his loyalty to the people comes to the fore,
when he rejects, emphatically, the idea of him being the line through which the
promises shall come. This display of loyalty wins special significance against
the foil of the people's previous attitude to his leadership abilities in the desert!
His intercessory activities are not limited to the Israelites, which, interestingly,
appear only after the establishment of the covenant (Exod. 24).[81] In the plague
episodes Moses time and time again prays for the ceasing of the curses and so it
happens. All this legitimises Moses' special role and office. He alone has the
ability to avert God's wrath or judgement. Jer. 15:1 reflects the later perception
of Moses, together with Samuel, as a paradigmatic intercessor. A further expression of the close relationship between Moses and Yhwh, considered by
Rendtorff, is the central verse, Exod. 14:31, which calls Moses a 'servant of
Yhwh' (cf. also Deut. 34:5). This 'title' appears in the remainder of the Old

---

[81] Following Schart 1990, 50f, Rendtorff finds the reason for this in the new legal responsibility of the people being covenanted to Yhwh and, thus, in a new legal relationship.

Testament especially in conjunction with two thematic areas, the Torah, given at Sinai, and the promise of the land. It seems to be a retrospective attribution as it features strongly at the end of important narrative blocks (e.g. Num. 12:7; Deut. 34:5; Josh. 1:1-2) and summary notices throughout the Old Testament. As it does not appear strongly in Exodus, I will only discuss it briefly when examining Exod. 14.

In conclusion, Rendtorff mentions Moses as Israel's paradigmatic leader: "[Die] erste Führungsfigur – eine Herrschergestalt, aber ohne institutionalisierte Herrschaftsgewalt."[82] Moses is the one in whom all later leadership functions of Israel's society are united. He is the one giving the prerequisites for Israel being a people by leading them out of Egyptian domination. Moses gives, as it were, the people their identity. Most important for his legitimation is that for everything he receives his orders straight from God; this was not the case for the different offices in Israel's later years. According to Rendtorff this is the key to Moses' uniqueness. In connection with these remarks, Rendtorff touches upon the rhetorical effects on the reader. For this reader it would now be obvious that Israel needs a leadership which is in intimate contact with Yhwh. Later kings need prophetic appointment and legitimation, something not necessary for Moses. When it comes to the 'kingship' of Moses, Rendtorff, rightly, highlights two aspects: contrary to the ancient Near Eastern king Moses is never the giver of the law and he never acts as priest.[83] The Aaronic priesthood can never be traced to a any kind of successor of Moses (cf. Num. 16–17).

As the communicative function of the Pentateuch's presentation of the character 'Moses' Rendtorff summarises:

> So zeigt sich unter den verschiedensten Aspekten, daß Mose eine paradigmatische Gestalt ist. Er hat in vielen Bereichen eine Vorbildfunktion, die jedoch religiös so überhöht ist, daß sie von keinem späteren Inhaber eines der Ämter erreicht werden kann. In der Gestalt Moses sind Idealformen bestimmter Ämter und Institutionen entworfen und in die Frühzeit Israels transponiert worden, an denen ihre späteren Inhaber und Verwalter gemessen werden, ohne sie je erreichen zu können.[84]

In addition, commenting on the conclusion of Deuteronomy he says:

> Dies ist eine der entscheidenden Botschaften der Überlieferung von Mose an die israelitische Nachwelt: daß Israel eigentlich nur von einem Menschen geführt werden kann, der in unmittelbarer Beziehung zu Gott steht und der daraus die Weisungen für die Leitung dieses Volkes empfängt, von dessen besonderer Stellung unter den Völkern das Deuteronomium in so hohen Worten geredet hat. Mose ist mehr als ein Prophet, aber er ist auch mehr als alle, die nach ihm das

---

[82] So states Rendtorff in his summarising remark on Moses' role for Israel as described in the Pentateuch (Rendtorff 1999, 85).

[83] Only in the context of the appointment of the Aaronic priesthood (Lev. 8) is Moses shown as bringing offerings himself.

[84] Rendtorff 2001, 134f.

Volk führen werden: als Josua, die Richter, Samuel und die Könige. Er setzt Maßstäbe, an denen die nach ihm Kommenden sich messen lassen müssen, die aber von keinem von ihnen erreicht werden.[85]

Moses is paradigmatic in that his religious example is so super-elevated that no one can ever reach him. Nevertheless, Moses' characterisation does not idealise him – we do not read a hagiography of Moses.[86] Rendtorff has provided a good starting point for the discussion of the rhetorical implications of the portrayal of Moses in Exodus. His results are, nevertheless, a little dissatisfying as they do not go beyond the remark that the Pentateuch is hoping for leaders in Israel who are sustaining an intimate relationship with God. There remains a set of questions awaiting treatment: What are the reasons for elevating Moses so high that no-one ever can reach this benchmark? Is that not a counter-productive strategy? How would a later king read this paradigm? Why *not* write a hagiography of Moses? Why does Moses need so much legitimation – posthumously?

Conclusion

This summary of research on the rhetorical use of the literary character Moses suffices to show the need for a further rhetorical-critical investigation. All authors make assumptions about certain rhetorical effects of the texts they discuss, but none of them gets beyond very general conclusions. The *desideratum*, here, is a more detailed analysis of the implications of the portrayal of Moses in Exodus including inferences on their communicative effect. Of critical importance are the following themes. A first theme is the need to define a reading level on which the character Moses works for the implied reader. Greßmann and Coats offer two different models, one trying to separate the fictional from the factual, the other one attempting to define a literary genre which preconditions the reading process. Rendtorff comes closest to a rhetorical-critical or reader-centred approach with his distinction of the story level and the level of the implied reader.[87] A second theme is the importance of the literary relationship between Moses and Yhwh and between Moses and the people, which is obvious in all the works previously discussed. A third theme, which is implicitly included in the previous, is one of the nature of Mosaic authority. As a fourth theme I wish, together with Crüsemann, Watts and Rendtorff, to highlight the importance of certain sociological offices for the presentation and perception of Moses in the texts. In the following I shall attempt to discuss the Mosaic picture emerging

---

[85] Rendtorff 1999, 85.

[86] "Mose ist so wenig eine Idealgestalt, wie es die Erzväter sind oder irgendeine andere Gestalt in der Hebräischen Bibel" (Rendtorff 2001, 135).

[87] This is of course a subjective comment, based very much on the shared pessimism about the validity of hypothetical source-critical or redaction-critical divisions. All other authors arrive at some sort of reader-centred interpretations, but in their case of texts of doubtful existence.

from the final shape of the book of Exodus, something which has not been done extensively yet, as the previous review tried to show. The themes highlighted will reappear at the relevant points in the discussion, which attempts to follow the natural reading sequence of Exodus.

Opening the Mind – the Introduction of Moses as a Character in Exodus

As I have shown in the chapter on Yhwh, the introduction of a character into the plot of a narrative is of utmost importance for the rhetorical effect of the entire portrayal. The first *rendezvous* between a character and the reader provides a background against which every action and development will be evaluated. This conditioning of the reader might well go unnoticed in the reading process, but it is present and, at times, will surface, especially when themes and motifs reappear in the plot. In the following paragraphs I intend to make explicit what may be implicit for the reader and thus provide a backdrop for the subsequent discussion of the different communicative focal points of the Mosaic portrait in Exodus.

The Making of a Hero?

First, I will consider the birth-narrative of Moses, which provides the initial point of contact between the reader and this character. After this 'initiation' passage I will go on to look into the rhetorical effect of the description of Moses' very first deeds (Exod. 2:11-22). All this material prior to the call narrative (Exod. 3:1–4:17) introduces us to Moses.

Moses has a rather unspectacular start for a biblical character of his later grandeur. In his birth story (Exod. 2:1-10)[88] the reader does not even learn about a proper family tree – except the note that his parents belong to the tribe of Levi. At his birth, there is no name given to the little boy. Women dominate the entire scene:[89] Moses only survives because of the care of his mother (בת־לוי), his sister, the princess (בת־פרעה) and her servants. The pharaoh's daughter adopts[90] this little child, but his real mother is allowed to spend a few more years with her boy as his professional wet-nurse. The entire setting seems almost surreal. But reading the brief pericope in its context, a perceptive reader

---

[88] Cf. Siebert-Hommes 1992, for some very intriguing insights into the structure of the first two chapters of Exodus and, also, for some remarks on the role of women (esp. the daughters) in the narrative.

[89] Cf. Weber 1990, 56ff.

[90] Adoption seems to be what is in view here. The naming of the child by the Egyptian princess and the payments to the nurse strongly suggest that the woman adopted Moses formally and took up responsibility for him.

will instantly realise the use of irony here.[91] All of the many women act – apparently quite deliberately – against the specific orders of the pharaoh (Exod. 1:22). His own daughter adopts a Hebrew male child. Even the narration of Moses' mother betrays the author's deep sense of humour, as the mother actually casts her son into the Nile just as the command prescribed. The Nile, however, is, for Moses, a place of saving and not of death. Another example of irony, this time not at the expense of the pharaoh but probably of Moses himself, is the etymology given at the end of the story. The text derives the name 'Moses' from a Hebrew root (משה drawn out) but – as is widely known – in Egyptian 'Moses' means 'son'.[92] The presentation of the Hebrew etymology serves the author as a device of concealment. The pleasure of the reading process is raised when the reader discovers the twist at the end of the story.

But more than that is achieved. Reading the brief pericope within the context of comparable motifs from ancient Near Eastern literature,[93] it becomes clear that this example of a birth story does not go beyond the very first steps of this genre. Willi-Plein observes rightly:

---

[91] Contrary Childs 1976, 18f. His argument for the favourable portrayal of the princess is not convincing at all. It would rather support the mocking of the Egyptian king, whose own daughter is forced by the appeals of a small child to act against the king's clear commands. On irony in Exod. 1–2 see also Weber 1990, 73–75.

[92] Cf. the very interesting comments by Willi-Plein 1991, 115–118. She offers an intriguing study of this brief pericope, highlighting the importance of the dominating root ילד and the cognate nouns. Willi-Plein argues, convincingly, that the author of the passage must have been aware of the Egyptian meaning of 'Moses.' On the Egyptian name see p.117, n.17. An important contribution on the semantic puns in Exod. 1–2 is given by Weber 1990. He suggests that there is an implicit, rhetorically motivated, link between the Egyptian name Moses and the *Leitworten* of these chapters.

[93] For an informative discussion of the parallel accounts of birth stories cf. Schmidt 1988, 55–57. I follow him in his judgement that the similarities and differences between the legend of Sargon and Moses' birth-narrative point only to an indirect dependency, probably via a common tradition. Coats 1988, 43 and 222, n.2, provides English literature on this subject. An interesting contribution comes from Zlotnick-Sivan 2004. Motivated by a possibility for a more precise dating (530-525) of the latest redactional layer of Exod. 1–2, she sets out to suggest a political function of this narrative in the relations between the post-exilic Israel and the Persian Empire. The base of her argument rests in a comparison of Herodotus' account of Cyrus' birth myth and the Mosaic one. Her venture shows, at least, the need for a very careful and methodologically well-argued interpretation of intertextual (and, between the lines, historical) relationships across literary and cultural borders. It is appealing to find links between biblical descriptions of certain events and otherwise well-attested events – this gives the feeling of more historical substance. But, sometimes, it seems better advice to admit historical agnosticism because of the lack of more than mere hypotheses.

Aus der angebahnten Karriere wird jedoch weiter nichts als eine Namenserklärung
– danach bricht der Erzählzusammenhang fast abrupt ab. Es handelt sich wirklich
nur um eine Geburtsgeschichte, nicht um eine Kindheitsgeschichte.[94]

A reader familiar with a birth story like that of Sargon of Akkad (approx. 2350–
2294)[95] would easily perceive that a similar story is initiated here. The hero (or
king) is born and miraculously preserved from imminent death in the waters.
Here, the author suggests to his reader that a similar career has begun. The end
of the pericope (v.10), then, comes as an anti-climax: the child is, simply, called
'son', i.e., not even a real name is given to him. Willi-Plein suggests that the
sole interest of the author would then be to give reason for the Egyptian name of
the Levite Moses.[96] In the light of the previous discussion, this seems to
understate the importance of the pericope, but it, certainly, demonstrates that
reading Moses as only partly and very quietly introduced as the book's hero is
not too erroneous.[97]

---

[94] Willi-Plein 1991, 116.

[95] Cf. ANET[3], 119 or Beyerlin 1985, 123f. Cf. Childs 1976, 8–10, who, rightly, points to
the literary function of the Sargon legend, which is still open to discussion. Whatever
the actual setting or function of this legend, as long as the reading of this text induces a
mental picture of a hero, the communicative strategy of the Exodus author was successful. Rendtorff 1997, 12, remarks on the characteristics of the birth-narrative and goes in
a similar direction, without referring to any motif from ancient Near Eastern sources:
"… a very peculiar story, so that the reader expects something extraordinary." Although
the legend is set in the life of Sargon of Akkad, its surviving fragments are of the Neo-
Assyrian and Neo-Babylonian periods (7th-6th cent. B.C.). This, of course, poses a dating problem. But there is no good reason to doubt the existence of Sargon's legend as
well as similar stories from other cultures prior to the 7th century. Donald Redford finds
32 examples of this type scene throughout the Ancient Near East (Redford 1967).

[96] She maintains that the actual function of the text is "das Entscheidende Stück Vorge-
schichte, Vorspiel zur Befreiungsgeschichte Israels. Noch einmal wird mit dieser Geburt
eine Familiengeschichte erzählt wie in der Genesis, aber sie führt in die Volksgeschichte
ein." (Willi-Plein 1991, 118) Hence: "Nicht um die Aussetzung, nicht um die Kindheit,
ja, nicht einmal primär um die Bewahrung des Kindes, sondern um die *Geburt* geht es."
(118, italics in the orig.) This is in total contradiction to Coats' reading of this narrative
(cf. Coats 1988, 43f). Of course, Coats has a strong interest in viewing the account of
Moses' birth as the best example of the heroic genre he proposes for all Moses traditions: "A birth that foreshadows the conflict at the center of the hero's life work typifies
the structure of heroic saga" (48). His arguments cannot convince: Coats has to strip the
story of its narrative context to arrive at his conclusion – something which I am very
hesitant to do.

[97] Hoffmeier 1997, 138, dismisses all notions of the extraordinary and thinks that this
text and all other texts which use a similar motif simply "reflect the ancient practice of
committing an unwanted child, or one needing protection, into the hands of provi-
dence." This may be the social and cultural reality behind the text, but the author of Exodus, certainly, makes more of it on the literary/rhetorical level.

Why, then, does the author use this ambivalent start for the introduction of his main (human) character? Admittedly, the reading proposed above points to some very subtle markers as justification. This subtlety, however, seems to be intended by the author. It is my conviction that the author presupposes a very positive Moses-picture on the part of his implied readers and that his attempt is to deconstruct this image. A reader 'knowing' that Moses is the hero of Israel's founding period would probably miss the subtle question marks introduced by the author in playing with the genre of 'the birth and miraculous saving of the hero'. Subsequently, the reader assumes that right from birth Moses is destined to become a hero, the hero he, the reader, always knew.[98] As I proceed with the argument it will become obvious that the author deconstructed Moses. Here the question arises: why, exactly, did the author not do so from the outset in the straightforward manner in which he continues? As has been observed above, the hesitant introduction of Yhwh into the plot of Exodus[99] is a good rhetorical advice which does not offend the reader from the start but, rather, gets the unpleasant message to him through the back door. The critique of one's preconceptions is always an unpleasant message, so it takes some skill on the part of the author to keep his reader with him – and, ultimately, to achieve his communicative goal. The reader, who has a less overly positive picture of Moses, might well recognise the subtle hints offered to him in the narrative and will, most likely, take much pleasure in discovering how the author proceeds with his task.

Of course, one can read the entire introduction of the character Moses with an entirely different set of preconceptions, as will become clear when I discuss the first actions of Moses recorded in Exodus.

Exod. 2:11-22 can and should be viewed as a unit.[100] The connection to the previous birth-narrative is only a loose one, as a number of interesting details go neglected.[101] The author, it would seem, intentionally created this gap in order

---

[98] Cf. the many embellishments provided by the later Jewish tradition showing the anxiety to mark Moses' birth as a most special event: his father, Amram, knew (Miriam, as well, had visions before) before conception that a deliverer would be born; at his birth the house was filled with light; Moses was of outstanding beauty, ability and *charme*; some Rabbis interpret the chronological remarks in the text as pointing to a "seventh-month child", which was, always, understood to have an extraordinary career. For references cf. Houtman 1993, 273f.

[99] See p.60.

[100] Cf. Siebert-Hommes 1992. For her 2:16-22 forms a sequel to 2:11-15, parallel to the two narratives in 1:8-14 and 1:15-22. See, already, Weimar 1980, 19f, n.9, from a different point of view.

[101] For example, how did Moses know that he originally belongs to the Hebrews? What did he know about his ancestors? How old was he? Where did he live? What kind of education did he receive? What kind of relationship did he enjoy with his Egyptian mother? That these questions were of interest to many readers of the text is clear from the answers given, mainly, by Jewish rabbis but, also, by Christian exegetes. For refer-

to focus the attention entirely on Moses' loyalty toward his people and his awareness of their oppression. This theme unfolds in telling of two contrasting stories found in Exod. 2:11-15 and 2:16-22.[102] The contrast, which lies on the story level, regards the success of Moses' actions. Structurally marked – and hence accentuating the content – in the first episode is the threefold chaining of the verbs נכה (to hit) and הרג (to kill). The iteration builds to the climax of the death sentence by the pharaoh (the last occurrence of הרג), which is of importance for the subsequent plot (cf. 4:19). The second episode balances Moses' failed attempt to avert injustice and violence with an account of success. In this scene, he reacts to a situation of injustice much more appropriately than in Egypt. There are more features supporting this contrasting reading of the two parts. Moses is no longer a refugee, but, rather, finds a new home together with a family. In the first part, Moses acts explicitly as an Israelite (v.11 "he went out to his brothers"), but, in Midian, he was considered to be an Egyptian, albeit one who does not oppress but who delivers from oppression. The pharaoh and Reuel/Jithro – both of whom are leaders – are, also, polarised in their attitudes towards Moses ('expulsion from the country' vs. 'warm reception in the family').

The author presents two events in Moses' life before his encounter with God. Thus arises the question: What communicative function do they serve in the portrayal of Moses?

Ari Zivotofsky asks exactly this question and answers it along the lines of the midrashic interpretive tradition. He reads the text as providing the reason for Moses' election by God as the leader of his people. For Zivotofsky איש becomes the key-word for the character of Moses. The author wanted to present Moses as a *man*, someone who really cared and took his responsibility for law and justice. In a fascinating reading, which includes the different Jewish traditions on the 'pre-history' of Moses, Zivotofsky presents a well-rounded presentation of the Mosaic character as the perfect leader and proves this by displaying the most important precondition of a leader: active empathy. Some *midrashim* present a more embellished version, adding a lot of detail and entirely new stories, while others use the standard devices of Jewish exegesis to extract from the text their desired meaning.[103] But Zivotofsky is not merely driven by an encyclopaedic interest in Jewish *midrash*. He, further, asks why the Rabbis felt the need for these embellishments. The claim is that a double motive lies beneath this literary strategy. On the one hand, the text was seen as dangerous for the common

---

ences cf. again Houtman 1993, 287–290, 298.

[102] The syntactic break between 2:15 and 16 is marked by the nominal beginning of v.16 (ולכהן), whereas the preceding and following sentences are firmly chained by waw consecutive forms.

[103] These un-embellished *midrashim* would provide a sufficient base to claim that the biblical text actually meant what the others tried to support with their embellishments (cf. Zivotofsky 1994, 264).

reader who could have copied Moses' actions, including the use of violence, and, therefore, followed this great man's precedent. So the prevention of misguided zeal was achieved by removing the original Mosaic situation as far as possible from normal reality and everyday experience. But, on the other hand, the Rabbis wanted to present Moses as a role model for moderated zeal and included further, less dangerous, examples for this in their commentary.[104] The Rabbis, and with them Zivotofsky, thus, implicitly, understood the text's most important communicative function as the exhortation to copy the exemplary attitude of Moses, the archetypical *Man*.

Quite a different reading is to be found in an article by Trent Butler. Working with the form-critical apparatus, he traces some inner biblical traditions originating from a polemic against Moses.[105] Butler takes his lead from Coats[106] and considers Exod. 2:11-25 as an originally independent narrative. But this is nearly the only point of similarity between Butler and Coats. Butler reads the narrative as an essentially non-heroic tale, whereas Coats stresses the heroic display of Moses. The separation of the passage from its present Pentateuchal context allows one to perceive its Moses-critical attitude: "Moses, the presumptuous pretender ... protecting his own interests ... willing to slay both Egyptian and Hebrew in his desire for power and position."[107] The second part of the narrative (v.16-22) is also interpreted as polemic against the national hero of Israel. Butler suggests reading the story as commenting on Moses' relationship with Midian[108] and putting the entire initiative for this connection in the deliberate will of Moses.[109] Butler, trying to clarify the criticism, writes with an ironic undertone: "The great heroic act of Moses is that he can deliver Midianite women from unidentified shepherds, while passing himself off as Egyptian."[110] Other narratives subsumed under Butler's 'anti-Moses tradition' are Exod. 4:24-26; 18:5-12 and 18:13-24. All of these texts are critical of Moses, to some extent,

---

[104] Zivotofsky 1994, 265.

[105] Cf. Butler 1979, 9.

[106] Coats 1973. Coats categorises Exod. 2:15b-22 on a form-critical basis as an old marriage story, which explains the relation between Moses and his Midianite relatives.

[107] Butler 1979, 10. Coats is quite opposed to Butler's interpretation (cf. Coats 1988, 49f). He views the killing of the Egyptian as foreshadowing the content of Moses' later call, not as an act of murder, but part of his heroic attitude. Coats does not sufficiently explain the reaction of the Hebrew who benefited from this heroic act (v.14).

[108] Coats 1988, 224, n.23, explicitly, disapproves of Butler's interpretation by arguing that Num. 25 does not set a principle against intermarriage between Midianites and Israelites. Hence, the national aspects of Moses' marriage would then be essentially of a neutral nature.

[109] Butler understands the whole point of the narrative being v.21, Moses agreement to stay with the priest. Moses' designation as Egyptian would then be read as Moses distancing himself from Israel since Israel and Midian were arch-enemies.

[110] Butler 1979, 11.

and appear to be the work of a group of people, probably from a priestly background, trying to undermine Mosaic authority. "[They] sought to show the true Moses as unqualified for any of Israel's positions of leadership."[111] The Pentateuchal image of Moses then reflects the domination of the pro-Moses party over against the anti-Moses polemics. Butler fails to explain why both traditions were ultimately brought together; he only suggests some sort of debate which he does not specify further. Nevertheless, his reading of some texts in Exodus which deal with the character Moses seems at many points appropriate.

These two readings demonstrate the range of interpretation which is possible. Some critically-trained scholars try not to smooth out the varied pictures of Moses presented in the Pentateuch and explain the final text by calling upon the services of textual genesis. Others try to harmonise their preconceived picture of Moses with the texts. I suggest that, reading the texts in their final shape, both options are inappropriate as the author, consciously, desired this ambivalence regarding the portrayal of Moses. Thus, the mixed presentation of Moses should be regarded as part of the author's rhetorical strategy of opening the minds of his readers towards his communicative aims.

The essentially rabbinic reading of Exod. 2:11-22, as exemplified by Zivotofsky, is certainly a possible reading, especially as it makes sense on a rhetorical level, as well. But does the text on its own, without midrashic additions, recommend this very positive interpretation of Moses at the beginning of his career? This question invites a negative answer.[112] Indeed, as Zivotofsky rightly observed, the theme of the pericope develops two issues: whether or not Moses is a righteous man and whether or not he qualifies as leader and judge. Because the author concentrates on these themes, other questions the reader might have remain unanswered. For example, does the author approve of Moses killing the Egyptian or not?[113] Both sides can be argued, but a sure conclusion can, in my opinion, not be reached. It seems viable to use the concept of two reading levels and to include in the discussion the level of the implied reader with his previous and presupposed knowledge.[114]

---

[111] Butler 1979, 14. Recently Ber has taken up this line of thought from Butler in his examination of Exod. 18, where he consciously goes about finding possible tensions in the narrative which often has been interpreted in a harmonistic way (cf. Ber 2008).

[112] Fretheim 1991a, 42–46, for example, attempts to read the text this way. He concludes that Moses' actions anticipate God's actions in the later plague narrative. True, there are key terms that are used with both subjects, but the results are very different from each other. It appears to be a rather selective reading of the texts.

[113] Cf. Houtman 1993, 300. Along the way, he mentions several very inventive stories, trying to justify Moses' act of violence from many traditions. For a review of different commentators and their ethical judgement on Moses' act of violence cf. Childs 1976, 40–42.

[114] This has been done very fruitfully by Rendtorff 1997. Cf. above (p.143f).

The three situations in which Moses is described here paint a picture of him open to many interpretations. The reader is left to decide. Firstly, Moses acts on behalf of oppressed Israel, which, surely, provokes some sort of sympathy on the part of the reader. Secondly, Moses wants to assume a high position of justice but cannot achieve it, because of another character. Thirdly, Moses, again, tries to help the underdogs and does so wisely; hence, he is blessed with a new home, family and children.

Exod. 2:14 presents us with the thematic climax of the first pericope (2:11-15): the brief dialogue between the guilty Hebrew and Moses. Not only does biblical dialogue often have a literary function of emphasis, but even the words, themselves, are important for the author's argument. In this brief discussion the idea that Moses, essentially, takes on the position of a judge builds from the first verse. Initially, there is only the rather untechnical description (in legal terms) of an attempt to restore justice (v.11b-12). Then, in the second scene, Moses' concern with justice comes to the fore, more explicitly, as the text uses the technical legal term רשע (v.13).[115] Finally, the Hebrew's reply focuses merely on Moses' endeavour to be a judge and hence to assume leadership functions (שר ושפט). The Hebrew speaks as judge, commenting on Moses' earlier murder and his motives. Rendtorff remarks: "At this point it is just a rhetorical question that has to be answered by 'No one did.' But later on we learn that God did exactly that: He made Moses a judge over his people (18.13-27)."[116] This is a valid interpretation only at the second level of interpretation which takes into account the assumed knowledge of the reader. Then, it is most likely that the reader realises this implication instantly while reading this dialogue. Of course, the reader – from any time in Israelite history – must have known that Moses was judge and something like a political leader.[117] At the plot level we merely observe the irony of a self-assuming judge becoming the judged.[118] The rhetorical effect, here, is clearly the undermining of the Mosaic (self-)presentation of a man of justice. This happens at the plot level but also exerts influence at the second level.

But, before I discuss this further, I want to include the next scene (Exod. 2:16-22) which is even more ambivalent. Moses, on the one hand, does a positive deed displaying, again, his concern for the oppressed, but, on the other hand he deserts his fellow-Israelites to live a life of quietness while adjusting himself into a Midianite family. At the plot level a few words suffice the author

---

[115] Cf. Childs 1976, 30.

[116] Rendtorff 1997, 13.

[117] If he had known and had made the mental connection, this aspect would then have been intended for the pleasure of a reader who, smiling insightfully, is satisfied that he knows more than the characters inside the story. This is, certainly, a rhetorical device which betrays the skill of the author.

[118] Butler 1979, 10.

to sketch the situation.[119] The climax is, again, a dialogue in which not even Moses has a voice. The rhetorical effect of this conversation between the father and his daughters is to evaluate Moses' assistance. It recapitulates events and highlights the exceptionality of Moses' deeds: he not only drove away the shepherds but even drew water for the animals. The rebuke by the father also underlines this – it was a great mistake not to invite Moses. The ambivalence of the portrayal of Moses is created when he, apparently, pretends to be an Egyptian and, of course, when he settles in with a foreign family and even marries the daughter of a heathen priest. At the second level of interpretation the reader who knows Moses as the deliverer of Israel must find it odd that Moses does not seem to show a great interest in the deliverance of the Hebrews from slavery – especially after reading of their troubles in bondage and the remarkable story of Moses' birth.[120] A glimmer of hope might arise when Moses' first son is named. Moses seems to recognise that he lives in a foreign land and hence does not intend to assimilate entirely into Midian. At the story level it could, nevertheless, mean that he considers the Hebrews as his (ideological) home or Egypt as his (physical) home country. Reading on the second level there is a hint of irony: Moses seems to perceive his stay in Midian – inside the plot – as being away from home, either the Hebrew people or the land of Egypt. This is Moses' perception. The implied reader, on the other hand, must surely recognise that the Israelites' 'official' home is Canaan. This reading can be supported by the next three verses (Exod. 2,23–25), which seem quite unrelated to the previous verses.[121] The link is made, here, between the patriarchal covenant together with its land promise and the situation of Israel in a land not promised to them. But this is only an afterthought; the story of Moses, for now, ends typically at the naming of his offspring. Thus, the introduction of Moses as a character into the plot of Exodus ends "without any prospect of a better future," as Rendtorff[122] remarks.

"With biblical man ... there is usually a distance – and often a clash – between the impression produced on his first appearance and the one left after his last."[123] Is Sternberg's generalisation appropriate for the portrait of Moses? Let

---

[119] It even seems to be written consciously in a non-elevated style; cf. the not very creative iteration of the verb בוא in Exod. 2,16–18a (came ... came ...).

[120] The mention of the different nationalities involved in the two pericopes (2,1–10 and 2,11–22) – Hebrew, Egyptian and Midianite – provides support for my reading of the passage. One can observe a certain development: in the beginning it is very clear that Moses is a Hebrew, a fact that becomes more and more clouded until he lives as "a semi-Egyptian shepherd in the service of a certain Midianite," as Rendtorff 1997, 14, succinctly, puts it.

[121] Exod. 2,23–25 have commonly been ignored in interpretation on the grounds that they represent a later insertion by P (cf. Rendtorff 1997, 14). For their rhetorical and theological importance cf. above p.61.

[122] Cf. Rendtorff 1997, 14.

[123] Sternberg 1987, 326.

me offer a rhetorical-critical reading of the first impression Moses leaves on the reader of Exodus. I shall assume the preconception of Moses' role in early Israel on the part of the implicit reader. There is no straightforward way to develop a rough sketch of this implied knowledge. All there is to achieve this aim are the hints provided by the text itself. The ambivalence in the portrait of Moses in Exod. 2 has lead to quite a span of contradictory readings, as has been just shown. These readings are, of course, based largely on the readers' biases and responsibilities to their interpretive communities.[124] But, the ambivalence is already intended in the text itself, giving the reader a lot of room (and responsibility!) to fill in the gaps and to pass judgements.

As has been argued above,[125] Exod. 2:1-10 is probably the attempt to take up the reader's knowledge of Moses as *the* leader and hero of Israel. The passage alludes to the ancient Near Eastern genre of birth-story and leads the reader into thinking that he can expect the portrayal of a hero, only to disappoint the reader in the following passage. The author begins Exod. 2:11-22 positively by telling of Moses' concern for his own people, but the plot does not continue to picture Moses as going from strength to strength. The reader observes how the right man with the right attitude completely fails to bring deliverance to the people he recognises as his brothers. The killing of the Egyptian does not bring about the recognition of his authority by his fellow Israelites – a theme that runs through the entire wilderness tradition (I will come back to that). Moses' attempt to ensure justice among the two Israelites fails precisely because of this earlier murder. Thus, the author sows a seed of disquiet in the mind of the reader as to whether or not Moses really is the man for the job. His moral waistcoat has a stain, his leadership abilities are certainly not great, as he could not even handle a situation as small as this, and the identification with the people erodes when he flees the country out of fear. Having read this story the reader must wonder how Moses actually achieved his great position in the tradition.

As we will see Sternberg's claim is true: there is a discrepancy between the introduction of the Mosaic image in Exodus and the later literary development. Reading to Exod. 2:22 Moses' career appears as a non-starter; his promising birth disappoints and his self-appointment as leader and judge utterly fails. Further reading will provide the reasons for this literary strategy. At the rhetorical level, the tactics of the author seem to create an openness to reconsider the early history of Israel. The major concern in the introduction of the character Moses, certainly, refutes an overly positive conception of this man.

---

[124] For this phenomenon cf. the illuminating essay by Wenham 1994.

[125] Cf. p.151, esp. the remarks on the subtle undermining of the portrait.

The Call of a Mediator

As observed above (cf. p.63), the call narrative (Exod. 2:23–4:31), with its lengthy dialogue mainly introduces Yhwh into the plot of the book. Nevertheless, Moses' portrait acquires a new quality in that he is, now, introduced as the mediator between Yhwh and his covenant people. In the following I shall restrict myself to relevant results of my earlier discussion and focus on a couple of points in more detail.

In the call narrative two characters come together who will dominate the remainder of the plot of Exodus. This literary meeting enables the author to contrast the two characters so that the reader will, unavoidably, compare the two. That this comparison (and its theological content) is the main function of the narrative is very different from the picture Houtman presents.[126] He constructs a reader who is drawn into suspense and emotional involvement as he wonders whether Moses will actually take on the job of deliverer or not. I suspect that this reading does not do justice to the likely previous knowledge on the part of the implied reader. The reader *knows* that Moses was the leader who actually brought out Israel from Egypt. So he will only wonder how he did so and, certainly, what enabled him to do this. This is not to rule out Houtman's reading, categorically, for a novice to Israelite history will, indeed, read the story as Houtman describes the process. But the concrete rhetorical features of the text seem to serve better the more reflective and evaluative communicative goal, as I defined it.

I have already argued that Moses is a figure serving mainly as the foil against which Yhwh's portrait takes shape. The most stark example of this contrast is found in 3:11.14: Moses is a nobody ("Who am I?"), whereas Yhwh is most sovereign ("I am who I am").[127] This, of course, does not mean that Moses remains a nebulous, minor figure. On the contrary, for a biblical character he gets quite a detailed portrayal. This picture, though, is not an overly positive one. Having widened the reader's horizon in the previous narratives to accept a deconstruction of the heroic Moses, the author now attempts to develop his picture of the more important and more-wonderful character in Israel's history, Yhwh. In the end, it becomes clear that Moses is who he is only because of the one God authorising him and enabling him to do what he does.[128] So, we witness a deconstruction in the implied reader's conception of Moses. After read-

---

[126] Cf. Houtman 1993, 322–326.

[127] Other examples of this contrast may be found above (p.63). Most striking is the issue of forecast/fulfilment: Moses' predictions fall flat, but Yhwh's succeed (cf. above p.68).

[128] Cf. my discussion of the idea of the transcendent authority developed by McBride (above p.134).

ing this text, it is not possible to speak of Moses as an authority in himself, as the able and willing leader or as the loyal and obedient servant. I shall now support this thesis by looking into some of the rhetorical features of Exod. 2:23–4:3, developing the narrative in its canonical shape.

THE FIRST THEOPHANY AT HOREB

After the short, but crucial, passage in Exod. 2:23-25, which opens a new dynamic of events in the plot of Exodus,[129] the author takes up the thread of Moses' story. Exod. 3:1 recalls the past situation: Moses' name, his father-in-law, his profession are all mentioned. After the heavenly scene (2:23-25), overloaded with meaning and allusions, the author, seemingly, goes back to the trivialities of life, only to present his reader shortly afterwards with the first theophany of the story. He continues to use allusions which must have been known by his implied reader. The mention of Mt. Horeb was surely known as the place of the later, more impressive theophany and of the giving of the law. Jacob comments tersely: "Der Dornbusch ist der Vorgänger des Sinai."[130] This association prepares the reader for one of the most significant theological points made in Exodus, namely, that the exodus from Egypt and the covenant established at Sinai belong together. In these two very brief scenes (2:23-25 and 3:1-6) the author manages to bring into contact Moses, the man of no success, and Yhwh, the God determined to rescue his people. The divine meets the human and a new narrative dynamic is developed.[131]

Is Moses' call indeed a "radical break with the past" as Childs suggests?[132] Childs might be influenced here by Karl Barth's views on revelation, but he highlights a feature of the text which deserves great attention in the framework

---

[129] Cf. above p.61. Jacob views the four appearances of 'Elohim' in 2,23–25 as preparation for the name 'Yhwh' in 3:2 (and for the entire theophany) and, hence, as a linking device between the two texts (Jacob 1997, 42).

[130] Jacob 1997, 45. Jacob offers a very lucid and insightful interpretation of the passage, whilst dismissing some of the astonishing rabbinic interpretations of the event.

[131] Or as Childs 1976, 72 puts it powerfully: "The intertwining of God's redemptive purpose for Israel with the reaction of his chosen vehicle forms the warp and woof of the call narrative." Jacob makes quite a lot of the last part of 3:6: "Der folgende Satz scheint überflüssig zu sein, zumal der Abschnitt mit Handlung sehr sparsam ist. Aber er ist bedeutsam für die Haltung Mose [sic!] während des folgenden Gesprächs und ganz besonders bezeichnend für den Charakter des Mannes, daher auch die singuläre Sprache." (Jacob 1997, 48). The conclusion for Moses' character is that even he, the one with whom God converses 'face to face,' has the piety and appropriate fear to cover his face and dismiss all seeing in order to hear. This interpretation seems somewhat far-fetched given the constant contrast between Moses and Yhwh constantly in speech; it is not an expression of piety. The presence of the divine always evokes some sort of shock and a feeling of inadequacy, which is exactly what the author narrates.

[132] Cf. Childs 1976, 73, with reference to von Rad's discussion of the prophetic calling (cf. Rad 1965, 62ff).

of a rhetorical reading. As the author tries to create in his reader's mind a certain picture of Moses, we are on the verge of a new development. After the more or less negative introduction to the character Moses, the reader now observes a typical theophany. Does this event change Moses' life forever? Or can we observe a degree of continuity? To a certain extent, Moses' situation changes radically. He cannot continue to pasture the flock of his father-in-law because he has been called to meet the current pharaoh face to face and to provoke a major conflict will affect Egyptian state interests. On the other hand, the author provides some important points of continuity within the person of Moses by linking Exod. 2 with 3+4. The theme linking the two narratives is Moses' authority. What Yhwh feels toward his people is similar to what Moses' felt toward his people when he went out to his brothers (אל־אחיו) in Exod. 2:11. Moses *saw* (ראה) them in their *corvée* (סבלות) just as Yhwh saw (also ראה)[133] them in their overly hard labour (עבודה).[134] Moses might have displayed the right attitude, but he has failed to do his brothers any good. He acted in his own authority which was no authority as is made obvious by 2:12+14.[135] Now, Yhwh attempts the same, and he wants Moses to act on his behalf to bring about deliverance. Apart from these, more implicit, invitations to compare the two situations, the author uses Moses' first words in reaction to Yhwh's call (3:11) to make it abundantly clear that, by now, even Moses knows that he has forfeited his authority for this job. Firstly, the reader is almost led to think of Moses as the born hero, but, then, he is left unsure as to whether or not this character can stand up to his destiny. Now, the reader sees that Yhwh is still confident in this man. At this point Child's proposed 'radical break' is expected by any reader. But does Moses now – having received his call – go from strength to strength and fulfil his divine duty with style and elan? The author does not seem to be finished with his deconstruction of an idealised concept of the Moses figure.

THE DIALOGUE

Moses resists his call with a direct refusal (Exod. 4:13) and is, clearly, not showing himself in the most positive light. His authority is non-existent; he does

---

[133] There is an interesting clustering of the verb ראה in 3:2-6, which has been observed quite often (cf. only Cassuto 1967, 32; Childs 1976, 70; Robinson 1997, 117). I think there might well be a deliberate link between 2:25, Yhwh seeing the sons of Israel (a very marked use of the word!), and the repetitive use in 3:2-6. One could draw all sorts of theological conclusions (e.g. when Yhwh sees man, man will see Yhwh' actions), but in the end I think it is simply a rhetorical device of *repetitio* or *polyptoton* (the repetition of a word in different grammatical functions) which heighten the anticipation of the reader or directs his attention to the central aspects of the story.

[134] This forced labour is described as 'groaning' (2:24), as 'affliction' and 'sufferings' (3:7), and as 'oppression' (3:9).

[135] Moses had to kill the Egyptian in secrecy because he, himself, had no authority to pass a death sentence (cf. Childs 1976, 31). The rhetorical force of the Hebrew's speech has been discussed already.

not know the divine name; he doubts his positive acceptance by the people and confesses that he is not a man of words.[136] Out of his own mouth Moses disqualifies himself from being what God wants him to be. These objections are not only literary cues for determining the subjects of the divine speeches.[137] Yhwh's responses get a lot of narrative space and go in their content well beyond what Moses wanted to know. Childs' formulation of the rhetorical effect is worth citing in full here:

> [T]he writer shows remarkable skill in sketching his portrayal of resistance. Moses raises five sets of objections to his commission. These are not logically connected, although they do begin with a personal focus. The progression of the dialogue is more visceral than rational. Each time in which the objection is fully met, a new one springs up, unconnected with the later. No visible gain is ever made. The picture emerges of one person trying to reason with another who is throwing up arguments, but basically whose will, not mind, is resisting the call. Moses' initial objection points to his own inability. Soon, however, his objection can flatly contradict God and attribute the worst to the people. In the end he is trapped and his real doubt emerges. … In contrast to the disconnected objections, God's answers move solidly along the one track.[138]

The contrast is obvious: a determined Yhwh remains astonishingly patient in his confrontation with an unwilling Moses. The image of Moses, which is further developed by this dialogue,[139] continues to build on the previous portrayal of him as the unlikely hero.

---

[136] Cf. my earlier discussion of this point on p.131.

[137] This is suggested by Coats 1988, 68f for Moses' fifth objection. This objection does not disqualify Moses or diminish his heroic qualities but should only be understood as part of the stereotype in use in the dialogue. "[This objection] is a literary construct that introduces Aaronic tradition into the Moses story." (69) This may be if we view the text from a form-critical position, but the reader will automatically understand it on the surface level: Moses is not eloquent enough to do the job effectively. This facet of Moses will, then, be built into the reader's perception of the character. From a different angle Moses' disability can be viewed as a physical impairment, which in the narrative construction of the character, is used in situations when Moses' integrity and commitment to either the Egyptians or the Hebrews is questioned. This was proposed by Junior and Schipper 2008. Their general presuppositions and some of their results appear to be a valid reading of the text with a refreshing attention to the rhetorics of the narrative. I suspect their suggested strong connection between disability and ethnic or cultural identity as being a little overemphasised, but their claim to achieve greater interpretive nuance has clearly been achieved. Certainly true is the rhetorical effect of subtly casting more doubts on Moses' character and commitments. In the Exodus narrative Moses *becomes* a mediator, he *is not* such from the beginning.

[138] Childs 1976, 71.

[139] Exod. 4:10 demonstrates irony when Moses reflects at a meta-level on the previous discussion with Yhwh. Moses' contributions to the dialogue are indeed not brilliant. When he realises that he does not convince Yhwh, as a last resort he tries to use this rhetorical failure for his good but fails again.

But we, also, have Yhwh's part of the dialogue to balance the picture. If there were a choice, the implied reader might not be willing to tolerate Moses as leader of his people.[140] God, on the other hand, is apparently willing. This willingness, of course, has an influence on the reader's perception of Moses. Yet the narrator does not offer in the Yhwh-speeches a rehabilitation of Moses, thereby going against his earlier characterisation.[141] His balanced view is also expressed through the voice of Yhwh (4:14). The expression of Yhwh's emotions tells the reader more about Moses than about Yhwh. The brief specification of Yhwh's reaction (וַיִּחַר־אַף יְהוָה בְּמֹשֶׁה) serves to back up the author's portrayal of Moses from the highest authority available to him, Yhwh. Despite all this, Moses becomes a leader, but only on the grounds of Yhwh's enabling him and vesting him with authority. Yhwh will be with him (3:12): he provides the message which Moses is to deliver both to the pharaoh and to the Hebrews (3:14-22), he endows him with a set of signs to underpin his authority (4:2-9), and, finally, he promises him help in the upcoming conversations (4:11-12.14-16). Moses is totally dependent on Yhwh, which is exactly what the implied reader should understand. Moses, the national hero of Israel, is no hero, in and of himself, but only because of divine legitimation and enablement.[142]

MOSES ON HIS WAY TO EGYPT

Having no room for further objections, Moses acts on Yhwh's call and goes. The verbs הלך (3x) and שוב (5x) dominate the first half of Exod. 4:18-23. The author stresses the movement Moses is making and, hence, his obedience. This notion of obedience is further emphasised with the almost verbatim repetition of 4:17 in 4:20b. Moses fulfils the final words of Yhwh's speech by taking the staff, which signifies his authority as divine messenger. The reader is then reminded of Moses' task and thus Yhwh's intentions (4:21-23), including a rhetorically powerful forecast of the last plague, the killing of the Egyptian firstborn.[143] This brief statement by Yhwh underscores the pervasive notion that what Moses is about to do ultimately comes from Yhwh.

---

[140] This is quite contrary to what Zivotofsky would be doing (cf. p. 152 above).

[141] This would equally portray Yhwh as an unreliable character, according to Kissling's definition (cf. Kissling 1996, 20f; see also Rimmon-Kenan 1983, 100f). A reliable character is in line with the author's point of view, so that the author can be heard directly through this character. The author disassociates himself from the actions and thinking of an unreliable character. Yhwh's being an unreliable character seems very unconventional for a book which essentially promotes Yhwh and, also, uses divine speech to communicate important content, thereby, taking advantage of this character's implicit reliability and authority.

[142] Cf. Cheon 1997, 325.

[143] The sole mention of the killing of the firstborn is probably to be understood as *pars pro toto* for the entire plague narrative. I will touch upon this brief passage in greater detail when it comes to the characterisation of Israel.

The exegetical headaches produced by Exod. 4:24-26 have been numerous over the centuries. For a review of the attempts to relieve the pain caused by this dark passage cf. Houtman.[144] I roughly follow his interpretation which, in my point of view, avoids gross overinterpretation and source-critical uprooting from the present context. Obviously, the author of Exodus used some old material here[145] and placed it strategically at this point in the narrative. The reason behind his logic, however, is vague. 4:22bβ-23 might be the clue as Yhwh mentions his relationship with Israel in the terms of a father and firstborn son. Apparently, Moses was criticised for not circumcising his own son or, perhaps, for not having been circumcised himself, if one understands the touching of Moses' genitals by Zipporah as a substitution for his actual circumcision.[146] This failure provoked God's attack, for why else should God refrain from killing Moses after his son had been circumcised?[147] What does this brief and puzzling passage contribute to the reader's perception of the characters?

The author never reflects the pressing question why Yhwh attacks the person he had just had great difficulty in convincing to be his emissary. As the context makes clear, Moses, though passive and never mentioned directly in the text, is the most important figure.[148] Moses, having suggested all kinds of personal shortcomings to disqualify himself, fails to see the crucial one. This is life-threatening for him. What saved his life is that he again has a woman at his side to look after him (cf. Exod. 2!). There might be some subtle irony in this depiction of Moses. The enigmatic phrase אז אמרה חתן דמים למולת (26b) should not be understood as a brief etiological remark showing that Zipporah's action explains circumcision, as many modern interpreters who follow Wellhausen and Greßmann understand the function of the passage. As Childs argues, the text in its present context explains whatever Moses' wife did as circumcision.[149] The

---

[144] See Houtman 1993, 439–447 and also in his succinct style Childs 1976, 95–101. Including the more recent literature see also Ber 2008, 158–161.

[145] Cf. Houtman 1993, 448, who finds traces of the antiquity of the text in the author's use of the term חתן דמים (along the same line: also Childs 1976, 100).

[146] That circumcision was a widespread rite and, also, present in Egypt does not rule out this interpretation. Even if Moses had been circumcised according to Egyptian culture, it had not been done according to Israelite rites and, hence, could not be meaningful in Israelite religion. This argument, of course, rests on the assumption that Gen. 17 is known to the implied reader of the passage, a conjecture I made earlier when focusing on the likely previous knowledge of the implied reader.

[147] Up to this point I am also following Childs 1976, 101. Another suggestion would be to see the action of Yhwh as a result of some sort of suppressed anger upon Moses' stiff-necked responses to his call in Exod. 3–4 (cf. Lapsley 2004, 125). This reading fails to the leave the event-level and carries a psychologising tone which prevents the exegete from seeing the theological connections and implications.

[148] Coats 1988, 70f, is convinced of the opposite and excludes this text from his corpus of Moses traditions.

[149] Cf. Childs 1976, 100f.

importance of the theme 'circumcision' to the author becomes clear, and so we should ask why. The preceding context suggests that Gen. 17 might be providing the uniting framework: it establishes the connection between the covenant of Abraham and all his descendants and the rite of circumcision, a sign established to signify who belongs to the covenant party. So one aspect of the text is to highlight the ultimate continuity between the Covenant-God of Abraham, whose covenant marker was circumcision, and the God now bringing about the deliverance of Israel from Egypt. Moses, as the leading character of the subsequent events, must be placed inside the covenant, and to show this the author could use (or had to use) this enigmatic part of Israel's tradition.[150] Again, the portrayal of Moses is tainted by a negative strain. Moses is now willing but apparently he is not quite fit for the task, for he had not submitted himself entirely to the old covenant on which the whole action is based. This failure even endangers his life which is saved by a woman who does what he should have done long ago.

"Moses is now circumcised and in the company of Aaron. In every respect he is suited for his task. The work can begin."[151] Houtman captures, nicely, the brevity of the account. And the work does begin: Exod. 4:27-31 abounds with *Leitmotiven* from Exod. 3–4 to remind the reader of the corresponding passages in the dialogue. Yhwh sends Aaron to meet Moses (4:27a – cf. 4:10-17); they meet at the mountain of God (4:27b; cf. 3:1); reference is made twice to the words and to the signs given by Yhwh (4:28+30; cf. 3:14b-22 and 4:1-9); and, lastly, the reaction of the sons of Israel is mentioned according to Yhwh's prediction (4:31; cf. 3:18aα).[152] Moses' obedience and his success is described very tersely, indeed. The effect of this brief text on the reader's image of Moses is, again, two-edged. As to be expected, it is a little negative, for all of Moses' fears – the disbelief on the part of the Hebrews, the lack of convincing arguments, etc. – prove ill-founded. The necessary counterpart to this is of course Moses' success. The implied reader might now begin to feel that Moses will, indeed, be an effective man for the job, even though he already knows this to be the case historically. But, having read the previous narrative, an unbalanced, overly heroic picture of Moses is no longer possible.

Conclusion

What has been the impact of the first *rendezvous* between the reader and Moses in the course of the reading process up to this point? As the review of recent literature on Moses has already exemplified, the portrait of Moses is far from

---

[150] Houtman 1993, 425 and 448 views the circumcision as an act of final preparation and consecration of Moses for his task.

[151] Houtman 1993, 426.

[152] Greenberg 1969, 122 observes a similar linkage.

being clear cut and unambiguous. The various interpretations testify to this fact. The final form of the texts opens up several legitimate possibilities for how the character Moses can be understood. Ultimately, it is the reader who decides which image of Moses he prefers.[153] I hope I have shown that the author deliberately used this ambiguity in the portrayal of Moses as a rhetorical device. The author's use of this strategy seems to have been motivated by the implied reader's preconceptions. As a strategy it opens the mind of the reader by forcing him to review his preconceived picture of the man called Moses. The new horizon the text creates for the reader is a rather realistic image of Moses, far removed from any heroic glorification or idealistic elevation. This is done in a subtle manner so as not to lose the reader from the start, but it is, nevertheless, done forcibly. One could probably speak of a deconstruction of a particular Mosaic image. Why does the author deconstruct the preconceived image of Israel's hero? When one compares the portrayal of Moses to that of Yhwh, it becomes clear that, in the end, Yhwh should emerge as the hero of Israel, with Moses as the mediator who can only achieve things by Yhwh's authority. The reader who does not bring a heroic picture of Moses to the text will, of course, be much more open to appreciate the small clues given by the author and will probably enjoy the texts on a more aesthetic level. This double rhetorical effect of instruction or correction, on the one hand, and of literary gratification, on the other hand, shows the rhetorical skill of the author. In view of my conclusion, the continuity of the varied material in Exod. 1–4 makes a source-critical or redaction-critical creating of new contexts for parts of the material unnecessary.

As argued above in chapter two, Exod. 4:31 marks the end of the introductory part of Exodus. The following section up to Exod. 7:7 constitutes a transitional pericope which ties up a couple of loose ends from the introduction but, mainly, foreshadows events and themes of the plague cycle. In any case, the introduction of Moses in the manner described above is not continued. The heroic Moses' deconstruction is not carried further in the telling of his second attempt to bring deliverance to Israel (Exod. 5:1-23), which, again, ends in failure.[154] It is not Moses' fault that the labour situation of Israel worsens; he only

---

[153] This is not necessarily a statement from a reader-response perspective, which assumes that any given text only means what a given reader brings as meaning to the text. On the contrary, my reading of the texts with regard to the character Yhwh should have shown that I prefer a hermeneutic which allows for the text to limit the likely possibilities of interpretation. Meaning is not entirely arbitrary and there is such a thing as misinterpretation.

[154] The situation is very similar to the days when Moses was sowing his wild oats (2:11-22): again Moses' authority and intentions are questioned (5:21). Cf. Weimar 1980, 21, who refers to *Stichwortverbindungen* between the two narratives. The differences are, nevertheless, clear: earlier Moses was a self-appointed judge and now he acts on Yhwh's behalf. Only the results are similar.

does what Yhwh tells him to do.[155] Indeed, Yhwh warns that the situation will worsen (3:19-20), but the Hebrews, nevertheless, blame everything on Moses and Aaron. That the author recorded this accusation might lead us to think that the deconstruction of Moses is carried further.[156] But, as the upcoming treatment of the character 'Israel' will show, it would not be good for the author to make Israel utter his own opinion. It appears more advantageous for the narrator to partake in and, thus, benefit from divine authority. This is exactly what has been done in the present pericope: the divine prediction of the heightening conflict with the Egyptian king finds its counterpart in the report of 5:1-23. Thus, implicitly, a balanced picture emerges, one which neither displays Moses as a complete failure nor as a fully-developed heroic figure. Exod. 5:1–7:7 should not be read as the continuation of the introduction but rather as the beginning of a climactic story which builds up the conflict to a point where only a divine intervention can bring about a denouement.

Moses is, from here on, portrayed in his mediatorial role, standing between Yhwh and Israel (cf. the complaint 5:21) as well as between Yhwh and the pharaoh (cf. the name issue "Who is he?" 5:2). He seems to be caught in the middle, not really having much control over what happens. The author demonstrates Moses' dependence on God's determination to do what he said he would do, but he does things in his own time and manner. This tension proves to be the driving force in Moses' various relationships to the other characters in the story, especially to Yhwh and to Israel. The transition narrative portrays Moses as *acting* out his new position of mediator. On the literary level, the most important result of acting out his vocation is the Israelites' indictment (5:21). This accusation provides a further key in understanding the function of the passage as transitional in that it foreshadows a recurrent theme of all later murmuring pericopes in the wilderness tradition. Throughout the Pentateuch, Moses struggles with his authority, and it is only God's repeated authorisation of his position as mediator, that prevents him from not fulfilling his divine vocation.

The transitional function of the passage is supported by the striking parallel to the earlier call narrative, which might be called the second call of Moses (6:2–7:7). Why this repetition? Though it is the traditional historical-critical consensus to view this text as a Priestly insertion of a parallel account, it seems,

---

[155] One might be tempted to discuss Moses' and Aaron's rhetorical skill betrayed in their argumentation, but since we most likely do not have the entire conversation, it is futile to do so in detail. The first address to the pharaoh appears rather blunt, whereas the second is much more moderate, trying to argue and picture a possible scenario. In the present context this is pure irony, as Yhwh will not diminish the Israelites or send them plagues. These threats are the Sword of Damocles hanging above the Egyptians.

[156] The conclusion of Houtman's comments on Exod. 5:22–23 might betray such a reading of the text: "Once again the fact that Israel's liberation is not man's but purely Yhwh's doing is etched all the more into the mind of the reader who has now become familiar with Moses' disenchantment." (Houtman 1993, 499)

also, to be the consensus that the function of the text in its present context has changed to one of confirmation of the promises given earlier (esp. Exod. 3).[157] At the story-level of the narrative this makes sense as Moses has every right to complain to Yhwh. In turn, for the sake of his discouraged agent the complaint is likely to provoke Yhwh's affirmation of his earlier promises. At the author-reader-level, it is, nevertheless, not necessary to elaborate so extensively on this aspect, as it, basically, represents a repetition of what was already emphasised. Biblical narrative is usually quite economic with narrative space, and I propose that together with the generic similarities to the later murmuring narratives and the genealogical introduction of Aaron and Moses (6:13-27), this 'second call narrative' presents the reader with a clear signal that the deconstruction of a heroic Moses is complete and a new argument has begun. This new argument involves a new communicational intention and new rhetorical strategies. The implied reader will, by now, be aware that Moses and Aaron act only on Yhwh's behalf and thus mediate divine communication to both the Egyptian rulers and the oppressed Israelites. This will be assumed for the ongoing plot, as new themes are built upon this ideational foundation. The contrasting of Moses with Yhwh has come to an end. New themes of conflict – between Yhwh and "the greatest of earthly kings"[158] and the discontent of the Israelites – are foreshadowed.[159]

Caught in the Middle – Moses the Mediator

Even though the sketch of Moses in Exodus undergoes certain developments, Moses is, from this point forward, pictured as the mediator between the people and God. Commenting on Exod. 6 Greenberg writes perceptively: "In a newly assumed role, Moses no longer waits for God, but, exploiting his intimacy with him, returns on his own initiative to give vent to his anguish over his people's worsened state. His own frustration is bound up with his people's agony; he thus becomes their spokesman."[160] First, he communicates God's will to the pharaoh; then he communicates Israel's agony to Yhwh, and, finally, he communicates the divine promises and instructions to the people. Deuteronomy makes this explicit in its recollection of the events around the great theophany:

> Yhwh spoke with you face to face at the mountain, out of the midst of the fire, while I stood between Yhwh and you at that time, to declare to you the word of Yhwh. (Deut. 5:4-5a)

---

[157] For the history of research cf. Childs 1976, 111–114.

[158] Wenham 2003, 4. See also Rendtorff 2001, 55, who regards Yhwh and the pharaoh as conflicting parties as well.

[159] Even the covenant formula appears in Exod. 6:7 and, thus, a clear indication that the patriarchal covenant – which has been mentioned implicitly and explicitly time and time again before – is intended to include the entire people.

[160] Greenberg 1969, 128.

The author portrays Moses' mediatorial role as developing. The aim of the following discussion is to trace the implications of this development for the rhetorics of the character and hence the communicative effects.

Moses and Yhwh

As my review of research on Moses has shown, the relationship between Yhwh and Moses is a recurring area of scholarly interest. Earlier, I defined the literary dependency between the two characters as a contrasting pair. The portrayal of Moses becomes the foil, against which the character Yhwh receives his profile. Now Moses, assuming his role as mediator, comes into focus as a character in his own right. The transitional aspects of Exod. 5+6 have already been mentioned. Moses is now introduced anew,[161] including his family tree and a chronological note informing the reader of Moses' and Aaron's ages.

Rhetorically important for this new 'beginning' of Moses' career are two aspects or themes. Firstly, there is the theme of obedience which is introduced at this point in the narrative in an emphasised manner: 7:6 כאשר צוה יהוה אתם כן עשו (they did just as Yhwh commanded them), which is followed up by 7:10 ויעשו כן כאשר צוה יהוה (and they did just as Yhwh commanded). The first incident is very general and there is debate as to which divine command it really refers.[162] The second is very specific and even presents the reader with an almost verbatim repetition,[163] noting the enactment of the divine order. It is, probably, only intended to help the reader realise that an important theme appears here in the narrative. But, it is the first note, especially in its indeterminate point of reference, which provides the rhetorically effective hint for the obedience theme which becomes important for the remainder of the book. It betrays the qualities of a mediator when he is faithful to the parties between whom he mediates.

The second theme important for one's understanding of the following text is Moses' elevated position between heaven and earth. The renewed commission of Moses and the brief account of Aaron's staff swallowing up the magicians' staffs (Exod. 7:1-13)[164] function as the conclusion to the 'second call' of Moses, as well as the anticipation of the plague cycle. The theme of obedience intro-

---

[161] Cf. esp. the emphasis in the framing הוא אהרן ומשה – הוא משה ואהרן of Exod. 6:26-27.

[162] For a brief discussion cf. Houtman 1993, 529.

[163] Here, we find an incident of repetition without much variation, which always stresses the reliability of the characters involved, whether they are the ones predicting or the ones carrying out orders (cf. Sternberg 1987, 387ff).

[164] Exod. 7:1-13 concludes the 'second call' of Moses and gives a prospect of the plague cycle. The first part (1-7) states the theme in a theoretical manner, whereas, the second (8-13) gives a foretaste of the later narrative pattern of the stereotypical plague description.

duced here, is not the only part of the Mosaic portrayal with which the author equips the reader before entering the plague cycle. Right at the beginning of the divine commission, as detailed in this pericope, a clear definition of Moses' role in relation to the Egyptian king is given: 7:1 "See, I have made you god to the pharaoh (נתתיך אלהים לפרעה), and your brother Aaron shall be your prophet." This notion of Moses as a person closely linked with the divine sphere is only hinted at in Exod. 7–11, but it receives further development throughout the progression of the narrative. Both themes will be traced throughout the book of Exodus. I will, also, reflect on the question of whether it is possible to find a concrete socio-historical background in the prophetic office for this portrayal of Moses, or if it is more appropriate to treat the emerging picture as singular. As usual, I will discuss, throughout, the consequences of this particular depiction of Moses for the guidance of the reading process.

MOSAIC OBEDIENCE

As argued above, the main theme of the plague cycle, which represents the first major progression in the plot after the 'second call' of Moses, is the conflict between Yhwh and the Egyptian king which centres around the knowledge motif. Moses and Aaron are ever present throughout the narrative, but never gain any substantial momentum in terms of bringing about the plot's unfolding. Moses, and, even more so, Aaron, are, merely, representatives of the Israelite God who is determined to unleash a sequence of terrible signs and judgements. As Yhwh never communicates directly with the pharaoh, it is always Moses who is the divine mouthpiece.[165] Hence, we find the distinctively prophetic phrase "Thus speaks Yhwh …" (כה אמר יהוה) clustered in this part of Exodus.[166] By, massively, repeating the same basic narrative pattern ten times over, the author makes it abundantly clear, though only between the lines, that Moses did his job faithfully. His predictions are always paired with a report of their enactment. As the main communicative effort in these chapters concentrates on the portrayal of Yhwh, the theme of Mosaic obedience does not take up much of the reader's attention. But, as the theme was hinted at in Exod. 7:1-13 and will feature strongly in the later narrative, it seems justified to observe the subtle effect of the plague narrative on the construction of the Moses-picture of Exodus. Even in narrative art, constant dropping wears away the stone.

---

[165] It may astound the reader when he remembers the Mosaic complaint that he, himself, is not a man of words and the divine promise of Aaron to take up that role (cf. Exod. 4:10-16; 6:12+30). In the depiction of the plague narrative, Moses does the speaking and Aaron wields the rod. Of course, there is no need to suspect different sources or traditions behind this discrepancy, as the plague narrative takes many shortcuts in order concentrate on what the author deemed to be important. It just shows that the uncircumcised-lips-theme has done its duty for the narrator and gives a further hint, that with Exod. 7, a new perspective on Moses is in force.

[166] See Exod. (4:22; 5:1); 7:17.26; 8:16; 9:1.13; 10:3; 11:4; (32:27).

The portrayal of the obedient Moses is further emphasised by the use of a formulaic expression.[167] The communication in Exodus, with its numerous repetitive passages, appears to be strongly concerned with the theme of obedience. A simple indication of this is the use of the recurring clause "and he/they did just as Yhwh commanded him/them" (כאשר צוה יהוה) at significant places in the narrative (Exod. 7:6.10.20; 12:28.50; [14:4]; 16:34; 34:4; 39:1.5.7.21.26. 29.31.43; 40:19.21.23.25.27.29.32). The reader of Exodus is often made aware that characters act in accordance to a previously defined or prescribed way – or else they do not act so, as the account of the midwives tells (1:17: they "did not do as the king of Egypt commanded them" ולא עשו כאשר דבר אליהן מלך מצרים). This particular sentence begins the sequence with the conjunction כאשר and a verb of speech. The narrative, in itself, suggests, between the lines, that the midwives did not act according to the kingly commands. Thus, to formulate it, explicitly, and hence to create redundancy, the author marks their disobedience to the royal decree as an important fact in his communicative intentions. Disobedience to the pharaoh, in this case, equals the fear of God and, consequently, obedience to him. Throughout the remainder of the book there is no other direct mention of disobedience using this same formula, but many statements of obedience are expressed in this way. At the beginning of the plague episodes Moses and Aaron are obedient (Exod. 7:6.10.20). Later, in the preparation of the Passover ritual, the Israelites do just as Yhwh told them (Exod. 12:28.50); this obedience is strongly stressed in an almost refrain-like manner in Exod. 39 and 40.[168]

In Exod. 35–40 it seems to be more appropriate to speak of a 'compliance formula' instead of an 'obedience formula'. The connotations of obedience with its static and "literal" aspects are probably misleading. Jacob goes a bit too far in his interpretation, but, certainly, he goes in the right direction when he writes:

> Allgemein wird dies als ein Lob verstanden, daß sie alles *genau so* ausgeführt haben, wie es in A [sc. Exod. 25–31] vorgeschrieben war. Nun aber wird die Vergleichung zeigen, daß dies in *keinem einzigen Falle* zutrifft! Jedes Parallelstück weist Abweichungen auf, die öfter so stark sind, daß wir fragen müssen, *wo* denn Gott dem Mose solches geboten habe. ... Eine bloße Kopie war auch bei der verschiedenen Tendenz von A [sc. Exod. 25–31] und B [sc. Exod. 35–40] gar nicht möglich, so daß man eher sagen müßte: Sie machten nichts genau so wie ER dem Mose in A geboten hatte![169]

---

[167] The characterisation of Israel – which will be discussed later in its own right – is inextricably linked with this phraseology.

[168] See Dohmen 2004b, 395, who considers all occurrences of the verb צוה, with Yhwh as subject, as instances of this formula: 25x, Exod. 35:1.4.10.29; 36:1.5; 38:22; 39:1.5.7.21.26.29.31-32.42-43; 40:16.19.21.23.25.27.29.32. It makes more sense to restrict the designation 'correlation formula' for the phrases where correlation is actually expressed, i.e. where כאשר or כ is used with צוה (Exod. 39:1.5.7.21.26.29. 31-32.42-43; 40:16.19.21.23.25.27.29.32 + 36:1; 38:22 with just אשר).

[169] Jacob 1997, 995 (his emphasis).

Jacob, probably, overstates his point for the sake of the argument. Important, however, is that the deviations from the divine picture of the tabernacle do not allow the reader to qualify Israel's obedience as something static or even legalistic. The report of the construction work (Exod. 35:4–39:43) together with the explicit mention of the contribution of skills, material and craftsmen's qualities (חכם, Exod. 35:10.25; 36:1-2.4.8) highlights the artistic creativity of the project. It seems as if the author includes this positive element on the part of the Israelites to offset the golden calf incident, which, of course, is presented as an act of outright disobedience (cf. esp. the summary statement in 39:43).

By noting the construction כאשר צוה יהוה, the reader can perceive a movement from Mosaic obedience to Israelite obedience. Israel, in this respect, seems to be transformed by the exemplary attitude of their leader. The rhetorical strategy behind this presentation expressly links the two characters, Moses and Israel, and gives insight into the likely intention of the author which is to provoke the reader to imitate the attitudes of both. 'Israel' represents another character in transition, exemplifying the same movement which the author hoped to achieve with his audience. Of course, the theme of obedience features in Exodus more often than the obedience formulae do. Especially, the notions of listening (שמע) and believing (אמן-hiph) must be mentioned in this regard, but as these themes are mainly relevant for the portrayal of Israel, I will delay the detailed discussion for the moment.[170]

It is likely that Moses' acting in compliance with the divine will serves as a model for the reader. By following Moses, Israel becomes, at least in the very end, a people obedient to God and, thus, secures the divine presence with them. This, of course, is related to Israel's calling to be a kingdom of priests (19:5-6), that is to act as mediators between Yhwh and all the nations. Again, the discussion of this has to wait until I focus on Israel. Nevertheless, it is obvious that obedience is essential for fulfilling the role of a mediator. Moses is portrayed as obedient once he accepts his calling.

This characterisation of Moses is supported in many ways throughout the narrative. Brief mention of the more important of these will suffice for my present purpose. Firstly, there is Moses, the capable debater.[171] Exod. 10:29 has been described as "a masterpiece of subtle restraint,"[172] and it can be taken as an ironic statement or a pun on 10:28, where Moses attempts to make a forecast, himself. At the literary level, this initiative appears hurried, as Yhwh immediately afterwards corrects it by mentioning that yet another plague (עוד נגע

---

[170] See p.221 below.

[171] The rhetorical analysis of Moses' disputes with the pharaoh would be an interesting and rewarding exercise, deserving a study of its own, but I suspect that the outcome would not be relevant enough to justify a discussion in the present context.

[172] Childs 1976, 136. Cf. also p.133, where Childs suggests that there is source-critically relevant textual tension (contrary to Greßmann or Noth), thereby, leaving these verses open to contribute to the Mosaic portrayal.

אחז) will come upon Egypt. In the context of obedience this is a minor but significant sign, that Moses should only mediate what Yhwh tells him. For the reader, this scene serves to highlight the importance of strict obedience, especially after reading about Passover ritual when the pharaoh summons Moses and Aaron one more time (12:31).

Just before the Horeb theophany the story, emphatically, pauses and the author narrates how Moses must double-check that the requirements are met for the people's holiness (19:21-25).[173] Even though this brief passage contributes, mainly, to the understanding and emphasis of the divine standards, it also characterises Moses as obedient to Yhwh, well beyond the point of comprehension: Moses, again, communicates to the people what they already know (cf. 19:12-13).[174]

Exemplary for all the minor notices that Moses mediates to the people every word from Yhwh, I want to mention 34:32 and 34:34. Both appear in the context of the description of Moses' shining face. The first notice is part of the initial encounter between the shining face of Moses and the people, whereas the second belongs to the part detailing the habitual transmission of the divine word by Moses.

The cumulative weight of these passages provides a glimpse into the reliability of the mediator Moses and is enough to shape the reader's perception of this character. The contrast between the stubborn Moses of the call narrative in Exod. 3–4 and the obedient Moses who fulfils his god-given role is striking. At the rhetorical level it provides an example to the reader that change is possible. Having described the introduction of Moses into the plot of the book as a deconstruction of an idealised Moses, we need to note the rehabilitation of Moses – a new idealised picture but an exemplary character, at least when it comes to his obedience. In this respect, Moses appears as a paradigmatic character in Exodus.

MOSES IN THE DIVINE SPHERE

The second theme mentioned above which dominates the perception of Moses is his close proximity to the divine sphere. The earlier deconstruction of a heroic Moses makes this shift in his portrayal quite astonishing. To establish the effect of this change, I will examine the passages in which Moses is divine categories or in which Moses crosses the border into the divine sphere.

---

[173] Cf. Houtman 1996, 460f for a discussion of the literary effect of the passage.

[174] The concretion of the divine command to include the priests (19:24) might give a rationale for its repetition. But the mention of 'priests' is an anachronism anyway; the stress is not so much on the fact that priests might be in danger of violating the mountain's sacredness. Rather, the emphasis is on telling the reader how seriously Yhwh takes his own requirements; even the people usually allowed in the holy realm are not to interfere.

Exod. 7:1 states that Moses is to function as *god* to the pharaoh (נתתיך אלהים לפרעה). The metaphorical character of this attribution is obvious,[175] for if the sentence were taken literally, we would encounter a marked inconsistency to the literary introduction of a human Moses. What, then, does the metaphor communicate here?[176] The vehicle of the metaphor clearly is the phrase אלהים ל – this is the element which marks the metaphor for the reader[177] – but the tenor of the metaphor, i.e. the relationship between Moses and the pharaoh, remains open for discussion. In the parallel passage, Exod. 4:16b, the case seems more obvious, as the relationship of Moses and Aaron is expressed with a more precise metaphor: Aaron being the 'mouth' and Moses, the divinity. Moses speaks authoritative words and Aaron mediates these to the people as a prophet would, something which is spelled out, explicitly, in 4:16a. This function of Aaron is, also, explicated in 7:1b, the text at the centre of our present interest. The context of 7:1, however, complicates the issue, as Yhwh expects Moses to take on the role which has been assigned to Aaron in 4:16 and also in 7:1b – i.e. he has to communicate every divine word to the king of Egypt (Exod. 6:29). So, in a single dialogue, Moses functions in two capacities: as prophet and as god. Hence on a rhetorical level, the metaphor in 4:16 is less marked by the tension between focus and frame[178] than the metaphor in 7:1a.

What connotations are to be understood when Yhwh says to Moses, "I am making you a god to the pharaoh"? Bearing in mind the following verse 7:2, the meaning of the metaphor seems to go in a direction identical to 4:16 – Moses is Yhwh's messenger and Aaron, in turn, is Moses' messenger. Houtman, rightly, notes that this interpretation does not explain the use of an unmarked אלהים to denote Moses.[179] There must be more to it. Does the metaphor indicate a divine being possessing supernatural abilities? Or, is אלהים tobe translated as 'judge'

---

[175] Dawes 1998, 48ff collects criteria for the detection of a metaphor.

[176] The literary theorists writing on metaphor have been very productive over the past 30 years, and the debate is still open. A working definition of metaphor which shows rhetorical awareness can be found in Richards 1936, 93: "[W]hen we use a metaphor we have two thoughts of different things active together and supported by a single word, or phrase, whose meaning is a result of their interaction."

[177] That a tension is present here, can be seen clearly in the attempts of the targumim to find a way around the literal translation by providing interpretations like 'master' (TO; TNf marg.), 'master and sovereign' (TNf) or the elaboration of TPsJ: 'Why are you filled with fear? I have already made you an object of fear for Pharaoh, as though you were his god' (cf. Houtman 1993, 523). They close down the metaphor, leaving no room for their readers to perceive the tension, and, hence, they prohibit the active participation to which the reader of the Hebrew text is invited.

[178] This terminology from Black 1979 refers the constituent parts of any given metaphor. The 'focus' being the word(s) used non-literally and the 'frame' denoting the remainder of the sentence which is understood literally.

[179] Houtman 1993, 524f. Rather איש האלהים should then be expected as in Deut. 33:1; Josh. 14:6 *et al.*

or 'ruler' as Rashi, apparently, understood the text? The definition given in the BDB lexicon – "divine representatives at sacred places or as reflecting divine majesty and power"[180] – reflects what most commentators make of the metaphor. In the words of Childs: "Moses is made as 'god to Pharaoh', that is to say, he is to function with divine authority before Pharaoh, and like God, make known his word through his prophet."[181] What understanding is best here? Monroe C. Beardsley's[182] principle of plenitude – a metaphor means all it can mean – is in force for the reader of the present text. The indetermination of meaning in a metaphor is something which must not be overlooked in rhetorical analysis, as it leaves room for the reader to fill in gaps and for the author to play with allusions in a very subtle way. Thus I am hesitant to narrow down the meaning of this metaphor to just one of these options. This, of course, is a theoretical apprehension, although it is important from my rhetorical vantage point. Beyond this, however, Exodus itself suggests at several points that the boundary between the immanence and the transcendence is less obvious for Moses than for other characters. With the metaphor the reader is made aware that this character is far removed from a simple portrayal, and he is likely to look out for further details to establish a more coherent picture.

Childs touches on this aspect of the plague tradition when he discusses the nature of the prophetic Moses as displayed in Exod. 7:14–11:10. He detects a certain detachment from reality, which he calls "the strange atmosphere which surrounds the plague stories, ... [their] sense of historical distance."[183] True to his form-critical vantage-point Childs considers different possibilities for a *Sitz im Leben* of the prophetic portrayal of Moses. For Childs, the most likely possibility is that the plague story should be read as an example of the recurring situation in Israel's history of prophet versus king.[184] Moses, as the paradigmatic prophet, would naturally have attracted an analogous depiction in his encounter with the pharaoh. Childs, then, highlights numerous parallels between the 'plague cycle' and the 'prophetic legends'. "The importance of the prophetic word to the genre of the prophetic legend is further apparent by the concern of the narrative to report its fulfilment."[185] This would be true for the occurrences of the genre in Kings, for example, but here in the plague cycle, Childs asserts that the emphasis is different: "The plague is produced by the direct action of Moses and Aaron, not by the prophetic word which ultimately brings an event to pass, but in the prophet himself who possesses the charisma to unleash at will."[186] Thus, Moses' role is not pictured as the messenger of the divine word but, first

---

[180] BDB, 2570.

[181] Childs 1976, 118.

[182] For a brief summary of his work on metaphors refer to Dawes 1998, 40ff.

[183] Childs 1976, 142.

[184] Cf. Buber 1952, 76ff.

[185] Childs 1976, 145.

[186] Childs 1976, 145.

and foremost, as a man of 'charismatic power' who transports divine power by so-called signs.[187] Childs' quest for the strange nature of the narrative ends in negatives: "Now it is apparent that the essential problem with which we began is not ultimately form-critical in nature, but profoundly theological. The interpreter is still faced with the task of penetrating the mystery of God's power before human pride."[188] This last remark is an allusion to the hardness of the pharaoh's heart: no matter how great and cruel the signs brought upon Egypt by Moses, the king never feels forced to let the Israelites go. The narrative, though it pictures Moses as a powerful master of mighty deeds, remains adamant that only Yhwh, himself, brings forth the deliverance, neither Moses nor the pharaoh can take the credit for this. Childs' attempt to find the reason for the awkwardness of the plague tradition in form-critical assumptions fails. No merging of different genres or conflation of different traditions or different *Sitze im Leben* can resolve the tension. In my opinion, there is no need for a resolution. The texts draw a picture of Moses – be it the institutional prophet or the charismatic miracle worker – which does not fit later sociological reality. To a certain extent, Moses is in limbo, between the divine and the human.

Further hints which support this conclusion can be found in the text of Exodus. Whenever Moses acts as mediator the divine presence is manifest in him. There are several points in the narrative when this theme surfaces.

Throughout the plague narrative, Moses never takes on a royal role. The story makes it quite clear that he is, merely, the representative of Yhwh, mediating the divine utterances, and that he does so, not in an institutionalised manner, but in a spontaneous and immediate way. Despite the emphasis on the conflict between Yhwh and the Egyptian gods, including the pharaoh who was divinised in the Egyptian world-view, Moses plays an astonishingly divine role, and, if Hoffmeier is right in his interpretation of Moses' shepherds staff, he plays a pharaonic role as well![189] Hoffmeier believes that Moses uses his rod to challenge the pharaoh's rulership because pharaohs used an abstraction of a shepherds rod as sceptre.

In the context of the two theophanies described in Exodus (19/24 and 32), the mountain of God signifies the divine sphere and is not to be violated by any human or animal (cf. esp. 19:11-13).[190] Exod. 24:12 speaks of 'the mountain' in

---

[187] For Childs these two concepts of the prophetic office reflect their chronologically separate origin: the prophet possessing powers is an earlier concept and has been gradually replaced by the prophet acting purely as a messenger. Thus, it cannot be the prophetic legend which gave the plague cycle its form (cf. p.146). Nevertheless, Childs has to account for the presence of the messenger formula in the plague story and opts for the solution that it is only secondarily introduced. Hence, the prophetic legend only provides a secondary setting for the narrative and this only in the J source.

[188] Childs 1976, 149.

[189] Cf. Hoffmeier 1997, 154.

[190] The one exception is Exod. 33:6, where חורב מהר obviously includes the camp.

apposition to the divine 'me' (אלי ההרה), thus making explicit what was clear from the narrative anyway – Moses is able to enter a sphere which is usually out of bounds for human beings. In the middle of the great and fearful theophany, Moses approaches Yhwh with no apparent hesitation (19:20 and 24:15-18). Later on, Moses desires an even closer view of God in order to assure the divine presence for the people after the breaking of the covenant; God partly grants him this wish (34:2-3[191] and 34:5-7). The only incident, so far as the author tells us, which excludes Moses from a divine manifestation, is the sanctification of the tabernacle in Exod. 40:34-35.[192] In the course of the Exodus narrative, Moses is the only one bridging the two spheres of the divine presence on the top of the mountain and the camp. Together with Moses, the reader moves between the two spheres, as the narrative, generally, focuses on Moses.[193] The effect of this literary attachment of the reader to Moses is that the reader becomes an insider in the matters of mediation and in the tensions between the divine and the human. The rhetorical effect of this intimacy will be discussed later, as additional material must, first, be considered.

That Moses is, partly, of the divine sphere and, thus, one may infer, partly removed from the 'normal life' of the Israelite camp is an aspect of this character which is emphasised strongly in the description of his shining face (34:29-35).[194] Dozeman[195] has shown, convincingly, that the shining face of Moses, as well as the veil covering his face, can be understood as ritual masking. As such, it has a semiotic value for the onlookers and also for the readers of the text: Moses' private identity dissolves and he functions only as the divine messenger. The transformation of Moses' face sets him apart from the other Israelites, so much so that they flee from him just, as they did from Yhwh in the first theophany (Exod. 20,18f). Though Dozeman stresses, rightly, that this masking does not mean that Moses is deified in substance, I would hold that, on a semiotic level, Moses is portrayed somewhere between the human and the divine. The shining face and the veil function as signs of Moses' removal from the rest of

---

[191] Cf. the parallels in the wording of the preparations for the first theophany.

[192] For a discussion of the importance of this brief pericope for the reading of Exodus cf. p.23ff. That this is an exception to the previous description of Moses' familiarity with the divine sphere, of course, marks and emphasises the rhetorical effect of the passage as the conclusion of the book. Park 2002, 179, draws our attention to an interesting aspect of the narrative progress in Exodus. The local separation (mountain vs. camp) of the divine/human spheres is not permanent. When the people move on, the mountain loses its holiness. Consequently, the cloud settles in the tabernacle inside the camp amongst the people. Park notes that this expresses the ongoing movement in the narrative which stresses that Mt. Horeb/Sinai is not the final destination of the people.

[193] Cf. Park 2002, 180, who notices this movement but does not make much of it.

[194] See also Moberly 1983, 109 and following him Scoralick 2002, 88f, who observes the parallels between the golden calf and his shining face of Moses. The bottom line is that Moses is just what Israel wanted to gain when they created the god-image.

[195] See my summary of Dozeman's position on p.141.

Israel and, hence, point to his special position in relation to God. The text is, clearly, concerned with the ongoing mediating role of Moses as the speaker of the divine word. The obvious anachronistic placement of the pericope (esp. 34:34-35) – the tabernacle is not finished until Exod. 39/40! – suggests that the stress, here, is on the continuous presence of Yhwh with the people.[196] The tabernacle functions as the 'portable Sinai'; Moses' going back and forth between the tent and the camp recalls his ascending and descending the literal mountain; and Moses' shining face is the continuous 'theophany' which mirrors the glory of Yhwh.

What is the rhetorical force of portraying Moses this way? I suggest that in the almost super-human Moses the author establishes what McBride called 'transcendent authority'.[197] Mosaic authority is not based on natural abilities, outstanding charisma, or access to the divine realm. The author removes Moses from normality and places him close to the divine in order to provide a constant factor for the people in their move from the divine mountain to the land of promise. It is this promised land where his implied readers are, and for them the author records the divine word, which he claims to have received from God via Mosaic mediation. Of course, this way of narrating early Israelite history gives its own authority, but it also places the reader firmly inside the patriarchal covenant, which was renewed at Sinai for the entire people. Hence, the author creates an immediacy between the God of this covenant and his own readers.

Another point of ambiguity for the reader is the identity of the divine messenger in the closing passage of the book of the covenant, Exod. 23:20-23. The text begins with an exhortation to obey the messenger (מלאך) in all that he does and says so as not to forfeit the divine presence. That Yhwh's presence is meant becomes clear in 23:22, where the messenger's words are equated with Yhwh's words.[198] Furthermore, the reference to the place which has been prepared by Yhwh (כון hif + מקום) does not clearly point to the land of Canaan, the land of the promise. The context makes clear that Canaan is meant, but this phrase commonly refers to the holy place, the temple, the tabernacle, or the altars, i.e. the places of divine presence.[199] That the divine presence it at stake here, in the exhortation to obey the stipulations of the book of the covenant, is crucial for the overall composition of Exodus, as the remainder of the material in the book circles around the themes of securing and endangering this presence. It is, never-

---

[196] Timmer 2009, 129–130 is convinced of the opposite: he seems to take Moses shining face as a symbol of the transitoriness of the divine presence until the completion of actual tabernacle (the light on Moses' face fades with time!). Clearly, Timmer allows for two constructions in the wilderness, the tent of meeting and the tabernacle.

[197] Cf. McBride 1990.

[198] Cf. Crüsemann 1992, 210: "Typisch für eine Reihe von Texten ist es, daß genau wie hier eine unklare, offene und überraschende Nähe zu Gott selbst bis hin zur Identität besteht."

[199] Cf. Crüsemann 1992, 210ff, who argues, convincingly, for this interpretation.

theless, awkward that this is not expressed explicitly. Why the detour via the מלאך? In Exodus, the one mediating between Yhwh and the people is, for the most part, Moses. Yet, we also find the pillars of cloud and fire physically leading the way in the desert, which seems to be part of the messenger's role.[200]

But several observations suggest that Moses, and not some supernatural being or manifestation, is meant here. Firstly, communicating the divine word, as described in Exod. 23:22, is something only Moses does in the account of Exodus. Secondly, we find the very intriguing root מרה.[201] This is a key word in the wilderness tradition (Exod. 15:22–18:27 and Num. 11ff), where we find a collection of similarly-structured narratives featuring the people rebelling (מרה) against Moses' leadership.[202] These murmurings are interpreted, by the author, as rebellion against the divine programme of bringing the people out of Egypt to the land of the promise and, hence, as rebellion against Yhwh himself. Exod. 23:20-23 takes up, exactly, this theme and throws light on the implications of opposing Moses, the divinely chosen leader. Here, the divine realm merges with the human realm of Israel, and the messenger is in the middle representing Yhwh and his presence.[203] Given this interpretation, we can assume that the guarding function (לשמרך בדרך v.20) is more an ideational protection concerned with the content of Yhwh's words for his people, rather than a physical protection by the messenger. The tangible protection is something Yhwh does not delegate to a messenger, for it seems to be his mere presence which protects: "I will be the enemy of your enemies" (v.22).

Why this rather indirect communication at the end of the book of the covenant? Even given the validity of the interpretation above, the identity of the מלאך remains undecided. This מלאך, certainly, has divine attributes and authority. Given the previous discussion of Moses' close relation to the divine sphere, it is likely that the author thought of Moses here. The author, clearly, presupposes the close linkage between the Torah and the person of Moses. To obey Moses means to obey the law. Both are of divine authority and both are mediators of the divine presence. The present ambiguity of Exod. 23:20-23 seems to

---

[200] Similarly, Watts 1999, 51f, 107 links Exod. 14:19 with the present text and concludes that the past experience, hinted at via the verbal link מלאך, grounds the promise of future success in the land. Another option, mainly held by Jewish interpreters, is the angel appearing to Joshua in front of Jericho (cf. Jacob 1997, 738). Childs 1976, 487 draws the attention to Maimonides who establishes a connection between the מלאך and the prophet of Deut. 18:18. Given that Moses is the prophet of all prophets, this link supports my interpretation.

[201] This follows LXX and Syr in addition to almost all modern commentators who all refer to Gesenius 1985, §67y, reading in v.21 אל־תמר instead of MT (מרר).

[202] Cf. the more detailed discussion which follows on p.179f.

[203] Cf. Hilbrands 2006, esp. 93f. Hilbrands, also, concludes convincingly that the divine messenger can often, if not generally, not be distinguished from the actual divine presence.

be a strategy to provoke the reader to come to his own conclusions and, thereby, to encourage the mental linkage between the reader's preconceptions and the author's message. This, as a strategy of participation, helps to effectively initiate deep understanding with the reader.

Moses, however, is limited to his familiarity with the divine side of his mediating role. His intimate connection with Israel will be the subject of the following discussion.

Moses and Israel

Greenberg, as quoted above, speaks of Moses as "exploiting his intimacy" with Yhwh on the people's behalf. Some aspects of this close relationship have just been discussed; now I intend to focus on the rhetorical shape and function of the relationship between Moses and the Israelites. The two textual blocks in which this relationship surfaces most prominently are the wilderness episode (Exod. 15:22–18:27) and the incident with the golden calf (Exod. 32–34).

The pre-sinaitic part of the wilderness wanderings (Exod. 13:17–18:27) consists of seven episodes, which are, primarily, concerned with viewing Moses' leadership qualities from different perspectives. This theme is carried throughout the entire book, beginning with his calling (Exod. 3–4). The people question whether or not Moses is a competent leader in the different situations they face. From the start, the reader, looking through Moses' eyes, gets a preview of the problems that the Israelites will have with the leadership of Moses (Exod. 2:14;[204] 3:13; 4:1), but Yhwh will prepare and authorise him (4:2-5). After initial difficulties (Exod. 5:20f), the people accept him as leader. Throughout the exodus and plague narratives, Moses always mediates Yhwh's will and judgement; only the last plague, the killing of the firstborn, is not mediated by Moses (12:29). So, in the context of actually leaving Egypt, the author can report Israel's obedience to Moses (12:50-51). The initial doubts about the integrity and reliability of Moses that the people had when they were between Egypt's forces and the sea (14:11-12) contrast and, thus, reinforce the statement of faith given in 14:31. Now, the reader, especially after hearing the psalm of Exod. 15, expects the people to have learned their lesson about Yhwh's abilities and Moses' just claim of leadership. The reader, however, is disappointed: the three murmuring episodes in Exod. 15:22–17:7, undoubtedly, show Israel's continuing problems with their leader.[205] Nevertheless, time and time again Yhwh confirms Moses' position by using only him as the mediator of his help (15:25; 16:4-12; 17:6). The 'war against the Amalekites' episode (Exod. 17:8-16) functions in a similar way: The author highlights, graphically, the people's dependence on Moses. As long as he keeps doing whatever he does there on the mountaintop, they prevail; when he stops, the Amalekites dominate.

---

[204] Cf. p.157 above.

[205] For this thrust of the wilderness narrative cf. Schart 1990, 53f.

These five threats to Israel's existence form an obvious thematic chiasm:[206]

A   military threat: Egypt (Exod. 13:17–15:21)

   B   problem of supply: water cannot be drunk (Exod. 15:22-26)

      C   problem of supply: no food (Exod. 16)

   B'   problem of supply: no water (Exod. 17:1-7)

A'   military threat: Amalekites (Exod. 17:8-16)

Despite the large textual range of this chiasm, the five parts are marked off so clearly and the resemblances are so obvious that a listener could distinguish them easily and, thus, note their structural relationship. The parts B, C, B' clearly form a unity. This is true on three distinct levels. First, on a formal level, they are all of the narrative pattern or type-scene[207] called 'murmuring narra-

---

[206] Schart's chiastic structure for Ex 15:22-18:27 (Schart 1990, 53ff) is not convincing. His headings for the parts of the chiasm only vaguely represent their actual content. The central position of the water out of the rock episode is not even interpreted. Finally, the conclusions he draws from the structure do not depend on the structure at all.

The present chiasm stresses the centre, Exod. 16. Its central position is not only based on the structure, but also on its form and narrative length, in comparison to the two framing pericopes. In this murmuring narrative the solution to the threat contrasts those of the two other narratives: Yhwh does not enable Moses to perform a miracle but, rather, interfers directly and thus proves to be a trustworthy provider for his people (cf. Houtman 1996, 317). Nevertheless, Yhwh communicates with his people only through the mediation of Moses, who, thus, does not loose his special position. An important theme besides Yhwh's provision is the introduction of the Sabbath law. A similar feature is being used in the Mara pericope (Exod. 15:25b), except that there no specifics are given about the contents of the laws that have been instituted. On the rhetorical effect of such *prolepsis* Milgrom writes: "There can be no doubt that anticipation is a key technique in the redactor's art. It peaks the curiosity of the reader, sustains his attentiveness, and prods him to read on so that he can discover the full meaning of each allusive prolepsis."(Milgrom 1989, xxx) Of course, Milgrom is referring, here, to the redactor of Numbers, but, given the overall unity of the Pentateuch, this also applies to Exodus. Additionally, the twice mentioned כבוד־יהוה (16:7.10) becomes significant, since the two framing episodes omit the report of the presence of Yhwh's glory, a part usually present in this narrative pattern. This becomes even more striking when the murmuring narratives in Numbers are considered as well. There the כבוד־יהוה is a regular element (Num. 14:21; 16:19; 17:7; 20:6). Highlighting this notion of centrality, Ruprecht argues, convincingly, for a mediating function of Exod. 16: it refers back to the exodus in portraying Yhwh as saviour, and it points forward to the Sinai episode in mentioning Yhwh as giver of divine law (cf. Ruprecht 1974, 290ff).

[207] I am following A.B. Lord's definition, as quoted in Ska 1990, 36: "Type-scenes contain a given set of repeated elements or details, not all of which are always present, not always in the same order, but enough of which are present to make the scene a recognizable one." Robert Alter also speaks of type-scenes for recurring narrative patterns (cf. Alter 1981, 47–62).

tive.'[208] Second, on a verbal level, they share the rare verb לוּן (to moan: 15:24; 16:2.7.8; 17:3)[209] and, also, the verb נסה (to test: 15:25; 16:4; 17:2.7). Lastly, on the content level, they all deal with the problem of supply.[210] A and A' both describe a similar kind of threat. However, especially with regard to their narrative length and form, they differ considerably. As Otto suggests, chiasms often serve a summarising function for the plot.[211] This seems true for the present texts. Their exemplary nature, together with their structural placement, make it possible for the writer to hint at certain aspects of the characters involved. Schart has observed the structural similarities of these murmuring pericopes in a convincing study,[212] and he concludes that the confirmation of Moses as leader and mediator is at the heart of these stories. His paraphrase of the typical murmuring scene expresses this nicely:

> Aus Anlaß eines Mangels entsteht ein Konflikt zwischen Mose und Volk. Das Volk bestreitet Moses Legitimität als Führer. Diesen Konflikt entscheidet Jahwe zu Gunsten Moses, wobei die Ausnahmestellung des Mose darin gegenüber dem

---

[208] The three texts are only a part of the murmuring stories in the Pentateuch; they find parallels in Num. 11–21, i.e. the latter part of the wilderness wanderings (Num. 11:1-3; 11:4-34; 11:35–12,:15; 12:16–14:45; 16; 17:6-28; 20:1-13; 21:4-9).

[209] This verb, with the preposition עַל, signifies more than unhappiness; it is an active opposition to a person who seems to be the cause of the present course of events (cf. *ThAT* 2, 870-72, Coats 1968, 24 and Houtman 1996, 307).

[210] See Houtman 1996, 299ff, who views Ex 15:22–17:7 as a 'three panel strip' without a climax, and thus he does not find a chiastic structure.

[211] Cf. Otto 1989, 8.

[212] Childs 1976, 258–264, who suggests two distinct kinds of murmuring stories, has influenced a number of studies, among which Lohfink 1981 is important (see esp. his p.18). These scholars believe that the difference between the stories is the appropriateness or inappropriateness of the murmuring. I suggest that all murmuring is qualified as inappropriate by the author and that the difference lies, not so much in the form-history of each story, but in their narrative placement inside the Pentateuch. Schart 1990, 48f, suggests that all existing murmuring stories are variations on one single type-scene. According to Schart, the typical elements of the murmuring stories of the Pentateuch are:
   (1) Situation: The cause for the complaint – usually a threat to the life of Israel – is described.
   (2) Actual complaint: The people complain to their leader, accuse him of incompetence and utter some sort of unrealistic desire. The people suggest a solution involving the return to Egypt.
   (3) Moses: Moses reacts either with intercession or despair.
   (4) Yhwh (who only ever speaks with Moses or Aaron): God offers a solution to lift the threat, announces judgement, or executes judgement immediately, and thus legitimises the leaders.
   (5) Moses: Moses mediates between Yhwh and the people.
   (6) Consequences: In the end, the lifting of the cause for the complaint or the mitigation of the divine judgement is described.

Volk manifest wird, dass Jahwe nur zu ihm *spricht*, während er am Volk nur *handelt.*[213]

The murmuring episodes provide excellent opportunities for the author to illustrate how he perceives the interrelationship between Yhwh, Moses and Israel. A conflict, usually, arises between only two characters, and the more complicated conflicts can often be reduced to a binary opposition. This is certainly true for the conflicts in Exod. 15–17, as they are ultimately conflicts between the people and Yhwh. Moses, however, is accused from both sides and therefore suffers, which provokes the sympathy of the reader. This ambivalence can be traced throughout Exodus; Moses is not continually linked with just one side. Before I provide some detail in support of this conjecture I will briefly comment on Exod. 18.

The remainder of the pre-Sinai desert narrative in Exod. 18 does not belong to the observed chiasm. It is, rather, attached as a summary and conclusion of the wanderings. The detailed report of Jithro's visit (Exod. 18:1-12), which is motivated by the curiosity to learn more about the experiences of Israel (18:8), is an invitation to the reader to review the past events from a theological perspective: despite many difficulties Yhwh proves to be a trustworthy provider and guardian. The reader learns "that there is another way than the ruin of non-Israelites to make people acknowledge the greatness of Yhwh: learning of Israel's redemptive blessings, the history of Yhwh's mighty deeds,"[214] as Houtman contrasts the Egyptians and Amalekites with this Midianite delegation. And, thus, the Israelites, as well as the well-meaning and impressed foreigners, celebrate a great feast in Yhwh's honour.[215]

Exod. 18:13-27 records lively dialogues which focus on the leadership role of Moses. He is portrayed as a busy and committed leader who is trying to cope with everyday duties.[216] The criticism offered by Jithro is described as valid, compared to the criticism of the people in the moaning episodes of the previous chapters. Thus, the author shapes his reader's evaluation of Moses' leadership abilities: he is, indeed, a competent leader, though somewhat over-committed. Jithro reminds Moses of his limited strength and suggests a better, decentralised management system. So, both parts of Exod. 18 confirm, in retrospect, Moses' leadership position. Yet, apart from this evaluation, there is also a cataphoric element in Exod. 18. Houtman in his commentary even appropriately gives this

---

[213] Schart 1990, 49 (emphasis in the original).

[214] Houtman 1996, 395–396.

[215] There may be a contrast between the lack of celebration on the part of the sons of Israel after Exod. 15 and their impressive song of praise. This is probably a strategy of the writer to comment on the addressees' lack of thankfulness.

[216] Ber offers a detailed discussion of this chapter, possible interpretations and arrives at a nuanced view of the involved characters and the correspondent literary and theological implications. He assigns Moses a much more passive role in the entire chapter (Ber 2008, 163ff), but, this needs not to conflict with the present perspective on the text.

chapter the heading: "Initial Appraisal – Moses' Position Delineated."[217] Moses fulfils his mediating role in a way not possible under the former centralised management structure. It becomes Moses' duty to concentrate on representing the people before Yhwh and communicating God's decisions to them. From the reader's point of view, 18:19 is the central verse of this chapter. It prepares one for the remainder of the book, which mainly consists of Moses' walking up and down the mountain and, thus, fulfilling his role. Or, to quote Houtman, "the writer, by describing the revamping of the system of delivering justice, indicates that just before the revelation at the Sinai the conditions were created for insuring an effective communication between Yhwh and Israel."[218] The reader's curiosity is raised in expectation of how Moses will put this advice into practice.[219]

I will, now, return to my proposal that Moses is not continually linked with either Yhwh or Israel. The believe-motif (אמן hif.; cf. Exod. 4:31; 14:31; 19:9) positions Moses, clearly, in the proximity of the divine; that is, the people's trust in God is mirrored in their behaviour towards Moses.[220] The same thrust can be found in the reaction of Moses and Aaron to the people's lament: "Your grumbling is not against us, but it is against Yhwh – who are we?" (16:8; cf. also 17:2!) The entire plot of Exodus makes it clear that following Moses means following Yhwh – the link is made through the role of the mediator. Moses delivers the divine word and, hence, represents Yhwh, the god who brought them out of Egypt, who re-established the old covenant of their fathers with them, and who gave them instructions for securing his presence with them. This emphasis may, also, be the reason why the author constructed a close literary association between the seeming 'loss' of Moses and the desire for 'new gods' in 32:1:

> When the people saw that Moses delayed to come down from the mountain, the people gathered themselves together to Aaron and said to him, "Up, make us gods who shall go before us. As for this Moses, the man who brought us up out of the land of Egypt, we do not know what has become of him."

---

[217] Houtman 1996, 393.

[218] Houtman 1996, 396.

[219] Exod. 18 is another narrative in Exodus which serves as a literary hinge between larger blocks of material. The beginning is predominantly a recapitulation of Yhwh's protection and provision for his chosen people, and the end is a catalyst for the reader's expectations about the things awaiting Moses in his newly-defined leadership role.

[220] Cf. Blum 1990, 47. Dohmen 2004b, 65, also, speaks of the influence of this conjunction between Yhwh and Moses as important for the characterisation of the mediator of the divine revelation. It is God who speaks, but it is Moses through whom the Israelites hear. Thus, the author can speak of 'believing Moses', not just because of the divine wonders he could perform, but also because of the revelation he mediated.

For the people it is obvious that the mediator is missing[221] and, thus, he needs to be replaced in order to secure their safety and the divine presence among them.[222] The irony is that they cause the exact opposite; they endanger if not entirely forfeit the divine presence as the later dialogue between Moses and Yhwh makes clear.[223] Moses cannot be replaced because he is the divinely-chosen representative and mediator. This fact, in part, leads to the harsh reaction of Yhwh to the people with their golden calf. Dohmen understands the focus of 32:1-29 as, not so much the violation of the laws on god-images (Exod. 20:4.23), but, rather, as the *modus* of divine presence in Israel, the options being god-image and divine revelation.[224] The god-image created by Aaron on behalf of the people is balanced on the literary level by the emphasis on the divine revelation in 32:15–16. Here, the stone tablets are referred to in a highly redundant manner. The emphasis is on what they are (the referent to העדת)[225] and their origin (מעשה אלהים). Moses, the mediator, holds God's words in his hands. Thus, to reject Moses is to reject the divine word and to reject the divine word is to reject Yhwh. This, clearly, represents the violation of the covenant of Exod. 24 and contradicts the divine desire, expressed in Exod. 25–31, to dwell among the people.

In addition to associating Yhwh and Moses using the theme of divine revelation, the author constructs a similar effect by talking of Moses as the one who brought the people up (עלה hif) out of the land of Egypt (17:3; 32:1.7.23; 33:1(.12)). Only in the direct speech of the people and of Yhwh is Moses assigned this role in the exodus events. The author's comments, however, only mention Yhwh's bringing the people up out of Egypt. That the people perceive reality in this way is, mostly, due to the necessities of the narrative. To place this same notion in Yhwh's mouth (32:7; 33:1), however, works on a different level. In the scene of the golden calf, Yhwh seems to distance himself from the

---

[221] Fretheim 1991a, 281 uses the term 'leadership vacuum' to describe the issue which provoked the rebellion. See also Coats 1988, 111.

[222] Cf. Plaut 2000, 331. He, succinctly, notes the idea of the calf replacing Moses, but he fails to draw the obvious conclusion that this has an enormous effect upon the position and importance of Moses. The author is of the opinion that a calf cannot and should not replace Moses as mediator of the divine presence.

[223] On this refer to p.69ff above, where I discuss the nature of the 'sin' described in Exod. 32.

[224] Cf. Dohmen 2004b, 292f, 305.

[225] Of course, the precise content is an issue of considerable debate, and there is no consensus in sight. The reference to the content is nevertheless clear in the use of the roots כתב (4x) and חרת (1x). The emphasis is that there is something *written* on them, that they are intended to be a document. The material stone may be of some importance in that the reader could assume, here, a metaphor for the longevity of the content ('engraved in stone'). But, as Moses almost immediately destroys these solid stone tablets, it becomes clear that even they cannot secure the reality they represent – the covenant – which, again, points toward the emphasis on their role as referent, to use semiotic terminology.

people and to associate them closely with Moses, their leader. It appears that the author intended to parallel the distance created by the Israelite's sin with a withdrawing God.[226] This rhetorical device is underlined by the marked use of the term עמך ("your people") in 32:7-14 and, emphatically, in 33:13+16 and 34:9 (with ונחלתנו "and takes us for your inheritance"). The suffix refers either to Yhwh or to Moses, depending on who is speaking.[227] Before the scene of the golden calf, Yhwh identified closely with Israel as the covenant formula illustrates (Exod. 6:7; 19:5-6 and also 29:45-46).[228] Now, Moses is to identify with this people, and this he does. Again, for the reader, a picture of Moses emerges which depicts him as a mediator who stands between the frontlines: Yhwh wants to withdraw from the people, but Moses feels the responsibility to interfere and to try to avert the consequences.

As the context of the exodus makes clear, Moses is strongly associated with the people. The author records that Yhwh rebukes Moses for crying out to him just before the people walk through the *yam suf* (14:15: מה־תצעק אלי). In context, the rebuke is striking, because Moses never cries out, but the people do.[229] This tension in the plot is obvious, and a reader must recognise it as bringing Moses and the people into a close relationship. The phrasing of Yhwh's question is clarified in Moses' discussions with Yhwh on the people's behalf. The reader learns of Moses' strong commitment to the people. This has been expressed in 14:15 *in nuce*: the people are seen in Moses as their representative. In the murmuring stories before Sinai, the Mosaic intercession is not the centre of attention. It is the golden calf episode which gives full detail to the portrayal of the Mosaic commitment to the people (32:7-14.31-34; 33:12–34:9).

Even if the relationship between Moses and Israel was ambivalent before the golden calf incident, Moses now sides unequivocally with them. Moses is indeed "exploiting his intimacy" with Yhwh to convince Yhwh that forgiveness is the only option left.[230] Exod. 32:9-10 evokes a picture of Moses as the faithful remnant, parallel to Noah or Abraham (cf. Gen. 6:7-8; 12:2). Yhwh suggests to

---

[226] Cf. Dohmen 2004b, 303.

[227] Fretheim 1991a, 283 reads these forms as ironic statements, i.e., God mimics the Israelites in their ascription of the exodus. As God never 'mimics' the people's difficult attribution of the exodus to the calf, I would not consider God's words ironic here. They, rather, verbalise a very real distance between God and the people.

[228] The expression לעם הזה or העם הזה is, compared to the suffigated form, less marked but may also carry a slightly derogative notion, mainly, because of the context in which it appears.

[229] Even John Calvin, who cannot be accused of an overly enlightenment-critical attitude, wants to place 14:15 before 14:13-14 (cf. Houtman 1996, 266 for more solutions for smoothing out the text).

[230] See, also, the wonderful discussions of Moses' appeals to Yhwh's grace in the rabbinic tradition. For an introduction cf. Bloch 1963, 125–129. On Moses as intercessor cf. also Joosten 1991 and Dozeman 1984.

replace Israel by and to start anew with Moses. The words ואעשה אותך לגוי גדול (Exod. 32:10b) are reminiscent of the patriarchal promises (Gen. 12:2; 18:18; 46:3) and are, thus, preparing the reader for the climax of Moses' reasons for why Yhwh should spare the Israelites in Exod. 32:13. In the light of an imminent discontinuation of the chosen people Israel, Moses appeals to the continuity of Yhwh's promises to the fathers and to the notion of a growing nation. In Exodus, this growth is a sure sign of Yhwh's blessing at work in Israel (cf. Exod. 1–2; also the credo Deut. 26:5). Furthermore, the exodus from Egypt only makes sense if Yhwh does not destroy Israel – *his* people, as Moses stresses. In all this, Moses never justifies Israel's sin. He urges the Levites to restore the violated holiness of the camp (Exod. 32:25-29), and he confesses their sin, including himself under their guilt (34:8-9), and he, even, appeals to their status and position in relation to God. Through Moses' argument the reader is equipped with a way to think about Israel, an Israel which is far from the ideal described in 19:5-6 but remains God's people, nevertheless. Thus, in Moses' perception of the nature of Israel the author provides an important element of continuity in Exodus. Moses – given the narrative development – becomes the character who voices the author's opinion of Israel.

Beyond this link to the patriarchal promises, a further element of continuity in the argument of Moses is the conception of holiness, as expressed in Exod. 25–31.[231] The atonement, desired by Moses (32:30b), centres around the divine presence among the people. In the end, Moses is prepared to accept only God's continuous presence (33:13-16), thereby he appeals implicitly to the seminal passage 29:43-46, and, finally, achieves his aim. The emphasis on divine presence dominates the narrative from 32:30 onwards. The first allusion to this theme can be detected in Moses' desire to quit his job as leader if Yhwh decides not to forgive (32:32). To be blotted form Yhwh's book includes the removal from God's presence or as S.R. Hirsch formulates:

> „Lösche mich aus dem Buche, das du geschrieben", heißt danach nichts anderes, als: tilge mich aus der Zahl der dir bedeutsamen Existenzen, enthebe mich meiner Zukunft, die du mir in deinem Weltenplane zugedacht.[232]

Dohmen supports this interpretation which rules out the notion of Moses being willing to die a vicarious death in place of the people:

> Vielmehr wird in der Alternative, die Mose aufstellt, eine Gegenüberstellung von Volk und Mose eingeleitet, so dass man den Gedankengang, der durch die Buchvorstellung und das betonte „doch" [אך, SK] umschrieben wird, wie folgt paraphrasieren kann: Du kannst nun entweder dem Volk seine Sünde vergeben, oder wenn nicht, dann behandle mich wie einen Sünder, der mit dir nicht mehr in

---

[231] For an intriguing treatment of this issue cf. Dohmen 2004b, 322,323f.

[232] Hirsch 1986, 478.

Verbindung steht (gestrichen ist!). Mose spricht also Gott für den Fall, dass Gott dem Volk nicht vergeben will, – modern gesprochen – seine „Kündigung" aus.[233]

As a consequence, Moses refuses to be the leader of a people which is cut off from their destiny as a divine people. That Israel is the divinely-chosen people is marked, mainly, by Yhwh's presence with them. Moses, here, emphatically expresses that the future of Israel is only imaginable if Yhwh is with them (33:16). Arguing from the future prospect of Israel becomes the dominant feature in the unfolding discussion.

Throughout the dialogues of Exod. 32–34 the author uses Moses' speeches to bring into immediate contact the divine commitment to Israel, as expressed earlier in the story, and the inevitable consequences which result from the breach of the covenant. Moses maintains that part of the purpose of the exodus – i.e., that the Egyptians should know Yhwh and his commitment to Israel (cf. Exod. 7:5), would be void if the people were destroyed in the desert (32:12). Moses upholds the patriarchal promises (32:13). Moses reminds Yhwh of the special position of Israel compared to other nations (33:16; 34:9b). Moses refers back to the divine-human encounter, already realised on the mountain with the representatives of the people (compare 24:9-11.17 with 33:18). This strategy enables the author to describe Israel as a very special possession of the Holy One, while recognising the sinful inclinations and the actual covenant breaches that taint the history of this people. The theological solution to the apparent tension is divine compassion, graciousness, kindness and reliability (34:6-7). The role of the mediator is of utmost rhetorical importance, if one is to come to the conclusion which violates neither Israel's special position, nor Yhwh's integrity as a holy God.

Conclusion

The portrayal of Moses as the one character in whom the divine and the human spheres merge seems to be quite contrary to the earlier deconstruction of this character which I proposed. My observations on Mosaic obedience have shown that the communicative function of the later picture of Moses is not a new idealisation; it is, rather, an example to follow and, thus, serves a paradigmatic function. But, what is the reason for the portrayal of a semi-divine Moses? As the narrative progresses, Moses becomes so detached from reality that he, eventually (Exod. 34:29-35), serves as a sign for the continuous divine presence.

---

[233] Dohmen 2004b, 326. See again Hirsch 1986, 478: „Ohne diese Verzeihung giebt [sic] es für ihn keine Zukunft mehr, ist sein Dasein und seine Sendung zu Ende, giebt [sic] es für ihn kein חתנ weiter." See also Houtman 2000, 673: "Moses tells YHWH that, should YHWH not forgive Israel – and Israel has forfeited her life – life for him has lost all meaning – so much he feels himself one with Israel! – and no longer wants to live."

Many interpreters note the strangeness of the Mosaic portrayal throughout Exodus, and they offer numerous possible solutions to this problem. That this picture reflects certain elements of the later office of the prophet is one of the more popular solutions; Crüsemann and Childs, especially, pursue this line of thought. Both of them conclude that Moses does not perfectly fit any of the societal roles which he appears to assume. The Moses of Exodus is larger than life, at least after his dubious beginning. He is not a prophet in the sense of the classical prophets. He is not a judge, in the sense of the later institutions of the monarchical period. Further, he definitely is more than a priest, although he, constantly, bridges the gulf between the divine and the human realms. To note what Moses is not is helpful to some extent. I will now try – on the basis of the previous observations – to arrive at positive conclusions regarding what Moses is in Exodus.

The final form of the book pictures Moses as a person who is exceedingly familiar with Yhwh, even to the point of merging with the divine on a semiotic or metaphorical level. From a rhetorical perspective, the reader is left with a singular character who does not suit any particular known reality. The observation of the obedience theme, certainly, enables us to say that Moses can, to some extent, function as a paradigmatic character, providing an example of conscientiousness for every possible reader. His close association with the divine sphere, however, restricts this paradigmatic function. Moses is special, and no one after him quite lives up to his stature, as Deuteronomy puts it with reference to the immediacy of his relationship to God: "And there has not arisen a prophet since in Israel like Moses, whom Yhwh knew face to face ..." (Deut. 34:10). But, in Exodus his being special never leads to his glorification.[234] Thus, even Moses' great intimacy with Yhwh does not contradict his introduction into the plot, which I interpreted as the deconstruction of a heroic conception of Moses. The Moses of the exodus from Egypt and of the wilderness wanderings and of the events of Sinai does not become a hero but a faithful mediator.[235]

The relationship between this faithful mediator and Israel, which was discussed in the second part of this secton, can be described at least two hermeneutical levels. At the story level, it is clear that Moses, from Exod. 6 onwards, is fully committed to both Israel and Yhwh. Thus, he perfectly fulfils the role of the mediator. His exemplary attitude tries to bring together the interests of both groups. At the level of author and implied reader, the former communicates a very nuanced picture of Israel's relationship to Yhwh through the character Moses. Through the words of Moses, the author balances the justifiable divine

---

[234] This is contrary to the Hellenistic and Palestinian Judaism of the intertestamental period (cf. Vermès 1963).

[235] Markl 2004 offers a similar reading in highlighting the reception of the twofold Mosaic profession as a mediator (speaking the words of Yhwh and acting the symbols or signs commanded by Yhwh) in the literary framework of Deuteronomy (1:1 and 34:10–12). This shows how balanced even Deuteronomy perceives this outstanding character.

reaction to the breach of the covenant with the people's special status as divinely-chosen nation.

Moses: a Restored Character

The results of the present enquiry into the character Moses in Exodus reflect a twofold rhetorical strategy. Firstly, the author presented us with a rather negative picture of Moses, possibly in an attempt to deconstruct his implied reader's overly positive picture of Moses. This should have opened the mind of the reader to learn anew about Moses and his role in Israel's history. Secondly, from Exod. 6 onwards the author fleshes out his own view of Moses and, thereby, develops a picture of a thoroughly committed mediator between Yhwh and Israel. I have, thus, shown that Sternberg's general assumption for the biblical portrayal of human characters is true for Moses in Exodus, "With biblical man ... there is usually a distance – and often a clash – between the impression produced on its first appearance and the one left after his last."[236] The overall picture that emerges is a complex one, and, in the end, Moses leaves the reader with a positive impression that is balanced by earlier critique. One could speak of this development as Moses' restoration or rehabilitation. In the following paragraphs I attempt to trace the way in which this renewed judgement of Moses is suggested to the reader. There are a number of rhetorical features which seem to prompt an evaluation of Moses by the implied reader. Of these, I want to highlight just two, the evaluation by other characters inside the story and Moses' self-evaluation.[237]

We already observed how the Hebrew culprit's accusation that Moses acts out of self-interest could initiate a mental reaction on the part of the reader (Exod. 2). The text necessitates that a judgement on Moses' attitude to actions be made. I argued that the author tried to sow a seed of disquiet in the reader.[238] Nevertheless, beyond this rather tentative directive, the reader must make up his own mind. Exod. 5:21 records the Israelites' handing over of Moses to divine judgement, clearly indicating their negative verdict. The reader is not inclined to agree with this devastating judgement, as he knows what's happening behind the scenes, especially Yhwh's prediction of the pharaoh's refusal (4:21-23). But

---

[236] Sternberg 1987, 326.

[237] The only incident when the author passes a judgement on Moses, Exod. 11:3, is less a characterisation of Moses than of the Egyptian people and the court officials. Jacob 1997, 347–359, argues well for an understanding of 3:21-22; 11:2-3 and 12:35-36 which holds both the Israelites and the Egyptians in a positive light. Hirsch 1986, 93, argues similarly from the typical 19th century morality point of view. The counterpart to the Egyptians is the pharaoh, who regarded neither Israel nor Moses highly. One might argue, justifiably, that these verses propose a rehabilitation of the Egyptian people, including their officials, but obviously excluding their king. This is, probably, along the lines of the many positive statements on Egypt made by the later prophets.

[238] See p.157 above.

certain doubts might remain as to whether or not Moses acted wisely during his first meeting with the king. Again, leadership issues are raised by the characters in the narrative.

Something very similar happens when the reader hears the people's reasons for their rebellion in the wilderness episodes of Exod. 15–18.[239] Here again, an explicit judgement is being passed on Moses by a character inside the story. The subject questions the ability and authority of Moses to lead the people. In Exod. 14:11, with the Egyptian army in sight, the Israelites question Moses' integrity and leadership qualities. The reader is not drawn into the people's tension and fear, as he knows Yhwh's purposes in the situation (14:3-4). Hence, he is not tempted to doubt Moses' leadership abilities. At the end of the pericope, the character Israel follows suit: "Israel saw the great power that Yhwh used against the Egyptians, so the people feared Yhwh, and they believed in Yhwh and in his servant Moses." (14:31) This conclusion, together with the divine forecast, distinguishes the *yam suf*-pericope from the other murmurings in the wilderness. I already mentioned aspects of these type-scenes. They also invite the reader to decide whether or not he deems the people's complaints regarding Moses' authority and leadership qualities justified. Yet, the freedom of the reader is now, noticeably, diminished by the close association between Moses and Yhwh, something which is specifically highlighted in Exod. 16:7-8 and 17:2. In emphasising the congruence between Yhwh and Moses, the author himself evaluates the entire situation and thus encourages a positive outcome for the character Moses. As has been shown above, Moses is positioned between the different demands of Israel and Yhwh. In the wilderness episodes, Yhwh always sides with Moses and rehabilitates him in his leadership skills. This divine approval must influence the reader's perception of Moses.

Another contribution to Moses' leadership skills is Jithro's refinement of Moses' self-management. Exod. 18:18 presents the reader with another evaluation of the character Moses: Jithro believes that an unwise Moses overworks himself and, thereby, cannot do justice to the people nor to his divinely-given role as mediator of special revelations. Here the reader must decide how to understand the effect of Jithro's counsel: does Moses prove his leadership qualities by accepting criticism or does he prove that he is not able to see clearly in this situation? Whatever the reader concludes,[240] a certain critique of Moses is present, especially, given the link to 2:14 and 5:21 via the key word שפט (18:13. 16.22.26).[241]

---

[239] One could include under this heading the brief passage just before the crossing of the *yam suf*.

[240] Carpenter 1997, 95.97, using literary devices, depicts the relationship between Moses and his father-in-law as peaceful, familiar and friendly. Given this ambience created by the narrative, the reader might be drawn to the first option.

[241] Beyond these references, this root does not appear in Exodus!

A further rhetorical device to invite the reader to evaluate the character Moses are the self-characterisations put in his mouth. The most explicit and rhetorically very effective was already discussed above – Moses' negative *Imponierformel* in Exod. 3:11 מי אנכי.[242] As shown above, the reader cannot but affirm Moses in this case: Who is he?[243] The reader witnesses, so to speak, Moses' disqualifying himself as leader (2:11-22), he hears Moses confessing his speech impediments (4:10), he must understand Moses as refusing to accept God's calling (Exod. 3–4), he learns about Moses' not being circumcised (4:24-26), and he, finally, understands from the first meeting between Moses and the pharaoh, that Moses did not achieve anything (Exod. 5). The brief phrase מי אנכי expresses all these negative points. That these words come directly from Moses' mouth intensifies the force of its influence upon the reader. The last two verses of Exod. 5 record Moses' perception of himself and of his actions up to that point.[244] The devastating judgement is that he feels responsible for the increased burden upon Israel's shoulders (5:23a).[245] It seems significant that Moses' voice ends the part of Exodus which promotes a rather negative picture of him. As the self-perception of Moses coincides with the cumulative evidence of the other, the reader may now be inclined to adopt this deconstructed picture of Moses.

Exod. 6 provides a new start for the developing picture of Moses. To put it in Houtman's words:

> [...] Moses is not placed in unfavourable light as in 4:13f.; he is despondent, however, and has misgivings (6:12. 30), but it is no longer the same Moses as in chaps. 3–4; whether he is prepared to act as God's envoy is no longer under discussion; he goes to the people without objections (6:9) [...][246]

But, again, the reader hears from Moses' mouth a comment on his abilities. Exod. 6:12.30 are part of the brief framework around Moses' and Aaron's genealogy which roots them firmly in the priestly tribe of Israel Levy. Both portions of this framework firstly mention the divine message that Moses is to bring to the pharaoh, and then Moses' response, which includes the reference to his speech impediment:

> So Yhwh said to Moses, "Go in, tell the pharaoh, the king of Egypt, to let the people of Israel go out of his land."

---

[242] See pp.39 and 158 above.

[243] I follow Houtman and do not take this expression as signifying Mosaic humility (cf. Houtman 1993, 361).

[244] The question "Why did you ever send me?" (5:22) refers the reader back to the call narrative (Exod. 3–4) and, thus, invites one to compare the outcome with the forecast.

[245] That this includes 5:21, the people's accusation, only means that Moses accepted this accusation; it does not diminish the radicalness of his own statement.

[246] Houtman 1993, 496f.

But Moses said to Yhwh, "Behold, the people of Israel have not listened to me. How
    then shall the pharaoh listen to me, for I am of uncircum-
    cised lips?" (6:10-12)

Yhwh said to Moses, "I am Yhwh; tell the pharaoh, the king of Egypt, all that I say
    to you."
But Moses said to Yhwh, "Behold, I am of uncircumcised lips. How will the pha-
    raoh listen to me?" (6:29-30)

This repetition is fairly literal, yet a semantically relevant alteration may be
found in Yhwh's command. Exod. 6:29 is more pressing because of the inclusion of אני יהוה, whereas Moses' answer seems less marked because the reason
(הן בני־ישראל לא־שמעו אלי) has been omitted.[247] Moses' double statement here in
Exod. 6, seems to thwart my argument for a new, less critical start in the
portrayal of Moses. There is, however, a significant difference between Exod.
4:10 and 6:12.30. In the earlier statement, Moses reasons from a state of potentiality, whereas in Exod. 6 he argues from a real experience of rejection (6:9).
The reader will, thus, be more likely to grant this excuse. Furthermore, the later
hesitation is balanced by a very compact note stressing Moses' loyal obedience:
"Moses and Aaron did so; they did just as Yhwh commanded them." (7:6) I,
therefore, propose that the framework around the genealogy mainly provides
continuity between the character Moses of Exod. 2–5 and the Moses of Exod.
6–40.[248]

There are not many self-reflections of Moses to be found in the remainder of
Exodus. The only exception is Exod. 33:12b (ידעתיך בשם וגם־מצאת חן בעיני – I
know you by name, and even you have found favour in my eyes). Moses here
quotes a statement by Yhwh and, thereby, applies the content to himself. There
is no specific referent for this phrase in Exodus. Note, however, that the narrative expresses Moses' intimacy with Yhwh, which is commonly linked with the
theophanies (19:9; 20:21; 24:18), especially with 33:11a, with its metaphor of
friendship describing the relationship between Yhwh and Moses.[249] This, rather

---

[247] Cf. Houtman 1993, 523.

[248] This may be supported from the eye-catching phraseology of 6:26-27: הוא אהרן ומשה –
הוא משה ואהרן. The reader is forced to link the earlier narrative with the Moses and Aaron
introduced by the genealogy.

[249] For a recent and interesting discussion of the concept of friendship between Moses
and God, see Lapsley 2004. Lapsey comes from a more psychological approach and focuses, mainly, on the event level of the portrayal of this relationship. The tension between the highly unusual encounter of humans seeing the face of Yhwh, as seen with all
other characters in the Hebrew Bible, and the customary, even everyday, occurrence of
Moses' encounter with the divine highlights the rhetorical force of this phrase in its context. Given all the valuable observations Lapsey provides, she draws too far-reaching
theological conclusions from them. The friendship metaphor remains fairly singular and

indirect self-characterisation of Moses, is emphasised by the divine affirmation of it in 33:17.[250] The lack of a referent for Moses' quotation and God's later affirmation of its content create a powerful rhetorical tension for the reader. Firstly, the reader will inevitably question whether Moses' claim is justified – i.e., whether God, really, has such a positive perception of Moses – or if it is only part of Moses' own rhetorical strategy to convince Yhwh.[251] But, when Yhwh affirms Moses' claim in this close literary proximity, the reader cannot but agree with Yhwh and think of Moses as someone who found divine favour. Hence, the notion of Moses' exploiting his intimacy on the people's behalf, as established above, is supported here. Moses' outstanding connection with Yhwh is, also, expressed by this character's self-characterisation.

In view of the above argument, it becomes clear that the reader is constantly invited to judge Moses by Moses' own evaluations and also by those of other characters. Another area serving the same rhetorical purpose, already dealt with in depth,[252] is the display of the Mosaic willingness and obedience. Bringing all these aspects together, I have shown that there is a considerable gap between Exod. 2–5 and 6–40 regarding the text's influence on the reader and his judgement. The earlier part of Exodus suggests a negative evaluation of Moses and the latter part, an increasingly positive one.

The Reader and Moses – a Conclusion

The previous discussion of Moses' portrayal has shown that the implied reader plays a dominant role, so dominant that a modern reader can develop a rough picture of this implied reader. The preconceptions of the reader, with regard to Moses' historical role in the events of the exodus from Egypt, apparently, led the author in the *inventio* of his book. These preconceptions are part of the rhetorical situation of the book. The history of research has shown that the rhetorical situation of Exodus is, mainly, discussed with regard to Moses. Clearly, the

---

despite its emphasised position I like to suggest that it, mainly, carries an illustrative force to exactly communicate this: the relationship between Moses and God is singular. As I have shown, the personality of Moses steps into the background as the story-line proceeds. The emphasis is on the function (mediator) and this guides the reader's perception of the details in the Mosaic portrayal. I find it hard to conceive of a friendship, in the common sense of the term, which is abstracted from personality. Hence, I would not over-emphasise the notion of friendship in this context.

[250] Some ancient versions have stressed the link to 33:17 by creating obvious verbal parallels to 33:12 (see LXX and TNf; cf. Houtman 2000, 696f).

[251] That Moses' rhetorics as displayed here, in Exod. 33–34, are outstanding is obvious. Dohmen 2004b, 346 characterises Moses' style as "sehr weise, feinsinnig und hintergründig." Unfortunately, I cannot provide a thorough investigation of Moses' rhetorical strategy here.

[252] Cf. p.170.

designation of the Torah as biography of Moses has contributed to this perspective on Exodus. Even if the centrality of Moses for the Torah is inescapable, the most important character for Exodus is not Moses, but Yhwh. The deconstruction of an overly positive picture of Moses, together with his mediatorial portrait, pointed in this direction. The three questions raised earlier[253] that impinge on the relationship between the implied reader and Moses can now be answered.

With regard to Moses' paradigmatic function for the implied reader we have to consider the amount to which the text invites identification with the character. Two aspects are present in the character Moses: the creation of distance and the invitation to identify. Moses as a singular figure in Israelite history, endowed with a singular task and a breathtaking closeness to God, certainly, contributes to a perception of him as a removed, unreachable 'super'-man. This notion of Moses is, however, balanced by numerous passages that focus on his failures, his fears, and his indebtedness to Yhwh. The often mentioned introduction of him into the plot contributes to this picture. But, the mere nature of his role as mediator between God and the pharaoh and between God and Israel implies a more approachable character. Another aspect, not yet mentioned, is the narratorial strategy of the book. The author lets his readers look over Moses' shoulders, as it were. Large parts of Exodus are, at the story level, Yhwh's direct speech to Moses. The Israelites, themselves, only perceive Yhwh's visible actions and later his mediated words. Thus, the author decides to lend Moses' perspective to his readers, at least for a good amount of the text. The effort the author makes to enable reader-identification with Israel is astonishing, as will be shown in the next chapter. The reader is, thus, brought to a level of intimacy with God which is akin to Moses'. It is, on the one hand, a privileged perspective, but, on the other hand, it also implies a higher amount of responsibility for the things heard or read.

This last consideration, already, points to Moses' paradigmatic quality which can be put in concrete terms. As mentioned by Childs, Crüsemann and Rendtorff, Moses fulfils a number of societal roles of Israel.[254] Among these are Moses as prophet, as judge, and as priest. These later offices are all present in the literary Moses, though not necessarily in their ultimate fullness. Moses' relationship with Yhwh is one dominated by obedience, prayer, intercession[255] and intimacy. Rendtorff claims: "It is not only a Deuteronomic tradition to call Moses a prophet, but … it is an intrinsic element of the Moses tradition from its earliest beginnings."[256] His call[257] and the face-to-face encounters with Yhwh carry prophetic overtones. The prophetic role is dominant in the Mosaic figure

---

[253] Cf. p.125.

[254] Cf. p.188.

[255] On this see also Rendtorff 2001, 128–131.

[256] Rendtorff 1997, 19. Cf. also Rendtorff 2001, 126f.

[257] On the signs to confirm/legitimise the prophetic office see Childs 1976, 78.

and is further developed in Numbers and Deuteronomy. Closely linked to his picture as prophet is the priestly portrayal of Moses. Here, his mediatorial role must be mentioned, which, of course, includes his intercessory practice and the various leadership functions regarding holiness issues concerning Israel which lives in the divine presence. His societal function as judge (see esp. Exod. 18) connects him closely with the law which he mediates. The role of king, however, is not ascribed to Moses. As has been shown above, in Exodus the only legitimate king is Yhwh.

Rendtorff sees the key for understanding the singularity of Moses' endowment with all these 'offices' in the fact that he always and only acts upon direct divine directives (see p.189ff). Thus, Rendtorff rightly summarises the communicative interest of the Torah with the character Moses: "Israel bedarf einer Führung, die in unmittelbarer Beziehung zu Gott steht. Der 'Prophet' Mose hat diese Aufgabe paradigmatisch erfüllt. Aber nach ihm gibt es keine Führungsgestalt mehr, die diesem Anspruch gerecht wird."[258] The literary character Moses is exemplary for any future leaders of Israel. He is the expression or embodiment of a part of the author's political and religious vision for Israel.

If we consider the Torah as a biography of Moses, the focus of this biography is on a complex figure who, to a certain extent, can fulfil the function of an archetype. But, as Gelin rightly cautions, the book of Exodus – if not the entire Pentateuch – does not provide a detailed study of the historical character.[259] Moses is never portrayed as a personality in his own right. He is a person with a task and this God-given task is more important. Hence, one must not read Exodus, or even Exodus through Deuteronomy, as a biography in the modern sense of the term.

---

[258] Cf. Rendtorff 2001, 133f.

[259] Gelin 1963.

CHAPTER 4

ISRAEL – BETWEEN IDEAL AND REALITY

In Exodus, we as readers, witness the birth of a nation. The literary focus on this foundational time of Israel provides an abundance of opportunities to influence the identity of the reader – if he considers himself as belonging to this people. I will argue that the implied reader of Exodus is influenced in exactly this way. Exodus creates what Assmann calls 'cultural memory', a memory which has shaped Israel's identity ever since the book was written.

If it were not for Israel, there would have been no exodus, no Moses and no tabernacle. Israel is the very first literary character introduced in the plot of Exodus. Nevertheless, the presence of the character Israel is so obvious and natural that it is easy to ignore the influence of its portrayal during the reading process. All the more important is it to reflect on this character, which surely provides the most natural contact and continuity between the reader and the text. Whatever is said to the Israelites inside the story has, by implication, been said to the implied reader's ancestors and, thus, indirectly to this reader himself, especially, as he is part of a historically conscious culture.

In the opinions of the other characters, Israel is far from being straightforward. Moses doubts that they will believe him or Yhwh (Exod. 4:1), and he finds them stiff-necked and resistant to better insights (cf. 15:22 –17:16 and 32–34). One pharaoh thinks that they became too numerous and, therefore, are a potential threat to his own people (1:9), whereas the other finds them idle and unwilling to work (5:8.17). The Egyptians, on the other hand, find them to be nice people or, at least, they accept them (12:36). Yhwh considers them to be his people, the people of the fathers' covenant, and he does everything to fulfil his desire to live among them (3:7-8 *et passim*). The Israelites picture themselves as being a misled and miserable lot – better off in Egyptian slavery than wandering in the wilderness (14:12; 16:3) – and as inadequate hearers of the divine voice (20:19). Inevitably, the reader will either side with Israel or turn away in disgust. He may criticise the author for being unfair to his ancestors, or he may be motivated to do better than they did. In the following chapter I shall try to explicate the author's strategy of portraying Israel the way he did. The emphasis will be on a rhetorical-critical analysis of the phenomenon of reader-identification in Exodus.

I will open with a review of some positions and insights from previous studies, in order to highlight the issues that may provide avenues into the subject.

Again, a section will be devoted to a reflection on the influence of the first contact between the reader and the literary Israel. The subsequent larger part will be concerned, firstly, with the development of the character Israel throughout the narrative and, second, with the contribution of the legal sections of Exodus to the picture. In these two major parts, the contrast between the ideal conception of Israel as promoted by the reader and the narrative description of their reality will play an important role. The conclusion attempts to identify what the text does with the implied reader regarding his own identification with the literary Israel.

The Rhetorical Function of Israel – Some Perspectives

When discussing 'Israel' most commentators or biblical theologians refer to the historical aspects of the sociological entity, and, usually, they admit that the Old Testament account is, mainly, concerned with theological issues revolving around the relationship between Yhwh and Israel. This set of issues is, then, typically discussed in Old Testament theologies and related monographs. Between the lines, so to speak, these studies display a certain understanding of the texts' rhetorical function and the role of the literary character Israel. There is little work explicitly discussing the literary or rhetorical implications of Israel's portrayal in the Old Testament,[1] let alone in Exodus. Therefore, I will consider a few representative views on the literary Israel and concentrate on the consequences for the rhetorical function of Israel in Exodus.

P.D. Hanson 1986

Hanson's study is an appropriate starting point, as he draws together results from mainstream biblical studies and concentrates on Israel as it is described in the Old Testament texts. He is concerned with the sociological outcome of the exodus event. In the Bible, he finds an almost utopian view of what Israel should be.[2] The ideal would be an egalitarian society of freed slaves without any social stratification. Hanson shows that this social structure is inseparable from the religious distinctiveness of the biblical authors' articulation of their Yhwh-faith. Especially the divine attributes of holiness and faithfulness informed the perception of Israel's ideal society. Hanson defines the Israelite self-conception as a response to Yhwh's elective act which finds expression in their

---

[1] One article approaches a literary aspect of the portrayal of Israel coming from a structuralist vantage point (Kunin 1999). Kunin, however, concentrates mainly on Genesis and the Talmudic perception of the genealogical lists in Genesis; esp. Edom and Amalek are his focus.

[2] Hanson notes the widely shared ancient Near Eastern ideological context of an ontologically founded inequality, which necessarily finds its expression in social reality. Some humans were created to dominate others and to supersede them in the acquisition of riches and power. For an introduction to these matters see Wright, C. J. H. 2004, 54ff.

exodus experience.[3] The crucial task for the Israel of the exodus is to communicate the experience of their own liberation to their neighbours. Hence, the biblical story focuses on the realisation of divine justice and compassion.

For Hanson, the rhetorical strategy of Israel's portrayal in Exodus is a paradigmatic one. The paradigm works at two levels, theological and empirical. The first level utilises the divine behaviour towards the Israel of the exodus as example for the desired ethical behaviour, or the *imitatio dei*. The second level reasons from the experience and, thus, history of Israel, and in the description of this it consciously supports the ethical ends of the law, localised in the context of the exodus-events. In other words, the reader is addressed in a pre-moral realm. Certain emotions are aroused by the narration of other characters' behaviour. Hanson would, therefore, probably approve of an epideictic genus for large parts of Exodus. Whether the social ideal of Exodus is, indeed, an egalitarian society appears doubtful, but Hanson has certainly raised important issues and opened up potentially fruitful avenues for a rhetorical evaluation of the text.

J. Assmann 1992

In his influential book on cultural memory, the Egyptologist Jan Assmann discusses, among other things, how ancient cultures formed and secured their identities. That political identity is a theme of Exodus is apparent. Whatever one may think about Assmann's philosophical abstractions, his material contributions highlight aspects that earlier might have gone unnoticed. Assmann's main thesis is that the past provides meaning for the present. But the past is not just present; it must first be created by remembering. Memory is dependent upon the needs and conditions of the present; everything which is not thought of as important will fall into oblivion.[4]

For Israel, Assmann notes the key terms *covenant* (ברית) and *election* (בחר, ידע) which describe Israel's relationship with God. Assmann rejects the concept of a "Wohngemeinschaft" (house-sharing) – in favour of the two terms just mentioned – as characterising the Yhwh-Israel relationship. His reason is the

---

[3] "In essence there was already revealed in this event both the nature of the God Yahweh, and the nature of the community of faith that Yahweh's nature implied ... In the deliverance from Egyptian slavery, Israel encountered a God whose nature and whose corresponding plan for reality stood in diametric opposition to the gods of the Pharaoh ... Thus a new notion of community was born with the exodus. In compromising or denying it, as Israel repeatedly would, Israel would compromise or deny its own essential being as a people called by God, a community of freed slaves within which the pyramid of social stratification consigning certain classes to lives of ease and others to relentless suffering and deprivation was to be banned forever." (Hanson, P. D. 1986, 21.23)

[4] Cf. below my comments on Kratz, who takes up Assmann's work and finds his own conclusions with regard to the 'cultural memory' of Israel.

contrast between the static nature of divine indwelling in Egyptian temples and the Israelite God whose earthly presence is always "unmittelbar und unvermittelt, aber unstet, unverfügbar und unzugänglich."[5] Assmann concludes that immanence is unthinkable for the transmundane God Yhwh.[6] Just like Hanson, he finds the foundations of Israel's social ideals in theological convictions about the nature of their God. The exodus event plays an important role in his argument. Nevertheless, as I will show later, all three concepts – covenant, election *and* 'house-sharing' – feature strongly in the literary unit Exodus, and none of them suffers under the weight of the others. That Assmann concentrates only on the first two of these is rooted in his assumption that the character of Israel's identity is based in the *Erinnerungsfigur* of the exodus from Egypt; the narratives about the tabernacle are not mentioned in his argument.

For Assmann, the historicity of the event does not contribute to its importance, but the significance of it in Israelite memory does. Both Israel and their god find their identities in the exodus. The centrality of the exodus event in Israel's reconstruction of its past reflects their self-perception, their aims and their hopes. At the heart of Assmann's argument is Morton Smith's suggestion of a "Yhwh-alone-movement", which opposes the heritage, culture and religion of the early Israelite people.[7] The exodus from Egypt symbolises the dissociation of religion and culture desired by this "Yhwh-alone-movement". The *Erinnerungsfigur* exodus stands for the 'exodus' from the profane, unclean, oppressive, conformist attitudes of their own culture. Hence, according to Assmann, we observe Israel – as we know it from the Hebrew Scriptures – to be a separate people because of their adherence to a monotheistic ideology. This is the heart of the Israelite identity which excludes all other faiths; it is an iron wall cutting through Israel's own culture, where the entrances and exits are defined along religious lines.[8] These demarcations, nevertheless, influence culture and every day behaviour, as Assmann, unmistakably, points out:

> Diese Mauer wäre nicht so hoch, die Grenze nicht so scharf gezogen, wenn sie nicht innerhalb der eigenen Kultur verliefe. Denn die so ausgegrenzte Lebensform muß sich gegen die selbstverständliche Alltagsroutine durchsetzen. Daher wird sie auf die Basis einer elaborierten Gesetzgebung gestellt, der jede Selbstverständlichkeit abgeht. Wer nach diesen Gesetzen lebt, vergißt keinen Augenblick, wer er

---

[5] Assmann 1992, 197.

[6] In an interesting move, he takes the deuteronomic phraseology of the divine *name* indwelling the temple to mean that God himself does not live there. In general, one has to make allowance for Assmann's less than up-to-date familiarity with Old Testament research.

[7] This is not the place to unfold the entire debate on monotheism provoked by Assmann 1997 in the last decade of the past century. It will suffice to concentrate on Assmann's view of the role of the exodus event.

[8] Cf. Assmann 1992, 205f.

ist und wohin er gehört. Diese Lebensform ist so schwierig, daß sie nur in der
Form unaufhörlichen Lernens und Bewußthaltens realisiert werden kann.[9]

Even though Assmann also perceives the importance of the theology and the
exodus event, the communication of the author whom he imagines for our texts
works quite differently. Like Hanson, he presents, by and large, a paradigmatic
reading, but with an emphasis on separation. This leads to the exact opposite result: the withdrawal of one person from another. As we have seen, Hanson focuses more on the acceptance of the other person as a driving principle behind
the Israelite social ideals. For Assmann, Israelite distinctiveness pervades all aspects of every day life and he would concede that the book of Exodus strongly
supports this abnormality. The role of these texts would be to cement Israelite
identity by not allowing their reader to deviate from the ideal, unless they
wanted to forfeit their identity. The texts are, thus, part of a rhetorical situation
marked by conflict. The written form of this communication is important to
Assmann, as only written texts can achieve canonical status and, hence, serve as
a standard which can be imposed.

I shall argue, below, for an ambivalent and complicated picture of Israel in
Exodus, which accounts for the complex reality of Israel and betrays a certain
rhetorical strategy. Assmann, however, concentrates narrowly on an ideal Israel
and, in so doing, does not give enough consideration to its effects on reader
identification. Anyone reading the texts as Assmann wants them to be read will
be offended by the ideals and demands of monotheism, just as Assmann himself
is offended.[10] Only in a rhetorical situation in which the canonical quality of the
text can be assumed would this strategy work. It is doubtful, however, that the
author had such in mind when writing his work – even when one allows for a
heated dispute between polytheistic traditionalists and a "Yhwh-alone-group".
A more likely rhetorical situation is one of persuasion and not one of pressure
and threat. Nevertheless, Assmann's contribution nicely balances Hanson's
views with the introduction of a different rationale for the distinguishing elements of Israelite society and culture. Especially, the assumption that there are a
number of possible reconstructions of Israel's past – and, thus, also of its religion and identity – is an important aspect which needs to be taken into account.
Furthermore, Assmann's overall argument highlights the importance of the
choices made by the authors who put the cultural memories in writing.

J. Schreiner 1995

Of the Old Testament theologies I want to mention in the present context, Josef
Schreiner displays a helpful awareness of rhetorical intricacies of the texts. He
is, further, convinced of the centrality and importance of the notion that Israel is
the people of God for the understanding of Old Testament thought. Schreiner

---

[9] Assmann 1992, 206.

[10] Cf. esp. Assmann 1997.

regards the historical reasoning of Israel's national existence as the root of any further theological development.

The earliest textual layers show that it is Yhwh's protective and liberating act on which Israel founds its national existence, which is expressed by the phrase עם יהוה.[11] Schreiner directs our attention to the way in which this concept is introduced: "Es ist bezeichnend und für die Frage nach der Entstehung des Volkes Jahwes wichtig, daß es innerhalb des AT zum ersten Mal, und dazu noch in der Gottesrede Ex 3,7.10 in den Blick kommt."[12] He infers that, apparently, it was important for the author to root the national identity of Israel in an adoptive formula which includes the imminent promise to act on their behalf. This promise is followed by the description of the act. The initiative was Yhwh's, and the ensuing acts, the inevitable consequences of an established relationship.[13]

A different rhetorical aspect is touched upon by Schreiner when he concludes his discussion of the so-called Deuteronomistic covenant formula "You will be my people and I will be your God." It, necessarily, remains open whether this formula should be translated in the present tense or the future tense, or whether it constitutes an appeal. All three are possible, depending in which situation the reader finds himself. In this communicational complexity "kann die Bundesformel auf Wesentliches aufmerksam machen, das nicht übersehen werden darf."[14] It functions as a rhetorical shortcut which invokes elementary issues of Israel's faith in any given situation. Another dominant theme, closely linked with the mentioned covenant formula, is the tradition of Israel's election. Schreiner understands this concept to be pre-Deuteronomic, although it features strongly in Deuteronomy and DtH. Schreiner points to an important semantic link to the root ידע, which in significant contexts (e.g.Am. 3:1-2; Exod. 3:7) may well be translated as 'choosing/electing.'[15] God knows his people and, thus, is in a special relationship with them; this provokes him to act favourably on their behalf. Of course, this requires the divine demands on the entire people; here, the concept of holiness is filled with theological and practical significance for the everyday life of the people.

This notion leads Schreiner, consequently, to a discussion of Exod. 19:5-6. Here, again, he demonstrates rhetorical awareness and stresses the importance of placing these propositions on Israel's *Wesen* in relation to the Sinai pericope:

> Gerahmt vom Verkündigungsauftrag (V. 3b. 6b), der auf die grundsätzliche Bedeutung der folgenden Worte hinweist, folgt der Rückverweis auf die Gottestat

---

[11] Cf. Schreiner 1995, 18ff who approaches the entire issue via the phrase *'m yhwh*.

[12] Schreiner 1995, 19.

[13] Schreiner points in this context to Exod. 6:7 and 15:16 which provide different angles on the same issue. Of course, Schreiner follows the common historical-critical source division for all texts he discusses, but he does not make much of it in the present context.

[14] Schreiner 1995, 23.

[15] Along the same line cf. also Nicole 1997 on the root בחר.

beim Exodus, die Zielangabe der göttlichen Führung und die Aufforderung zum Gehorsam gegenüber dem Herrn.[16]

This provides the framework for the divine requirements of Israel, the people's position and their responsibility. There is no need to review Schreiner's comments in detail, but it is good to remember his focus on the *locus* of the call narrative passage for our later discussion.

Unfortunately, the historical-critical separation of textual layers obstructs Schreiner's view of the complexity created by the unity and diversity – or exclusiveness and inclusiveness – of the people Israel in the view of Exodus.[17] The tensions in the final shape of our text lead, rhetorically, to a very fragile, but effective, balance in the concept of Israel, which disappears, for example, when a priestly layer is removed from a Deuteronomic one. But this issue will be postponed until later. In sum, Schreiner's remarks on 'Israel' bear the marks of a thorough exegetical treatment of the relevant texts – with an emphasis on Deuteronomistic theology – which guides the reader through the form of the texts. Schreiner's discussion, probably, was never intended to be a rhetorical analysis, but mentioning his work was nevertheless fruitful. Thus, Schreiner gives several good hints as to what deserves our attention in this present work.

R.G. Kratz 2000

R.G. Kratz's recent article may serve here as typical example for the traditional historical-critical views on Israel, and, as such, his study is marked by its consistent argument. For Kratz, the historical beginning of everything were the two, historically tangible, distinct monarchies of Israel and Judah. "Die Israel und Juda umgreifende, die politische Einheit transzendierende Größe 'Israel', die 'in der Sprache des Bekennens und Glaubens' ihren Ort hat, erscheint demgegenüber als künstlich und also sekundär."[18] In other words, the name *Israel* represents the unity of the twelve tribes and is a theological ideal which is devoid of any historical or social reality.[19] Any vague sense of belonging together in a

---

[16] Schreiner 1995, 27.

[17] Except for a very brief reference to the אהל מועד there is no mention of any Exodus text in Schreiner's discussion (cf. Schreiner 1995, 31–33), which is astonishing given the abundance of material in Exodus on the subject.

[18] Kratz 2000, 3.

[19] Quite opposed to Kratz, Brevard Childs concludes that the term Israel "is not an ideal or theological construct, but refers primarily to an empirical people, indeed to a nation." (Childs 1993, 138) This notion is based on the historical experiences on which Israel bases its peoplehood, but it, also, encompasses its religious identity. The idea that Israel is Yhwh's people precedes and succeeds its political reality and can be found in the covenant formula and its expansion in Exod. 19,1–6, but it "is most thoroughly developed in the book of Deuteronomy." (Childs 1993, 139) Also, in Exodus, Childs finds a strong emphasis on the covenantal character of the relationship between Yhwh and Israel, including the signs and the logic of this special mode of affiliation.

pre-state or a pre-monarchical setting, is for Kratz, a myth needed for our own pre-critical, psychological[20] security. Even Wellhausen felt the need for a pre-monarchical idea of a unified Israel, which found its expression in a covenant formula ("Jahve der Gott Israels und Israel das Volk Jahves") dating from Mosaic times.[21] But this notion of unity would only be due to a sort of creative 're-membering', also known as Assmann's 'cultural memory'.[22] But, where does the memory come from, if there was no unity initiating it, Kratz asks? As an initial attempt at an answer, Martin Noth proposed his, now obsolete, amphictyonic theory: a religious alliance between the twelve tribes.[23]

Kratz, himself, finds no other option than to concede that "insofern Jhwh der Gott des Reiches Israel war, ... Israel hier zum ersten Mal zum 'Volk Jhwhs' [wurde]."[24] *Israel* would, then, signify nothing other than an inhomogeneous population under the unifying roof of a monarchical state, a common god, and a shared ideology.[25] Thus, there is a difference between the historical Israel and the Israel of confession and faith ("Israel des Bekennens und Glaubens"). This difference provides the exegete with his task of tracing the developments of the 'ideal Israel' – the self-reflection of Israel – throughout the history of the theological reflections which found expression in the Old Testament.[26] Kratz does so, first, in brief sketches of the Chronistic history, and, then, he mentions the importance of the imagination of a unified Israel for all preceding literary strata. The election of Israel in pre-monarchical times, its integrity secured by Torah-observance, and its fate determined by the monarchy delineate this idea. In the beginning were the two kingdoms, the north and the south, which were brought together on an ideological level. In Kratz's reconstruction, one step leads to the next in a logical sequence of theological explanations for the present *status quo*

---

[20] Kratz interprets the history of research on this subject along psychological lines. For quite distinct reasons, scholars felt the need to uphold the concept of a united twelve-tribe Israel.

[21] This concept, however, must not be mistaken as the fully-fledged legal covenant of the priestly redaction, which, according to Wellhausen, must be dated in the fifth century B.C. The earlier relationship would be some sort of natural bond. (See Childs 1993, 135f for a brief discussion of Wellhausen's ideas.)

[22] For this term see above and refer to Assmann 1992.

[23] Cf. Noth 1986.

[24] Kratz 2000, 5.

[25] Schmidt 1996, 157ff also raises the question of what constitutes Israel's unity. He discusses the election by Yhwh, certain sociological/political factors, and certain cultic practices and concludes that before the kingdom there must have been some sort of awareness that the tribes belong together. This would, of course, not be Kratz's conclusion, but the aspects in which unity should be found are similar.

[26] Cf. Kratz 2000, 6. He quotes von Rad: "Jede Generation stand vor der immer gleichen und immer neuen Aufgabe, sich als Israel zu begreifen. Jede Generation mußte erst in einem gewissen Sinne Israel werden" (Rad 1962, 132).

of the divided kingdom. The Deuteronomist, together with Deuteronomy, would present the clearest expression of the unity of the two states.[27]

But there must have been something before exilic times which led to Israel being the name of the ideal, unified, mythical state, Kratz suspects. Here, we come to the texts of more interest for my present concern. The narrative of the exodus from Egypt betrays, on all proposed redactional levels, the togetherness of the names Yhwh and Israel.[28] Thus, the designation of Israel as "my people" or "this people", which belongs to a later redaction, is only a development and formulation of an already present idea.[29] In this narrative, we find a version of the history of Israel reaching back in time to the pre-national and, thus, patrilineal clan of Jacob, without any reference to the northern kingdom. The need for this development arose when the knowledge of where one belongs, whether in Israel or in Judah, was lost. This would be the case after 720 B.C., after the downfall of the northern kingdom.[30] Dating issues are not my immediate interest here, so I will focus on the rhetorical implications of Kratz's analysis.

We can extract the communicational objective of the redactors of these 'earlier' narratives, the patriarchal- and the exodus-narratives: they attempt to provide their readers with a reasoning for an identity beyond any national particularity. "'Israel das Volk Jhwhs' – das meint hier also das Staatsvolk ohne Staat, das allein auf sich und seinen Gott gestellt ist, der zugleich der Nationalgott des noch bestehenden Reiches Juda ist."[31] The reader is invited to feel at home in a people who are without a state, but still Yhwh's people. The overall rhetorical strategy behind the texts, according to Kratz's reconstruction, is to build up a flexible and stable definition of Israel, or, in other words, to provide a new and theologically reflected national identity in the middle of national uncertainty. Unfortunately, Kratz does not go into any detail to describe how this aim is pursued in the texts, but his few hints, certainly, provide starting points for our inquiry. Of course his entire argument rests upon the historical-critical

---

[27] Here Kratz uses the term "Schicksalsgemeinschaft", which binds the two together in their participation in the same sins, the violation of the unified worship, both locally and theologically.

[28] Cf. Kratz 2000, 13.

[29] According to Kratz, one has to distinguish between the patriarchal narrative and the exodus narrative and their respective views on the origin of Israel. The former speaks of Israel as having always been in Canaan and always linked genealogically with its neighbours, whereas the latter prefers an entry from the outside, from the East-Jordan, without touching Judah (cf. Kratz 2000, 14).

[30] "Das Ende des Reiches Israel war der Anfang der theologischen Tradition." (Kratz 2000, 17)

[31] Kratz 2000, 15.

paradigm regarding the literary origin of the texts. A different and more clearly developed picture will emerge when one considers the final shape of Exodus.

J.A. Davies 2004

Exod. 19:6, with its direct epithets on Israel, undoubtedly plays a crucial role in the portrayal of Israel in Exodus. Davies devotes his entire monograph to a 'newer' literary critical reading of the verse in its present context. Basically, Davies argues that ממלכת כהנים and גוי קדוש are epexegetical comments on the enigmatic designation relating to Israel's special position before God – סגלה (19:5) – which is the divine grant expressed as covenant in the surrounding framework. Compared with the other solutions to this notoriously difficult passage, his reading appears very balanced and is especially convincing because of its attention to the literary context. Davies' comments on this contextual level provide some valuable insights for my present subject. Much of the material following Exod. 19 makes sense if viewed through the lenses offered with these metaphors of royalty and priesthood. Exod. 24:1-11 can be read as the ordination rite for the priesthood of the community of Israel, which is followed by the meal on the mountain "as consummation of royal-priestly intimacy in the court of the divine king."[32] The instructions in Exod. 25–31 describe the cult, with special attention to the priests and then provide a model for the royal-priestly status of Israel as a whole.[33] The official priests represent the community, and this, together with the ascriptions of Exod. 19 and the understanding of the tabernacle as a restored cosmos, provide the rationale for concluding that Israel is intended to fulfil priestly duties before God for the sake of humankind.[34] Minor points may be added to Davies' argument, but it has become clear that, for him, the centrality of Exod. 19:5-6 controls most of the material of Exodus, and, thus, the rhetorical function of Israel in Exodus is decisive.

To base the entire picture of Israel upon the ideal expressed in 19:5-6, however, seems to overload the passage exegetically. In Exodus there is more to Israel than the formulation of some characteristics of an exemplary nation before God, even if these aspects are central. For the sake of the implied reader, Israel emerges as a character torn between ideal and reality, as soon will be argued. The value of Davies' thesis lies in its careful attention to the narrative connections between the royal-priestly metaphor and the surrounding material. The shortcoming, at least from a rhetorical-critical point of view, is that the emerg-

---

[32] Davies, J. A. 2004, 136. This interpretation, Davies argues, stands equally justified parallel to the understanding of Exod. 24 as a covenant ceremony.

[33] Cf. Davies, J. A. 2004, 164ff.

[34] "The priest is the living symbol of blessing and well-being, of life in the fullest, of all that humanity should be and could become in relation to God." (Davies, J. A. 2004, 168)

ing picture of Israel only concentrates on the ideals. Attention to the reader will
help to balance this bias.

Conclusion

The works referred to above represent the current thinking on the literary portrayal of Israel. None of them ventures deeply into the actual role the picture of
Israel plays in the communicative process, nor do any of them utilise an explicit
rhetorical-critical approach – the *desideratum* is obvious. Only Schreiner mentions a couple of textual intricacies where the concern for the means of reader-
guidance is explicit. Beyond this, it was my aim to try to unearth how these
studies perceive the relationship between author and reader and the means by
which the reader is guided in his understanding of Israel. The themes or aspects
raised above reappear at the appropriate places in the subsequent investigation.
The importance of the relationship between Israel and God, namely the God of
the exodus, for the portrayal of Israel is one of the points upon which virtually
all commentators agree. Another common point is the relationship of Israel to
their own history or the memory of their own past. Again, this concept is inextricably linked with the exodus from Egypt.

   In the following paragraphs I will emphasise the aspects of Exodus that I
have not yet widely discussed, especially as they relate to the processes of
reader-identification. The discussion will concentrate on the introduction and
development of Israel as character, the various expressions of their relationship
to Yhwh, and the rhetorical influence of the picture of Israel as it is drawn in
Exodus.

The Introduction of Israel Into the Plot of Exodus

After reading my previous chapters one will not be surprised that I deem the introduction of Israel to be of major importance for the shaping of the reader's understanding, especially as it concerns his previous preconceptions. As already shown, the first contact between a character and the reader provides the author with the opportunity to create a backdrop against which the character's development can be evaluated.

When first introduced in Exodus, the character Israel is not even a people as such.[35] The Israel mentioned in Exod. 1:1 is, clearly, the individual known from the Genesis narrative, Jacob. Toward the beginning of the present study, I argued that it seems very likely that the author of Exodus assumed his implied reader knew Genesis. Evidence of this are the link between the beginning of Exodus and the end of Genesis (especially Gen. 46), the individual names of the twelve sons of Israel (Exod. 1:1-6), and the allusions in Exod. 1:7 to the patriarchal promises.[36]

In very few sentences the reader perceives the emergence of a people and the creation of a literary character. Rendtorff expresses this when he talks of a change in perspective from the individual and clan levels to the national level, where collective concepts dominate: the people as a whole act and suffer.[37] This literary abstraction from the individual to the collective is maintained throughout the entire book of Exodus. Even when the elders of Israel (זקני בני ישראל) are mentioned,[38] they are merely representatives for the entirety of the people and do not develop a literary existence of their own.[39] The only Israelite individuals playing roles in their own right are Moses and Aaron. Moses was covered in greater detail above. Aaron tends to step back behind the figure of Moses in the first part of Exodus,[40] and, later, in the context of the golden calf episode, the

---

[35] There is discussion of how far one can speak of any ancient Near Eastern collective as a nation or people in a modern sense. Von Soden, the renowned assyriologist, holds that the only such entity in the Ancient Near East which comes close to a national self-understanding, based on genealogy and thus historical thinking, would be Israel (cf. Soden 1985, 13). Block (Block 1997) argues roughly along the same lines, but is more hesitant, as there is, presently, not enough material from sources other than the Old Testament to discern other peoples' national self-consciousness. In the present context I will use the term 'people' in the sense of a sociological unit, which is distinguished, mainly, by descent and which forms some sort of national identity where there are insiders and out-siders. For a summary of the issues around the name Israel and its usage and cognates, see Houtman 1993, 110f.

[36] This has been discussed in detail above (see p.21).

[37] Cf. Rendtorff 1999, 32.

[38] Exod. 3:16.18; 4:29; 12:21; 17:5-6; 18:12; 19:7; 24:1.9.14. Furthermore, the division of Israel into tribes plays no role in Exodus (cf. Houtman 1993, 220).

[39] On the use of the 2nd person singular in the legal parts of the book, cf. p.234 below.

[40] On Aaron as 'mouth' and prophet, cf. p.173 above.

reader is left uncertain as to Aaron's role in the sin of the people (32:23-24).[41]
In summary, the implied reader of Exodus is, generally, confronted with the status and the behaviour of the *people* of Israel. The rhetorically important assumption is that he will consider himself as part of this still existing people;
hence, there is considerable potential for identification with the collective literary character of the story. The reader will know a very concrete reality which
carries the name 'Israel', and this reality becomes, inevitably, part of the reading process as a foil against which the literary character takes shape. Thus, the
literary Israel becomes relevant for the evaluation of the reader's present reality.

Interestingly, it is the second character which appears in the book, the pharaoh of Exod. 1–2, who is the first to call Israel עם (1:9). Neither the omniscient
narrator nor, Yhwh utter the obvious. The pharaoh recognises Israel's growth
and, thus, the nascent national quality of the immigrants and, of course, the possible threat this poses to his own nation.[42] With this strategy, the author introduces the tension which carries the plot until the drowning of the Egyptians in
the *yam suf*. The pharaoh is also the one to express that the national identity of
Israel is based on ethnicity (עם בני ישראל). Rendtorff observes that the pharaoh
does not refer to the sons of Israel as the family of Joseph (or Jacob), which betrays that he, himself, does not acknowledge any official representative for this
ethnic entity. At this stage of the story the people, although numerous and
strong, do not have anyone to lead them out of misery: "Es [sc. the people] ist
stumm der Unterdrückung ausgesetzt. Und auch Gott schweigt."[43] The reader
observes that after the ups and downs described in Genesis Israel is now a people, even a vigorously growing one. But it is without a defence against its op-
pressors, and there is no one to represent their interests to the Egyptians: "So
beginnt die Geschichte Israels als Volk in der konturlosen Gestalt des Sklaven-
volkes in Ägypten."[44]

Thus, the character Israel is portrayed in Exod. 1 as passively exposed to the
fear-driven whims of the Egyptian monarch. The only action it takes is repro-
duction, which takes centre stage in the construction of the chapter. The key
terms of the text clearly point in this direction (esp. ילד – בת – בן – ינק [hif.]),[45]
as do the growing fears of the pharaoh. But any reader immersed in the ancient
Near Eastern cultural background will immediately have recognised the element
of divine benevolence which finds expression in the abundant growth of the Is-

---

[41] Cf. Dohmen 2004b, 310.

[42] The prospect imagined by the king (ועלה מן־הארץ, 1:10) is not so much that the people
of Israel might leave the country (so that the Egyptians had to do the work themselves),
but, rather, that they might 'rise up from the land' and, thus, overthrow the existing government. "At this point of the narrative there is no reason for them to 'escape'."
(Callender 1998, 78, n.4).

[43] Rendtorff 1999, 32.

[44] Rendtorff 2001, 54.

[45] Cf. Weber 1990, 50f.

raelite populace.[46] Hence, in the end, the multiplication is not their own activity but God's, as 1:20f make explicit. The passivity of Israel, together with the fulfilment of the divine promises to the patriarchs, draws a picture of Israel as a people dependent on God's intervention on their behalf. Exodus begins with the potential of the people. Later, the author becomes more explicit in his understanding that the people's potential is rooted in the divine covenant with the fathers and in Yhwh's resolution to rescue his people (Exod. 2:24-25). The emphasis on Israel's passivity prepares the reader for the fact that Israel's identity and independence could be realised only by the later historical developments leading to the exodus from Egypt, and not by some inherent quality of the people itself.

At the beginning of Exodus, the author takes his implied reader back to the formative time of their common national background: Once there was a time when there was no Israel. Although the implied reader, certainly, has a very concrete conception of what 'Israel' is, the author attempts to start from scratch and build up this character anew. The strategy involved is one of distancing the reader from the character. The passive role allocated to the emerging Israel postpones the inevitable reader identification, so that the plot can properly develop before Israel plays a major role. Israel's passiveness directs the reader's attention to the more active characters in this part of the story, namely, the pharaoh and Yhwh. The same happens with the concentration on one Israelite in Exod. 2, Moses:[47] Israel remains, largely, in the background while the role of Moses (2–4) and the conflict between Yhwh and the pharaoh (5–14) take the foreground. The author's opinion and development of a characterisation of Israel are postponed. At least thirteen chapters pass before Israel becomes alive, so to speak. These thirteen chapters, however, provide a plethora of opportunities to influence the reading process and, thus, to shape the reader's later per-

---

[46] The argument of Eslinger 1991, 53, n.1, is similar, but it has a different twist at the end: "In Exod. 1.7 the narrator pounds the allusion into the readers' minds so that they will not fail to see that it is exactly the fulfilment of the blessings and promises that leads to the Israelites' enslavement in Egypt." Eslinger attempts to answer the question – who is responsible for the oppression of Israel in Egypt? – and concludes that Yhwh carries the ultimate responsibility: "The Egyptian king and his reasonings are only cogs in the machine engineered and run by God." (53, n.1) To my understanding, this text is not very concerned about the reasons for the Israelite's enslavement. Especially, given the complex theology behind the notion of the pharaoh's hardened heart, it appears a bit shallow just to blame Yhwh for the difficulties. This remains true even in the light of Eslinger's interpretation of the hard heart (Eslinger 1991, 56f; he accepts the interpretation of Gunn 1982 on this issue).

[47] Although, as Weber 1990 has shown impressively, Exod. 1 and 2 are distinctly linked on multiple literary levels. The theme might be the same, the counteraction of the life-threatening behaviour of the Egyptian king, but the focus in Exod. 2 is, clearly, not on the Israelites but on Moses, or, to be precise, indirectly on Moses through the women who clearly focus on him as a baby (cf. Exum 1983, 52).

ception of Israel. As matters of priority, Yhwh and his mediator Moses are of more importance to the author than the people are. That this could have been different is shown in the historical credo: "A wandering Aramean was my father. And he went down into Egypt and sojourned there, few in number, and there he became a nation, great, mighty, and populous." (Deut. 26:5) This is quite a different summary of Israel's founding period, and not just because of its brevity.

Later on, however, the author constructs a multilayered literary character who is far from being flat and simplistic. In the following paragraphs I intend to trace the evolving character Israel.

The Development of Israel in Exodus

The rhetoric of Exodus maintains a distinct tension in its portrayal of Israel. The tension builds between two sets of poles: doubt versus faith and ideal versus reality. After the initial passivity, the description of Israel's actions – including the record of its speeches and the comments on its reactions, its status and its role – covers the fields between these poles. The reader is led into this field and has to decide how he views himself and where he wants to be. As the following discussion will show, the author did not just favour the ideals, but he also recognises the reality of human nature and its inclination away from the ideal. In allowing this horizon to influence his portrayal of Israel, the author provides an effective rhetoric to persuade his reader to strive for the ideal. It would be bad rhetorics to provoke and shatter all presuppositions of the reader in order to create some sort of *tabula rasa*. It is much more effective to attempt a restructuring of what is already known, to allow the horizons to merge and to provoke both rational and emotional approval.[48] The complexity of the picture of Israel in Exodus serves, exactly, this communicative aim. The implied reader is not forced into acceptance of some ideal, but the text creates an opportunity for him to decide on his own position with relation to the proposed ideal.

I assume that, in Exodus, the argument is structured along movements which guide the reader through the work and establish a conceptual framework for the understanding of the single pericopes of the book. With regard to Israel, we can find three lines of literary development in Exodus.

- The first line reaches from the unit Exod. 1–15 to the pivotal point which highlights Israel's inclusion in the old covenant of the fathers: Israel is to serve Yhwh and not some other god or human king (Exod. 19–24). The obvious overarching movement of Israel is the leaving of slavery (עבדה) in order to serve (עבד) Yhwh at the mountain and to return to the place which their fathers left. It is a transition from being slaves to one king to "being honoured royal guests in the court of an-

---

[48] Cf. Eco 1972, 184f.

other [sc. God]."[49] This new status is expressed, explicitly, in numerous ways in Exod. 19–24, but even the first chapters of Exodus prepare one for this thought.[50] This results in the tension between the actual condition of Israel and its election by God, which is also expressed in its shifting between faith and doubt.

• The second line of Israel's literary development concentrates on the tension between ideal and reality in the covenant setting. The issue through which this tension finds expression in Exodus is the cohabitation of Yhwh and Israel, i.e., the issue of divine presence in a human community. The tension is created by the juxtaposition of 19–31 (the theophany together with the covenant and the concept of the divine dwelling place) and 32–34 (the violation of the covenant and its reinstitution with a focus on divine presence).

• The third movement is not so much a progressive development but a consolidation of the ideal as described in Exod. 19–31: the newly found basis of divine graciousness and forgiveness. The reality of the human inclination to turn away from God is connected to the ideal, and the inevitable tension is resolved. Thus, the text moves from 32–34 to 35–40 and culminates in a final theophany, sanctifying the dwelling place among the people. In this last movement the author portrays Israel more in the likeness of the later Moses, and, hence, Israel's priestly role, as mentioned in 19:6, already finds its literary expression in Exodus.

These lines, along which the character Israel is shaped, cover the entire conceptual field mentioned previously. The reader will find numerous instances with which he is familiar but also ones that challenge him and lead him to a new understanding of his own cultural and religious background. The concrete rhetorical strategy behind this threefold delineation of Israel, which is the concern of the following paragraphs, will help us to gain insight into the ideational context of the reader (only the one anticipated by the author, of course) and to understand the contribution these structures make to our understanding of the message the author attempted to convey.

Between Ideal and Reality

The status of Israel as the divinely-chosen people which is mentioned in the first line of development, has inherent implications for the concept of such a people. What makes them special? How can they be distinguished from other peoples?

---

[49] Davies, J. A. 2002, 158.

[50] For a more detailed discussion on the rhetorical aspects of the plague story see p.53 above.

Exodus gives the answer in the reaffirmation of the covenant with the people (Exod. 19–31).

The one theme that holds together the diverse material in these chapters is the divine presence with the people. It begins with the requirements of the theophany, includes the establishment of the mediator, sets the requirements for regular worship, connects blessings with the divine presence, and, finally, provides the blueprints for the cult and the construction of the holy place. After the people fail to realise the ideal (Exod. 33–34) the discussion revolves around this very theme,[51] since Moses is keen to secure the divine presence with the people as the hallmark of Israel's status as the chosen nation. Later, I will be looking into the legal parts of Exodus which contribute to the portrayal of Israel (see p.234ff); it is, therefore, in the present context sufficient to concentrate on the general picture which the text evokes in the reader's mind. The radical turning away from the ideal (Exod. 32:1–6), as set out in the laws, betrays Israel's reality. The ensuing resolution of the conflict discussed in 32:7–34:28 shows a way forward to deal with this reality.

Bernd Janowski writes in the preface to his collection of essays *Gottes Gegenwart in Israel*:

'Gottes Gegenwart in Israel' – nicht das Problem, ob Gott existiert, sondern die Frage seiner Gegenwart hat das alte Israel immer wieder umgetrieben. Die Antworten die es darauf gab, entsprechen seinem dynamischen Gottesbild. ... Eine ähnliche Dynamik prägt auch die Rede vom Handeln JHWHs – der erschafft und erhält, der erlöst und vergibt, der aber auch sein Angesicht verbirgt und dem Schuldigen zürnt.[52]

This, nicely, captures the centrality of the theme of the divine presence, together with its implications for the divine relationship with humans in the Old Testament. Janowski's general comment is brilliantly expressed in the unity of the material collected in Exod. 19–34 (and, also, 35–40).[53] As has been shown above, the ideal of Israel – as presented in the legal parts of Exodus – sheds a

---

[51] The people want to secure the divine presence with the creation of the calf (32:1+4). The central text of Exod. 32, v.15–16, highlights the issue at stake: Is Yhwh present in a god-image or in his word? The text leaves no doubt as to the answer. For a general discussion of divine presence in the ancient Near East and in Israel cf. Pitkänen 2003. The centrality of divine revelation is also emphasised by the redundant explanation of Moses' role as the mediator communicating Yhwh's words to the people (34:27–35). Along with the mention of the long stay of Moses on the mountain, we have a *inclusio* referring us back to the early troubles (Exod. 32:1).

[52] Janowski 1993, v.

[53] Of course, Janowski would not consider Exod. 19–34 a homogeneous unit and, thus, would not attempt to develop this thought from this text alone. It does not fit his diachronic assignment of the various literary layers of the texts. In his essays, he mainly discusses the metamorphosis of the picture of Yhwh that manifests itself in the theme of divine presence; his focus is on late Israelite history and second temple Judaism.

good deal of light on the character Yhwh. The ideal is, clearly, oriented along the lines of the *imitatio dei*; it is rooted in the divine nature and divine concerns.[54] The conclusion is that the divine presence in Israel requires an amount of compatibility between the people and their God. 'Holiness', 'justice' and 'compassion' are terms of significance.[55] For the reader, a picture of Israel develops which is inextricably bound with divine concerns and perspectives on certain issues. It is an ideal picture of Israel, painted in colours of close acquaintance with Yhwh. Klein comes to the conclusion that the entirety of Exodus attempts to achieve this one aim, "that Yahweh might dwell among his people. Life in the presence of God is clearly considered to be an ideal existence."[56] The basis of this familiarity between Israel and God is expressed in the covenant:

> I will dwell among the people of Israel and will be their God. And they shall know that I am Yhwh their God, who brought them out of the land of Egypt that I might dwell among them. I am Yhwh their God. (Exod. 29:45f)

Given this paradigm, the people's failure to realise the ideal could not have been chosen more fittingly: by creating and worshipping the golden calf, the people violate the exclusiveness of their relationship with Yhwh[57] and, thus, forfeit Yhwh's willingness to dwell among them.

In my discussion of the rhetorical role of Moses' intercession for the people after the incident with the golden calf,[58] I concluded that the author maintains a balance between the status of the people – because of their inclusion in the patriarchal covenant – and their sinful reality, which, rightfully, led to Yhwh's proposed solution of killing the people and starting anew. Moses achieves his aim; the continuous presence of Yhwh with Israel is based on his willingness to forgive. The literary strategy of how this has been expressed in Exodus is important for the message. Instead of a lengthy discussion (Exod. 32–34), one could imagine a rather short statement of Yhwh's preparedness to grant a second chance, a new beginning. This, however, would have neglected the com-

---

[54] Wenham 1997, 26f, argues the same point from a different direction. He proposes that there is a gap between biblical law and the ethics of the writers of the Bible. Law expresses the minimal consensus important for any society whereas the positive expression of what is good behaviour is spread across genre lines and found in narrative, wisdom or poetic literature.

[55] See p.91 above.

[56] Klein 1996, 271.

[57] Cf. also Scoralick 2002, 86. She collects numerous links between Exod. 19–24 and 32–34. Among these are the references to חטאה and the reason Moses gives for the theophany in 20:18-21: "Do not fear, for God has come to test you, that the fear of him may be before you, that you may not sin." Moses interprets the golden calf as just this, a חטאה גדלה in 32:30. The connections between Israel's sin andthe beginning of the decalogue have long been noticed.

[58] See p.187.

plex reality of the relationship between Israel and its god.[59] The assumption is that the imagined reader himself feels the tension of continuous deviation from Yhwh's ways and from the ideal which marks this very same people as special and chosen. In this rhetorical context, the character Moses reminds Yhwh – just as he does the reader – of the divinely intended ideal which is defended against the logical consequences of sin in the relationship with their god. A holy god needs a holy place in which to dwell, for his presence is dangerous for anything profane.[60] A concretion of this point can be found in Dohmen's comments on 32:26-29:

> Die Sünde des Volkes, die durch die Aktion der Leviten bewertet wird, wird also auf die gleiche Stufe wie ein Einbruch in den Bereich der Heiligkeit gestellt. ... Theophanie und Bund haben Israel in eine besondere Gottesnähe hineingenommen, was nur durch eine besondere Form der Heiligung (vgl. Ex 24) ermöglicht worden ist. Die Abwendung von Gott, wie sie sich in der Geschichte vom Goldenen Kalb darstellt, bedeutet deshalb nicht nur das Verlassen einer bestimmten Situation oder die Rückkehr zu einem Ausgangspunkt, sondern sie impliziert im Kern das 'Entfernen' des Heiligen, also ein Entweihen.[61]

The qualification of the people's sin as desecration points to the underlying concept of the need for a holy Israel. This has, already, been expressed strongly in the preparation of the covenant in Exod. 19 and, again, in very similar words just before the renewal of the covenant in Exod. 34:1–4.[62] Furthermore, it is

---

[59] For a more detailed discussion of the issues revolving around judgement and forgiveness, see my comments on Exod. 34:6-7 (p.43) and the conflict between Yhwh and Israel (p.69ff) above.

[60] Cf. Exod. 33:5. An interesting aspect is raised by Dozeman 2000, 34, who interprets the removal of jewelry in 33:4b as signifying the acceptance of imageless worship as prescribed in the 'pre-priestly' texts.

[61] Dohmen 2004b, 313. There are a number of interpretations of the nature of the sin, which is described in Exod. 32:1-6. Fretheim 1991a, 281f, argues that the sin is not explicit idolatry but, rather, a replacement of the 'lost' messenger with a new visible messenger. Only in the ascription of the exodus to this new messenger comes the idolatrous notion into the people's actions. The problem is one of confession. "Yahweh is not being set aside. At least this is what Aaron understands by the 'feast to Yahweh' in verse 5. Aaron's proclamation to that effect suggests that the people also view the matter. The people also proceed to engage in acts of worship that, except possibly for the 'play', are appropriate, indeed reserved for Yahweh. Hence, the messenger of God has been elevated to a status alongside Yahweh in the allegiance of the people (and hence the plural reference to 'gods')." (282) Although I do not follow the entire argument, Fretheim, certainly, highlights important aspects. See also p.73 above for a different angle on the issue.

[62] Jackson 2000, 250–255 argues that the sin of the golden calf, though it represents a severe breach of the covenant, never actually abrogated it. Therefore, he rejects the term 'renewal' for what is described in Exod. 34. To a certain extent, his argument is consistent, but his own solution is, from a rhetorical-critical perspective, not very different to a renewal of the covenant in Exod. 19 or 24. Clearly, Exod. 34 does not speak of an entir-

verbalised in detail in Exod. 25–31. An ideal Israel, holy and pure, would find no difficulties in realising Yhwh's presence in its midst. The obvious sinfulness and 'stiff-neckedness' of the people (32:9; 33:3.5; 34:9), however, is in conflict with the divine presence. Thus, the author uses the voice of Moses to express his solution to the apparent problem. The solution lies in the patriarchal promises, which are put in concrete terms using the allusions to the people's growth in (32:13) and the exodus Egypt (32:12).

The rhetorical strategy of having Moses challenge the divine attitude toward his people – on the grounds of the ideas expressed earlier by Yhwh, namely their election as a special nation – enables the author to sustain the picture of a gracious god who is willing to forgive beyond human understanding. At the same time, the author's strategy does not diminish the seriousness of the Israelite's misbehaviour. This tension is expressed explicitly in Exod. 34:6-7 – both sides are part of the divine nature.[63] In keeping this intricate balance, the author builds a bridge for his implied reader to feel part of the ideal people of Exod. 19–31. This bridge is necessary because Israel's reality in the present – the time of the writing of the text – is far from the ideal conception of Exod. 19.[64] The tension between the ideal Israel and the sinful, but forgiven, Israel enables the author to invite his reader to identify with the challenging ideal, while at the same time allowing for the factual reality of this reader.[65]

To conclude the description of this second line of character development, it is important to note that the possible, and likely, deviation from the ideal is included in the portrayal of the character Israel in Exodus. This inclusion, however, is not at the expense of downplaying the importance of the ideals, as they are set out in the legal texts and also in the cultic instructions of Exod. 25–31, which is highlighted by the repetition of central aspects of the covenant in 34:10-35.

A Change of Masters

Fretheim makes a relevant theological point when he states that the election of Israel is never a theme in Exodus, but their vocation is.[66] It is true that Israel's

---

ely 'new' covenant but, again, of a reaffirmation of the Israelites into the old covenant of the fathers, something which Jackson also argued for strongly and rightly.

[63] See my reflections on this passage on p.43ff above.

[64] Given the picture of Israel, as we find it in both the former and latter prophets, this is true for virtually all periods of their existence.

[65] See also Wenham 1997, 28: "[The biblical writer's] ideal was a holiness like God's, yet they did not believe in legal intervention to punish offenders, unless they fell crassly below it. Their idealism was combined with realism in dealing with human weakness."

[66] Cf. Fretheim 1996, 114. He also observes the notion of the change of masters and evaluates the issue theologically (Fretheim 1991a, 20).

election by God is never questioned, nor is it dependent on their keeping of the law. In following the narrative, however, the reader becomes quite aware of the author's concern with the covenant of Abraham, Isaac and Jacob. This, of course, has to do with divine election in a very intimate way. Jackson argues, convincingly, that the narrative of Genesis shows that the Abrahamic covenant is a hereditary covenant. The numerous covenant renewals featured in Genesis and Exod. 19–24 have to be understood in exactly the same way. Jackson is unrelenting in his belief that the term 'renewal' needs to be understood as confirmation: "If there is anything new, it is not the covenant but those committing themselves to it."[67] The parties recognise that they are already bound by the covenant, and, for one reason or another, they reaffirm their commitment to it.

When approaching Exodus with these reflections in mind, it becomes clear that Israel is understood, from the start, as participating in the Abrahamic covenant. Exod. 2:23-25 formulate this explicitly. Jackson comments:

> At this point, an Opponent is presented, who threatens to impede Performance. The attitude of the new pharoah [sic] is presented not simply as an incident in the changing fortunes of the Israelites, but as directly relevant to the Contract God has undertaken.[68]

The arrival of a new king occasions a point at which the promise is reconfirmed to a new generation. Precisely this is narrated using the term for remembering (זכר) in 2:24.[69] Given the situation of Israel in the story, the reader will evaluate the reality of the contract between Yhwh and the people and will probably doubt that the divine promise is still in force. But, as the author allows the reader to perceive the reaffirmation of the contract as a divine initiative, the reader will understand that Israel – despite its present state of being without political sovereignty and territory – is still part of the patriarchal covenant, including its promises. The highest authority available to the author, Yhwh, understands Israel in this way, so the reader will, most likely, follow suit. Throughout the plague story the reader is constantly reminded of Israel's status by the phrase עמי,[70] which is essentially part of the covenant formula: "I am your God and you are my people."[71] The reader will understand from the beginning that Israel is Yhwh's people, and he will, thus, judge the pharaoh's claim on Israel as a political misconception.

Consequently, the change of masters from the Egyptian monarch to Yhwh does not mean for the character Israel a change in status before Yhwh. The ten-

---

[67] Jackson 2000, 233.

[68] Jackson 2000, 244.

[69] For the immediate rhetorical effect of the use of this root see p.62 above.

[70] Cf. Exod. 3:7.10; 5:1; 7:4.16.26; 8:16-19; 9:1.13; 10:3-4. 22:24 is the last occurrence of the phrase in Exodus but it serves an entirely different communicative purpose there.

[71] Exod. 6:7; 19:5-6 and also 29:45-46. See also my summary of Schreiner's very insightful rhetorical-critical comments on p.201f above.

sion, however, between the character's theological status and its social reality is still present, and although the reader is likely to adopt Yhwh's view of Israel, he is drawn into an emotional turmoil through the framework of the plague story. Exod. 5, in describing vividly the darkest hour of Israel's oppression,[72] leaves out any mention of divine intervention. The utter helplessness of Israel must arouse the anger of the reader. The reader is drawn into the tension between faith and doubt, which at certain points in the narrative is expressed through the character Israel.[73]

The faith of Israel is one of the main subjects of the dialogue in Exod. 3–4. Moses questions the people's belief, but Yhwh never doubts their initial acceptance of Moses' message.[74] The tension is between 4:1-9 and 3:18, together with the report of their reaction in 4:31, which goes well beyond the mere mental appreciation of the message, but anticipates the frequently-stated purpose of their exodus from Egypt, the worship of Yhwh (ויקדו וישתחוו). The doubts raised by Moses prove unfounded, and the reader might develop high expectations regarding Israelite responsiveness to divine messages. Knowing the later portrayal of a fearful and doubtful Israel,[75] it might well be that the author attempted to

---

[72] Cf. p.54 above.

[73] Joosten 1996 (esp. in his 4th chapter), also, understands the exodus as a change of master in a slave-master scheme, and he draws important theological conclusions from his study of the Holiness Code, which are, ultimately, linked with the covenant formula. The change to Yhwh as the new master indicates a total alteration of the political constitution of Israel. It is now a people totally dependent on Yhwh, i.e., it receives its land from him, obeys his rules, and expects blessings and curses from his hand alone. This implies that Israel should not be subject to any other power, neither god, nor nation. Those far-reaching transformations are traced back solely to the exodus event by the author of the Holiness Code. According to Joosten, this relationship is expressed in the covenant formula. Of course, there are further conclusions, but these have more to do with the moral and religious conduct of Israel than with its political status. Further theological and social implications, especially for the post-apartheid South Africa, are highlighted by Bosman 2005.

[74] See my notes on this above (p.68).

[75] This movement in the narrative can be traced with the belief-motif in the Pentateuch. Sailhamer 1992, 270 offers some interesting insights into this motif, but I do not follow his theological conclusion on the author's critical evaluation of the law in the Pentateuch. Sailhamer writes in summary: "The narrative strategy of the Pentateuch contrasts Abraham, who kept the law, and Moses, whose faith was weakened under the law. This suggests a conscious effort on the part of the author of the Pentateuch to distinguish between a life of faith before the law (*ante legem*) and a lack of faith under the law (*sub lege*). This is accomplished by showing that the life of God's people before the giving of the law was characterized by faith and trust in God, but after the giving of the law their lives were characterized by faithlessness and failure. Abraham lived by faith (Gen. 15:6), in Egypt the Israelites lived by faith (Exod. 4), they came out of Egypt by faith (Exod. 14:31), and they approached Mount Sinai by faith (Exod. 19:9). However after the giving of the law, no longer was the life of God's people marked by faith. Even their

heap flattery upon the reader: he may feel pride that his ancestors' reaction proved Moses' expectations wrong.[76] Clearly, the unfolding development paints a less positive picture of Israel. Doubts arise in response to the new measures brought upon the Israelites after the first encounter between Moses and the pharaoh. (I already mentioned the rhetorical effect of Exod. 5.) After the narration of the plagues, in which Israel plays no substantial role, the author returns to the response Israel is making in the light of the divine action on its behalf.[77] The response in 12:27b is clearly an immediate reaction to the forecast of the tenth plague, whereas 12:28 may also include the institutionalised response, which future generations are to practice (12:24-26).[78] Here the reader is implicitly included in the story and, depending on his own cultic traditions,[79] the bridge to his (people's) past is firmly established. The narration of the actual exodus, with its intertwined cultic material (12:14-20.25-27b.43-49; 13:1-16),[80] constitutes a similar effect; the compositional strategy embraces both the narrated time and the reader's present. Israel has thus a double function in the author's strategy: it is a character inside the story world, but it is also the addressee of the texts.

The author thus manages the feelings of his reader in order to create a sense of historical reality and immediacy in the reading process. With this strategy the narrative conveys much more than the theological concept of Israel being under the terms of the Abrahamic covenant. Indeed, the emotional involvement of the reader even threatens the perception of this theological point in that he feels that the described reality of Israel does not support a concept of Israel as the chosen people of God. The communicative opportunity is, of course, that no simplistic notion of a mechanistic world-view can arise. There is no easy connection to be made between the people's condition and their theological status. In other words, the hereditary quality of the old covenant is not threatened by the pharaoh and his oppression of Israel. What is threatened, however, by the situation

---

leaders, Moses and Aaron, failed to believe in God after the coming of the law." (270) In the light of my study, this picture of the rhetorical function of the mentioned characters appears too sketchy. A more differentiated picture emerges which does not comment so much on the law, as such, but rather on the nature and tendencies of the participants of the covenant.

[76] This, of course, has a significant effect more upon the emerging picture of Moses than on the picture of Israel.

[77] McBride 1990, 232, n.8 notes, perceptively: "For P, significantly, it is preparation for Passover that marks the beginning of Israel's responsiveness to divine instruction mediated through Moses and Aaron. (12:28)." This is true for the reading of the final work Exodus as well.

[78] Cf. also Exod. 12:50, phrased very similar to v.28, which again seems to be a comment on the reaction of the later generations.

[79] Even if Exodus imagines or promotes an idealised cult, the reader is, nevertheless, addressed directly, as he is, inevitably, part of the narrative's future conception.

[80] Cf. Childs 1976, 195–206, who offers an insightful analysis of the work of the last redactor together with some significant theological reflections.

is, as Jackson makes clear, the performance of the contract. This becomes the driving force of the narrative up to the time when Israel leaves Egypt. After the actual exodus and after the pharaoh's last attempt to jeopardise the performance,[81] Exod. 15 provides the poetic denouement, allowing the reader to participate in the joy of the saved Israelites.[82] The performance of the father's hereditary covenant is not yet completely fulfilled (the land of the promise has not been reached), but it is much more likely that Yhwh will achieve what he has promised. As already mentioned, the author suggests an element of continuity that dominates the particularities of Israel's history. I concluded that this continuity was ensured by Yhwh's self-binding promise to the hereditary covenant, together with his willingness and potency to bring it into fruition for his people. The portrayal of Israel, as we find it in Exod. 2:23–15:21, draws the reader into the story and, thus, enhances his willingness to accept the theology just expressed, a theology which might well ring true to the implied reader's ears as he experiences his own historical situation.

The passages dealing with the desert wanderings, prior to the arrival at Mount Sinai, are of some importance for the portrayal of Israel as it develops a character of its own. I, nevertheless, covered this material in my discussion of the character Yhwh because of the dominant role he plays in these narratives[83] and will restrict myself to a few comments on the specific outcome for the portrayal of Israel. Doubt and disbelief mark the events of this period of Israelite history. Three occasions of conflict are used to narrate the relationship between Yhwh and Israel (Mara, Wilderness of Sin and Rephidim). These conflicts arise because the people cannot imagine God's ability to bring about the fulfilment of the patriarchal promises, in which case their existence is threatened. As argued in my chapter on Yhwh, these occasions provide sufficient opportunities for the reader to conclude that Yhwh, actually, deserves to be Israel's king: he can provide not only military success (14:19-31 and 17:8-16) but also an abundance of life's necessities. Thus, Israel functions, mostly, as a foil against which the character Yhwh is promoted. Nevertheless, as Israel is moved out of its passivity it, actually, initiates progress in the narrative. The murmuring calls into question Moses' intentions in bringing them into the wilderness, away from the wonderful life they enjoyed in Egypt. Obviously, the perspective of Israel is limited by the author, but the reader fully understands the theological impact of this murmuring against Moses. From the start, the reader interprets Israel's complaints

---

[81] Exod. 14:10-14 provides another example of the people's fearfulness and, hence, doubt about the Mosaic motivation to bring them out of Egypt. This brief pericope foreshadows the later murmuring stories and balances their "self-confidence" as they left Egypt (cf. Houtman 1996, 252 referring to 13:18). 13:17-18 provides an explicit rhetorical hint that fear is a character trait of Israel.

[82] The Israelites' breaking into song because of the disappearance of the pharaoh's host is a model for the readers (cf. Sternberg 1987, 112).

[83] See p.69 above.

as criticising God, because the reader was informed beforehand that the exodus from Egypt was not Moses' initiative but Yhwh's (restated for the people in 16:6b).[84] Especially after the song of Exod. 15, this lack of faith comes as a surprise.

Another surprise is the reaction of Yhwh to the grumbling people. Apart from the alleviation of the problem, there is no response to the obvious expressions of distrust and the lack of appreciation. That this could have been different is shown by the parallel pericopes which narrate the second leg of the wilderness wanderings after leaving Mount Sinai (Num. 10 onwards). This divine restraint in Exod. 15:22–17:7 underlines the just mentioned literary function of Israel as a background to the portrayal of Yhwh. The grumbling of the Israelites is not the focus of the author, hence there is hardly any literary evaluation, except for the contrast between the song of Moses and the complaints and the fact that it is Yhwh they are blaming for their circumstances. The reader, of course, evaluates the behaviour of Israel, but the author gives very little guidance in his text; one might consider this a literary gap which delegates responsibility to the reader. Again, just as in the case of Moses (Exod. 3–4), the first actions or initiatives of the character Israel in Exodus provide not much more than cues for the development of Yhwh's portrayal. The outcome is more likely negative for the perception of Israel.

In spite of its status as the divinely-elected people, Israel clearly does not appear as the positive example to follow. They sway back and forth between faith and doubt and, thus, display the typical instability of all human characters in the Old Testament. Here, we, again, find support for the already quoted claim of Meir Sternberg: "With biblical man ... there is usually a distance – and often a clash – between the impression produced on its first appearance and the one left after his last."[85] This effect is due to what he calls "the biblical poetics of ambiguity."[86] From the beginning, Israel is portrayed as the chosen nation and, as such, is part of the patriarchal covenant, but it is also full of doubt which betrays a great lack of knowledge regarding its covenant partner.

I suggested that the first line of the literary development of Israel is established by the change of masters: "Israelites are servants (*'bdym*) exclusively to YHWH, and therefore cannot rightfully be 'servants' of others, whether another god, a domestic or foreign king, or another Israelite."[87] Yhwh, the new אדני, managed to break the claims of the old one, the Egyptian monarch, and to bring the people successfully to his mountain and to re-establish the covenant (Exod.

---

[84] The narrative, clearly and explicitly, underlines this perception of the events; Moses comments that the exodus was not his 'fault' and therefore the people were actually grumbling against Yhwh (16:7-8; 17:2b).

[85] Sternberg 1987, 326.

[86] Cf. Sternberg 1987, 325 and his Ch. 5.

[87] Callender 1998, 79.

19–24). Israel is shown to have accepted this agreement, even before they heard any of the stipulations of the decalogue or the book of the covenant (19:8) – at least from the perspective of the reader.[88] This demonstrates, together with the important verses 19:5-6, that the change of masters is completed at this point of the narrative. Interestingly, the author, from this point on, drops the theme of doubt entirely and gives prominence to an enthusiastic and willing people. Rendtorff comments on Exod. 19–24: "Hier wird eine ideale Beziehung zwischen Israel und Gott dargestellt. Dabei ist ein wesentliches Element, daß Israel seinerseits den Bund 'bewahrt', wie es in 19,5 als Voraussetzung für dieses ideale Gottesverhältnis Israels ausgesprochen wurde."[89] This is a further hint toward the conclusion that this first line of character development comes between the poles of faith and doubt.

'And they did just as Yhwh commanded them'

The character Israel is pictured in relative passivity after its idolatry in 32:1-6, but the portrayal changes considerably when it comes to the narration of the implementation of the tabernacle (Exod. 35–40). Israel is busy contributing and constructing in the attempt to realise the dwelling place fit for its God. I already anticipated that, in this section of Exodus, we find not so much a progressive development, but more a literary consolidation of Israel's status as a holy and priestly nation, or, in other words, an expression of its realisation. The tension between ideal and reality, which sustains the movement in the second line of development, no longer plays a role. Nevertheless, the depiction of Israel in Exod. 35–40 is not entirely detached from the previous portrayal. The reader will remember Israel's covenant and its failure to maintain that covenant, and so the author uses certain elements to build a contrast to the Israelites of Exod. 32 and, also, to establish a line of continuity to the earlier Israel of the covenant (Exod. 24).

Moses gathers the entire assembly of the sons of Israel (ויקהל משה את־כל־עדת בני ישראל Exod. 35:1a) after the renewal of the covenant. Here, the author deliberately reminds the reader of the setting just before the covenant had been vio-

---

[88] Now, the reader has a disadvantage, as he was not informed by the author what the כל־חקיו כל־המחלה were, that is, what the people heard in the wilderness at Marah (15:26). This is a strange tension between the levels of the story and of the reading process. It may be that the reader was able to substitute from previous knowledge of any divine commands or statues; at least, the text suggests this to his implied reader by mentioning the event without giving any detail. This is, especially, so because of the main clause of the conditional statement ("I will put none of the diseases on you that I put on the Egyptians" 15:26bα) which, greatly, arouses the interests of any reader: if this is the outcome, then I am really motivated to abide by the law. But what exactly is the law?

[89] Rendtorff 1999, 55.

lated by the Israelites: ויקהל העם על־אהרן (32:1).[90] This initial similarity prompts the reader to compare the two gatherings. Fretheim highlights a number of contrasting elements between the golden calf incident and the narration of the construction of the tabernacle: human initiative versus divine initiative, Aaron's demand for gold versus the request for a generous contribution, no planning versus painstaking preparations, quick construction versus lengthy building process, immediate accessibility versus safeguarding of the divine holiness, a visible God versus an invisible God, and an impersonal object versus a personal god.[91] The people attempt to replace the mediated presence of God – which they think is missing in Moses' absence – with the construction of the calf, resulting in the need for forgiveness. Exod. 35:1b pictures Moses, again, in his main role as mediator of the divine words. Now the people construct a dwelling place for the actual presence of God in answer to the divine forgiveness. Exod. 40:34-38 fittingly records the success of their efforts: as the golden calf was supposed to go before them (אלהים אשר ילכו לפנינו 32:1), now, Yhwh goes with them (40:36-38).

An important aspect of the very positive portrayal of Israel in Exod. 35–40 has been noted by Klein: "The commands to construct the tabernacle are given in seven speeches of Yahweh to Moses, but it is the people who erect the tabernacle, in perfect obedience to the divine command, and then present it to Moses."[92] He observes the rhetorical effect of the frequently used 'compliance formula' (כאשר צוה יהוה).[93] As has been shown above, the correspondence between the heavenly model, described in Exod. 25–31, and the actual building is not exact. The record of the building process testifies to much creativity, and imagination is part of the often noted connections between Gen. 1:1–2:4 and our text[94] and is, thus, an expression of the joyfulness in the people's response. Exod. 35–40 reports the answer of the people to the gracious divine willingness to dwell among them. The compliance formula neither expresses ritual obedience nor lifeless conformity to the heavenly archetype. Rather, an equivalent to the archetype, in terms of essence or spirit, is expressed here.[95] A precise corre-

---

[90] קהל appears only in these two sentences in Exodus.

[91] Cf. Fretheim 1991a, 267.

[92] Klein 1996, 265.

[93] The German term is 'Entsprechungsformel.' See my discussion of this formula in the excursus above (p.170f).

[94] For a recent and important contribution see Janowski 1990. Another significant work is Krochmalnik 2000.

[95] See Dohmen 2004b, 395 ("Entsprechung im Sinn") and 391 which states: "Die Entsprechungsformel in Ex 35–40 darf man deshalb auch nicht als überflüssiges 'Gleichheitszeichen' verstehen, sondern muss den darin enthaltenen Hinweis auf eine Analogie erkennen, die das nun errichtete Heiligtum als Antwort Israels auf Gottes Zuwendung – auch und gerade nach der Sünde des Volkes mit dem Goldenen Kalb in Ex 32 – deuten will."

lation in this regard is necessary as a contrast to the golden calf incident. The recapitulatory passage 39:32-43 encourages the perception of this contrast with a specific marker:

And as soon as he came near the camp and **saw** the calf and the dancing, Moses' anger burned hot, and he threw the tablets out of his hands and broke them at the foot of the mountain. (32:19)	According to all that Yhwh had commanded Moses, so the people of Israel had done all the work. And Moses **saw** all the work, and behold, they had done it; as Yhwh had commanded, so had they done it. Then Moses blessed them. (39:42-43)

The reactions of Moses to each of the people's constructions could not be more different. In the first, he broke the tablets to signify that Israel had broken the covenant; in the second, he blesses Israel. Hence, the evaluation of the people's actions by a character inside the story turns out to be very positive. The overall literary strategy – including the reiteration of the 'compliance formula' and the contrast with Exod. 32 – suggests that the implied reader should follow this internal evaluation of Israel.

A further effect of the compliance formula was noted above while considering Mosaic obedience: the emergence of certain parallels between Israel and Moses. I wrote that the reader perceives a development in Israel's obedience. At the end of Exodus, Israel, in this respect, seems to be transformed and copies the model attitude of their leader. The character 'Israel' clearly is a character in transition, exemplifying the same transition which the author hoped to achieve with his audience. As has been shown above, this transition was initiated by the divine decision to forgive and the subsequent willingness to dwell among the people. The ideal expressed here is one of thankfulness for God's choosing them as his special people. This thankfulness, also, finds expression in the abundance of freewill contributions (כל־איש אשר־נשאו לבו וכל אשר נדבה רוחו אתו) for the tabernacle construction (35:20–36:7) – so much material was provided that the donations had to be stopped. But, the association between the portrayals of Moses and of Israel in Exod. 35–40 goes much deeper than mere thankfulness: Israel is here pictured as fulfilling their call to be a priestly nation, i.e., mediators – like Moses – of the divine presence among all other nations. Israel begins to come to terms with their ideal status, even as Moses eventually did. The emphasis on the priestly garments in Exod. 39[96] and the divine directions on the assembly of the tabernacle along with the report of their immediate fulfilment in Exod. 40, are further hints that Israel is to be a *priestly* nation (19:6).[97] The concentration on the Aaronic priesthood, which is most likely the actual reality

---

[96] Here and also in Exod. 40 the 'correlation formula' is used excessively, which may be an indicator for the importance of the priestly aspect for the author.

[97] See my discussion below (p.229).

known by the implied reader, serves as a significant point of balance to the contributions given by the entirety of the people. The communicative strategy is to remind the reader, by mentioning the normality as an afterthought, that all of Israel are supposed to be priests and to live this ideal by contributing skills and wealth. Krochmalnik writes:

> Die Schrift zählt in diesen Kapiteln mehr als einmal peinlich genau das ganze Inventar der gespendeten Edelstoffe – Hölzer und Steine – und die daraus verfertigten Geräte auf. Wenn man das Buch Exodus als Heldenepos liest, dann sind solche Kapitel langweilig, wenn wir es aber als Gemeindeutopie verstehen, dann erfüllt die Veröffentlichung der Spendenaufrufe und des Ertrages der Spendenaktion ihren Zweck als Vorbild und Anstoß.[98]

Krochmalnik uses the term *Gemeindeutopie* to refer his readers back to Exod. 19–24. The contribution of materials and skills of the entire assembly of the sons of Israel mirror the people's reply in Exod. 24:3b: ויען כל־העם קול אחד ויאמרו כל־הדברים אשר־דבר יהוה נעשה.[99] The author guides the reader from the initial acceptance of this *utopia* (to use Krochmalnik's terminology) through a devastating failure and, finally, through the response of a whole community to the re-establishment of the covenant, which would ensure the divine presence.

Krochmalnik notes an interesting association between our present texts and the ancient Near Eastern cultural context:

> Waren doch die Tempel Gipfel und Krönung der menschlichen Kunst und Kultur (gerade in unseren Abschnitten wir das Zeltheiligtum als regelrechte göttliche Neuschöpfung durch menschliche Kunst beschrieben) – und zugleich meistens als Sklavenwerk.[100]

The temple, as an expression of the divine presence on earth, served in all cultures of the Levant as a symbol of national identification, to use a term with possible anachronistic undertones.[101] The god(s) linked with the community lived among the people, and, thus, the temple and the running of it provided opportunity to develop a 'national' unity – the greater the political claims of the community, the greater the temple. Krochmalnik, rightly, draws our attention to the involvement of slaves (again, to be understood apart from any anachronistic notions!) in the process of the temple construction. As I described the plot-development of Israel as a change of masters, it becomes an intriguing thought,

---

[98] Krochmalnik 2000, 151.

[99] Cf. Dohmen 2004b, 394.

[100] Krochmalnik 2000, 134.

[101] 'Nation' – in a narrow, modern sense – is, of course, an enlightenment/post-enlightenment development of European statehood (cf. Graf 2003). To use the term for ancient Israel clearly cannot embrace this notion, especially as Israel is pictured without a territory. The etymological roots of 'nation' (lat. *nasci* – being born; *Natio* – the goddess of birth), with their emphasis on genealogical unity, nevertheless provide enough reason to use this term.

how far the building project of Exod. 35–40 can be viewed as parallel to the ancient Near Eastern social function of the temple. Exodus envisages an Israel, bound by contract with Yhwh (as Yhwh's voluntary 'slaves'), building together a national sanctuary, a *Gemeindeutopie* which must have been very appealing to any reader.

The notion of work, just mentioned, gives rise to another observation regarding a common Israelite identity: the influence of the Sabbath, the abstinence from work as a lasting covenant symbol.[102] Exod. 31:12-17 finds its parallel in 35:1-3. As has been shown above, both texts serve as framing devices and point the reader to the habitual aspects of the cult. To remind the reader of the Sabbath just before the report of the work at the tabernacle is a strategic device to bring together the temporal tabernacle and the reader's present (לדרתיכם, 31:13). Dohmen puts it succinctly:

> [Der Sabbat] war zum Abschluss der Instruktionen von Ex 25–31 vorgestellt und eingeschärft worden, weil er als *das* Zeichen schlechthin für die Verbindung zwischen JHWH und Israel gilt, und durch ihn der Bund vom Sinai in alle weiteren Generationen getragen wird. ... Der Schabbat soll und wird das Zeltheiligtum überdauern, weil dieses seinen Sinn darin hat, Gottes Gegenwart auf dem Weg vom Sinai ins Gelobte Land zu ermöglichen.[103]

The Sabbath functions as a symbol of Yhwh's covenant (ברית עולם, 31:16) and, thus, also as a symbol for his continuous presence among Israel. God's consecration of or taking possession of the tabernacle (40:34-35; described as another theophany parallel to the one in 24:15-18) makes it the movable Sinai, a locally unrestricted place of revelation: "Damit ist das Heiligtum sichtlich ein Sinai geworden."[104] The cloud motif, the explicit mention of the journeys (בכל מסעיהם), and the collapsing and reconstruction of the tabernacle (40:36-38) all point to further wanderings, and, thus, they provide a link into the future. The reader lifts his eyes beyond the horizon of Exodus toward the land of the promise. Whether he lives in Canaan or not, the continuity between the text and his own present is established. He is part of this worshipping community, that keeps the Sabbath as prescribed here. This, of course, helps him identify with the Israel of the story and thus increases the possibility of his reading the text as relevant for his own situation. Exod. 35–40 shows the successful portrayal of the ideal community, defined in 19:6 – a picture that strengthens Israelite identity and provides vision for the implied reader.

---

[102] See the recent monograph by Timmer, who studies, carefully and in depth, this so called sabbath frame, always with a firm eye on its biblical theological facets (Timmer 2009).

[103] Dohmen 2004b, 393 (emphasis in the original).

[104] Jacob 1997, 1032.

Conclusion

I spoke of the merging of horizons as part of the author's rhetorical strategy in developing the character Israel in Exodus. The ideal Israel presented – which I will discuss in the following section – is connected to the reader's reality, so that identification is enabled through the construction of the plot. The need for forgiveness is the context in which the ideal finds expression, especially, in the common effort of the construction of Yhwh's dwelling place. In the last part, it becomes clear that the author includes numerous points of contact between the present of his implied reader and the past of Israel, which he presents in his plot. These links are all tied to cultural and religious identification markers: The tabernacle provides an imaginative concept for all later places of worship in Israel;[105] the installation of the Aaronic priesthood must be controlled by genealogical records throughout the generations; and the sign of the covenant, the Sabbath, has a continuous effect upon every day life. The literary use of these concepts in Exodus serves the overall aim of reader identification with the collective Israel that emerged from the clan. The concern with cultural and religious identification markers and literary identification points is fitting for a book that presents a picture of the formative period of this people.

This discussion has shown that Israel has been developed along three threads, each overlapping with the other two. In the end, a picture of Israel as a people emerges a picture that in its complexity and differentiation encourages the rational and emotional identification of the reader with the character. This picture also provides avenues for the establishment of a 'national' identity along the lines of the concept of covenant. I have, already, mentioned the ideal Israel in several places but have yet to give an account what this ideal is, how it is communicated, and how its presentation influences the reading process. This will be the concern of the next section.

---

[105] The record of the building of the tabernacle as counterpart to the instructions for it suggests that these instructions are not intended for all later sanctuaries in Israel. Dohmen 2004b, 242, from a rhetorical-critical view point, makes a relevant observation: "Mit diesem exemplarischen Charakter der Beschreibung von Ex 25–31 – in Verbindung mit Ex 35–40 – öffnet der Text sogleich den Blick darauf, dass hier auf 'Leser' und eben nicht auf 'Konstrukteure' hin formuliert worden ist." This means that, when confronted with these instructions, the reader is faced with a staging of the sacred space which he will inevitably attempt to reconstruct before his mind's eye. Dohmen speaks of the 'work of imagination' (*Vorstellungsarbeit*) which has to be done by the reader. The reader conceptualises the tabernacle and the idea of Israelite worship.

The Ideal Israel

The last section showed that the author developed his character Israel specifically to enable his reader to identify with this literary unit. It, also, became clear that Exodus attempts to shape the reader's understanding of the social entity Israel. Here emerges a picture that deals with ideal concepts of Israel's society and, because of the author's profound theological interests, with the relations between this community and Yhwh, its national god. Above, I expressed the doubt that the mere presentation of an ideal is good rhetorical practice.[106] The previous results, which have shown the author's attempts to enable the reader's identification with the character Israel, provide the context in which the author wants the ideals in Exodus to be understood. The character Israel is, clearly, not an ideal character, but the divine speeches dominating Exod. 19–31 present the reader with some insights as to what the author thought could match the peoples status as divinely elected and covenant bound.

The author's ideal finds expression, mainly, in two aspects of Exodus. Firstly, the author delineates his concept of Israel in epithets that voice specific and often abstract qualities or characteristics of Israel. Secondly, and much more concretely, the legal parts of Exodus contribute to the picture of the ideal Israel. Both aspects of the portrayal of Israel will be discussed below from a specific rhetorical-critical vantage point.

Israel – Between Ideal and Reality

James Watts, again, provides a starting point in noting the three roles that the people of Israel have in the Pentateuch: vassals, citizens and priests – all under one king, Yhwh.[107] Rhetorically, roles can serve as condensation nuclei for identification as they can overcome chronological distance in their concentration on more abstract notions. Roles are less dependent on concrete circumstances and, thus, give the reader the freedom and, also, the responsibility to draw the concrete implications himself.

ISRAEL AS VASSAL

The first role mentioned by Watts – Israel's portrayal as vassal under the king Yhwh, bound by the covenant re-established at Sinai – has already been touched upon, above, in the discussion on the change-of-masters-metaphor (cf. p.215). Although they are oppressed and without political independence or even a territory of their own and despite their tendency to return to Egypt displayed

---

[106] Cf. p.200.

[107] Cf. Watts 1996, 6, n.18. The kingly aspects of the divine portrayal in Exodus have been discussed above (see esp. p.85).

in the wilderness, the Israelites are and remain the recipients of the covenant of the fathers. Rendtorff formulates: "Die 'Erzväter' sind und bleiben die 'Väter' schlechthin, und Israels Identität ist zuallererst dadurch bestimmt, daß dieses Volk die Gemeinschaft der Nachkommen dieser Väter ist."[108] Israelite identity is based on their covenant relationship with Yhwh. This finds expression in the text that reports the reinstitution of the father's covenant in the context of the first personal encounter between Israel and Yhwh, the theophany of Exod. 19. The covenant stipulations play a major role,[109] and the people, explicitly, agree on them to be binding for both parties of the covenant: Yhwh, Israel's king, and Israel, Yhwh's vassal. That Exodus uses the metaphor of covenant and the ensuing roles of overlord and vassal establishes the same relationship for any reader who identifies with Israel. The identification leads the implied reader to conceive of himself as being bound to Yhwh because of the very same covenant. Thus, a certain immediacy is created in the reading process which overcomes the usual distance between literary character and reader. The implied reader clearly becomes part of the story and, through this story, he becomes part of the covenant.[110]

THE ISRAELITE AS CITIZEN

The second role of the character Israel in Exodus, their status as citizens, is a concept based more on the individuals of the community. However, that Israel is presented as vassal, clearly, transcends individuality. The picture of Israel in Exod. 1 describes the dawn of a nation, the first prerequisite of citizenship. In my discussion of the report of the people's construction of the tabernacle (Exod. 35–40), I highlighted the aspects of the text which concentrate on the communal effort or the *Gemeindeutopie*, as Krochmalnik put it. In the laws of Exodus we

---

[108] Rendtorff 2001, 41. Having said this, I do not hold that Israel begins to be the divinely chosen people only with the establishment of the covenant in Exod. 24, as C. Park seems to think: "The importance of the covenant is that God and the people enter a new status of relationship by means of it. Until now, Yahweh was rather the God of their ancestors. God saved the people as he remembered the covenant with Abraham, Isaac and Jacob. Indeed, Yahweh called Israel as 'my people' even before the covenant with them was made. Still, however, this relationship is indirect, mediated by the patriarchs. The covenant changes this indirectness into the directness: ... Through the consent of the people to the covenant stipulations, they fully become the people of God." (Park 2002, 171). The narrative, leading up to Exod. 24, seems to indicate that, for the author, the people are already included in their father's covenant; they have been Yhwh's people all along.

[109] These stipulations will be discussed below (p.234).

[110] One might even consider the appropriateness of the category 'speech act' for this rhetorical strategy. The text of Exodus includes any Israelite reader in the covenant it describes and thus establishes an ideational reality for this reader. This clearly coincides with the theological notion of the Torah as word of God which establishes reality for its readers.

find numerous allusions to the גר,[111] which implies that the author imagined Israel as non-גרים, i.e., forming a political and social entity made of citizens. The national identity of Israel, touched upon in the previous paragraph, has a definite influence on the individual Israelite in that he is part of a community. There is an inside and an outside with regard to Israel[112] and the implied reader, clearly, wants to remain inside. Assmann based his entire argument on the assumption that the driving force of the conception of Exodus is Israelite distinctiveness which pervades all aspects of every day life.[113] Identity can be sustained by separation, and, here, Assmann makes an important point regarding the political identity of the Israelites: their awareness of belonging together is structured along the lines of cultural distinctiveness and theological self-confidence expressed in the notion of divine election. The implied reader of Exodus is, clearly, urged to conform to the pattern or ideal outlined in the law which generally addresses individuals rather than the 'nation'. A citizen of the Israel presented in Exodus will, without a doubt, know when he is part of the in-group, as Assmann rightly stated: "Wer nach diesen Gesetzen lebt, vergißt keinen Augenblick, wer er ist und wohin er gehört."[114] A definition of what it means to be an Israelite is possible, even when there is no political sovereignty and no territory. The integrative force of the laws will be discussed below.

Israel's role, as vassal, centres around the covenant relationship with Yhwh; the portrayal of the people in terms of citizenship emphasises their distinctiveness from other nations. But, election and separation, alone, do not constitute the author's full conception of an ideal Israel. I already mentioned that both Hanson and Assmann reflect two aspects of the textual reality. Assmann's emphasis on distinctiveness needs to be balanced by Hanson's understanding of the inclusiveness. This important aspect finds expression, primarily, in the third role suggested by Watts: Israel as priests.

ISRAEL: A PRIESTLY NATION

Exod. 19:5-6, clearly, concerns Israel's identity. It is a priestly identity which denotes the modus of their being as different from all other peoples. There has been a considerable amount of dispute over the interpretation of this priesthood of Israel.[115] I follow Steins and Dohmen in understanding the term "kingdom of

---

[111] Cf. Exod. 12:19.48-49; 20:10; 22:20; 23:9.12.

[112] This finds direct expression in the metaphor 'cutting off from the people', which is included in the punishments for a number of breaches of the law (Exod. 12:15.19; 30:33.38; 31:14).

[113] See my review on p.198ff above.

[114] Assmann 1992, 206.

[115] For a recent review of important contributions see Steins 2001, 21–30. J.A. Davis devotes an entire monograph on these two verses (Davies, J. A. 2004). Kooij 2006 offers insights into ancient Jewish interpretation (LXX and the Targumim) and presents his own reading concluding that the phrase reflects some sort of priestly conception of the

priests" (ממלכת כהנים, 19:6) essentially as a metaphorfor the people's proximity to the divine, a relationship established at Mount Sinai.[116]

The importance of the passage 19:3b-6 justifies a more detailed presentation of the view adopted here.[117] The following table includes the masoretic text and my translation, and it, already, betrays my reading of the passage.

³ᵇ כה תאמר לבית יעקב	³ᵇ So you shall say to the house of Jacob
ותגיד לבני ישראל:	and declare to the sons of Israel:
⁴ אתם ראיתם	⁴ You yourselves have seen
אשר עשיתי למצרים	what I did to Egypt.
ואשא אתכם על־כנפי נשרים	Then I carried you on vulture's wings
ואבא אתכם אלי:	and brought you to myself.
⁵ ועתה	⁵ But now,
אם־שמוע תשמעו בקלי	if you truly listen to my voice
ושמרתם את־בריתי	and keep my covenant,
והייתם לי סגלה מכל־העמים	then you will be for me a possession among all peoples.
כי־לי כל־הארץ:	Although the whole earth belongs to me
⁶ ואתם תהיו־לי	⁶ you will be for me
ממלכת כהנים וגוי קדוש	a kingdom of priests and a holy nation
אלה הדברים אשר תדבר אל־בני ישראל:	these are the words you shall tell the sons of Israel.

Exod. 19:3a marks the section as a divine speech with the common introductory messenger formula (3b) and the corresponding closing formula (6b). This unit is quite set apart from the following preparations for the theophany, and there are no explicit links made between the two passages. Dohmen makes a relevant point when he emphasises the independence of the passage from the theophany in temporal terms: Exod. 19:3-8 looks back on the past (... אתם ראיתם) and, also, well beyond Sinai into the future (ועתה ... אתם תהיו ...).[118] Thus, this divine speech points the reader beyond the book of Exodus (which ends with the people still at the place of theophany) and at the same time reminds him of the need to keep together the exodus events and this expression of his people's identity. Blum, rightly, speaks of a *geschichtlichen Konkretion*[119] of the lasting identity of Israel. In other words, the author rejects the interpreta-

---

political constitution during latter days of the kingdom period of Israel. Timmer 2009, 89–92 discusses mainly the multiple aspects of קדש in this context.

[116] Cf. Steins 2001, 31 and Dohmen 2004b, 62, who takes up Steins' study to a large extent. This runs parallel to Israel's cultural context: access to the divine in ancient Near Eastern thought is normally attributed to the king or his surrogates, the priests.

[117] There is no need, however, to repeat the discussion of the numerous other possibilities for reading this text.

[118] Cf. Dohmen 2004b, 49.

[119] Cf. Blum 1990, 192.

tion of Israel's Sinai experience that only views the people as fulfilling the ideal then and there.[120] This continuity is not just communicated by the closed framework and, thus, the structural independence of the pericope. The need for the continuous realisation of divine proximity is closely connected in Exod. 19 and 24 with the hearing of God's voice.[121] Dohmen puts it nicely with respect to the prominence of Israel among the nations: "Jedoch gilt die Hervorhebung Israels nicht generell, sondern nur insofern Israel den Gotteswillen realisiert. Dann und nur dann entsteht eine – ansonsten Priestern vorbehaltene – besondere Gottesnähe bzw. einzigartige Gottesbegegnung."[122] The implication is that the author perceives the need for Israel to become what they are then and there at Sinai and throughout their history.

The second expression of Israel's identity in Exod. 19:6, implicitly, relates to the theophany: they shall be a holy nation (גוי קדוש). The preparations for the divine descent are clearly concerned with the holiness of the people. It is obvious that both expressions of Israel's identity found in 19:6 are not only structurally but conceptually parallel: In the ancient understanding of gradual holiness, priests, of course, had to achieve high standards. Divine proximity always requires a 'holy nation'. The offerings of the young men (Exod. 24:5) and the elders' meeting with God (24:9-11) provide two examples that the ideal has already been achieved once. The sprinkling of the entire people with blood (24:8), a ritual usually reserved for the consecration of priests in Israel, underscores this narrative portrayal of an ideal Israel, then and there at Sinai.[123] The reader, however, will soon be informed about the danger of divine proximity, as expressed in the remainder of Exod. 19, in the requirements for the preparation of the theophany. Later, he will encounter the terrible expression of impurity and thus the people's distance from Yhwh because of the creation of the golden calf. The tension between ideal and reality remains, of course – but, as the book ends with the specific mention of Yhwh indwelling the mobile sanctuary, the continuity is provided and 24:3-11 is not a singular exception. The ideal of 19:6, viewed in the context of the book, is an ideal which can, actually, be realised and, thus, can only exert influence on the implied reader.

---

[120] Houtman 1996, 426, seems to go in this direction, though he is never explicit in this point. (See also his translation of v.6 – "You, however, are destined to be consecrated to me..." – which appears to narrow down this verse to the preparation of the theophany.)

[121] Cf. Steins 2001, 36: "Von Israel eigentlich gefordert ist das 'Hören', das zu neuem Tun führt: Das Hören wird sowohl in Ex 19,5 durch die doppelte Nennung des Wortes, wie auch in Ex 24,7 durch die unerwartete Endstellung des Ausdrucks akzentuiert: 'Wir werden tun – und wir werden hören.'" See also Jacob 1997, 749 with reference to an intriguing Midrash on the passage.

[122] Dohmen 2004b, 63.

[123] See also Davies, J. A. 2004, 119ff who views Exod. 24:1-11 as priestly ordination rite.

Up until now, I have discussed the contribution of the metaphor ממלכת כהנים to the status of the people only. Steins, expressly, limits the semantic value of this metaphor to just this: the statement of Israel's privileged proximity to Yhwh.[124] The functional component of the expression – i.e. the answer to the question 'What has Israel been called out for?' – would only be a later development, found in Isa. 60–62. The genuine priestly task of the mediation of the Torah comes into view for the entirety of Israel only in the post-exilic Trito-Isaiah, so says Steins.[125] In the context of Exodus, however, I propose that the implied reader should, also, be pointed to the functional aspects of Israel's priestly identity. I have shown in a number of places that the author of Exodus presupposed a good deal of previous knowledge on the part of his implied reader. Part of this previous knowledge seems to be based upon the previous reading of Genesis, especially when it comes to the concept of the covenant. The allusions to this covenant in Exodus are abundant. Exod. 19:5, explicitly, mentions the context of the nations (כל־הארץ and כל־העמים). This broadening of the horizon well beyond "Gott und Israel ganz unter sich,"[126] is, clearly, intended to remind the implied reader of the functional aspect of the patriarchal covenant mentioned in Gen. 12:3.[127] The patriarchal covenant which God is about to reestablish with Israel was never just for the benefit of Abraham's family, and so it is only natural to transfer this thought to the integration of Israel in Exod. 19–24. Given this contextual background and also the common understanding of the roles and functions of priests in the reader's cultural context, it is difficult to limit the metaphor to, merely, the close connection with the divine sphere that the priesthood enjoyed.

Thus, I conclude that the priestly defined holiness promised to the people also includes their investiture with this job. "God's universal rule is the setting in which the holiness of the nation is meant to function. The people of God must take on the role of priests to the entire world."[128] The innovation in this concept of the people's responsibility can be described as the democratisation and extension of the duties which are usually limited to a professional priesthood. Obviously, I do not assert that all Israelites were priests in the technical

---

[124] Cf. Steins 2001, 33f. "Eine priesterliche Mittlerfunktion ist hier nicht im Blick." (34, n.68).

[125] Cf. Steins 2001, 36.

[126] Steins 2001, 34. This is what Steins thinks is in view only in Exod. 19.

[127] Gen. 12:3 moves structurally from the direct, individual blessing for Abraham to the blessing mediated through Abraham for the whole world (cf. Hamilton 1997, 667 who even translates: "*so that* all peoples on the earth will be blessed through you"). כל משפחת האדמה clearly points the reader to the table of nations (Gen. 10). IfGenesis 12–50 can be read as showing the gradual fulfilment of the divine promises to the patriarchs, then the blessing of the nations will be part of this (see Gen. 30:27; 39:5), and any reader will be reminded throughout what the blessing actually was at the beginning.

[128] Dozeman 2005, 127.

sense of cult officials – this should have been sufficiently communicated by the designation of the phrase as a metaphor – but they all should attempt to mediate God's benevolent presence to the nations around them and thus bring blessing into their world. According to Exodus, this blessing is mediated through the Torah, together with the practice of the Torah as an example for the nations. By listening to the Torah and living it, Israel becomes what it is.

In my remarks on the exemplary attitude provided by the character Jithro, I concluded that, in him, one of the communicative functions of the narration of the exodus from Egypt was realised: he recognised Yhwh for who he is (Exod. 18:11).[129] This picture is closely linked to the priestly role. Israel was supposed to know Yhwh, i.e., to have close contact with him in order to determine his will and, also, to know his history ('Torah' includes both parts!) and to communicate this knowledge to the 'laity'.[130] As has been shown, the 'knowing-Yhwh motif' dominated the first part of Exodus, with the concluding example of Jithro in Exod. 18. In the latter part of Exodus, this theme returns to the narrative level, its foundation having already been laid prior to Exod. 19. Implicitly, it surfaces in the notion of Israel's priesthood and, explicitly, in the seminal passage Exod. 29:45-46: "I will dwell among the people of Israel and will be their God. And they shall know that I am Yhwh their God, who brought them out of the land of Egypt that I might dwell among them. I am Yhwh their God." The close proximity of priests with God and their knowledge of Yhwh are bound together.[131] This fits nicely with the rhetorical function of large parts of Exodus which were developed above: a new picture (or a new *knowledge*) of Yhwh will be communicated persuasively, which can serve as a basis for any future living in Israel.

For the rhetorical strategy of Exodus, it follows that the image of Israel as a priestly nation provides a literary thread which strings together the various parts of the book and, thus, guides the reader to deduce its overall message. With the image's close link to the ideal conception of Israel, it also contrasts the implied reader's reality. In this regard, however, it is important that the text is not read as an affront against the reader: even though the image of Israel's priesthood expresses a conditional ideal, dependent on the people's Torah-abiding practice, this portrayal also honours the people, as well as the implied reader, who is a part of this people. Specifically the emphasis on the distinguished position of Is-

---

[129] Cf. p.58f above. See, also, my comments on the direct address of the reader in Exod. 10:1-2 (p.53).

[130] An interesting observation supporting my argument is that Jithro is designated as *priest* whenever he enters the plot (Exod. 2:18; 3:1; 18:1).

[131] On the whole see Rendtorff 2001, 55ff.

rael is bound to be an effective rhetorical strategy in any shame-oriented culture that values acceptance, honour and prestige.[132]

Up until now, I have highlighted numerous points in Exodus that encourage the reader's identification with the literary Israel. This identification enables the author to maximise the reader's willingness to accept his concept of an ideal Israel. This ideal shall be further discussed in the following section.

Israel in the Laws

The discussion of the legal portrayal of the character Yhwh, above, has already provided considerable detail to the ideal Israel as it is expressed in Exodus. The shaping of the law in Exodus as divine speech and the numerous elements of single laws point the reader in the direction of an ethics based on the concept of *imitatio dei*.[133] The specifics of this rhetorical design do not need to be repeated here, and, thus, I will concentrate, straight away, on the contribution of the legal passages to the image of Israel in Exodus.

The legal collections in Exodus clearly contribute to the author's conception of an ideal Israel: they describe Israel as Yhwh's people. Nevertheless, the mere existence of laws anticipates their violation. That the people needed these instructions implies that the author imagined them capable of doing the opposite. This rather indirect but, also, obvious characterisation of the people's inclinations is in tune with the rebellious attitude the author describes in the story of their wilderness wanderings.[134] "The Pentateuch's characterization of Israel serves to enhance and to justify its persuasive rhetoric. ... By depicting such an audience [sc. a rebellious Israel], the Pentateuch defends its rhetorical strategies

---

[132] Cf. Wiher 2003, 222 and p.111ff above where I already discussed certain aspects of shame-oriented cultures like Israel. Davies, similarly, observes that the theophany at Sinai "enhances the prestige of the people who witness the event (as it did for any king who received such a revelation)" (Davies, J. A. 2002, 158). Janowski's conclusions on the emerging picture, especially when reading the priestly accounts of creation and the construction of the tabernacle, suggest a similar effect upon the reader. Janowski speaks of the "Neuschöpfung Israels" which started off with the exodus and finds its fulfilment in the tabernacle (Janowski 1993, 240). The ideal world finds expression in the Israelite cult, in particular the tabernacle. This is a very enthusiastic conception of the worldwide role of Israel, appealing to any Israelite convinced of his people's uniqueness: "Das Heiligtum ist nicht nur für die Entstehung der Welt, sondern auch für deren Geschichte/Fortgang konstitutiv: als Ort der Begegnung zwischen Gott und Mensch bzw. zwischen JHWH und Israel." (Janowski 1993, 246)

[133] This is something very much stressed by Hanson 1986. He also attributes great importance to the strong linkage in the Pentateuch between socially concerned laws and the cult.

[134] Cf. Watts 1999, 108f and Patrick 1994.

as necessary for the people's survival."[135] Obviously, the author felt the need to introduce his concept of Israel and its history and to set it all in the framework of the divine covenant relationship. He, apparently, anticipated resistance from his implied reader, and, therefore, he attempted to communicate the ideal in a framework which allowed the reader to decide for himself whether or not the text personally addresses him.[136] Despite this openness, the text is clearly constructed to win the reader, and in this regard it should be considered as a persuasive text, even in its legal parts. Before I discuss this I will look, firstly, into the connections between the priestly status of the people and the laws they receive. This will be followed by a discussion of the intersection of history and law and finally by a focus on the unity of the people which was mentioned previously.

A PRIESTLY KINGDOM READING LAW

The effect of the mixture of cultic and profane regulations on the reader's perception of Yhwh, the law speaker, has been discussed above (p.116f). The same phenomenon also has its effects on the portrayal of Israel: "YHWH's claim on Israel's exclusive worship (Exod. 20:3; 22:19; 23:13; 34:14) may depend in part on the depiction of the entire people as a priesthood consecrated to God's service (Exod. 19:6; cf. 22:31; Lev. 19:2; 20:26)."[137]

The special requirements for a people with exceptionally close relations to the divine realm indeed find expression in the legal collections of the book. Not only the notion of exclusive worship of Yhwh is part of this but also the altar law (Exod. 20:24-26), the regulations on firstfruits (22:27-30), the cultic calendar (23:14-19) and the epilogue of the book of the covenant with its specific links to Yhwh's presence (23:20-33). The location of these passages at structurally emphasised points is an important guide in the reading process: the introduction consists of the altar law; then, 22:19 marks the high point by setting the theme for the second part of the *mišpaṭīm,* with its concentration on community values; and the greater part of the cultic regulations dominate the end of the book of the covenant. All of the 'profane' legislation is embraced by a cultic framework, so that the reader cannot but perceive the entirety of the book of the covenant as religiously relevant and impinging on the status of the people as a priestly and, thus, holy nation. The law collection only presents the reader with a select choice of representative regulations, leaving large parts of everyday life untouched. The implication is that the reader is left to decide for himself how he is supposed to live his life as part of the covenant people, without endangering the divine presence and, hence, the divine blessing for himself and his fellow Israelites.

The renewal of the covenant in Exod. 34:11-26, after almost forfeiting the divine presence among the people, includes many parallels to the epilogue of the

---

[135] Watts 1999, 109.

[136] See my discussion of the direct address below (p.242).

[137] Watts 1996, 7; cf. also 6, n.22.

book of the covenant. Both texts deal with the future of the literary character Israel and, thus, with the present of the implied reader. The odd ending of both with the memorable phrase "You shall not boil a young goat in its mother's milk" (23:19b; 34:26b), is an unmistakable rhetorical device for creating a mental link between the two collections: all of the book of the covenant is meant in Exod. 34. God requires exactly the same of his people before and after the covenant renewal. The manner in which Israel is to live in the presence of Yhwh does not change in any way; the ideal Israel pictured for the exodus generation is the same ideal Israel pictured for the implied reader.

This remarkable continuity can be established from another example of a, more or less, legal genre in Exodus, the regulations concerning the sabbath. The references to the sabbath in Exodus are clustered in four passages: Exod. 16; 20:8-11; 31:12-17; 35:1-3. I will start with the couplet around the golden calf narrative because of its structurally accentuated position. The sabbath must be considered as *the* perpetual sign of the covenant:

> Er [sc. the sabbath] war zum Abschluss der Instruktionen von Ex 25–31 vorgestellt und eingeschärft worden, weil er als das Zeichen schlechthin für die Verbindung zwischen JHWH und Israel gilt, und durch ihn der Bund vom Sinai in alle weiteren Generationen getragen wird. ... Der Schabbat soll und wird das Zeltheiligtum überdauern, weil dieses seinen Sinn darin hat, Gottes Gegenwart auf dem Weg vom Sinai ins Gelobte Land zu ermöglichen. Demgegenüber soll der Bund Gottes, den der Schabbat repräsentiert ('ein Zeichen für immer'), unabhängig vom Aufenthaltsort Israels zu jeder Zeit bewahrt werden.[138]

Rhetorically, it is very telling that the hints at the perpetuity of Israel's worship connected with the sabbath are grouped around the pericope narrating the near loss of divine presence among Israel. Hence, the continuity is not only provided beyond the existence of the tent sanctuary, as Dohmen rightly stressed, but, also, beyond the people's failure to adhere to the covenant. The rhetorical emphasis is clearly on the implied reader's identification with the exodus generation, which is based on the perpetuity of the eternal covenant. Thus, the regulations on the sabbath – which affect everyday life, as Exod. 16 makes abundantly clear – serve as a constant reminder of the bondage of Israel to Yhwh. Exod. 31:13-14 and, also, implicitly 20:8-11 draw the connection between the Sabbath and Yhwh's intent to sanctify Israel.[139] The idea of holiness takes the reader again to Exod. 19:5-6 and thus to the ideal Israel.

---

[138] Dohmen 2004b, 393f.

[139] See, again, the study by Timmer, who takes the sabbath in Exodus as signifying sanctification. This aspect is balanced by his interpretation of the tabernacle as signifying divine presence and forgiveness. Taken together, one can readily see the interpretative value here for the difficult literary relationship between the two parts of the tabernacle account and the golden calf episode (cf. Timmer 2009, 137ff).

THE INFLUENCE OF PAST EXPERIENCE

In Exodus, the reader finds numerous connotations to the semantic field of servitude.[140] Above, I suggested that the portrayal of Israel develops from slavery in Egypt to its service to Yhwh, both finding expression in building projects (Exod. 1:11b and 35:1–39:43). When it comes to the legal corpus in Exodus, the past slavery in Egypt is called upon in two motive-clauses, creating a framework for the laws related to the community values of Exod. 22:20–23:9(12):

> You shall not wrong a sojourner or oppress him, for you were sojourners in the land of Egypt. (Exod. 22:20)

> You shall not oppress a sojourner. You know the heart of a sojourner, for you were sojourners in the land of Egypt. (Exod. 23:9)

Their past experience should inform their present behaviour. I already touched upon this issue, above, and concluded that the strategy behind this composition of the laws is one that utilises the appeal to emotions, which in this case is compassion.[141] A further hint in the same direction may be found in Exod. 20:2, at the pronounced place at the beginning of the decalogue ("I am Yhwh your God, who brought you out of the land of Egypt, out of the house of slavery [מבית עבדים]"). This specific apposition to Egypt is designed to prompt the reader to recall the difficulties in Egypt, especially as the Hebrew phrase, noted above, is linked with the consecration of the firstborn (Exod. 13:3.14 – also מבית עבדים). One can assume that the liturgy in Exod. 12+13 was known to the reader and that it was there to remind him to continue the practice. The beginning of the section, with its mention of מארץ מצרים מבית עבדים, serves as an additional mnemonic shortcut to all the events narrated in Exod. 1–15 and, thus, also to the described historical reality of the implied reader's ancestors.[142] The author created inner-textual connections in order to utilise his previous narrative for further persuasive purposes. The mental connection is made between the Egyptian cruelty, described most vividly in Exod. 1–2 and 5, and the potential maltreatment of foreigners by Israelites, envisioned in 22:20.

I propose that the very same rhetorical strategy informs the *dispositio* of the book of the covenant, with the leading position of the slave-laws (Exod. 21:2-6.7-11) in the *mišpatīm*.[143] After the first part of the cultic framework of the

---

[140] For an overview of various aspects of slavery in Israel and the ancient Near East cf. Chirichigno 1993 and also Callender 1998, who emphasises the broad range of social realities connected with the root עבד.

[141] See above p.104f and 111f.

[142] Cf. Callender 1998, 77, who thinks that the "exodus narrative formed the basis of Israel's socio-cultural identity, which it forged from the memory of harsh servitude, 'slavery' in Egypt."

[143] Slavery was a regular theme of any ancient Near Eastern law collection, and thus it is not surprising that the book of the covenant covers this subject as well. But the follow-

book of the covenant, the author includes the heading 21:1 – ואלה המשפטים אשר
תשים לפניהם: – in order to introduce the subsequent collection of regulations as
belonging to the message Moses had to convey to the Israelites.[144] The placement of the slave laws at the very beginning of the book of the covenant has
been considered as relevant in a number of studies. The interpretation commonly given alludes to the Israelite's slave-existence in Egypt.[145] As a more recent contribution Dohmen voices the issue here:

> Die um das Thema der Sklavenbefreiung kreisenden Gesetze zu Beginn des Bun-
> desbuchs werden folglich nur vom Exodusgeschehen, der Befreiung Israels aus
> der ägyptischen Knechtschaft, verständlich. Die Freiheit, die Gott Israel geschenkt
> hat, bleibt dem Einzelnen letztlich auch dann erhalten, wenn er sich durch
> Verschuldung in eine Form der Unfreiheit selbst verkaufen muss.[146]

The emphasis on the Israelite individual[147] is supported by the formcritically
unexpected second person singular תקנה in 21:2. After v.1, this can only refer to
an Israelite of the exodus generation.[148] Given the term 'Hebrew slave' (עבד
עברי), the addressee of the law clearly belongs to the Israel of the exodus. The
liberation, by God, provides the basis of their existence: "Die Freiheit, die Gott
Israel geschenkt hat, bleibt dem Einzelnen letztlich auch dann erhalten, wenn er
sich durch Verschuldung in eine Form der Unfreiheit selbst verkaufen muss."[149]
From the sub-cases that unfold under the present law, Dohmen argues, convincingly, that the right to self-determination has to be taken most seriously (21:5).
The same applies to the female 'slave' who has the right to demand to be
treated like a regular wife (21:10). Sprinkle is correct, when he writes concerning the slave laws: "This kind of regulation, far from being 'casuistic law', is a

---

ing considerations set 21:2–11 apart from their cultural background.

[144] There is considerable dispute as to which block of text the heading should serve. Behind this debate often lies the desire to separate certain parts of the book of the covenant
and to date them. Crüsemann 1992, 200 might serve as an example: "Vor allem durch
das an die Spitze tretende Altargesetz (Ex 20,24–26) wird das Ganze betont als
Gottesrede eingeleitet, was sich in 22,20ff fortsetzt und durchhält. Lediglich die
Mischpatim fallen aus dieser Redehaltung heraus, abgesehen von der Ergänzung
21,13f." Whatever one might think about the secondary nature of the *mišpatim*, in the
present composition, the entire corpus of law belongs together and is deliberately
presented as Yhwh-speech addressed to Moses who then promulgates this text to the
people. Thus, I follow Dohmen 2004b, 159 and include everything up to the end of B
(23:33) under this heading.

[145] Cf. e.g. Chirichigno 1993, 187–196; Sprinkle 1994, 62ff; Jacob 1997, 624; Jackson
2000, 153.

[146] Dohmen 2004b, 161.

[147] I follow Houtman 1997, 78f, who takes עברי as *nomen gentilicium* and as an allitera-
tion to עבד (denoting the social status).

[148] Cf. also Exod. 20:22 where the addressees – the Israelites – are explicitly mentioned.

[149] Dohmen 2004b, 161.

humanitarian prescription that depends not on the courts, but on persuasion for its performance."[150] The persuasive element is again the appeal to the experiences in the past, hence the appeal to compassion, together with an emphasis of the freedom gained from Egyptian oppression. That any slave is much more than a chattel shines through in other regulations (Exod. 21:20f.26f), which oppose the excessive punishment or other maltreatment of slaves.[151]

Neither the decalogue, nor the book of the covenant presents the reader with some sort of universal law (like Kant's categorical imperative) or an early expression of human rights. The reasoning is quite different. It functions as the provision of a set of representative requirements for the people of God who experienced a very specific past. This past should inform their present, even if this past is a mediated and remembered one (as opposed to an experienced one). The continuity between past and present is established by the covenant and passed on through the rituals as previously described.

ESTABLISHMENT OF A UNIFIED PEOPLE

Weisman rightly observes: "The view impressed upon the reader everywhere throughout the Pentateuch is that it was the entire people who took laws and judgements upon themselves even prior to their settlement in the land of their forefathers."[152] And, reflecting on Deuteronomy, he writes: "Responsibility for maintaining and upholding them was placed upon the people, as a collective whole, a single people. The national destiny of Israel, for good or ill, for blessing or curse, depended on their observance of them."[153] Patrick observes the very same idea of collective responsibility in Deuteronomic law.[154] His term for this Deuteronomic innovation, as he calls it, is 'collectivisation.' The rhetorical situation of this collectivisation is, according to Patrick, the Josianic reform. The goal of Deuteronomy would hence be to convert mildly polytheistic, influential men to its Yhwh-alone theology.[155] Following von Rad, Patrick contrasts the rhetorical strategy of Deuteronomy with the other law collections in the Pentateuch. In the book of the covenant, on the one hand, he finds the form of distributive address dominating the collection, i.e., the laws address the individual and not the community.[156] The decalogue, on the other hand, being influenced

---

[150] Sprinkle 1994, 66.

[151] It has often been, rightly, noted that the book of the covenant does not demand the abolition of slavery as such – it was a social given – but it was concerned with the mitigation of possible negative effects.

[152] Weisman 1995, 407. Even though Weisman does not think that this reflects historical reality, he, rightly, makes the point; this is, indeed, what the Pentateuch suggests.

[153] Weisman 1995, 408. The following argument is based partly on Weisman's observations, especially those regarding the people as a collective.

[154] Cf. Patrick 1995.

[155] Cf. Patrick 1995, 435f.

[156] The exceptions are Exod. 21:13-14.23-25, where Patrick detects a foreshadowing as-

by Deuteronomic circles, provides examples of collective address (e.g. Exod. 20:1.4-6).

Although the present study differs from Patrick's – especially regarding the literary stratification of the Pentateuch – his argument is, nevertheless, relevant for my present question. Patrick attributes the need for collective responsibility to the (Deuteronomic) notion of Israel's otherness: Deuteronomy "seeks to instil pride in their unique position in the world. ... No other nation had been so favored by the one universal God (10:14-15); thus it would be foolish, even suicidal, to renounce one's obligations to the relationship."[157] This reminds me very much of Exod. 19:3b-6. Reading Exodus on the level of the *Endtext*, a reader cannot miss the point that the wholeness of the community is endangered when the covenant is violated. Each individual has to live out the covenant in his private life, and, consequently, he has responsibility for the community.

The same idea is communicated by the distinct notion that in Exodus all law is divine law. In the narrative, the reader finds the people passive and accepting of whatever God communicates to them as law. The law is divinely given; it is from heaven. Though Moses adjudicates the people before the actual giving of the law in Exod. 20–23 (cf. Exod. 15 and 18), Exodus, in its silence about the specific content at these places, stresses that the law is God-given and not of human origin. That the law appears only after the arrival at Sinai is probably not the author's concept of the historical reality of the origin of Israelite law, but it, distinctly, communicates the theological link between the law and the covenant: the law is part of the covenant and an therefore an expression of it. The special status of the people (cf. 19:5-6) defines Israel as a nation set apart; the legal collection puts this status in concrete terms: "[The] Pentateuchal law defines the nation of Israel, rather than the nation defining the scope and jurisdiction of its laws."[158] What follows is Israel's collective responsibility to uphold the covenant. To establish this connection to a necessary part of any culture – the legal regulation of everyday issues – proves to be a very important rhetorical strategy in Exodus. Exod. 19:8, as well as 24:3+7, picture the entirety of Israel responding together to the offer of the covenant. The reader, as part of the people, is included in the covenant and is, thus, also held responsible for keeping law and order throughout the community of Israel. Parallel to what Patrick found to be true in the rhetoric of Deuteronomy,[159] Exodus does not look to a king or to other individuals for the realisation of the covenant throughout Israel, but it attempts to persuade every reader to do his share, to be part of a unified people, and, thus, to move Israel forward to what it is, God's special possession among the nations.

---

pect of the Deuteronomic mode, and 22:20-26; 23:9 with their communal motivations (Patrick 1995, 432).

[157] Patrick 1995, 436.

[158] Watts 1999, 108.

[159] Cf. Patrick 1995, 436.

The rhetoric of Exodus, which is moving toward a unified people also finds expression in the details of the law, especially in its concern with the treatment of the weak and underprivileged. I have already discussed some aspects of this concern in the book of the covenant (p.101ff). As argued there, the $y^e šallem$-laws (Exod. 21:37–22:16) have a high regard for private property. In contrast to other ancient Near Eastern regulations concerning the payment of reparations, which is the emphasis of Exodus, the private person is not distinguished from institutions like the temple or palace; nor are there any distinctions in social status relevant for the adjudication of property offences. It follows that Exodus imagines an egalitarian society with regard to property. The treatment of recompensation is a point in which the people are unified across social and economic borders.

When discussing the idea of benevolence in the book of the covenant and its implications for the portrayal of Yhwh (p.103f), I showed that the misuse of the laws by the powerful, at the expense of the underprivileged, undercuts the intentions of the laws. Limbeck termed this notion 'binding benevolence',[160] for E. Otto it is an 'ethic of solidarity'.[161] Both of these terms express the ideal of a unified Israel, who, only in its togetherness and mutual solidarity, reflects its special status as God's people. I, also, showed that the legal texts work on the level of rhetoric, rather than on an executive level; the author relies, solely, on the power of his text to promote his ideal.[162] Hence, the communication takes place in the pre-moral sphere of emotion. The pressure is on the conscience and the threat is shame. And, as shame is a more group-oriented sanction – what do the others think of me? – it is quite appropriately used here in the promotion of a unified Israel.[163]

---

[160] Cf. Limbeck 1997, 26ff.

[161] Cf. Otto 1991, 167.

[162] This has been noticed and heavily criticised by Sneed 1999, who suspects the ruling classes in Israel merely paid lip-service to a fashionable idea of concern for the oppressed. Sneed, however, seems to define rhetoric very narrowly and *per se* as something morally reproachable.

[163] See my comments on shame as sanction above (p.111f). Assmann 2000, 140f rightly points out that shame only works properly when the violation of ideals is visible. Unrecognised violation, a problem of every society, is usually solved by establishing guilt-oriented sanctions. With guilt, however, it does not matter whether it is seen or not; guilt accumulates and needs to be redeemed. This solution only works when the members of society internalise the law, when it is written on their hearts. Conscience, of course, relates to shame. One can see that the concepts of guilt and shame cannot be easily divided in any real society. Exodus, however, utilises the necessity and constructs a paradigm in which both concepts are combined.

These laws are part of the second major section of B, the section, mainly, concerned with foundational values beginning with Exod. 22:17.[164] Dohmen summarises his interpretation of 22:17-19 as follows:

> So wie das Leben als höchstes Gut in Ex 21,12–17 behandelt wird und grundlegend für den ganzen darauf folgenden Teil des Bundesbuches ist, so sind die Handlungen und Haltungen, die Einheit und Zusammenhalt der Volksgemeinschaft garantieren, die entscheidenden gesellschaftlichen Grundwerte, die in Ex 22,17–19 als solche erfasst werden und die die Grundlage für die weitere Entfaltung der sittlichen Werte im nachfolgenden Teil des Bundesbuches bilden.[165]

And, indeed, Exod. 22:20 and 23:9 provide a rationale for the concern for the unity of Israel's society.[166] This motive-clause should form an attitude within the reader (as opposed to a motivation of certain single acts). It is based on the golden rule, and recollects the shared experience of being foreigners in Egypt (see p.237f above). Hirsch speaks of a principle of equality before the law and a considerateness for the needy as the underlying values behind the laws of 22:20–23:9.[167] The individual, as part of the covenant people, is linked by these values with the other members of the Israelite society which leads to the fundamental principle of solidarity.[168] Acting against this solidarity means to threaten the unity of the community, to threaten the ideal communicated throughout the law collection including the decalogue with its emphasis on securing the newly gained freedom and equality.

DIRECT ADDRESS OF THE IMPLIED READER

How does the reader engage with the legal passages just mentioned? Does he feel personally addressed by the regulations set in Yhwh's direct speech? The divine speeches, obviously, address the wilderness generation which stands there at Sinai. The reader, because of the narrator's mediation, stands beside these people and takes on the role of an onlooker. This could happen with any reader, ancient or modern, but was it the intention for the implied reader? Watts makes a relevant point, when he writes:

> The Pentateuch ... divides the audience in two. God and Moses (or, at least, God through Moses) address the people in the wilderness and also the readers who overhear their speeches. ... By providing knowledge unavailable to the Israelites in the story, the narrative alienates readers from wilderness Israel at the same time

---

[164] Authors recommending a two panel structure for the book of the covenant include Jacob 1997, 710; Schwienhorst-Schönberger 1990; and Dohmen 2004b, 169ff.

[165] Dohmen 2004b, 172.

[166] On the structure of this last part of the book of the covenant see p.121.

[167] Hirsch 1986, 305.

[168] Cf. Dohmen 2004b, 175f. The emphasis on equality, especially with regard to periods of rest (cf. 20:10; 23:10-12), supports the notion of a solidarity in Israel which disregards social status.

that the laws identify them with the audience in the story. The resulting tension strengthens the persuasive power of the Pentateuch's rhetoric.[169]

Watts finds the reason for the division of the audience, mainly, in the existence of different speakers – the omniscient narrator and the characters inside the story, including Yhwh – and in the different genres in the narrative. The last distinction, in my opinion, is the most important for our present discussion. A legal genre implies that the readers are part of the intended audience. But, one might object, the legal provisions of Exodus are part of the narrative, and thus the legal genre is dominated by the narrative genre, which, again, creates a distance for the reader, as just mentioned. The question is whether there are any signals in the text which allow us to determine how far the author wanted the story to dominate the law. I believe Watts is right to assume a consistency in the Pentateuch's strategy of using "multiple voices for purposes of persuasion".[170] That means we can expect the author to support his claims by the use of divine direct speech, the highest possible authority inside the story. It will probably, also, be the highest authority for the implied reader. This consideration helps to bridge the genre divide between narrative and law. Besides the desired identification of the implied reader with the literary Israel, that Yhwh speaks the law indicates that the author wanted to address directly the implied reader with the law collection.

The reader is faced with the decision whether he wants to accept the requirements of the legal collections of Exodus or whether he chooses to disobey and, thus, to place himself outside the covenant. Identification with the Israel of the story is necessarily followed by the identification with their covenant status which, hence, requires obedience to the law: "Readers are urged to feel as if they themselves agreed to the covenant at Mt. Sinai and heard Moses' sermon on the plains of Moab."[171] But the high standards of the law also alienate the reader from Israel, especially as portrayed in Exod. 15–16 and 32–34 as a rebellious and idolatrous people. The mere fact that Exodus has been written, including the legal collections, shows the author's hope that his implied reader will do better, that he will be the 'true Israel'.

The part of Exodus that may be termed 'legal' to a certain degree and that appears to be written most clearly as direct address of the reader are the regulations concerning the festivals. It appears that on the narrative level the Passover instructions in Exod. 12–13 are, largely, irrelevant for the wilderness generation. But these passages are highly relevant for the readers, as they describe what Israel is are doing – or at least what they should be doing. In a brief, innovative article, Steins develops a possible interpretive angle from which to un-

---

[169] Watts 1999, 101.

[170] Watts 1999, 104, n.8. He adopts a distinction introduced by M. Bakhtin.

[171] Watts 1999, 110f.

derstand Exod. 14 and other narratives relating miraculous events.[172] He argues that Exod. 12:1–15:21 represents a literary unit in which 13:17–14:31 is the actual narrative of the events at the *yam suf* framed by the instructorial section 12:1–13:16 (with only minimal narrative development) and the two songs in 15:1–21. The feature most interesting of these units are the anachronisms in the framing parts. After the announcement of the last plague (Exod. 11), the section 12:1–13:16 comes as a break in the chain of suspense. In its elaboration on the Passover rituals this text discusses and interprets the yet-to-be-narrated events around the actual flight from Egypt. In its detail, these instructions go well beyond the narrated time, forward into the times of the actual readers, established in the land and commemorating a past event. As already argued above with regard to Exod. 15, reader-identification is a specific function of inset hymns.[173] Steins summarises these two framing sections as establishing, firstly, a time of remembering and, in the case of Exod. 15 with its emphasis on the temple, a place for remembering.[174] Hence, he finds a "sacramental" strategy employed specifically to suggest the relevance of this past historical event of salvation for all subsequent generations: whoever celebrates the Passover and comes to the temple to worship the saving king Yhwh, himself passes through the *yam suf* into freedom and life.[175] This, clearly, is a liturgically-based form of directly addressing the readers.

Conclusion

In the end, the legal material refines the, already, observed image of Israel in Exodus. There is nothing substantially new added to the narrative climax of Exod. 19:5-6. The ideal is expressed more precisely, and certain aspects of the royal priesthood and the holy nation are highlighted. I have shown that during the reading of the law, the implied reader is drawn much deeper into accepting his identification with the character Israel, as Nasuti writes, perceptively, on a larger scale:

> Part of the function of the legal material in the Bible is precisely to keep the reader from 'getting on with the story.' It forces the reader to stop and consider who he or she is and what he or she does. It specifies who such a reader must be if he or she wants to read the text correctly."[176]

---

[172] Steins 2007

[173] Cf. p.77ff.

[174] Cf. Steins 2007, 234.

[175] Steins 2007, 235. Steins goes on to highlight some points of fresh hermeneutical observations, aiming to overcome traditional shortcomings on both sides of modern fundamentalist readings, as well as liberal interpretations.

[176] Nasuti 1986, 23.

After reading the law the implied reader will know ways in which he can and should fulfil the divine calling to be a holy people, especially when it comes to the sabbath, to festivals or to worship. He will, however, find the divine requirements in the profane sphere inextricably interwoven with the issue of holiness.[177] By including representative aspects of everyday life he expresses what Jenson calls 'graded holiness',[178] the holiness that goes beyond the actual sacred space out into the world and thus acts out the priestly role given to all Israelites.

The past experiences of Israel's sojourn in Egypt are to influence the implied reader's conscience. Here, the author utilises intratextual connections in that he, firstly, provides a certain picture of this past and, then, builds upon it to create a rhetorically powerful urge that lets the knowledge of the past inform the actions in the present. The key issues here are the social implications of being a foreigner and the poverty which leads to debt-slavery.

The implied reader is, constantly, urged by the laws to understand himself as being part of a larger entity – the people of God. The fellow Israelite is to be treated as a brother, bound by the same covenant which had been reaffirmed between Yhwh and his fathers. This should create, in the reader, an attitude of solidarity and consideration for the needy.

In a last step, I reflected the ways in which the reader – any reader, not just the one implied – is encouraged to read the text for more than mere information of some distant past. I concluded that the law is a good option for the creation of immediacy in the reading process. The reader will read the text correctly when he, actually, identifies with the literary Israel and, thus, accepts the challenge of the ideal set before his eyes. The issue of reader identification draws together the threads of the present chapter in an attempt to express concisely the rhetorical strategy the author of Exodus followed in the portrayal of his character Israel.

'Israel' and Reader Identification – a Conclusion

Exodus is all about retelling the beginning, providing a definition, promoting an ideal. The tension between this ideal and the reality of the relationship between Israel and its God, Yhwh, dominates the story line after the escape from the power of the pharaoh and the arrival of Israel in the land of their promise. The ideal relationship, as the author of Exodus perceives it, finds its direct expres-

---

[177] See also Kiuchi's conclusions on the practicability of biblical law (Kiuchi 2007). He concludes that biblical law, ultimately, reaches the level of an ideal which points towards the human incapacity of being holy in and of oneself. This may well be true for the summary statements of law in the Torah (as Lev. 19:18, which Kiuchi discusses; or the decalogue). In many other parts of the legal collection, however, I find a much more practical attitude which attempts to translate the undeniable ideal into everyday life.

[178] Cf. Jenson 1992.

sion in the ideas of Yhwh – cast in the direct speech which dominates the laws – which are in constant contrast with the depiction of the people's reality. Though there is no such thing as a perfect Israel in Exodus, the book presents a vision of a perfect Israel.

In the following, I wish to provide a brief recapitulation of the results so far, in order to highlight the effect the portrayal of Israel has on the reader.

The introduction of Israel into the plot of Exodus is, primarily, marked by passivity. Israel does little which could provide clues for the reader as to what the author thinks about Israel. Just like baby Moses, things happen to Israel and it cannot do much about them. That Israel has not been developed very much in the first thirteen chapters of Exodus delays, considerably, the reader's identification with this character. The only mode of identification possible, apart from the obvious genealogical identification with one's ancestors, seems to be the arousal of emotions such as pity and compassion. Even pride could be mentioned, because of their prolific strength, but this is obviously regarded as the result of divine blessing and is, thus, more a comment on Yhwh than on Israel. The rhetorical effect of downplaying Israel as an active and thriving character is the emphasis on the other characters, specifically, Yhwh. In his description of the beginnings of Israel's existence, the author starts with a literary and ideational focus on Yhwh. This sets the paradigm for the rest of his narrative or, in other words, provides the stained-glass window through which he wants his implied reader to perceive the history of Israel.

In a second step, I traced the development of Israel along three lines. The most important outcome was the specification of the rhetorical strategy used to enable reader identification with Israel. For reader identification to happen two horizons need to merge: the described character and the reality of the reader. The narrative needs to bring together the past and the present. The development of the plot provides numerous points of contact between these two horizons. The genealogical link between the exodus generation and the implied reader enables the author to assume that reading this text is important. But, more needs to be established in order to increase the willingness of the reader to accept the author's reconstruction of the past. Certain cultural, religious and literary identification markers are provided throughout the text that stress the continuity between the Israel described and the implied reader. The development of the literary Israel along three threads provides a picture of Israel, that in its complexity and differentiation, encourages the rational and emotional identification of the reader with the character. With this picture, the author endows the reader with possibilities for establishing a 'national' identity along the lines of the covenant concept. This is just what Assmann expects to happen when a foundational text becomes part of the cultural memory or, at least, expresses a version of this cultural memory.

The third move mainly reflected on the legal parts of Exodus and the ideal concept of Israel communicated in these sections. While the definition of ideals and the persuasive communication of them dominates this genre, criticism comes between the lines. The implication of any law is that it is necessary to formulate it, which is not, exactly, a compliment for the addressee. However, that the laws are included in a larger narrative framework, which does its best to encourage reader identification, reshapes the impact of this legislation on one who reads it as he should, as part of the larger text. In the chapter on Yhwh, I concluded that the law is presented in a way which, greatly, enhances the image or *ethos* of the lawgiver. The main function of the law, in its present context, is not necessarily the regulation of issues of justice, but rather the condensation of the characterisations of both the law giver and the law recipient. For Israel this means a society which reflects its status before God, their special position among all peoples as a royal priesthood and a holy nation. Core values are solidarity and compassion. The urge for the implied reader is to embed himself within this people, with all the necessary consequences.

It has been established that Israel is, indeed, the most paradigmatic character in Exodus. Reader identification with this character is not only a by-product of considering the book, but one of its specific communicative interests. The portrayal is one of a people who are struggling with the implications of the divine presence among them and who are granted forgiveness in the case of failure. This, positively, regards the possibilities of a nation under the rule of Yhwh. The text can be read critically, as an evaluation of a present development in Israel's society, but at the same time it may serve as an expression of hope in that it presents a vision without losing sight of reality. Exod. 40 concludes with a sense of achievement. Nevertheless, reading the book in its entirety, a utopian reading is inappropriate.

CHAPTER 5

SUMMARY AND CONCLUSIONS

At the outset of my study stood the question whether or not Exodus can sensibly be read as a book, i.e., as a single piece of communication. Understood as part of a communication process, the book was expected to show traces of how the author went about convincing his audience of his interpretation of the events surrounding the exodus from Egypt and the time at Sinai. The initial proposal was that a study of the literary characters provides insights into the rhetorical strategy of Exodus. The book's focus on the foundational period of Israel and, especially, on the relationship between Israel and their God suggested that this approach be made via the characters.

I have shown that the themes connected with each of the main characters and the rhetorical strategies of their respective literary portraits, indeed, open up the possibility of reading the book of Exodus as a consistent literary unit. The method employed, rhetorical criticism, enabled us to see aspects of the text inside the framework of a thoughtful and intentional composition. In this conclusion, I will summarise my view of the rhetorical strategy of Exodus. Furthermore, I will attempt to highlight future work which needs to be done in this area of research, but that went beyond the scope of the present enquiry.

Reading Exodus – How Does the Book Work?

The study of character helped to overcome a deficiency of many theologically concerned readings of Exodus, which often focus only on parts of the book. Studies, looking into the actual departure narrative, tend to arrive at claims on Yhwh's involvement in history. Studies of the so-called priestly material in Exodus often highlight creational aspects. Studies concerned with the covenantal parts of the book show great concern for the relationship between God and Israel, often leading to an impersonal, even contractual understanding of this relationship.[1] These theological dimensions are, without doubt, present in the book. However, my enquiry has shown that the whole is greater than the sum of its parts. The author structured and composed his material in a way which addresses each of these notions in one literary work. Rhetorical criticism, with its alertness to both form and content, helps to keep all of these aspects together –

---

[1] Cf. Fretheim 1996, 229.

at least, from the 'last redactor's' point of view. What we observed is the 'art of editing', as Amit calls it.[2] The concentration on literary characters has proven to be a fruitful approach for describing Exodus as an artifact which, apparently, resulted from a conscious and creative process of text production.

In the terminology of ancient rhetorical theory, the author of Exodus first collects available material at the stage of the *inventio* which is guided by his imagination of the communicative interests or by the ends he has in mind. As we have seen, the rationale for these decisions is often connected with the development of a character or with the effect this portrayal should have upon the implied reader. The generic and stylistic inhomogeneity of Exodus commonly leads to various source-critical and redaction-critical approaches. The same is true for the numerous instances of repetition inside the book. From a rhetorical-critical perspective, however, the inclusion of both of these literary features is subordinated to the intentionality of the rhetorical effect. This conviction is reflected in the methodological primacy of the reader. The interweaving of worship, law and narrative materials attempts to keep "God's activity front and center. ... [Law] parallels liturgy in that it becomes another way in which Israel responds to what God has done on its behalf."[3] At these two interfaces, theology and cult, history becomes timeless, in that it relates directly to the present reality of the reader.

The second step of classical rhetorical theory is the *dispositio*. The author arranges his material in a specific way, again, guided by the intentionality of the rhetorical effect. In Exodus, the *ordo naturalis*, i.e., the chronological order, has been chosen. Sometimes, however, we see glimpses into the future which clearly are a deviation from the *ordo naturalis* (e.g. the references to the sons and their sons, the festival regulations, the perpetuity of the tabernacle worship, and the glimpses of the land of promise). I have argued that this strategy is intended to bridge the gap between the narrative present and the reader's present. Again, we encounter how the author creates an immediacy for the implied reader.

It can be concluded that the text of Exodus, obviously, has an effect-oriented focus. Exodus does not merely satisfy potential historical interests of its readers; there is more to it than this archival function. I proposed that this piece of literature was composed specifically to convince the implied reader to adopt a certain theology, entailing implications for the ideational perception and practical fashioning of the reader's present.[4] By concentration on the characters, it was

---

[2] Cf. Amit 2003.

[3] Fretheim 1996, 231.

[4] Recently, Berge 2008 has tried to describe Exod. 1-15 as including parts of a genre called "sapiential didactic tales". This article is interesting in that it allows for inner-textual comments on how the redactors hoped their work to be understood. However, it also shows the difficulties of applied form criticism in describing the actual thrust of a given textual unit. Berge is rather generic and not very specific when actually interpret-

possible to put this abstract and general communicational purpose into more concrete terms. In the following, I will summarise my findings and evaluate their contributions to understanding the rhetorical strategy of Exodus.

Yhwh is pictured as *the* hero and king of Israel; this is the bottom line with regard to the divine character in Exodus. In my discussion of Moses I concluded that an overly positive perception of Israel's hero is deconstructed and that a decidedly mediatorial role is delegated to him. Against this background, Yhwh is established as the one on whom the entire exodus and the future security of Israel depends. To enhance this picture, the author paints Yhwh's role in 'kingly' colours. The song in Exod. 15 directly expresses the kingship of Yhwh; the other parts of Exodus do so indirectly, but unmistakably, for a reader sharing an ancient Near Eastern cultural background. To provide security in foreign affairs, to care for his subjects' life necessities, and to establish law and order among his subjects are the marks against which a king in the ancient Near East was evaluated. Exodus pictures Yhwh as fulfilling all of these requirements. Theology is, thus, constructed from primarily political notions. The influence of this kingly portrayal of the Israelite God can be traced throughout the literary and social history of Israel. To have a divine king superseding every human rule opens ways for public control and the evaluation of these political structures. There is always a higher standard against which human rule has to justify itself and against which it can be measured. The former and latter prophets in the Hebrew Bible do exactly this. The development of messianic expectations is another result of kingship based in the *imitatio dei*.

This higher standard is not Moses – a point made very clearly in Exodus. Moses, even though he is a paradigmatic character who fulfils many of Israel's social functions *in nuce*, is not presented as the one on whom Israel should build its identity. It is, also, not possible for Israel to base its identity in its own strength or piety. The people's identity is rooted, according to Exodus, in their inclusion in the patriarchal covenant (especially 19:4-6) and in God's willingness to forgive their covenant breaches (34:6-7).

That these options regarding Israel's identity are excluded so specifically in Exodus points us to the exigency which might have invited the creation of the book. The rhetorical situation determines the rhetorical choices made by the author. Amit concluded from her studies that

> [it] seems reasonable to assume that the biblical story was simultaneously addressed to all levels of the people, from the simplest person, who was presumably an auditor-listener, to the educated reader. One may go even further, and argue that it was not a story intended only for a small community of intellectuals, lovers and consumers of literature. Its writing within a historiographical setting was done

---

ing Exod. 1-15. The term "didactic" certainly is appropriate – even for the whole book – but it seems to be too broad to be of any concrete help in our present study. Which literature cannot be used in a didactic setting?

in order to transmit the ancestral tradition, and was intended to serve and to educate all levels of people.[5]

In the present study, I have highlighted numerous communicational and compositional devices working at these various reading levels. It has been shown that Exodus is coherent in its communication across these levels. Hence, reading Exodus at the level of the 'simplest person' should already enable us to envisage the message of the book. We find a retelling of the foundational period of Israel's social existence. The author, apparently, felt the need to promote Yhwh, from the start, as the one on whom Israel's existence depends. Furthermore, Israel's early history has, according to Exodus, existential implications for the continuing life of this people. The people are called to live in the presence of God, which requires a high standard of holiness from them. Moses is introduced as the faithful mediator who serves as a paradigm for the people's calling to be a royal priesthood. The ideal is, also, expressed directly in the legal parts of Exodus, which regulate exemplary issues to distinguish between insiders and outsiders. I have shown that large parts of this ideal are characterised by their reliance on the rhetorical force of the *imitatio dei*. Yhwh, as portrayed in Exodus, has concrete claims on every Israelite's life, his private or institutionalised worship, and his social connections. The standard, however, remains idealistic as the reality often looks different. That this is the situation of the implied reader is obvious from the emphasis of the golden calf narrative on divine forgiveness. This reader is encouraged to connect the described past with his own present, which probably highlights further breaches of the covenant. With its reference to the divine willingness to forgive Exodus provokes hope and, thus, encourages trust in this God, despite likely Israelite shortcomings. Exodus, however, is not just a simple message of consolation but also a powerful exhortation to adopt and live the ideals presented. This message is perceptible to any audience or reader, whatever their literary competence. A number of literary features are, however, designed to address more sophisticated readers. These features – such as irony, structure, metaphors, intertextuality, word plays etc. – emphasise the message just outlined and contribute depth and joy to the reading process. Furthermore, these features help the rhetorical critic to pin down the message with greater precision.

I mentioned the effect-oriented focus of my reading of Exodus. In this realm, classical rhetorical theory distinguishes the purposes of *persuadere*,[6] *docere*, *delectare* and *movere*,[7] all of which are found in Exodus. Thus, we find a considerable breadth of rhetorical features. Exodus aims to convince the reader at

---

[5] Amit 2003, 13.

[6] See, also, the distinctions given by Eco 1972, 179ff. He observes a threefold message: aesthetic, referential and persuasive. The latter is the unmarked, normal case. Here, Eco finds tensions between new information and redundancy, and between cognitive and emotional persuasion.

[7] Cf. e.g. Plett 1991, 4–6.

the intellectual level by providing historical facts, proposing a certain interpretation, thereof, and offering ethical rules which appeal to the intellect (*docere*). Furthermore – and here lies the main focus of this study – Exodus appeals to the emotional capacities of its readers through *ethos* (this purpose may also be called *conciliare*). The characters of the book invite identification or turning away, both of which are often guided more by sympathy – or the lack, thereof – than by logical reasoning. At the sophisticated reading level, Exodus also wants to 'please' (*delectare*). Contrary to classical rhetorical theory, I think that Exodus' *delectare* is not without any specific purpose (self-sufficient), but is there to reinforce the message – again, at an emotional level. The rhetorical use of intensive emotions (*movere* which is often linked to *pathos*), however, is not so dominant in Exodus. The closest we come to this effect-orientation is the golden calf episode, with its descriptions of the calf's creation and God's first reaction, and, of course, the song at the *yam-suf*, which urges the reader to join in the praise. Thus, *movere* is used sparingly at structurally exposed points in the narrative. The rhetorical strategy, clearly, involves the reader at multiple communicational levels. Any more *pathos* would probably be considered a violation of the chief rhetorical principle of *aptum* (appropriateness).[8] Only a detailed comparison with other ancient Hebrew literature would yield some certainty in this respect. That my conjecture is not too far off the mark is supported by the use of *pathos* in Judges and the prophets. In these works, the reader is often asked to side with Yhwh against other gods. In comparison, these prophets are much more concerned with the present than with the past.[9] Judges, like Exodus, uses the past to inform decisions in the reader's present, but it does so indirectly. In Judges the communication, however, is more intensified in its focus on the choice between Yhwh and Baal. In the end, we may say that Exodus avoids rhetorical extremes and, thus, aims to convince, using a middle level of style which appeals to cognitive and emotional factors. Viewed from a rhetorical-critical perspective, this is how Exodus 'works'; these are "the means by which [Exodus] establishes and manages its relationship to its audience in order to achieve a particular effect."[10]

This conclusion can only be drawn because of the presupposition that the book maintains a continuity between the textual and extra-textual worlds. This continuity removes Exodus from the realm of literary fiction.[11] Under the assumption that the implied reader is an Israelite, reader identification with the story becomes much more likely. These people in Egypt and in the desert are

---

[8] The use of *inaptum* can of course also functionally support the communication, but it is appropriate to do so because of the overall communicative interest.

[9] For studies pointing in this direction cf. Bluedorn 2001 on Judges and Möller 2003 on Amos.

[10] I return to the definition of rhetorical criticism adopted above (Patrick and Scult 1990, 12).

[11] Cf. Sternberg 1987, 159.

the reader's ancestors. This God of the exodus and of the covenant is the same God he is worshipping. This Moses is the Moses whose name he heard while listening to the oral traditions of his fathers. Basically, Exodus does what most persuasive communication does: it restructures the already known. Reading Exodus with a focus on the characters, on *ethos*, has been a fruitful way to understand how the book works. If Exodus were mere fictional writing, the present thesis would have to be written anew. The rhetorics outlined above are based on this 'spatiotemporal continuity' (Sternberg) and on the use of the entire book as it has been transmitted throughout the centuries.

Reading Exodus – Broadening the Horizon

My reading of Exodus is just one possible reading. I maintain that it is a consistent reading, based on the hermeneutics outlined at the outset. Nevertheless, it is just one reading because of its concentration on the literary characters, which, on the other hand, seems to be a perspective the text, itself, suggests. Different horizons, however, can be imagined. To try another avenue could help to verify or falsify my conclusions. In the following, I will highlight a number of further test-cases and, also, some issues arising from the present enquiry which could not be covered here but which logically follow from this enquiry and promise to be fruitful for the understanding of Exodus.

One central question in the canon of rhetorical criticism has been left untouched in this thesis: Did the book's rhetorical strategy actually work? Did the author achieve, with his readers, the purpose which motivated him to write Exodus in the first place? The evaluation of the effectiveness of persuasive communication suggests itself, and it is the concluding step in Kennedy's five steps of rhetorical analysis.[12] We do not have any extant witnesses telling us how Exodus was received by its first readers, or if the rhetorical strategy was effective. It cannot be verified whether or not the rhetorical utterance successfully modified the exigency that occasioned it. Thus, one has to resort ultimately to an area of research commonly called *Wirkungsgeschichte*. The reception of Exodus through time, as studied at the various interfaces of the text with other cultural products, should make clear whether or not the communicative purpose, as defined in this study, has been achieved. This, of course, is a massive venture which needs to be split up into smaller parts. I suggest starting with the question of whether or not the above argued bipartite vision of Moses, actually, achieved its purpose in deconstructing an overly positive image of the man. So far as I

---

[12] Kennedy's fifth step is, basically, a review of the four preceding steps and aims for the big picture without losing sight of the rhetorical detail previously examined. Kennedy writes: "Criticism too can be a creative act [as rhetorical and literary composition are], not only bringing the target text into clearer focus, but looking beyond it to an awareness of the human condition, of the economy and beauty of discourse, and to the religious or philosophical truth." (Kennedy 1984, 38)

can tell Exodus, did not achieve this goal in much of Jewish interpretive history. For the most part, Moses remains the superman of Israel's earliest times, in second temple Judaism, as well as in medieval Jewish thought.[13] This, however, does not mean that Exodus did not have the potential to convince its readers. My results regarding the communicative intentions of the author are not, necessarily, falsified by the actual reactions of the readers. The picture can probably be balanced by the later Jewish festivals which, in practice, affirm the interpretation of history according to Exodus. These festivals emphasise many aspects of the role of Yhwh, including the giving of the Torah as divine gift, which enables Jewish identity (e.g. *Simchat Torah* 'Rejoicing in the Torah', marking the completion of the annual cycle of weekly Torah readings).

Beyond these considerations, one must not forget that there, often, is a discrepancy between official, institutionalised religion, which usually calls for theological texts, and private, personal belief. But Exodus addresses more than theoretical, theological concepts or cultic reflections. Exodus, in its attempt to influence, specifically, the actions of its readers, consciously tries to shape the (intuitive) concepts underlying what is, actually, said and done. Thus, Exodus introduces a 'counter-intuitive' perspective on Israel's social world and on theological issues. This means that the rhetorical strategy of the book connects intuition and actual reality at various levels. Especially, the study of the metaphors for social entities – divine or otherwise – could yield a reading of Exodus which is aware of the described discrepancy between religious intuition and institution which finds expression in contradictory, but juxtaposed, 'discourses': God in heaven *versus* God on the mountain, in a fire, in the sanctuary; talking to God face to face *versus* "you cannot see my face, for man shall not see me and live"; immanence *versus* transcendence; God's willingness to forgive *versus* his readiness to punish. Many other ideas could be mentioned. *Wirkungsgeschichte* can offer an approach to Exodus which includes this rhetorical notion in its enquiry.[14]

Having discussed the actual reader of Exodus, historical questions come to mind. The prevalent one, from a rhetorical-critical point of view – because it addresses the possible relationships between author and reader – is: Against which historical background should Exodus be read? Given the present state of discussion of the religious, political and social history of Israel and the notoriously difficult issue of dating Exodus, it would be pretentious to try to pinpoint

---

[13] Cf. the collection of essays in Cazelles 1963, for an older overview. For a more recent study on the tradition of Moses as prophet see Galley 1996. See, also, the commentaries by Houtman and Jacob on Exodus and the stimulating analysis on the *wirkungsgeschichtliche* contribution in Assmann 1997. Fraade 2004, provides some insights regarding the post-biblical Judaic interpretation of Moses' role in mediating the law. Interestingly, the relationship between Moses and God and their respective authorities and abilities seems to have been a source for an ongoing debate among the rabbis.

[14] Cf. Pöttner 2004.

the one and only situation. An additional complexity is added in that Exodus seems to address a range of possible audiences, which, again, points in the direction of a quite differentiated Israelite society, socially and otherwise. One might, however, fruitfully inquire into various historical scenarios and ask how Exodus might have influenced these situations and how the respective readers might have responded to its communication. Nevertheless, one must always be cautious not to oversimplify with respect to the presuppositions of the readers. This danger is the reason for my hesitation to include such a valuable discussion in the present thesis.

More at a literary level lies the question of Exodus' contribution to the theme of the Pentateuch. Although I argued for treating the book separated from its literary context, the integration of Exodus in the Torah is a given which must not be neglected. The portrayals of the characters, discussed above, continue to be refined beyond Exodus, although I claim that nothing new is added, with the probable exception of Moses in some areas. This, already, suggests the contribution of Exodus to the Pentateuch. In Exodus, the main protagonists are introduced in the roles which they continue to assume throughout Israelite history. Yhwh is introduced as the God who has ultimate and justified claims on Israel, as his people. Israel is presented as a nation with a responsibility to the God who chooses to live in their midst and as having a specific function toward the other nations. Moses emerges as the paradigmatic mediator and, thus, serves as an example for many social functions. Hence, a detailed inquiry of the contribution of Exodus to the overall theme of the Pentateuch could start with the identity of Israel and its basic relation to Yhwh. This theme finds expression in the literary and imaginative tour of the tabernacle in Exod. 25–31. Exod. 35–40 prompts us to consider Exodus as an introduction to the institutionalised worship which dominates the central parts of the Torah in Leviticus and Numbers 1–10.[15] The sanctuary conception of Exodus, which is interwoven with its narrative context, thus, provides the foundational framework for the Israelite cult.[16] Based on the divine-human relationships described in this study and the imaginative sanctuary, further investigations could be made into the various theological shapes these conceptions take inner-biblically.

A further, and last, literary aspect should now be mentioned; it arises from this thesis and forms a nice *inclusio* with my introduction. Considering the work that has been done lately on the Old Testament legal collections and their implications on biblical ethics, I propose that there is still the need for approaching these issues with a strong emphasis on the literary and communicational function of these texts. The integration of law into foundational, historical narrative, as we have it in the Torah, is something which cannot be undone without doing harm to the whole. Biblical ethics are always informed by relational considera-

---

[15] Cf. Douglas 2002. She understands the tabernacle of Exodus as a spatiotemporal, imaginative blueprint for the structure of Leviticus.

[16] Cf. Dohmen 2004b, 399.

tions. I have highlighted aspects of this in my discussion of Yhwh's legal portrayal and of the ideal Israel. Many theological distortions and much ethical bias
could be avoided if the Pentateuch were read with attention to and appreciation
for its integration of different genres.[17] In this sense, I hope that the present
book may be considered a small step on the way toward a new understanding of
the Torah – to pick up an urgent and understandable desire of Georg Fischer.[18]

---

[17] A promising avenue has been pursued by Gammie 1990. He considers the compatibility in principle of literary genres commandment and paraenesis. Both are collections of
maxims.

[18] Cf. Fischer 2005.

BIBLIOGRAPHY

Albright, W. F.
    1924   'The Name Yahweh', *JBL* 43: 370–78.
Alter, R.
    1981   *The Art of Biblical Narrative* (New York: Harper Collins).
Amit, Y.
    2003   'Progression as Rhetorical Device in Biblical Literature',
                    JSOT 28(1): 3–32.
Assmann, J.
    1992   *Das kulturelle Gedächtnis: Schrift, Erinnerung und politische*
                    Identität in frühen Hochkulturen (München: Beck).
    1997   *Moses the Egyptian: The Memory of Egypt in Western*
                    Monotheism (Cambridge, Mass.: Harvard University Press).
    2000   *Herrschaft und Heil: Politische Theologie in Ägypten, Israel*
                    und Europa (Darmstadt: WBG).
Auffarth, C.
    2000   'Theokratie', in C. Auffarth, J. Bernard and H. Mohr (eds.),
                    Metzler Lexikon Religion: Gegenwart – Alltag – Medien,
                    Vol. 3 (Stuttgart, Weimar: J.B. Metzler): 485–86.
Auld, A.G.
    2002   'Samuel, Numbers, and the Yahwist-Question', in J.C. Gertz,
                    K. Schmid and M. Witte (eds.), *Abschied vom Jahwisten: Die*
                    Komposition des Hexateuch in der jüngsten Diskussion
                    (BZAW 315; Berlin: de Gruyter): 233–46.
Baker, D.L.
    2005   'The Finger of God and the Forming of a Nation. The Origin
                    and Purpose of the Decalogue', *Tyndale Bulletin* 56: 1–24.
Bartholomew, C.G., Evans, S.C., Healy, M.E., and Rae, M.A., eds.
    2003   *"Behind" the Text: History and Biblical Interpretation* (The
                    Scripture and Hermeneutics Series; Carlisle: Paternoster).

Barton, J.
1996   *Reading the Old Testament: Method in Biblical Study* ([1]1984;
            London: Darton, Longman and Todd).

Baum, A.D.
2003   'Zu Funktion und Authenzitätsanspruch der oratio recta:
            Hebräische und griechische Geschichtsschreibung im
            Vergleich', *ZAW* 115: 586–607.

Beach-Verhey, K.
2005   'Exodus 3:1–12', *Interpretation* 59: 180–82.

Bechtel, L.M.
1991   'Shame as a Sanction of Social Control in Biblical Israel
            Judicial, Political and Social Shaming', *JSOT* 49: 47–76.

Becker, J.
1999   'Zur "Ich bin"-Formel im Alten Testament', *BN* 98: 45–54.

Ber, V.
2008   'Moses and Jethro. Harmony and Conflict in the
            Interpretation of Exodus 18', *Communio Viatorum* 50: 147–
            70.

Berge, K.
2008   'Didacticism in Exodus? Elements of Didactic Genre in
            Exodus 1–15', *Scandinavian Journal of the Old
            Testament* 22: 3–28.

Berger, K.
1991   *Exegese des Neuen Testaments: Neue Wege vom Text zur
            Auslegung* (3. erneut durchges. und erg. Aufl.; Uni-
            Taschenbücher 658; Heidelberg: Quelle & Meyer).

Beulke, G.
2004   'O Quarto Mandamento e seu desafio para filhos e filhas',
            Estudos bíblicos 82: 15–27.

Beyerlin, W., ed.
1985   *Religionsgeschichtliches Textbuch zum Alten Testament* (2nd
            edition; ATD, E 1; Göttingen: Vandenhoeck & Ruprecht).

The Bible and Culture Collective
1995   'Rhetorical Criticism', in E.A. Castelli, S.D. Moore, G.A.
            Phillips and R.M. Schwartz (eds.), *The Postmodern Bible* (G.
            Aichele, F.W. Burnett, R.M. Fowler, D. Jobling, T. Pippin
            and W. Wuellner; New Haven: Yale University Press): 149–
            86.

Black, M.
1979   'More About Metaphor', in A. Ortony (ed.), *Metaphor and
            Thought* (Cambridge: Cambridge University Press).

Bloch, R.
1963   'Die Gestalt des Mose in der rabbinischen Tradition', in H.
            Cazelles (ed.), *Moses in Schrift und Überlieferung* (orig.

Moïse, l'Homme de Alliance, 1955; F. Stier and E. Beck, trans.; Düsseldorf: Patmos): 95–171.

Block, D.I.

1988 *The Gods of the Nations: Studies in Ancient Near Eastern National Theology* (Evangelical Theological Society Monograph Series 2; Jackson: Evangelical Theological Society).

1997 'Nations/Nationality', in *New International Dictionary of Old Testament Theology & Exegesis* (CD-ROM ed. Zondervan Pradis 5.13.0025. 2002. Print ed.: *New International Dictionary of Old Testament Theology & Exegesis*. Willem A. VanGemeren ed., 5, vols.; Carlisle: Paternoster, 1997).

Bluedorn, W.

2001 *Yahweh Versus Baalism: A Theological Reading of the Gideon-Abimelech Narrative* (JSOT.S 329; Sheffield: Sheffield Academic Press).

Blum, E.

1990 *Studien zur Komposition des Pentateuch* (BZAW 189; Berlin: Walter de Gruyter).

Booth, W.C.

1967 *The Rhetoric of Fiction* ([1]1961; Chicago: University of Chicago Press).

Bosman, H.L.

2005 'Origin and Identity : Rereading Exodus as a Polemical Narrative Then (Palestine) and Now (Africa)', *Scriptura* 90(3): 869–77.

Bottéro, J.

1992 *Mesopotamia: Writing, Reasoning, and the Gods* (Chicago: University of Chicago Press).

Brueggemann, W.

1994 *The Book of Exodus* (NIB; Nashville: Abingdon).

1998 *Theology of the Old Testament: Testimony, Dispute, Advocacy* (Minneapolis).

Buber, M.

1952 *Moses* (2nd edition, [1]1944; Heidelberg: Lambert Schneider).

Butler, T.C.

1979 'An Anti-Moses Tradition', *JSOT* 12: 9–15.

Callender, D.E.

1998 'Servants of God(s) and Servants of Kings in Israel and the Ancient Near East', *Semeia* 83/84: 67–82.

Carpenter, E.

1997 'Exodus18: Its Structure, Style, Motifs and Function in the Book of Exodus', in E. Carpenter (ed.), *A Biblical Itinerary. In Search of Method, Form and Content. Essays in Honour of*

George W. Coats (JSOT.S 240; Sheffield: Sheffield
Academic Press): 91–108.

Cassuto, U.
1967   *A Commentary on the Book of Exodus* (Hebr. 1951;
            Jerusalem: Magnes).

Cazelles, H., ed.
1963   *Moses in Schrift und Überlieferung* (orig. Moïse, l'Homme
            de Alliance, 1955; F. Stier and E. Beck, trans.; Düsseldorf:
            Patmos).

Chatman, S.
1978   *Story and Discourse: Narrative Structure in Function and
            Film* (Ithaca: Cornell University Press).

Cheon, S.
1997   *The Exodus Story in the Wisdom of Solomon. A Study in
            Biblical Interpretation* (Journal for the Study of the
            Pseudepigrapha. Supplement 23; Sheffield: JSOT Press).

Childs, B.S.
1963   'The Birth of Moses', *JBL* 84: 109–22.
1976   *The Book of Exodus: A Critical Theological Commentary*
            (3rd reprint of [1]1974; OTL; Louisville: Westminster).
1993   *Biblical Theology of the Old and New Testaments:
            Theological Reflection on the Christian Bible* ([1]1992;
            Minneapolis: Fortress).

Chirichigno, G.C.
1993   *Debt-Slavery in Israel and in the Ancient Near East* (JSOT.S
            141; Sheffield: Sheffield University Press).

Clines, D.J.
2007   'Being a Man in the Book of the Covenant', in J.G.
            McConville and K. Möller (eds.), *Reading the Law. Studies
            in Honour of Gordon J. Wenham* (Library of Hebrew
            Bible/Old Testament Studies, 461; New York, London: T &
            T Clark): 3–9.

Coats, G.W.
1968   *Rebellion in the Wilderness. The Mourning Motif in the
            Wilderness Tradition of the OT* (Nashville: Abingdon).
1970   'Self-Abasement and Insult Formulas', *JBL* 89(14–26).
1973   'Moses in Midian', *JBL* 92: 3–10.
1988   *Moses: Heroic Man, Man of God* (JSOT.S 57; Sheffield:
            Sheffield Academic Press).

Conrad, D.
1968   'Studien zum Altargesetz: Ex 20,24–26', Unpublished Ph.D.
            Diss. (Marburg: Phillips Universität Marburg.

Cox, D.G.
2006   'The Hardening of Pharaoh's Heart in Its Literary and
            Cultural Contexts', *Bibliotheca Sacra* 163: 292–311.

Cross, F.M., Jr.
1962   'Yahweh and the God of the Patriarchs', *HTR* 55: 225–59.
Crüsemann, F.
1992   *Die Tora: Theologie und Sozialgeschichte des*
              alttestamentlichen Gesetzes (München: Kaiser).
Dandamaev, M.A.
1984   *Slavery in Babylonia: From Nabopolassar to Alexander the*
              Great (626–313 BC) (revised ed.; V. Powell, trans.; DeKalb:
              Northern Illinois University Press).
Davies, J.A.
2002   'A Royal Priesthood: Literary and Intertextual Perspectives
              on an Image of Israel in Exodus 19,6', *TynBul* 53(1): 157–59.
2004   *A Royal Priesthood: Literary and Intertextual Perspectives*
              on an Image of Israel in Exodus 19.6 (JSOT.S 395; London,
              New York: T & T Clark).
Davies, O.
2006   'Reading the Burning Bush. Voice, World and Holiness',
              Modern Theology 22(3): 439–48.
Dawes, G.W.
1998   *The Body in Question: Metaphor and Meaning in the*
              Interpretation of Ephesians 5:21–33 (Biblical Interpretation
              Series 30; Leiden: Brill).
de Vaux, R.
1965   *Ancient Israel: Its Life and Institutions* (2nd ed.; J. McHugh,
              trans.; London: Darton, Longman & Todd).
Dentan, R.C.
1963   'The Literary Affinities of Exodus 34,6f', *VT* 13: 34–51.
Dijkstra, M.
2006   'Moses, the Man of God', in R. Roukema (ed.), *The*
              Interpretation of Exodus. FS Cornelis Houtman, Vol. 44
              (Contributions to Biblical Exegesis and Theology; Leuven,
              Paris, Dudley (Mass.): Peeters): 17–36.
Dohmen, C.
1993   'Der Dekaloganfang und sein Ursprung', *Bibl* 74: 175–95.
2004a   'Biblische Auslegung. Wie alte Texte neue Bedeutungen
              haben können', in F.-L. Hossfeld and L. Schwienhorst-
              Schönberger (eds.), *Das Manna fällt auch heute noch.*
              Beiträge zur Geschichte und Theologie des Alten, Ersten
              Testaments. FS Erich Zenger (Freiburg: Herder): 174–91.
2004b   *Exodus 19–40* (HThKAT; Freiburg: Herder).
Douglas, M.
1973   *Natural Symbols* (New York: Vintage Books).
2002 [1999]   *Leviticus as Literature* (Oxford: Oxford University Press).

Dozeman, T.B.
1984   'Moses: Divine Servant and Israelite Hero: A Study of Moses
               as Mediator Between Yahweh and Israel in Ex 32',
               HAR 8: 45–61.
1989   *God on the Mountain: A Study of Redaction, Theology and
               Canon in Exodus 19–24* (SBLMS 37; Atlanta: Scholars
               Press).
1996   *God at War: Power in the Exodus Tradition* (Oxford; New
               York: Oxford University Press).
2000   'Masking Moses and Mosaic Authority in Torah',
               JBL 119(1): 21–45.
2005   'The Priestly Vocation', *Interp.* 59(2): 115–28.
Durham, J.D.
1987   *Exodus* (Word Biblical Commentary 3; Waco, Texas: Word
               Books).
Eco, U.
1972   *Einführung in die Semiotik* (UTB 105; München: Fink).
1979   *The Role of the Reader: Explorations in the Semiotics of
               Texts* (Advances in Semiotics; Bloomington: Indiana
               University Press).
Eichrodt, W.
1961   *Theology of the Old Testament* (Theologie des Alten
               Testaments, [1]1933; J.A. Baker, trans.; Philadelphia:
               Westminster).
Ellington, S.A.
2005   'Who Shall Lead Them Out? An Exploration of God's
               Openness in Exodus 32.7–14', *Journal of Pentecostal
               Theology* 14: 41–60.
Eslinger, L.
1991   'Freedom or Knowledge? Perspective and Purpose in the
               Exodus Narrative (Exodus 1–15)', *JSOT* 52: 43–60.
Etheridge, J.
1968   *The Targums of Onkelos and Jonathan Ben Uzziel on the
               Pentateuch with the Fragments of the Jerusalem Targum:
               Genesis and Exodus* (2nd edition, [1]1862; KTAV).
Exum, J.C.
1983   'You Shall Let Every Daughter Live: A Study of Exodus 1:8–
               2:10', *Semeia* 28: 63–82.
Fischer, G.
2005   'Wege zu einer neuen Sicht der Tora', *Zeitschrift für
               altorientalische und biblische Rechtsgeschichte* 11: 93–106.
2007   'Gottes Offenbarung am Dornbusch. Und die Berufung des
               Mose (Ex 3–4)', *Bible und Kirche* 62: 227–31.

Fitzpatrick-McKinley, A.
1999   *The Transformation of Torah from Scribal Advice to Law*
            (JSOT.S 287; Sheffield: Sheffield University Press).
Fokkelman, J.P.
1998   *Major Poems of the Hebrew Bible at the Interface of*
            Hermeneutics and Structural Analysis, Vol. 1, *Ex. 15, Deut.*
            32, and Job 3 (Studia Semitica Neerlandica; Assen: Van
            Gorcum).
Ford, W.A.
2006   *God, Pharaoh and Moses: Explaining the Lord's Actions in*
            the Exodus Plagues Narrative (Paternoster Biblical
            Monographs; Carlisle: Paternoster).
Fraade, S.D.
2004   'Moses and the Commandments : Can Hermeneutics, History,
            and Rhetoric Be Disentangled?' in H. Najman and J. Hood
            Newman (eds), *The Idea of Biblical Interpretation. FS James*
            L. Kugel (Leiden: Brill): 399–422.
Franz, M.
2003   *Der barmherzige und gnädige Gott: Die Gnadenrede vom*
            Sinai (Exodus 34, 6–7) und ihre Parallelen im Alten
            Testament und seiner Umwelt (Beiträge zur Wissenschaft
            vom Alten und Neuen Testament, 160; Stuttgart:
            Kohlhammer).
Freedman, D.N.
1960   'The Name of the God of Moses', *JBL* 79: 151–56.
Fretheim, T.E.
1991a   *Exodus* (Interpretation; Louisville: John Knox Press).
1991b   'The Reclamation of Creation: Redemption and Law in
            Exodus', *Interp.* 45: 354–65.
1996   'Because the Whole Earth is Mine: Theme and Narrative in
            Exodus', *Interp.* 50: 229–39.
1996   *The Pentateuch* (Interpreting Biblical Texts; Nashville:
            Abingdon).
Futato, M.D.
2002   'ענן', in *New International Dictionary of Old Testament*
            Theology & Exegesis (CD-ROM ed. Zondervan Pradis
            5.13.0025. 2002. Print ed.: *New International Dictionary of*
            Old Testament Theology & Exegesis. Willem A. VanGemeren
            ed., 5, vols.; Carlisle: Paternoster, 1997): n.p.
Galley, S.
1996   'Moshe ha-Navi. Studien zur Überlieferung und
            Wirkungsgeschichte der Deutung Moses als Prophet',
            Unpublished Ph.D. Diss. (Berlin: Humboldt Universität).

Gammie, J.
1990   'Paraenetic Literature: Toward the Morphology of a
            Secondary Genre', *Semeia* 50: 47–77.
Geertz, C.
1973   *The Interpretation of Cultures. Selected Essays* (New York).
Gelin, A.
1963   'Moses im Alten Testament', in H. Cazelles (ed.), *Moses in
            Schrift und Überlieferung* (orig. Moïse, l'Homme de
            l'Alliance, 1955; F. Stier and E. Beck, trans.; Düsseldorf:
            Patmos): 31–57.
Gertz, J.C., Schmid, K., and Witte, M., eds.
2002   *Abschied vom Jahwisten: Die Komposition des Hexateuch in
            der jüngsten Diskussion* (BZAW 315; Berlin: de Gruyter).
Gesenius, W.
1985   *Hebräische Grammatik* (reprographischer Nachdruck der 28.,
            vielfach verbesserten und vermehrten Auflage Leipzig 1909;
            E. Kautzsch, Adapt.; Darmstadt: Wissenschaftliche
            Buchgesellschaft).
Graf, F.W.
2003   'Nation', in *RGG⁴ Vol. 6* (H.D. Betz, D.S. Browning, B.
            Janowski and E. Jüngel; Tübingen: J.C.B. Mohr): 66–67.
Graupner, A.
2005   'Vergeltung oder Schadensersatz? Erwägungen zur
            regulativen Idee alttestamentlichen Rechts am Beispiel des ius
            talionis und der mehrfachen Ersatzleistung im Bundesbuch',
            EvTh 65: 459–77.
Greenberg, M.
1967   'The Thematic Unity of Exodus III-XI', in *Fourth World
            Congress of Jewish Studies I* (Jerusalem): 151–54.
1969   *Understanding Exodus* (The Melton Research Center Series
            2,1; New York: Behrman House).
Greßmann, H.
1913   *Mose und seine Zeit: Ein Kommentar zu den Mose-Sagen*
            (Göttingen: Vendenhoek & Ruprecht).
Gunn, D.M.
1982   'The 'Hardening of Pharaoh's Heart': Plot, Character and
            Theology in Exodus 1–14', in *Art and Meaning: Rhetoric in
            Biblical Narrative* (JSOT.S 19; Clines D.J.A., D. Gunn and
            A. Hauser; Sheffield: JSOT Press): 72–96.
Halbe, J.
1975   *Das Privilegrecht Jahwes Ex 34,10–26: Gestalt und Wesen,
            Herkunft und Wirken in vordeuteronomischer Zeit* (FRLANT
            114; Göttingen: Vandenhoeck & Ruprecht).

Hamilton, V.P.
1997   'Genesis: Theology Of', in *New International Dictionary of
            Old Testament Theology & Exegesis* (CD-ROM ed.
            Zondervan Pradis 5.13.0025. 2002. Print ed.: *New
            International Dictionary of Old Testament Theology &
            Exegesis*. Willem A. VanGemeren ed., 5, vols.; Carlisle:
            Paternoster, 1997): n.p.
Hanson, B.
1977   *Application of Rules in New Situations: A Hermeneutical
            Study* (Lund: CWK Gleerup).
Hanson, P.D.
1986   *A People Called: The Growth of Community in the Bible* (San
            Francisco: Harper & Row).
Hardmeier, C., and Hunzinker-Rodewald, R.
2006   'Texttheorie und Texterschließung. Grundlagen einer
            empirisch-textpragmatischen Exegese', in H. Utzschneider
            and E. Blum (eds), *Lesarten der Bibel. Untersuchungen zu
            einer Theorie der Exegese des Alten Testaments* (Stuttgart:
            Kohlhammer): 13–44.
Hieke, T.
2007   'Ein Bekannter stellt sich vor.. Das Buch Exodus als
            vielfältige Quelle biblischer Rede von Gott', *Bible und
            Kirche* 62: 221–26.
Hilbrands, W.
2006   'Das Verhältnis der Engel zu Jahwe im Alten Testament,
            insbesondere im Buch Exodus', in R. Roukema (ed.), *The
            Interpretation of Exodus. FS Cornelis Houtman*, Vol. 44
            (Contributions to Biblical Exegesis and Theology; Leuven,
            Paris: Peeters): 81–96.
Hirsch, S.R.
1986   *Der Pentateuch*, Vol. 2, *Zweiter Teil: Exodus* (Jubiläums-
            Ausgabe, ^{5}1912; Tel-Aviv: Sinai).
Hoffmeier, J.K.
1997   *Israel in Egypt: The Evidence for the Authenticity of the
            Exodus Tradition* (Oxford: Oxford University Press).
Houtman, C.
1993   *Exodus Volume I* (Dutch 1986; Historical Commentary on the
            Old Testament; Kampen: KOK).
1996   *Exodus Volume II* (Dutch 1989; Historical Commentary on
            the Old Testament; Kampen: KOK).
1997   *Das Bundesbuch: Ein Kommentar* (Documenta et
            Monumenta Orientis Antiqui 24; Leiden: Brill).
2000   *Exodus Volume III* (Dutch 1996; Historical Commentary on
            the Old Testament; Leuven: Peeters).

Howard, D.M., Jr.
1994   'Rhetorical Criticism in Old Testament Studies', *BBR* 4: 87–
            104.
Howell, M.
1989   'Exodus 15,1b-18: A Poetic Analysis', *EThL* 65: 5–42.
Hurowitz, V.
1985   'The Priestly Account of Building the Tabernacle',
            JAOS 105: 21–30JSOTSup 115; Sheffield: Sheffield
            Academic.
1992   *I Have Built You an Exalted House: Temple Building in the
            Bible in the Light of Mesopotamian and North-West Semitic
            Writings* (JSOTSup 115; Sheffield: Sheffield Academic).
Hutter, M.
1996   *Religionen in der Umwelt des Alten Testaments I:
            Babylonier, Syrer, Perser* (Studienbücher Theologie 4/1;
            Stuttgart: Kohlhammer).
Iser, W.
1974   *The Implied Reader: Patterns of Communication in Prose
            Fiction from Bunyan to Beckett* (Baltimore: Johns Hopkins
            University Press).
1979   *Der implizite Leser. Kommunikationsformen des Romans von
            Bunyan bis Beckett* (2 Aufl.; UTB 163; München: Fink).
1984   *Der Akt des Lesens. Theorie ästhetischer Wirkung* (2.,
            durchges. und verb. Aufl.; UTB 636; München: Fink).
Jackson, B.S.
1984   'The Ceremonial and the Judicial: Biblical Law as Sign and
            Symbol', *JSOT* 30: 25–50.
1989   'Ideas of Law and Legal Administration: A Semiotic
            Approach', in R. Clements (ed.), *The World of Ancient Israel:
            Sociological, Anthropological and Political Perspectives*
            (Cambridge: Cambridge University Press): 185–202.
2000   *Studies in the Semiotics of Biblical Law* (JSOT.S 314;
            Sheffield: Sheffield Academic Press).
2006   *Wisdom-Laws: A Study of the Mishpatim of Exodus 21:1–
            22:16* (Oxford: Oxford University Press).
Jacob, B.
1997   *Das Buch Exodus* ([1]1935/1943; Hrsg. im Auftrag des Leo-
            Baeck-Instituts von Shlomo Mayer; Stuttgart: Calwer).
Janowski, B.
1990   'Tempel und Schöpfung: Schöpfungstheologische Aspekte
            der priesterschriftlichen Heiligtumskonzeption', *JBTh* 5: 37–
            69.
1993   *Gottes Gegenwart in Israel: Beiträge zur Theologie des Alten
            Testaments* (Neukirchen: Neukirchener).

1993   'Tempel und Schöpfung: Schöpfungstheologische Aspekte der priesterschriftlichen Heiligtumskonzeption', in B. Janowski (ed.), *Gottes Gegenwart in Israel: Beiträge zur Theologie des Alten Testaments* (Neukirchen: Neukirchener): 214–46.

Jenson, P.P.

1992   *Graded Holiness: A Key to the Priestly Conception of the World* (JSOT.S 106; Sheffield: Sheffield Academic Press).

Jobling, D.

1986   *The Sense of Biblical Narrative: Structural Analyses in the Hebrew Bible* (2nd ed., [1]1978; JSOT.S 7; Sheffield: JSOT Press).

Joosten, J.

1991   'The syntax of zeh Moseh (Ex 32,1.23)', *ZAW* 103: 412–15.

1996   *People and Land in the Holiness Code: An Exegetical Study of the Ideational Framework of the Law in Leviticus 17–26* (SVT 67; Leiden: Brill).

Junior, N., and Schipper, J.

2008   'Mosaic Disability and Identity in Exodus 4:10; 6:12,30', *Biblical Interpretation* 16(5): 428–41.

Kaiser, G.

2001   'War der Exodus der Sündenfall?: Fragen an Jan Assmann anläßlich seiner Monographie 'Moses der Ägypter'', *ZThK* 98: 1–24.

Kaiser, O.

2003   *Der Gott des Alten Testaments: Wesen und Wirken. Theologie des Alten Testaments*, Vol. 3, *Jahwes Gerechtigkeit* (UTB 2392; Göttingen: Vandenhoeck & Ruprecht).

Keil, C.F.

1983   *Genesis und Exodus: biblischer Commentar über das Alte Testament* (4.Aufl., Nachdr. d. 3., verb. Aufl. von 1878; Gießen: Brunnen).

Kennedy, G.A.

1984   *New Testament Interpretation Through Rhetorical Criticism* (Chapel Hill: University of North Carolina Press).

Kim, E.C.

2004   'The Purpose of the Book of Exodus : A Narrative Criticism', *Asia Journal of Theology* 18(1): 3–13.

Kinyongo, J.

1970   *Origin et signification du nom divin Yahvé à la lumière de récents travaux et de tradition sémitico-bibliques* (BBB; Bonn).

Kissling, P.J.
1996   *Reliable Characters in the Primary History: Profiles of Moses, Joshua, Elijah and Elisha* (JSOT.S 224; Sheffield: Sheffield Academic Press).

Kiuchi, N.
2007   'Commanding an Impossibility? : Reflections on the Golden Rule in Leviticus 19:18b', in *Reading Law. FS Gordon J. Wenham* (Library of Hebrew Bible, Old Testament Studies 461; J.G. McConville; London: T & T Clark): 33–47.

Klein, R.W.
1996   'Back to the Future: The Tabernacle in the Book of Exodus', *Interp.* 50(3): 264–76.

Klengel, H.
1992   *König Hammurapi und der Alltag Babyloniens* (Darmstadt: WBG).

Koch, K.
1955   'Um das Prinzip der Vergeltung in Religion und Recht des Alten Testaments', *ZThK* 52: 1–42.

Kooij, A.v.d.
2006   'A Kingdom of Priests : Comment on Exodus 19:6', in R. Roukema (ed.), *The Interpretation of Exodus. FS Cornelis Houtman*, Vol. 44 (Contributions to Biblical Exegesis and Theology; Leuven, Paris: Peeters): 171–79.

Köckert, M.
1989   'Leben in Gottes Gegenwart: Zum Verständnis des Gesetzes in der priesterschriftlichen Literatur', *JBTh* 4: 29–61.

Kratz, R.G.
1994   'Der Dekalog im Exodusbuch', *VT* 44: 205–38.
2000   'Israel Als Staat und Als Volk', *ZThK* 97: 1–17.

Kraus, F.R.
1960   'Ein zentrales Problem des altmesopotamischen Rechts: Was ist der Kodex Hammurabi?' *Aspects Du Contact Sumero-Akkadien, Geneva* 8: 283–93.

1984   *Königliche Verfügungen in altbabylonischer Zeit* (Leiden).

Krochmalnik, D.
2000   *Schriftauslegung. 3. Das Buch Exodus Im Judentum* (Neuer Stuttgarter Kommentar. Altes Testament 33; T. Heither, ed.; Stuttgart: Kath. Bibelwerk).

Kunin, S.D.
1999   'Israel and the Nations: A Structuralist Review', *JSOT* 82: 19–43.

Lang, B.
2001   'Theokratie', in H. Cancik, B. Gladigow and K.-H. Kohl (eds.), *Handbuch religionswissenschaftlicher Grundbegriffe*, Vol. 5 (Stuttgart: Kohlhammer): 178–89.

Lapsley, J.E.
    2004   'Friends with God? Moses and the Possibility of Covenantal Friendship', *Interpretation* 58: 117–29.

Leder, A.C.
    1999   'Reading Exodus to Learn and Learning to Read Exodus', *CTJ* 34: 11–35.

Lehrman, S.M.
    1951   *Exodus*, in *Midrash Rabbah* (H. Freedman and M. Simon; London & Bournemouth: Soncino Press).

Levinson, B.M., ed.
    1994   *Theory and Method in Biblical and Cuneiform Law: Revision, Interpolation and Development* (JSOT.S 181; Sheffield: Sheffield Academic Press).

Limbeck, M.
    1997   *Das Gesetz im Alten und Neuen Testament* (Darmstadt: Wissenschaftliche Buchgesellschaft).

Lohfink, N.
    1981   ''Ich bin Jahwe, dein Arzt' (Ex 15, 26): Gott, Gesellschaft und menschliche Gesundheit in der Theologie einer nachexilischen Pentateuchbearbeitung (Ex 15, 25b.26)', in Helmut Merklein and E. Zenger (eds.), *Ich Will Euer Gott Werden: Beispiele Biblischen Redens von Gott* (Stuttgarter Bibelstudien 100; Stuttgart: Katholisches Bibelwerk): 11–73.
    1990   'Das deuteronomische Gesetz in der Endgestalt - Entwurf einer Gesellschaft ohne marginale Gruppen', *BN* 51: 25–40.

Lundbom, J.
    1978   'God's Use of the Idem Per Idem to Terminate Debate', *HTR* 71: 193–201.

Markl, D.
    2004   'Ex 3f und Dtn 1,1; 34,10–12 als literarische Eckpunkte des pentateuchischen Mosebildes', in *Führe mein Volk heraus. Zur innerbiblischen Rezeption der Exodusthematik. FS Georg Fischer* (S. Paganini, C. Paganini, G. Fischer and D. Markl; Frankfurt: Lang): 15–23.

Mayer, R.
    1958   'Der Gottesname im Lichte der neuesten Forschung', *BZ NF* 2: 26–53.

McBride, S.D.
    1990   'Transcendent Authority: The Role of Moses in Old Testament Traditions', *Interp.* 44: 229–39.

McCarthy, B.R.
    2004   'The Characterization of YHWH, the God of Israel, in Exodus 1–15', in J.H. Ellens, D.L. Ellens, R.P. Knierim and I. Kalimi (eds), *God's Word for Our World, Volume 1:*

Biblical Studies in Honor of Simon John de Vries (London: T&T Clark): 6–20.

McConville, J.G.
2002   *Deuteronomy* (Apollos Old Testament Commentary; Downer Grove: InterVarsity Press).

McKeon, R., ed.
1941   *The Basic Works of Aristotle* (New York: Random House).

McNamara, M., Hayward, R., and Maher, M., trans.
1994   *Targum Neofiti 1: Exodus. Targum Pseudo-Jonathan: Exodus* (The Aramaic Bible: The Targums. Vol. 2; K. Cathcart, M. Maher and M. McNamara, eds.; Edinburgh: T & T Clark).

Meynet, R.
1998   *Rhetorical Analysis: An Introduction to Biblical Rhetoric* (JSOT.S 256; Sheffield: Sheffield Academic Press).

Milgrom, J.
1989   *Numbers: The Traditional Hebrew Text with the New JPS Translation, Commentary by Jacob Milgrom* (The JPS Torah Commentary 4; Philadelphia: The Jewish Publication Society).

Moberly, R.W.L.
1983   *At the Mountain of God: Story and Theology in Exodus 32– 34* (JSOT.S 22; Sheffield: JSOT Press).
2002   'How May We Speak of God? A Reconsideration of the Nature of Biblical Theology', *TynBul* 53(2): 177–202.
2007   'On Learning Spiritual Disciplines : A Reading of Exodus 16', in *Reading Law. FS Gordon J. Wenham* (Library of Hebrew Bible, Old Testament Studies 461; J.G. McConville; London: T & T Clark): 213–27.

Möller, K.
1999   *Presenting a Prophet in Debate: An Investigation of the Literary Structure and the Rhetoric of Persuasion of the Book of Amos* (Unpublished Ph.D. Diss.; Cheltenham and Gloucester College of Higher Education).
2003   *A Prophet in Debate: The Rhetoric of Persuasion of the Book of Amos* (JSOT.S 372; Sheffield: Sheffield Academic Press).

Muilenburg, J.
1969   'Form Criticism and Beyond', *JBL* 88: 1–18.

Nasuti, H.P.
1986   'Identity, Identification, and Imitation: The Narrative Hermeneutics of Biblical Law', *JLR* 4(1): 9–24.

Nicole, E.
1997   'בחר', in *New International Dictionary of Old Testament Theology & Exegesis* (CD-ROM ed. Zondervan Pradis

5.13.0025. 2002. Print ed.: *New International Dictionary of Old Testament Theology & Exegesis*. Willem A. VanGemeren ed., 5, vols.; Carlisle: Paternoster, 1997).

Niehaus, J.
1995   *God at Sinai: Covenant and Theophany in the Bible and Ancient Near East* (Carlisle: Paternoster).

Niehr, H.
1998   *Religionen in Israels Umwelt: Einführung in die nordwestsemitischen Religionen Syrien-Palästinas* (Neue Echter Bibel, Ergänzungsband zum Alten Testament 5; Würzburg: Echter).

Noth, M.
1978   *Das 2. Buch Mose* (6., unveränderte Aufl., [1]1958; ATD 5; Göttingen: Vandenhoeck & Ruprecht).
1986   *Geschichte Israels* (10., unveränderte Aufl., [1]1950; Göttingen: Vandenhoeck & Ruprecht).

Ogden, G.
1992   'Idem Per Idem: Its Use and Meaning', *JSOT* 53: 107–20.

Olson, D.T.
1985   *The Death of the Old and the Birth of the New: The Framework of the Book of Numbers and the Pentateuch* (BJS 71; Chico: Scholars).

Osswald, E.
1962   *Das Bild des Mose in der alttestamentlichen Wissenschaft seit Julius Wellhausen* (Theologische Arbeiten 18; Berlin: Evangelische Verlagsanstalt).

Osumi, Y.
1991   *Die Kompositionsgeschichte des Bundesbuches Ex 20,22b-23,33* (OBO 105; Freiburg; Göttingen: Universitätsverlag; Vandenhoeck & Ruprecht).

Otto, E.
1988   *Wandel der Rechtsbegründungen in der Gesellschaftsgeschichte des antiken Israel: Eine Rechtsgeschichte des "Bundesbuches" Ex XX 22 - XXIII 13* (Studia Biblica 3; Leiden: Brill).
1989   *Rechtsgeschichte der Redaktionen im Kodex Ešnunna und im 'Bundesbuch'. Eine redaktionsgeschichtliche und rechtsvergleichende Studie zu altbabylonischen und altisraelitischen Rechtsüberlieferungen* (OBO 85; Fribourg/Göttingen: Universitätsverlag/Vandenhoeck & Ruprecht).
1991   'Die Bedeutung der altorientalischen Rechtsgeschichte für das Verständnis des AltenTestaments', *ZThK* 88: 139–68.
1994   *Theologische Ethik des Alten Testaments* (Theologische Wissenschaft Vol. 3,2; Stuttgart: Kohlhammer).

2007   *Das Gesetz des Mose* (Darmstadt: Wissenschaftliche
                Buchgesellschaft).

Owens, L.R.
2004   'Free, Present, and Faithful. A Theological Reading of the
                Character of God in Exodus', *New Blackfriars* 85: 614–27.

Pannell, R.J.
2006   'I Would Be Who I Would Be! A Proposal for Reading
                Exodus 3:11–14', *Bulletin for Biblical Research* 16(2): 351–
                53.

Park, C.
2002   *From Mount Sinai to the Tabernacle: A Reading of Exodus
                24:12–40:38 as a Case of Intercalated Double Plot*
                (Unpublished Ph.D. Diss.; University of Gloucestershire).

Patrick, D.
1994   'Is the Truth of the First Commandment Known by Reason?'
                CBQ 56: 423.
1995   'The First Commandment in the Structure of the Pentateuch',
                VT 45: 107–18.
1995   'The Rhetoric of Collective Responsibility in Deuteronomic
                Law', in D.P. Wright, D.N. Freedman and A. Hurvitz (ed.
                by.), *Pomegranates and Golden Bells. Studies in Biblical,
                Jewish, and Near Eastern Ritual, Law, and Literature in
                Honor of Jacob Milgrom* (Winona Lake: Eisenbrauns): 421–
                36.

Patrick, D., and Scult, A.
1990   *Rhetoric and Biblical Interpretation* (Sheffield: Sheffield
                Academic Press).

Patterson, R.D.
2004   'Victory at Sea : Prose and Poetry in Exodus 14–15',
                Biblioteca Sacra 161: 42–54.

Perelman, C., and Olbrechts-Tyteca, L.
1969   *The New Rhetoric: A Treatise on Argumentation* (Originally
                published as La Nouvelle Rhétorique: Traité l'argumentation
                (1958); J. Wilkinson and P. Weaver, transl.; Notre Dame:
                University of Notre Dame Press).

Perry, M.
1979   'Literary Dynamics: How the Order of a Text Creates Its
                Meanings [with an Analysis of Faulkner's "a Rose for
                Emily"]', *Poetics Today* 1–2: 35–64; 311–61.

Phillips, A., and Phillips, L.
1998   'The Origin of "I Am" in Exodus 3.14', *JSOT* 78: 81–84.

Pitkänen, P.M.A.
2000   'Central Sanctuary and the Centralization of Worship in
                Ancient Israel from the Settlement to the Building of

Solomon's Temple: A Historical and Theological Study of the Biblical Evidence in Its Archaeological and Ancient Near Eastern Context', Unpublished Ph.D. Diss. (Cheltenham: University of Gloucestershire, Okt.

2003   *Central Sanctuary and Centralization of Worship in Ancient Israel: From the Settlement to the Building of Solomon's Temple* (Gorgias Dissertations 6; Piscataway: Gorgias).

Plaut, W.G., ed.
2000   *Schemot Exodus* (Die Tora in Jüdischer Auslegung 2; Gütersloh: Chr. Kaiser).

Plett, H.F.
1991   *Einführung in die rhetorische Textanalyse* ([1]1971; Hamburg: Helmut Buske).

Pöttner, M.
2004   'Wirkungsgeschichte', in G. Müller (ed.), *TRE 36* (Berlin: de Gruyter): 123–32.

Propp, W.H.C.
1999   *Exodus 1–18: A New Translation with Introduction and Commentary* (Anchor Bible 2; New York: Doubleday).

Rad, G.v.
1962   *Theologie des Alten Testaments. Band 1: Die Theologie der geschichtlichen Überlieferungen Israels* (4. Aufl., [1]1957; München: Kaiser).

1965   *Theologie des Alten Testaments. Band 2: Die Theologie der prophetischen Überlieferungen Israels* (4. Aufl., [1]1960; München: Kaiser).

Redford, D.B.
1967   'The Literary Motif of the Exposed Child (cf. Ex. ii 1–10)', *Numen* 14: 209–28.

Rendtorff, R.
1997   'Some Reflections on the Canonical Moses: Moses and Abraham', in E. Carpenter (ed.), *A Biblical Itinerary. In Search of Method, Form and Content. Essays in Honour of George W. Coats* (JSOT.S 240; Sheffield: Sheffield Academic Press): 11–19.

1999   *Theologie des Alten Testaments. Ein kanonischer Entwurf*, Vol. 1, *Kanonische Grundlegung* (Neukirchen-Vluyn: Neukirchener).

2001   *Theologie des Alten Testaments. Ein kanonischer Entwurf*, Vol. 2, *Thematische Entfaltung* (Neukirchen-Vluyn: Neukirchener).

Richards, I.A.
1936   *The Philosophy of Rhetoric* (The Mary Flexner Lectures on the Humanities: Bryn Mawr College; New York: Oxford University Press).

Rimmon-Kenan, S.
1983   *Narrative Fiction: Contemporary Poetics* (London:
            Routledge).
Robinson, B.P.
1997   'Moses at the Burning Bush', *JSOT* 75: 107–22.
Roth, M.T.
1997   *Law Collections from Mesopotamia and Asia Minor* (2nd
            edition; SBL Writings from the Ancient World Series;
            Atlanta: Scholars Press).
Roth, W.
1999   'Rhetorical Criticism, Hebrew Bible', in J.H. Hayes (ed.),
            Dictionary of Biblical Interpretation, Vol. 2, *K-Z* (Nashville:
            Abingdon Press): 396–99.
Römer, T.C.
2002   'Das Buch Numeri und das Ende des Jahwisten: Anfragen zur
            Quellenscheidung im vierten Buch des Pentateuch', in J.C.
            Gertz, K. Schmid and M. Witte (eds.), *Abschied vom
            Jahwisten: Die Komposition des Hexateuch in der jüngsten
            Diskussion* (BZAW 315; Berlin: de Gruyter): 215–31.
Ruprecht, E.
1974   'Stellung und Bedeutung der Erzählung vom Mannawunder
            (Ex 16) im Aufbau der Priesterschrift', *ZAW* 86: 269–307.
Saebø, M.
1981   'Offenbarung oder Verhüllung: Bemerkungen zum Charakter
            des Gottesnamens in Ex 3,13–15', in J. Jeremias and L. Perlitt
            (eds.), *Die Botschaft und die Boten. FS Hans Walter Wolff*
            (Neukirchen: Neukirchener): 43–55.
Sailhamer, J.H.
1992   *The Pentateuch as Narrative: A Biblical-Theological
            Commentary* (Michigan: Zondervan).
Sarna, N.M.
1991   *Exodus שמות* (The JPS Torah Commentary 2; Philadelphia:
            Jewish Publication Society).
Scharbert, J.
1957   'Formgeschichte und Exegese von Ex 34,6f und seiner
            Parallelen', *Bib* 38: 130–50.
Schart, A.
1990   *Mose und Israel im Konflikt: Eine redaktionsgeschichtliche
            Studie zu den Wüstenerzählungen* (OBO 98; Göttingen:
            Vandenhoeck & Ruprecht).
Schenker, A.
1990   *Versöhnung und Widerstand. Bibeltheologische
            Untersuchung zum Strafen Gottes und der Menschen,
            besonders im Licht von Ex 21–22* (SBS 139; Stuttgart:
            Kohlhammer).

Schmid, H.
1986   *Die Gestalt des Mose: Probleme alttestamentlicher*
            Forschung unter Berücksichtigung der Pentateuchkrise
            (Erträge der Forschung 237; Darmstadt: WBG).
Schmid, K.
2001   'Etappen der Forschungsgeschichte zu Ex 32–34 in seinen
            Kontexten', in M. Köckert and E. Blum (eds.), *Gottes Volk*
            am Sinai. Untersuchungen zu Ex 32–34 und Dtn 9–10
            (VWGTh 18; Gütersloh: Gütersloher Verlagshaus): 9–40.
2002   'Die Unteilbarkeit der Weisheit: Überlegungen zur
            sogenannten Paradieserzählung Gen 2f. und ihrer
            theologischen Tendenz', *ZAW* 114(1): 21–39.
Schmidt, W.H.
1988   *Exodus: 1. Teilband Exodus 1–6* (BKAT II/1; Neukirchen:
            Neukirchener).
1996   *Alttestamentlicher Glaube* (¹1968, 8., vollständig
            überarbeitete und erweiterte Auflage; Neukirchen:
            Neukirchener).
Schmitz, T.A.
2002   *Moderne Literaturtheorie und antike Texte: Eine Einführung*
            (Darmstadt: Wissenschaftliche Buchgesellschaft).
Schnabel, E.J.
1999   'Rhetorische Analyse', in E.J. Schnabel and H.-W. Neudorfer
            (eds.), *Das Studium des Neuen Testaments* (Wuppertal: R.
            Brockhaus): 307–24.
Schniedewind, W.M.
2004   'Explaining God's Name in Exodus 3', in *"Basel und Bibel"*:
            collected communications to the XVIIth Congress of the
            International Organizations for the Study of the Old
            Testament, Basel 2001 (M. Augustin and H.M. Niemann;
            Bern: Peter Lang): 13–18.
Schreiner, J.
1995   *Theologie des Alten Testaments* (Neue Echter Bibel, Erg. Bd.
            Zum AT 1; Würzburg: Echter).
Schwienhorst-Schönberger, L.
1990   *Das Bundesbuch (Ex 20,22–23,33): Studien zu seiner*
            Entstehung und Theologie (BZAW 188; Berlin: De Gruyter).
Scoralick, R.
2001   ''JHWH, JHWH, ein gnädiger und barmehrziger Gott...' (Ex
            34,6). Die Gottesprädikationen aus Ex 34,6f. in ihrem
            Kontext in Kapitel 32–34', in *Gottes Volk am Sinai.*
            untersuchungen zu Ex 32–34 und Dtn 9–10 (VWGTh 18; M.
            Köckert and E. Blum; Gütersloh: Gütersloher
            Verlagshaus): 141–56.

2002   *Gottes Güte und Gottes Zorn. Die Gottesprädikationen in*
               Exodus 34,6f und ihre intertextuellen Beziehungen zum
               Zwölfprophetenbuch (HBS 33; Freiburg: Herder).
Seebass, H.
1996   'Pentateuch', in G. Müller (ed.), *TRE 26* (Berlin: de Gruyter):
               185–209.
2004   'Mose in einem seiner Ausnahmegespräche mit Gott. Zu Ex
               33,12–23', in M. Witte (ed.), *Gott und Mensch im Dialog. FS*
               Otto Kaiser (BZAW 345; Berlin: de Gruyter): 301–31.
Seely, D.R.
2004   'The Image of the Hand of God in the Book of Exodus', in
               J.H. Ellens, D.L. Ellens, R.P. Knierim and I. Kalimi (eds),
               God's Word for Our World, Volume 1: Biblical Studies in
               Honor of Simon John de Vries (London: T&T Clark): 38–54.
Shaw, I., and Nicholson, P., eds.
1998   'Königtum', in *Reclams Lexikon des alten Ägypten* (Stuttgart:
               Philipp Reclam jun.): 151.
Shreckhise, R.L.
2007   'The Rhetoric of the Expressions in the Song by the Sea
               (Exodus 15,1–18)', *Scandinavian Journal of Theology* 21(2):
               201–17.
Siebert-Hommes, J.
1992   'Die Geburtsgeschichte des Erzählzusammenhanges von Ex I
               und II', *VT* 42: 398–403.
Ska, J.L.
1990   *Our Fathers Have Told Us: Introduction to the Analysis of*
               Hebrew Narratives (Subsidia Biblica 13; Rome: Editrice
               Pontificio Istituto Biblico).
Slivniak, D.M.
2008   'The Golden Calf Story : Constructiveley and
               Deconstructively', *JSOT* 33: 19–38.
Smend, R.
1959   *Das Mosebild von Heinrich Ewald bis Martin Noth* (Beiträge
               zur Geschichte der biblischen Exegese 3; Tübingen: Mohr).
Smith, M.S.
1997   *The Pilgrimage Pattern in Exodus* (JSOT.S 239; with
               contributions by Elizabeth M. Bloch-Smith; Sheffield:
               Sheffield Academic Press).
Sneed, M.
1999   'Israelite Concern for the Alien, Orphan, and Widow:
               Altruism or Ideology', *ZAW* 111: 498–507.
Soden, W.v.
1985   *Einführung in die Altorientalistik* (Orientalistische
               Einführungen in Gegenstand, Ergebnisse und Perspektive
               der Einzelgebiete; Darmstadt: WBG).

1985   'Jahwe "Er ist, Er erweist sich"', in (Ed. and comp.) H.-P.
              Müller, *Bibel und Alter Orient: Altorientalische Beiträge zum*
              Alten Testament von Wolfram von Soden (BZAW 162;
              Göttingen: Vandenhoeck & Ruprecht): 78–88.
Sperber, D., and Wilson, D.
1995   *Relevance: Communication and Cognition* (2nd edition;
              Oxford: Basil Blackwell).
Sprinkle, J.M.
1994   *The Book of the Covenant: A Literary Approach* (JSOT.S
              174; Sheffield: JSOT Press).
Steins, G.
2001   'Priesterherrschaft, Volk von Priestern oder was sonst? Zur
              Interpretation von Ex 19,6', *BZ* 45(1): 20–36.
2006   'Kanonisch lesen', in H. Utzschneider and E. Blum (eds),
              Lesarten der Bibel. Untersuchungen zu einer Theorie der
              Exegese des Alten Testaments (Stuttgart: Kohlhammer): 45–
              64.
2007   'Den anstößigen Text vom Durchzug durchs Schilfmeer (Ex
              14) neu lesen. Oder: Wie der Bibelkanon uns Gottes Rettung
              nahe bringt', *Bible und Kirche* 62: 232–37.
Sternberg, M.
1987   *The Poetics of Biblical Narrative: Ideological Literature and*
              the Drama of Reading (Indiana Literary Biblical Series;
              Bloomington: Indiana University Press).
Thiselton, A.C.
1992   *New Horizons in Hermeneutics. The Theory and Practice of*
              Transforming Biblical Reading (London: Marshall
              Pickering).
Tiemeyer, L.S.
2007   'The Compassionate God of Traditional Jewish and Christian
              Exegesis', *Tyndale Bulletin* 58: 183–207.
Timmer, D.C.
2009   *Creation, Tabernacle, and Sabbath: The Sabbath Frame of*
              Exodus 31:12–17, 35:1–3 in Exegetical and Theological
              Perspective (FRLANT 227; Göttingen: Vandenhoeck &
              Ruprecht).
Tomes, R.
2008   'Home-Grown or Imported? An Examination of Bernard
              Jackson's "Wisdom-Laws"', *ZAR* 14: 443–62.
Trible, P.
1994   *Rhetorical Criticism: Context, Method and the Book of Jonah*
              (Minneapolis: Fortress).

Vanhoozer, K.J.
2001   'From Speech Acts to Scripture Acts', in C. Bartholomew, C. Greene and K. Möller (eds.), *After Pentecost: Language and Biblical Interpretation* (Scripture and Hermeneutics Project 2; Carlisle: Paternoster): 1–49.

Vermès, G.
1963   'Die Gestalt des Mose and Wende der beiden Testamente', in H. Cazelles (ed.), *Moses in Schrift und Überlieferung* (orig. Moïse, l'Homme de l'Alliance, 1955; F. Stier and E. Beck, trans.; Düsseldorf: Patmos): 61–93.

Vialle, C.
2004   'La naissance de Moïse : essai de définition de la structure et de l'intrigue d'Exode 1,1–2,10', *Etudes Théologiques et Religieuses* 79(1): 51–63.

Watson, D.
1999   'Rhetorical Criticism, New Testament', in J.H. Hayes (ed.), *Dictionary of Biblical Interpretation*, Vol. 2, *K-Z* (Nashville: Abingdon Press): 399–402.

Watson, D.F., and Hauser, A.J.
1994   *Rhetorical Criticism of the Bible: A Comprehensive Bibliography with Notes on History and Method* (Biblical Interpretation Series 4; Leiden: Brill).

Watts, J.W.
1992   *Psalm and Story: Inset Hymns in Hebrew Narrative* (JSOT.S 139; Sheffield: Sheffield Academic Press).
1996   'The Legal Characterization of God in the Pentateuch', *HUCA* 67: 1–14.
1998   'The Legal Characterization of Moses in the Rhetoric of the Pentateuch', *JBL* 117: 415–26.
1999   'Reader Identification and Alienation in the Legal Rhetoric of the Pentateuch', *BibInt* 7(1): 101–12.
1999   *Reading Law: The Rhetorical Shaping of the Pentateuch* (The Biblical Seminar 59; Sheffield: Sheffield Academic Press).

Weber, B.
1990   '"Jede Tochter aber sollt ihr am Leben lassen!" Beobachtungen zu Ex 1,15–2,10 und seinem Kontext aus literaturwissenschaftlicher Perspektive', *BN* 55: 44–77.

Weimar, P.
1980   *Die Berufung des Mose: Literaturwissenschaftliche Analyse von Exodus 2,23–5,5* (OBO 32; Fribourg: Editions Universitaires Fribourg/University Press Fribourg).
1988   'Sinai und Schöpfung: Komposition und Theologie der priesterschriftlichen Sinaigeschichte', *RB* 95(3): 337–85.

Weimar, P., and Zenger, E.
1975   *Exodus: Geschichten und Geschichte der Befreiung Israels* (Stuttgarter Bibelstudien 75; Stuttgart: KBW).

Weisman, Z.
1995   'The Place of the People in the Making of Law and Judgement', in D.P. Wright, D.N. Freedman and A. Hurvitz (ed. by.), *Pomegranates and Golden Bells. Studies in Biblical, Jewish, and Near Eastern Ritual, Law, and Literature in Honor of Jacob Milgrom* (Winona Lake: Eisenbrauns): 407–20.

Wells, B.
2006   'The Covenant Code and Near Eastern Legal Traditions: A Response to David P. Wright', *Maarav* 13: 85–118.

Wenham, G.J.
1981   *Numbers* (TOTC 4; Leicester: Inter Varsity).
1986   'Sanctuary Symbolism in the Garden of Eden Story', *Proceedings of the World Congress of Jewish Studies: Division A, the Period of the Bible* 9: 19–25.
1994   'The Face at the Bottom of the Well: Hidden Agendas of the Pentateuchal Commentator', in *He Swore an Oath* (R.S. Hess, G.J. Wenham and P.E. Satterthwaite; Carlisle: Paternoster): 185–209.
1997   'The Gap Between Law and Ethics in the Bible', *JJS* 48: 17–29.
2003   *The Pentateuch* (Exploring the Old Testament; London: SPCK).

Westbrook, R.
1988   *Studies in Biblical and Cuneiform Law* (Cahiers de la Revue Biblique 26; Paris: Gabalda).
1994   'What is the Covenant Code?' in B.M. Levinson (ed.), *Theory and Method in Biblical and Cuneiform Law: Revision, Interpolation and Development* (Sheffield: Sheffield Academic Press): 15–36.
2003   *A History of Ancient Near Eastern Law* (2 Vols.; Handbook of Oriental Studies, Part One: The Ancient Near East and Middle East; Leiden: Brill).

Wiher, H.
2003   *Shame and Guilt: A Key to Cross-Cultural Ministry* (Edition Iwg - Mission Academics 10; Bonn: VKW).

Williams, T.F.
1997   'פקד', in *New International Dictionary of Old Testament Theology & Exegesis* (CD-ROM ed. Zondervan Pradis 5.13.0025. 2002. Print ed.: *New International Dictionary of Old Testament Theology & Exegesis*. Willem A. VanGemeren ed., 5, vols.; Carlisle: Paternoster, 1997).

Willi-Plein, I.
 1991   'Ort und literarische Funktion der Geburtsgeschichte des
                Mose', *VT* 41: 110–18.
Wright, C.J.H.
 2004   *Old Testament Ethics for the People of God* (Downers Grove:
                InterVarsity Press).
Wright, D.P.
 2003   'The Laws of Hammurabi as a Source for the Covenant
                Collection (Exodus 20:23–23:19)', *Maarav* 10: 11–87.
 2004a   'The Compositional Logic of the Goring Ox and Negligence
                Laws in the Covenant Collection (Ex 21:28–36)',
                ZAR 10: 93–142.
 2004b   'The Fallacies of Chiasmus: A Critique of Structures
                Proposed for the Covenant Collection (Exodus 20:23–
                23:19)', *ZAR* 10: 143–68.
 2006   'The Laws of Hammurabi and the Covenant Code: A
                Response to Bruce Wells', *Maarav* 13: 211–60.
Wuellner, W.
 1987   'Where is Rhetorical Criticism Taking Us?' *CBQ* 49: 448–63.
Yaron, S.R.
 1993   'Social Problems and Policies in the Ancient Near East', in B.
                Halpern and D. Hobson (eds.), *Law, Politics and Society in
                the Ancient Mediterranean World* (Sheffield: Sheffield
                Academic): 19–41.
Zenger, E.
 1971   *Die Sinaitheophanie: 'Untersuchungen zum jahwistischen
                und elohistischen Geschichtswerk* (Fzb 3; Würzburg: Echter).
Zenger, E., and Fabry, H.-J., eds.
 1998   *Einleitung in das Alte Testament* (3. neu bearb. und erw.
                Aufl., ¹1995; Kohlhammer Studienbücher Theologie 1.1;
                Stuttgart: Kohlhammer).
Zimmerli, W.
 1999   *Grundriß der alttestamentlichen Theologie* (7th ed., ¹1972;
                Theologische Wissenschaft 3,1; Stuttgart: Kohlhammer).
Zivotofsky, A.Z.
 1994   'The Leadership Qualities of Moses', *Jdm* 43: 258–69.
Zlotnick-Sivan, H.
 2004   'Moses the Persian? Exodus 2, the "Other" and Biblical
                "Mnemohistory"', *ZAW* 116: 189–205.

BIBLICAL REFERENCES

Genesis

1-2 22
1:1-2:4 227
1-11 39
1:20f.................................... 22
6:7-8 190
8:17.................................... 22
9:7...................................... 21
12:2................................... 190
12:3................................... 237
15:6.............................. 222n75
15:18.................................. 63
16:10.................................. 21
17.............................. 168n146
17:2.................................... 21
17:4.................................... 63
17:6............................... 21, 62
17:8.................................... 92
18:11................................. 238
18:18................................. 191
22:17.................................. 21
26:4.20............................... 21
28:3............................... 21, 62
30:27......................... 237n127
35:11............................. 21, 62
39:5........................... 237n127
41:44............................. 38n37
46...................................... 212
46:3................................... 191

46:8 20
48:4 21

Exodus

1 61
1:1 20
1:1-6........................... 20, 212
1:7................................. 21, 62
1:9 .... 201, 213
1:11............................. 22, 241
1:17...................... 61, 79, 175
1:20f................................... 61
1:22 154
1–2 .... 8n20
1:1–2:10.................. 22n72, 62
1–14 77
1–15 30
1–18 71
2:1-10....................... 153, 162
2:11-15............................. 158
2:11-22................. 39, 153, 156,
                          159, 162, 196
2:14 .... 184, 195
2:23-25........... 58, 64, 164, 221
2:23–4:31 162
2:24 .... 40n47, 62
2:24-25............................. 214
2:26 168
2–5 27

3.. 4
3:1-6 .... 64, 164
3:2.................................... 26, 42
3:6.. 79
3:7-10 .... 64f, 201, 206
3:10.................................... 149f
3:11.............................. 39, 196
3:12.................... 39, 150, 167
3:13.................... 39, 63, 184
3:13-15 .... 36, 57
3:14................... 47, 54, 79
3:14-22 167
3:15.. 35
3:16-22 66
3:17...................................... 77
3:19............................... 57n126
3:18-20 .... 54, 79, 222
3:1–4:17...................... 148, 153
3–4...................... 35, 41, 54, 64
4:1...............63, 149f, 184, 201
4:1-9 222
4:1-17 67
4:2-9 167
4:10........................... 149, 196
4:13............... 38n40, 149, 165
4:14.................................. 167
4:16.................................. 178
4:18-23 167
4:19.................................. 157
4:21............................. 54, 67
4:21-23 195
4:22-23 .... 67, 149f
4:24-26 .... 158, 196
4:27-31 169
4:31.................................. 188
5.. 54f
5:1-19 56
5:1-23 171
5:2................................. 38, 55
5:8.................................. 201
5:11.................................. 150
5:17.................................. 201
5:19-21 55
5:21.................................. 194f

5:21-23 ....55f
5:22.................................. 150
5:23.................................. 196
5:1–7:7............................58, 171
6 ....42, 58
6:1 56
6:1-8..............................56-58, 77
6:7 .... 92, 190, 221n71
6:12.................................. 196
6:13-27.............................. 172
6:26-27........................ 173n161
6:29.................................. 178
6:30.................................. 196
6–15.................................... 67
7:1 .... 173, 177
7:1-13...............................173f
7:5 192
7:6 .... 173, 197
7:10.................................. 173
7:13.................................. 53
7:17............................. 53, 150
7:22.................................. 53
7–11 174
7:8–12:32...................... 52, 56
7:14–11:10.......................... 179
8:6.11.15.18.......................... 53
8:16.................................. 150
9:1.................................. 150
9:10-11........................98n257
9:12.................................. 53
9:13.................................. 150
9:15-23........................... 24, 55
9:29.35.................................. 53
9:30.................................... 79
10 ....71n168
10:1-2.............................39, 52f
10:3 150
10:28-29.............................. 176
11:2..............................67n155
11:4.................................. 150
11:7.................................. 53
12:12 51
12:14-20.24-28 223
12:25 ....54n116

12:28.................................... 175
12:29.................................... 184
12:31.................................... 177
12:35-36 .... 67n155, 201
12:43-49 223
12:50f 184, 223n78
13:1-16 223
13:3.................................... 242
13:5...................................... 77
13:9............................... 57n126
13:17..................................... 70
13:21f 25–26
14.. 151
14:10-14 .... 224n81
14:11f 184, 195
14:12................................... 201
14:15................................... 190
14:19-31 .... 26, 71, 224
14:31................ 31, 77-79, 150,
                              184, 188, 195,
                                      222n75
14–15........................ 32n14, 77
15.............................. 4, 29f, 54
15:1-18 .... 27, 78
15:3...................................... 78
15:9-10.12-17 77
15:11....................... 51n98, 79
15:22f 150
15:22-26 98
15:25.......................... 26, 184
15:26.............. 70n165, 226n88
15–17.............................. 5, 69
15:22–18:27........ 183f, 185n206
16................. 71, 185n206, 240
16:3.................................... 201
16:4-12 184
16:6.................................... 225
16:7f 70, 188, 195
16:10.................................... 26
16:23............................. 38n41
16:28f 70n165
17:2.................. 70, 188, 195
17:2-3 150
17:6.................................... 184

17:8-16.......................... 71, 224
17:26................................... 150
18.............................. 87, 141
18:1-12................. 59, 158, 187
18:13-27............. 158, 160, 187
18:18................................... 195
19.. 23
19:1-6.......................... 90n228
19:3 .... 21n65, 94
19:5-6............73, 89, 176, 190f,
                               206, 210, 221n71,
                               226, 234f, 237,
                                      245, 249
19:6.................. 216, 228, 230
19:9 .... 188, 222n75
19:11-13.............................. 180
19:16.................................... 26
19:21-25.............................. 177
20:1-17................................ 81
20:2 ....49f, 90
20:2-6........................... 72, 99
20:4 .... 49, 189
20:5f..................... 29, 35, 49f
20:8-11............................. 240
20:18-21............................ 85
20:19................................... 201
20:20.................................... 79
20:22.................................... 93
20:23............................. 72, 189
20:24-26................. 92, 93n235,
                               94, 115, 240
20:22–23:33...... 50, 81, 84n207
21:1 .... 94, 127n370, 242
21:2-11.............................. 242
21:12................................... 113
21:21f.37............................ 114
21:37–22:16............... 102f, 245
22:3 114
22:17-19............................. 246
22:18................................... 113
22:19................................... 240
22:20........................241f, 246
22:20-26............. 104, 110, 118
22:26................. 108, 110, 116f

22:27-30 240
22:20–23:12................ 124, 126
23:1-8 .... 104, 106f
23:7.................. 108, 110, 116f
23:9.................... 90, 110, 117,
                            242, 246
23:14-19 .... 96, 240
23:20-33 .... 78, 90, 93,
                96, 100, 182f, 240
23:22................................... 115
23:24-26 96
24............................ 72, 74, 150
24:1.............................. 93n235
24:1-11 210
24:3................................... 229
24:7........................... 84n207
24:9-11 .... 59n136, 236
24:12................................ 180
24:15-18 230
25–31................................ 175
25–40................................ 22
28:35................................ 113
29:43-46 .... 53n107, 72, 92,
            190f, 221n71, 238
30:20f 113
31:12-17 .... 230, 240
32....................................... 150
32:1................................... 188
32:1-6 .... 46, 226
32:1-29 189
32:7................................... 189
32:7-14 .... 46, 190
32:9............................... 47, 71
32:10.......................... 46, 74
32:12................................ 192
32:23-24 213
32:25-29 .... 73, 191
32:27................................ 150
32:30............................... 73
32:31-34 190
32:35................................ 73
32–34.................. 4, 50, 69, 73
33:1................................... 189
33:1-6 73

33:3 71
33:11f............................ 47, 197
33:13-16........................ 190-192
33:19............. 38n41, 41, 44, 47
33:12–34:9 190
34 ....4f, 150
34:2-7............................ 44, 181
34:6f............ 29, 32, 35, 42f, 47,
                        49f, 69
34:9 .... 47, 71, 190f
34:10 .... 79, 90
34:11 .... 101, 115
34:11-26................. 73, 81, 240
34:14 101
34:29-35....................... 146, 192
34:32.34 177
35:1-3 .... 113, 226, 240
35–40 .... 175, 241
35:20–36:7 228
39:32-43 227
39–40 21
40:34-38................ 23f, 26,181,
                        227, 230

Leviticus
1:1 24
18–20 .... 104n280
19:18............................ 249n177
23–26 .... 104n280

Numbers
9:15-23............................ 23n76
10:10................................. 23
11 183
11:21-23............................ 5, 55
11:29 142
11–21 .... 186n208
12:6-8.............................. 150f
14:21 .... 185n206
16:19 .... 185n206
16–17 151
17:7 .... 185n206
20:6 .... 185n206
25 .... 158n108

Deuteronomy
1:9-18 141
4:6-8 86
5:4-5 172
10:18 .... 105n281
12:25 .... 88n222
13:1 145
13:19 .... 88n222
17:14-20 .... 78, 88n221
18:15 144
18:18 .... 183n200
21:9 .... 88n222
24:17 .... 105n281
25:1-3 .... 109, 117
26:5 .... 191, 215
27:5-6 .... 93n235
27:19 .... 105n281
28:27.60 .... 98n257
33:1 .... 178n179
34:5 150–51
34:10 .... 144, 193

Joshua
1:1-2 151
8:30-31 .... 93n235
14:6 .... 178n179
24:19 .... 101n266

1 Samuel
8:9-18 87
23:13 .... 38n40

2 Samuel
13:28 .... 38n37
15:20 .... 38n40

1 Kings
11:33 .... 88n221
19:2 (LXX) 38n37

2 Kings
8:1 .... 38n40
10:33 .... 88n221

2 Chronicles
19:5-7 141
20:32 .... 88n221

Isaiah
1:23 .... 105n281
40–49 38
47:8.10 .... 38n37
60–62 236

Jeremiah
7:6 .... 105n281
15:1 150
22:3 .... 105n281

Ezekiel
12:25 .... 38n41
22:7 .... 105n281
36:20 .... 38n41

Hosea
1:9 .... 40n49

Amos
3:1-2 206

Zephaniah
2:15 .... 38n37

Zechariah
7:10 .... 105n281

Malachi
3:5 .... 105n281

Psalms
146:9 .... 105n281

Job
21:15 .... 38n43

Proverbs
30:9 .... 38n43

GENERAL INDEX

Aaron 26, 52, 55n124, 56, 59,
    70n165, 137n29, 147, 151,
    166n137, 169, 170n155, 171–
    75, 177–79, 186n212, 188–
    89, 196–97n248, 212–13,
    219n61, 222n75, 223n77,
    227–28, 231
Abimelech 265
abnormality 205
Abraham 21, 58, 62–63, 74n177,
    97n253, 142, 149, 168–69,
    190, 221, 222n75, 223,
    232n108, 237, 279
abstraction 69n159, 180, 203, 212
accentuation 241
acceptance 39, 59, 76, 89–90,
    109n297, 117n326, 133n12,
    145, 149, 165, 176, 205,
    214n46, 215, 219n60, 222,
    229, 238, 250
actualisation 44
addressee 1, 9, 17, 94, 106n291,
    109, 115n322, 117, 187n215,
    223, 243, 251
administration 81, 88, 106n287,
    107, 141, 272
admiration 82, 84
adversary 49, 70
affront 238

agenda 10, 73, 77
aggrandizement 144
Akkad 136, 155
alienation 247–48, 284
alliance 208, 265–66
allusion 17–18, 20–21n65, 31n11,
    47, 59n135, 59, 73, 80, 91,
    94, 97n250, 115, 121, 126,
    136, 148, 162, 164, 179–80,
    191, 212, 214n46, 220, 233,
    237, 243
altar 92–93n235, 94n239, 95–
    98n255, 115, 125, 182, 240,
    242n144, 266
alteration 130, 197, 222n73
alternatives 19, 41, 46, 191
Amalekites 184–85, 187
ambiguation 4–5, 19, 30, 31n12,
    40n50, 57n126, 78, 83n205,
    106, 122n345, 130, 146, 170,
    182–83, 225
ambivalence 54n115, 97, 156,
    159–62, 187, 190, 205
anachronistic 59n137, 82,
    103n275, 182, 229, 248
analogy 17, 36, 40, 95n243, 179
ancestors 65, 75, 156n101, 201,
    223, 232n108, 242, 250, 258

announcement 49, 144, 186n212, 248

anthropologia 108, 116, 146n64, 272

anthropomorphism 62, 79

anticipation 12n40, 24–26, 28, 36, 55–57, 63–64, 75, 92, 133, 159n112, 165n133, 173, 185n206, 216, 222, 226, 239

apodictic 99, 110n301, 118n330

apologetic 13, 52n105, 144

appeal 15n49, 77n183, 81nn200, 202, 105, 106n285, 107, 109–11, 117–19, 154nn91, 93, 190n230, 191, 206, 230, 238n132, 242–43, 257

Appellstruktur 11

application 22, 81, 83n205, 114n315, 115n322, 128, 143, 271

archetype 17, 130, 200, 227

archival 254

Aristotle 3, 276

arousal 8n21, 17, 46, 54, 97, 109, 116, 203, 222, 226n88, 250

assimilation 14, 161

associative 122, 139

assonance 22

Assyrian 87n217, 96n247, 155n95

aesthetic 13, 272

audience 2–3, 8n21, 9–12, 14–15, 17, 18n54, 19, 52–53n110, 60, 103, 135, 138, 148, 176, 228, 239, 247, 253, 256–57, 260

auditor 17, 255

Ausnahmestellung 186

Ausschließlichkeit 50

authenticity 264, 271

authority 38, 142, 145, 268, 275

Baal 257, 265

Babylonia 87, 106n285, 155n95, 267, 272, 274

balance 9n24, 12, 15n49, 22n74, 32n14, 45, 59, 66, 72–75, 123n347, 125n363, 134, 136, 138–39, 142, 148n73, 157, 166–67, 171, 189, 193–94, 197, 199, 205, 207, 210, 218, 220, 224n81, 228, 234, 241n139, 260

binding benevolence 92, 94–99, 101–3, 106–8, 114n314, 213, 237, 245–46

biography 14, 130, 199–200

blueprint 36, 217, 261n15

bridging 28, 181

Canaan 20–21, 36, 63, 77–78, 95, 96n248, 97, 161, 182, 209n29, 230

canon 15, 20, 259, 268

canonical 13, 20, 43, 131n4, 132n5, 143, 163, 205, 279, 283

captatio 103

causality 45, 80, 133

centralisation 2, 52, 72, 76, 79, 94, 98, 129, 141, 185n206, 188, 199, 204–5, 210, 217, 278–79

characterisation 2–4n10, 7n19, 12, 16, 19, 27, 29–30, 33, 35, 39, 61n141, 63n145, 74, 76–77, 80, 82, 84–87, 90–93, 99–103, 105, 108, 110n303, 113, 115, 118n332, 121, 123n353, 132, 138, 143–45, 148, 150, 152, 167, 174n167, 176–77, 188n220, 194n237, 196, 198, 203, 214, 222n75, 239, 251, 256, 275, 284

chiasm 11, 67, 122, 124, 126n366, 185–87

circumcision 97n253, 168–69n150, 196

citizen 107, 232–34

closure 24, 97n251, 115

collective 28, 45n81, 111, 118,
    212–13, 231, 244–45, 264,
    278
collectivisation 244
commandment 50, 93, 98–102,
    105n284, 126, 262n17, 269,
    278
commemorative 124, 248
community 17, 93n235, 105,
    111n304, 118n333, 138n33,
    162, 203n3, 210, 216, 229–
    31, 233, 240–41, 244–45,
    247, 255, 271
compassion 45, 47n86, 49f, 76,
    104–5n281, 110, 117, 126,
    192, 203, 218, 242–43, 250–
    51, 283
compensation 103, 110, 111n307,
    113–14n316, 118, 119n336
competence 7n17, 15n49, 48n95,
    184, 187, 256
complement 25n83, 137
composition 263, 265, 270, 277,
    280, 284
concealment 145–46, 154
conceptual 7n19, 35, 46, 76, 79,
    101, 102n270, 128–29, 215–
    16, 236
conflation 36, 138, 145, 147, 180
conflict 6, 35, 46, 49, 52–53, 67–
    72, 75, 79, 136, 155n96, 165,
    171–72n158, 174, 180, 186–
    87n216, 205, 214, 217,
    219n59, 220, 224, 264, 280
confrontation 35, 55, 166
congruence 195
congruity 121
conjecture 17, 168n146, 187, 257
conscience 109n296, 116n325,
    193, 246, 249
consecration 22–23, 72, 127n369,
    169n150, 230, 236, 242
consistency 13–14, 18, 207,
    219n62, 247, 253, 259

consolation 256
consolidation 111, 119, 216, 226
constitution 83n205, 98, 222n73,
    234n115
contextual 9n23, 45, 75, 210, 237
continuity 25n82, 53n111, 66, 87–
    88, 165, 169–70, 191, 197,
    201, 224, 226, 230, 235–36,
    240–41, 244, 251, 257–58
contradiction 90, 162, 189, 260
contrasting 46, 157, 172–73
corrective 60
correlation 88n222, 175n168, 227,
    228n96
counterfoil 51
creation 8n21, 14, 20–22, 32n16,
    36, 43, 69–71, 79, 89,
    111n304, 118n333, 129, 143,
    199, 212, 217n51, 236,
    238n132, 250, 253, 255, 257,
    269, 283
creativity 176, 227
credibility 3–4
crisis 1n1, 26, 71, 142
cuneiform 112, 120–21, 275, 285
curiosity 138, 185n206, 187–88

decalogue 43, 49, 50n100, 72, 81,
    85n212, 94, 98–101n269,
    105n284, 127, 129, 145,
    218n57, 225, 242–44, 247,
    249n177, 263, 267, 274
deconstruction 18, 30, 41, 55,
    72n174, 83n205, 156, 163,
    165, 170–72, 177, 192–94,
    196, 199, 255, 259
deliverance 55–57, 65, 68n156, 99,
    161–62, 165, 169–70, 180,
    203n3
democratic 83n205, 125n364, 141,
    237
denouement 56, 171, 224
deuteronomic 199, 206–8, 244,
    275, 278

deviation 103, 175, 219–20, 254

diachronic 43, 93n235, 109n295, 116n324, 122n345, 146, 217n53

dialogue 27, 39, 48 54, 58, 60, 63–65, 67–68n157, 73–75, 148, 160, 162, 165–66n139, 169, 178, 187, 189, 192, 222

dimensionality 30

dispositio 2n3, 17, 242, 254

disqualify 136, 166n137, 168

distancing 31, 158n109, 214

distortion 12, 261

divinising 180

docere 11, 256–57

downplaying 66, 73, 220, 250

drama 17, 54n118, 60, 66, 76, 283

effective 3, 8n21, 19n60, 22–23, 48n93, 54, 59, 85, 98–99, 108, 111–12, 118, 120, 123, 138n33, 150, 166n137, 169, 173, 184, 188, 196, 207, 215, 238, 259

ellipsis 64

Elohist 36, 286

eloquent 4, 166n137

embellishment 55, 95n242, 156n98, 157

embodiment 200

emotion 11, 50, 54, 56, 74, 82n203, 99–101, 105–7, 109–11, 116–18, 138n33, 154n93, 163, 164n131, 167, 203, 215, 222–23, 231, 242, 246, 250–51, 256n6, 257

empathy 157

enactment 64n148, 173–74

enlightenment 5, 17, 37, 83n205, 111n306, 119n335, 133, 190n229, 229n101

epilogue 87, 90, 96, 100, 121, 240

epipher 24

episode 18n54, 46, 101, 150, 157, 184, 185n206, 190, 212, 241n139, 257

epithet 4, 27, 29, 35, 43, 46, 49, 69, 74–76, 79, 209, 232

equality 112, 119, 247

equilibrium 125, 135

establishment 2, 83n205, 111n307, 119n336, 141, 150, 217, 229, 231, 232n108, 244

ethics 1, 32n14, 48n96, 104, 106nn285, 287, 111, 113, 119–20, 159n113, 203, 218n54, 239, 246, 257, 261, 277, 285–86

ethos 3, 33, 68, 82–84, 89–91, 112, 120, 125, 127, 251, 257–58

etiological 140, 143, 168

etymology 35, 37, 42, 154

eulogy 79

excess 45, 87, 243

exclusivity 49, 95, 97, 129, 207, 213, 220, 235

exhortation 96, 106, 115, 158, 182, 256

exigency 10, 255, 259

existential 256

expectation 26, 37, 47, 54, 63–64, 188, 222–23, 255

explicitness 60, 75

extremes 25, 73, 112n308, 119n337, 257

factual 133, 152, 220

failure 4, 31, 39, 51, 77, 79, 109, 116, 121, 166n139, 168–71, 199, 218, 222n75, 226, 229, 241, 251

faithful 12, 49f, 69n160, 173–74, 190, 193, 202, 256, 278

fallacy 11

falsify 259–60

familiarity 8n21, 30, 181n192, 184, 204n6, 218

fantasy 133
festivals 74, 93n235, 96, 115n320, 248–49, 254, 260
fiction 7, 152, 257–58, 265, 272, 280
flattery 103, 223
foil 7n19, 39, 52, 62, 65, 69, 150, 163, 173, 213, 224
foreigner 19, 34, 102, 104–5, 110, 118, 161, 187, 225, 242, 246, 249, 255
foreshadow 172
foretelling 52
form 2, 9n23, 10n28, 11–15, 18–19, 22, 32n16, 34, 36–37n33, 40, 51n102, 52n108, 65n150, 69n159, 78, 92, 99, 101n267, 110n301, 113, 118n330, 121, 123–24n354, 126, 128, 133n12, 134n18, 135–36, 138, 140, 148n75, 158, 166n137, 169, 179–80n187, 185–86n212, 190n228, 191, 193, 204–5, 207, 219, 243–44, 246, 249, 253, 254n4, 265, 276, 279
formal 11, 36, 77n185, 91, 108, 121, 123n353, 125n358, 127, 185
frame 22, 50, 57, 71n166, 77, 79, 85, 97, 173n161, 178, 185n206, 230, 248, 283
framework 5n11, 16–17, 19n60, 22–23, 35, 43n70, 68, 90, 93n236, 106n287, 113, 114n315, 121, 123, 124n355, 125–27, 133, 147, 164, 168, 193n235, 196–97, 207, 210, 215, 222, 235, 239–42, 251, 253, 261, 273, 277
fulfilment 12, 20–21, 42, 47, 52–54, 57–58, 62–63, 66–68, 70, 72, 74, 77, 163n127, 165, 167, 171, 176–77, 179, 188, 193, 199–201, 210, 214, 224, 228, 235, 237n127, 238n132, 249, 255
function 29, 35, 131, 202, 265–66
functional 1n1, 8–12, 15, 22, 59n135, 64n148, 78, 84n208, 95n242, 121, 125n358, 135, 137, 236–37, 257n8

gap 30, 40n47, 51n103, 63, 105n283, 107, 145, 156, 162, 179, 198, 218n54, 225, 254, 285
genealogy 20–21, 172, 196–97n248, 202n1, 212n35, 229n101, 231, 250–51
generic 12–13, 29, 43n70, 97, 115n321, 121, 123, 127, 129, 135–36, 143, 172, 254
genre 12, 13n43, 27, 29, 33, 76, 77n183, 80, 85, 123, 129, 132, 134–36, 138n34, 139, 145, 152, 154, 155n96, 156, 162, 179–80, 218n54, 240, 247–48, 251, 254n4, 262, 264, 270
glorification 31, 70, 170, 193
Gorgias 279
government 81n202, 87, 213n42
graded 249, 273
gradual 38–39, 180n187, 236, 237n127
graphical 184
grumbling 149, 188, 225
guarantor 51, 87–88, 90
guardian 45, 81, 96n247, 110n301, 118n330, 183, 187
guidance 4–5, 12, 18–19, 22n73, 25–26, 53, 56, 60, 68, 76, 93, 96n247, 129, 158, 174, 198n249, 207, 210–11, 215, 225, 229, 238, 240, 254, 257

guilt 45, 50, 108–9n296, 112–13,
116–17, 120, 160, 191,
246n163, 285

hagiography 152
Hammurabi 82, 88, 123, 124n354,
274, 286
hardening 49–50n104, 52, 60, 67,
214n46, 266, 270
harmonise 54, 159, 264
hate 99–100, 104, 106
hero 1n1, 29, 41, 63n145, 128,
130, 133–36, 138nn33–34,
139, 143, 148, 153, 155–56,
158, 162, 165–67, 170,
183n200, 193, 229, 245, 255,
268
historian 133–34
historical 1, 5–6, 7n17, 8nn20–21,
12–14, 16, 18, 19n60, 22n74,
28, 37, 50, 51n102, 54, 57–
58, 62, 77n183, 85n212, 131–
34, 136, 140, 142–43, 146,
154n93, 169, 171, 174, 179,
198, 200–202, 205, 206n13,
207–9, 212n35, 214–15, 223–
24, 235, 242, 244n152, 245,
248, 254, 257, 260–61, 271,
279
historicity 135, 204
historiography 17, 131, 133, 255,
264
history 72, 213, 219, 263, 267,
269, 274, 277, 282, 284–85
Hittite laws 105n281, 124
holiness 38, 64, 72n173, 76, 79,
96n247, 97n253, 101, 113,
126–28, 139, 142, 177,
181n192, 182, 191–92, 200,
202, 206, 217–20n65, 222n73,
226–27n95, 230, 235–37,
238n132, 240–41, 249, 251,
256, 267, 272–73
holistic 90, 129

honour 48, 105n284, 111,
112n312, 114n315, 119,
120n341, 135, 187, 215, 238,
265–66, 276, 278–79, 282,
285
humour 154
hymn 78, 80, 105n281, 136, 248,
284
hymnic 32, 43n70, 44, 48, 50,
77n183, 78

ideal 1, 73, 81, 82n203, 83n205,
92, 105, 109, 113, 116n325,
117, 121, 201, 204–5, 210,
215–16, 220, 231–32,
246n163, 251, 256
idealisation 143, 146, 149, 152,
165, 177, 192, 223n79
idealistic 130, 170, 256
ideational 2, 12, 16–17, 58, 60, 73–
74, 76, 98, 101, 112–13, 115–
16, 120–21, 124, 127, 172,
183, 216, 233n110, 250, 254,
273
identification 1–2, 28, 48n96,
53n111, 59, 69, 80, 128, 138,
145, 162, 199, 201–2, 205,
211, 213–14, 229, 231–33,
239, 241, 248–51, 257, 276,
284
identity 1–2, 8, 38–39, 71–73, 76,
78n193, 146, 151, 166n137,
181–83, 201, 203–6, 207n19,
209, 212n35, 213–14, 230–
37, 242n142, 251, 255, 260–
61, 263, 265, 273, 276
ideological 14, 30, 34, 82n203,
112n310, 114n315, 120n339,
161, 202n2, 204, 208, 282–83
illocution 13–14
imagery 75
imagination 109, 117, 208, 227,
231, 254, 261

imitation 17, 48n96, 129, 137, 203,
    218, 239, 255–56, 276
implicitness 31, 106, 219, 272
Imponierformel 38, 196
impurity 236
inclusio 15, 21–23, 50, 57, 98, 100,
    101n267, 115, 124, 127, 197,
    215, 217n51, 218, 220, 254–
    55, 261
indetermination 173, 179
individual 17, 34, 55, 103, 122,
    212, 233–34, 237n127, 243–
    45, 247
individuality 233
inhomogeneity 208, 254
institution 34, 45n81, 58, 131,
    134n18, 138n33, 140–43,
    150–51, 193, 245, 260, 267
institutional 103, 126, 139, 151,
    180, 223, 256, 260–61
instruction 59n136, 69, 72n172,
    124, 125n358, 144, 170, 172,
    188, 210, 220, 223n77,
    231n105, 239, 248
instrumentality 137
integrity 166n137, 184, 192, 195,
    208
intention 10n31, 14, 18, 40, 43n68,
    57, 60, 66, 94, 97, 104, 142,
    167, 170n154, 172, 175f, 224,
    246f, 260
intentional 9f, 14, 18, 43, 156, 253f

intercession 44, 46n84, 47–48, 71,
    73–74n177, 148, 150,
    186n212, 190, 199–200, 218
intertextual 18, 22n71, 43, 154n93,
    256, 267, 282
intratextual 18, 249
intuition 18, 63, 260
inventio 10
irony 31, 53n108, 61nn141–42,
    154, 158, 160–61, 166n139,

    168, 171n155, 176, 189,
    190n227, 256
iteration 24, 157, 160n119
itinerary 23, 265, 279

Jacob 260n13
jealous 49f, 76, 99–101n266
Jehoshaphat 141
Jithro 59, 87, 133, 157, 187, 195,
    237–38n130, 264
judge 30, 61, 93n236, 107, 126,
    133, 141, 159–60, 162,
    170n154, 178, 193, 198–200,
    221, 257
judgement 4, 32, 70n165, 74n177,
    110, 117, 118n330, 150,
    154n93, 159n113, 184,
    186n212, 194–96, 198,
    218n59, 285
judgements 3n6, 4, 49, 82n203, 92,
    107, 110n301, 118n330, 162,
    174, 244
judicial 107, 141, 264, 272
jurisdiction 245
justice 1, 8, 10n31, 32n14, 81,
    82n204, 104–9, 111n306,
    113, 117, 119n335, 120f,
    124n354, 130, 134, 141, 157,
    160, 162–63, 188, 195, 200,
    203, 218, 251, 273

kingdom 40n49, 52n105, 127, 142,
    176, 208–9, 234–35, 240,
    274, 282
kingly 46, 76, 80, 83n205, 84,
    90n228, 112n310, 120n339,
    128–29, 144, 175, 232n107,
    255, 274
kingship 84, 89, 129, 151, 255

law 140, 204, 234, 243, 267, 274–
    75, 278
lawgiver 143–46, 251

Laws of Ešnunna 15n49, 111, 114n316, 119, 124
Laws of Hammurabi 15n49, 88, 91n229, 103n274, 111n307, 119n336, 123–24n354
lawsuit 104
leadership 24, 34, 135, 137n29, 149–51, 159–60, 162, 183–84, 187, 188n219, 189n221, 195, 200, 286
legend 135f, 154n93, 155n95, 179, 180n187
legislation 50, 82, 86–92n231, 99, 108n294, 125, 127, 129, 145–46, 240, 251
legitimation 87, 115n322, 131, 140–43, 150–52, 167, 186, 199n257
Leitmotiv 169
lex talionis 111n307, 114, 119n336, 270
liable 33
liberation 10, 33n19, 55, 171n156, 203, 205, 243
lists 31, 115n322, 121, 123, 202n1
liturgical 24, 69n159, 242, 249, 254
loyalty 60, 92, 95n245, 97–102, 109n300, 117n329, 150, 157

maltreatment 104, 110–11, 118, 242–43
manna 71, 267, 280
mediation 68, 74, 85, 96, 140, 145, 149, 171–73, 176–78, 180–84, 185n206, 186n212, 188, 199–200, 223n77, 227–28, 233n108, 236–37n127, 244, 247, 255, 260n13
mediator 34, 41, 70–71, 137, 139–40, 145–46, 148–50, 162, 166n137, 170–73, 176–77, 180, 184, 186, 188–90, 192–

95, 198n249, 199, 215, 217, 227, 256, 261
mediator 149
memory 263
merciful 41, 44, 46n84, 47–48, 71–74, 76
Mesopotamia 16, 46, 82, 84n208, 86, 88, 91n229, 103, 123n353, 265, 272, 280
messenger 39, 63n145, 68, 96, 136, 167, 178–79, 180n187, 181–83n203, 219n61, 235
metaphor 2, 25–26, 34n25, 46, 50, 75n181, 90n228, 127, 129, 177n175, 178–79n182, 189n225, 197, 210, 232–34, 236–37, 256, 260, 264, 267
metaphoric 34n25, 45–46, 177, 193
metaphysical 42, 79
Midian 59n135, 64, 157–58n109, 161, 266
Midianite 59, 64, 137n28, 158, 160, 161n120, 187
Midrash 157, 159, 236n121, 275
midwives 61, 79, 175
milieu 18
military 56, 71, 90, 128, 185, 224
mišpatim 87
mnemonic 99n260, 242
Moab 248
moaning 186–87
monarchy 140–42, 193, 207–8
monotheism 57n133, 204–5, 263
motivation 41, 85, 90, 92, 96, 100, 103, 106, 108, 110, 115n322, 116–18n332, 133, 138n33, 144, 224n81, 244n156, 246
murmuring 70–71, 150, 171–72, 183–87, 190, 195, 224
myth 51, 154n93, 207, 209

Nabopolassar 267
naming 153n90, 161

narrator 4, 8n21, 17, 26, 30–31n11,
    33, 53–55, 60, 133, 167, 171,
    174n165, 194n237, 213,
    214n46, 247
novelistic 4, 278

obedience 53n114, 85, 89–90, 96–
    98, 102, 104n280, 105, 108–
    10, 113, 114n314, 115–17,
    144, 163, 167, 169, 173–77,
    184, 192–93, 197–99, 206,
    227–28, 248
obligation 58, 244
omnipotence 30, 52, 79
omniscience 30, 213, 247
opposition 113, 120, 282
oppressed 32, 57, 64–66, 75, 99,
    104f, 159–60, 172, 204, 222f,
    232, 241-243, 246n162
oppressor 105, 110, 118, 213
oral 3, 9n23, 12, 36, 84n207, 132,
    258
oratio 264
orphan 81, 104–5n281, 110–11,
    118, 282
overinterpretation 168

paradigmatic 25, 28, 33n19, 47,
    71–72, 130, 142, 144, 148,
    150–52, 177, 179, 192–93,
    199–200, 203, 205, 251, 255,
    261
paradox 30
paraenesis 270
parallelism 25n83, 41, 65, 79n194
paraphrase 57, 108, 116, 186, 191
paronomasia 106
passiveness 61, 70, 77, 168,
    187n216, 213–15, 224, 226,
    245, 250
passover 175, 177, 223n77, 248
pathos 257
patience 46

patriarchal 20–22, 32, 42, 57–58,
    62, 66–68, 70–71, 76, 91,
    139, 161, 172n159, 182, 191–
    92, 209, 212, 214, 218, 220–
    21, 224–25, 233n108, 237,
    255, 267
personality 3, 59, 112, 120, 147,
    198n249, 200
perspective 8n21, 9, 15–16, 18–19,
    27, 30–31, 33, 52n108, 55,
    61n140, 63–64, 66, 77,
    82n203, 85n212, 91–92, 96,
    113, 120–22, 124, 126, 128–
    29, 140, 145, 170n153,
    174n165, 184, 187, 193, 199,
    202, 212, 218, 219n62, 224,
    226, 254, 257, 259–60, 267–
    68, 272, 282–84
persuasion 3, 8n21, 11, 32n16,
    116n322, 143, 205, 215, 243,
    245, 247, 256, 276
persuasive 10–11, 18, 56, 98, 108,
    112, 120, 143, 238–39, 242–
    43, 247, 251, 256n6, 258–59
pharaoh 53–55, 58, 60, 61n142,
    178n177, 179–80, 203n3,
    221, 266, 269–70
plot 2, 5, 12n40, 18, 21, 23, 33, 35,
    55–57, 57n135, 60, 69–70,
    75, 77, 80, 99, 101, 130–31,
    135, 145, 148n75, 153, 156–
    57, 160–64, 172, 174, 177,
    186, 188, 190, 193, 199, 201,
    212–14, 229, 231, 238n130,
    250–51, 270, 278
poetic 8n21, 25, 27, 29–30, 43n68,
    45, 53n106, 76–80, 98n256,
    129, 144, 218n54, 224, 269,
    272, 278
poetics 15, 29, 130, 225, 278, 280,
    283
polarise 33, 157
polemic 7n19, 32n14, 60, 158–59,
    265

polyptoton 106, 165n133
polytheistic 205, 244
portrait 4, 6, 27, 77–78, 80, 83–84, 128–29, 153, 161–63, 169, 199
portray 3–4, 30, 32–33, 61, 70–72, 75, 76n182, 82, 91, 110, 117, 135, 137, 138n33, 139, 143, 145, 149, 167n141, 171–72, 176, 181–82, 185n206, 187, 200–201, 213, 216, 225, 228, 248, 253, 256, 261
potentiality 197
pragmatics 135
prayer 43–44n70, 46n84, 47, 74, 150, 199
preconception 3–5, 8n21, 18, 31, 37, 66, 83, 99n260, 129–30, 133, 136, 156, 161, 170, 184, 198, 212
precondition 8, 16, 59n136, 93, 131, 152, 157
prediction 53–55, 63, 67–68, 73, 163n127, 169, 171, 174, 195
presence 72, 94, 142, 217, 230, 241, 263, 272–74
Priesterschrift 272–74, 280, 284
priesthood 83n205, 90n228, 147, 151, 210, 228, 231, 234, 237–38, 240, 249, 251, 256, 267
profanation 113
profane 125, 127–28, 147, 204, 219, 240, 249
progression 12, 40n47, 64, 166, 174, 263
prohibition 46n84, 49, 72, 95–96, 99, 102, 109, 116n325, 117, 145
prologue 22, 87, 90, 121
prophet 36, 76n182, 83n205, 141–42, 144, 148, 150–51, 174, 178–80n187, 183n200, 193, 194n237, 199–200, 212n40,

220n64, 255, 257, 260n13, 269, 276
prophetic 36, 37n34, 149–51, 164n132, 174, 179, 180n187, 199, 279
prose 77, 135, 272, 278
protagonist 139, 261
protection 26, 53, 80, 93n234, 96, 102, 110n301, 118n330, 155n97, 158, 183, 188n219, 205
prototype 130
pun 40n49, 42, 107n291, 176

rabbinic 156n98, 157–59, 164n130, 190n230, 264
readable 35, 134
reader 1–2, 5–6, 8, 14, 15n49, 16, 19, 28, 30, 33, 35, 37, 39, 40n49, 44, 53, 64, 77, 86, 98n257, 104–5n283, 114n315, 123n346, 132, 140, 148n75, 156, 159, 162, 178n177, 181–82, 198–99, 201, 209, 214n46, 224n82, 229, 231n105, 233n110, 247–51, 254, 256–57, 259–61, 268, 272, 284
reading 14, 272, 283
readings 19, 27, 32, 140, 159, 162, 249n175, 253, 260
rebellion 69n160, 70, 71n166, 183, 189n221, 195, 239, 248, 266
recipient 9, 27, 48, 66, 68, 77, 85–86, 89, 106, 133, 232, 251
recitation 12
recompensation 103, 245
redaction 54n115, 93n236, 96n247, 106n285, 112n311, 120n340, 122, 135–36, 138–39, 142n45, 143, 152n87, 154n93, 170, 208n21, 209, 254, 268, 277, 280

redactor 32, 57, 133–34, 138,
    185n206, 209, 223n80, 253,
    254n4
redundancy 39, 64n148, 65, 110,
    118, 175, 189, 217n51, 256n6
rehabilitation 130, 167, 177, 194–
    95
reintroduction 25, 58
repetition 12, 17, 22, 24n79, 25–
    26, 38, 52, 54, 56, 64n148,
    66, 79, 105n281, 110, 118,
    126, 144, 165n133, 167, 171–
    74, 177n174, 185n207, 197,
    203n3, 220, 239, 254
restitution 92, 101–3
restoration 103, 107, 111n307,
    114nn315, 317, 119n336, 160,
    191, 194, 210
restructure 215, 258
retelling 62, 132, 250, 256
retrospective 50, 62, 68n157, 87,
    110, 118, 151, 187
rhetor 3, 82
rhetoric 3, 10–11, 28, 60, 72, 94–
    95, 115, 125, 129–30, 132,
    143, 145, 215, 239, 245–47,
    265, 269–70, 276, 278–79,
    282, 284
rhetorical 9, 11, 13–15, 17, 19, 22–
    24, 29, 47–48, 63, 67, 72, 79,
    83n205, 84, 86, 89, 96, 98–
    99, 108–9, 111, 116–18, 123–
    24, 131, 154n92, 167, 173,
    196, 202, 207, 213, 232, 241,
    249, 253, 263–64, 272–73,
    276, 279–81, 283–84, 286
rhetorics 2n3, 15, 32n14, 58, 128–
    29, 166n137, 172, 198n251,
    215, 258
ritual 88n222, 93n233, 146, 175,
    177, 181, 227, 236, 244, 248,
    278, 285
royal 46, 84, 87, 89–90, 103,
    110n301, 118n330, 144, 175,

180, 210, 215, 249, 251, 256,
    267

sabbath 70n165, 71, 97n253, 127,
    185n206, 230–31, 240–
    41n139, 249, 283
sacred 1, 33, 79, 125, 177n174,
    178, 231n105, 249
sacrifices 94, 96, 125n362
saga 132–35, 137, 138n34, 139,
    155n96
sanctify 94, 216, 219, 241
sanction 43, 49, 85, 92, 105n282,
    108–20, 129, 144–45, 246,
    264
sanctuary 24, 26, 59n136, 71, 79–
    80, 93, 94n239, 95, 96n247,
    124, 147, 230, 236, 241, 260–
    61, 278–79, 285
Sargon 136, 154n93, 155
semiotic 13, 146, 181, 189n225,
    193, 268, 272
shame 56, 108–13, 114n315, 116–
    21, 238, 246, 264, 285
Šamaš 113, 120
šakānum 87
Simchat Torah 260
slave 62, 100, 103n275, 111, 113–
    14n316, 118, 126n366, 202,
    203n3, 215, 222n73, 229,
    242–43
slavery 20n63, 22n73, 58, 63, 87,
    99, 103n275, 104n280, 161,
    201, 203n3, 213, 215, 229,
    241–43n151, 242n143, 249,
    266–67
social history 277
society 14, 52n105, 112, 120, 275
spatiotemporal 52, 258, 261n15
statutory 87, 96, 103, 105, 111,
    118
stereotype 127, 136, 166n137,
    173n164
strophe 79–80

structural 7n17, 11, 24, 27, 50, 57,
    67n155, 77–78n190, 80,
    84n209, 90, 121, 122n345,
    123, 157, 183, 185–86, 215,
    234–36, 237n127, 240–41,
    253, 257, 269, 273
structuralism 13, 274
structure 2, 10–12n40, 14, 17, 19,
    21n65, 29, 32n16, 43n70,
    64n148, 65, 77n183, 96n249,
    98n256, 99n259, 106n287,
    108, 110, 116, 118, 121–
    24n355, 134, 144–45, 153n88,
    155n96, 185n206, 186n210,
    188, 202, 216, 246nn164, 166,
    255–56, 261n15, 265–66,
    276, 278, 284, 286
style 7n17, 10, 25, 43, 52, 56,
    65n150, 79, 95–96, 116n322,
    133, 160n119, 165, 167n144,
    198n251, 257, 265
stylistics 10, 17, 105n281, 131n4,
    254
subconscious 64, 127
subjectivity 20n61, 36, 122n345
suspense 8n21, 69–70, 74, 163,
    248
symbol 26, 182n196, 204, 210n34,
    229–30, 267, 272
symbolism 148, 285
sympathy 159, 187, 257
synchronic 1n1, 13, 109n295,
    116n324, 146
syntagmatic 25

tension 5, 27, 45–47, 50, 51,
    54n115, 60n139, 65n150, 70,
    73, 106n289, 129, 135, 137–
    38, 145–47, 159n111, 171,
    176n172, 178, 180–81, 190,
    192, 195, 197n249, 198, 207,
    213, 215–16, 219–22, 226,
    236, 247, 250, 256n6
theocracy 83n205, 263, 274

unambiguous 30, 42, 57n126, 169
utopia 202, 229–30, 233, 252

variation 17, 122, 137n28,
    173n163, 186n212
vassal 90, 232–34
victory 77, 79, 278
violence 57n126, 157, 159n113
virtue 150

wilderness wanderings 25–26, 50,
    69–70, 96, 97n250, 98, 184,
    186n208, 187, 193, 224–25,
    230, 239
Wirkungsgeschichte 106n285, 132,
    259–60, 269, 279
wisdom 17, 32n16, 46, 61n140,
    82n203, 84, 86, 144, 218n54,
    266, 272, 283
worship 46n84, 49f, 59n136,
    68n156, 76n182, 78, 80, 93–
    97n251, 100–102, 129,
    208n27, 217, 219nn60–61,
    222, 231, 240–41, 249, 254,
    256, 261, 278–79

Yahwist 20n63, 263, 270, 280, 286
yam suf 4, 6, 51n102, 69, 77–79,
    190, 195, 213, 248–49, 257
yešallem-laws 103, 245

Zipporah 168

ND - #0067 - 090625 - C0 - 229/152/17 - PB - 9781842277805 - Gloss Lamination